Investment Banking
Front Office Investment Banking

Michael Herlache, MBA
Investment Banking University
<u>www.InvestmentBankingU.com</u>

**For my soulmate,
Svitlana Herlache**

About the Author:

Michael Herlache is a seasoned professional in the investment banking and tech industries. He co-founded AltQuest Group, a lower middle market M&A advisory firm, during his time at Texas A&M University, where he pursued an MBA. With foundational training from the Investment Banking Institute and Wall Street Prep, Michael embarked on a career as an independent investment banker, providing advisory services across various transactions. He later transitioned into the tech industry's go-to-market side, where he continued to leverage his expertise in financial strategies and market analysis.

Michael has been a pioneer in democratizing investment banking education, creating independent investment banker training programs designed to open the doors of Wall Street to a broader audience. He advocates for progressive values such as diversity, equity, and inclusion and is passionate about empowering others to discover and express their unique voices.

Currently, Michael resides in Scottsdale, Arizona, with his wife, Svitlana. His professional experiences and personal values converge in his work, including the syllabus of the Investment Banking University (www.InvestmentBankingU.com), which is based on the content of this book.

Investment Banking University

Disclosure:

This book discusses financial and legal concepts however is in no way legal advice. Please seek the counsel of a legal advisor when implementing the processes and concepts discussed in the book.

Table of Contents:

Investment Banking University
All Rights Reserved

Investment Banking University

Investment Banking University

Chapter 134: Practicing Investment Banking & Equity Research

Appendix
Introduction to Data Science

Investment Banking University
All Rights Reserved

Preface

Preface

Investment banking stands at the forefront of the financial world, playing an instrumental role in the economic fabric by facilitating capital raising, mergers, acquisitions, and risk management. The field is both exhilarating and demanding, offering professionals the chance to engage in some of the most intricate and high-stakes transactions in the global marketplace.

This book, *Investment Banking: The Official Guide to Front Office Investment Banking*, serves as a comprehensive resource for those seeking to navigate the complexities of this industry. It is crafted for students aspiring to enter the field, job seekers aiming to secure positions, and seasoned professionals desiring to deepen their knowledge of investment banking's multifaceted nature.

Structure of the Book

The book is methodically divided into twelve parts, each dedicated to a crucial aspect of investment banking:

Part I: Introduction to Investment Banking
This section lays the groundwork, exploring the evolution of investment banking, the various types of investment banks, and an overview of the industry's compensation structures. It sets the stage for understanding the core functions and significance of investment banks in the financial ecosystem.

Part II: The Buy-Side Perspective
Focusing on private equity firms, this part delves into their investment strategies, operational frameworks, and the expected returns for their investors. It provides a glimpse into how these entities operate and interact with investment banks.

Part III: The Front Office Investment Banking Process
Here, readers are introduced to the practical aspects of getting started in M&A, viewing M&A as a product, and understanding the day-to-day realities of investment banking practice.

Part IV: Coverage
This section explains the process of choosing coverage areas, focusing on sectors such as the lower middle market and middle market. It also covers the construction of indices, the preparation of coverage reports, and the importance of marketing materials. Additionally, it discusses essential financial data sources and the different types of filings utilized in investment banking.

Part V: Mandate/Target Matching and Strategic Alternatives
This part guides readers through the process of identifying strategic and financial buyers and targets. It emphasizes the importance of aligning buyer and seller mandates and exploring various strategic alternatives.

Part VI: Origination and Pitching Strategic Alternatives
The focus here is on the nuances of origination, identifying key decision-makers, and the overall cycle of origination. It also discusses how to align strategic alternatives with the priorities of C-level executives and board members.

Part VII: Fee Structuring and Winning the Mandate
This section details how to structure fees for different services, including M&A transactions, and the components of a well-crafted engagement letter.

Part VIII: Underwriting the Strategic Alternative
A deep dive into financial modeling and valuation techniques, this part serves as a business case guide for implementing strategic alternatives.

Part IX: Packaging and Securitizing the Strategic Alternative
Here, the creation of essential documents like the pitch book, teaser, and Confidential Information Memorandum (CIM) is discussed, emphasizing their roles in the deal-making process.

Part X: The Buyer List
This section covers the development of buyer profiles, leveraging a buyer database, and effective outreach strategies.

Part XI: Deal Structuring
An exploration of the intricacies of deal structuring, including setting valuation ranges and deal terms, and managing interactions with sellers and buyers, especially in the lower middle market/middle market.

Part XII: The M&A Process
The final part guides readers through the M&A process, from due diligence and negotiation to closing the deal, providing a detailed roadmap for executing successful transactions.

Conclusion

Investment Banking: The Official Guide to Front Office Investment Banking offers a thorough and practical guide to the industry. Whether you are a student embarking on your career, a job seeker exploring opportunities, or a professional looking to refine your expertise, this book is an indispensable resource for mastering the complexities of investment banking and excelling in this dynamic field.

The Challenge

Navigating the Path in Investment Banking: From Data Analyst to Managing Director

The journey in investment banking is marked by a significant transformation in roles and responsibilities. Starting as an analyst, the primary focus is on data analysis, whereas, at the level of Managing Director (MD), the role shifts towards client engagement and strategic decision-making. This post explores the evolution of responsibilities in investment banking, the importance of data analysis, and the skills needed to succeed.

The Analyst's Role: Mastering Data Analysis

Foundation in Data Analysis At the beginning of an investment banking career, analysts are primarily data specialists. Their work involves the meticulous collection, cleaning, and interpretation of financial data. The analyst's role is foundational, as they provide the quantitative backbone for all financial models and reports. They apply various tools and techniques from data science, including statistical analysis, financial modeling, and forecasting.

Tools and Techniques Analysts use advanced software like Excel, SQL, and specialized financial databases such as Bloomberg and

Capital IQ. They are responsible for generating detailed financial models, performing valuation analyses, and creating presentations that summarize data findings for senior bankers. This stage requires a strong understanding of financial statements, market trends, and economic indicators.

Skills Development To excel, analysts must develop technical skills in data science and finance. They need to be proficient in creating complex financial models, understanding macroeconomic factors, and analyzing industry trends. Attention to detail and accuracy are crucial, as these analyses form the basis for significant investment decisions.

Transition to Client-Facing Roles: The Journey Towards MD

Building Client Relationships As professionals progress to associate and VP levels, their roles gradually shift from pure data analysis to include more client-facing responsibilities. They begin to take on roles that involve more direct communication with clients, discussing insights derived from data and helping to shape investment strategies.

Developing an Investment Thesis At this stage, the ability to develop and articulate an investment thesis becomes critical. This involves synthesizing data analysis into a compelling narrative that explains why a particular investment is sound. It's about connecting the dots between data insights and real-world market opportunities. The investment thesis must be backed by solid data and align with the client's strategic objectives.

Strategic Decision Making As bankers advance to senior levels, including the role of Managing Director, their focus shifts towards strategic decision-making. MDs leverage the insights generated by their teams to advise clients on high-stakes investment decisions. They are responsible for presenting and defending the bank's investment recommendations to clients, drawing on their deep industry knowledge and experience.

The Role of Managing Director: The Pinnacle of Client Engagement

Leadership and Strategy MDs play a pivotal role in the investment banking hierarchy. They lead client relationships and are responsible for securing new business. The ability to build and maintain strong relationships with clients is paramount. They also oversee the work of analysts and associates, ensuring the quality and accuracy of financial analyses and presentations.

Decision Tools and Client Convincing One of the critical responsibilities of an MD is to utilize decision-making tools and frameworks developed by analysts to persuade clients. They use these tools to present data-driven recommendations, highlight potential risks and returns, and guide clients through complex financial landscapes.

Client-Centric Focus MDs need to understand the client's perspective, including their risk tolerance, investment objectives, and strategic goals. They must tailor their communication and proposals to align with the client's needs, ensuring that the investment strategies presented are not only data-backed but also client-focused.

Conclusion: The Path to Success in Investment Banking

Success in investment banking requires a blend of analytical skills and client management abilities. Starting with a strong foundation in data analysis, professionals must develop their client-facing skills and strategic thinking as they advance in their careers. From mastering financial modeling as an analyst to leading client relationships as an MD, each stage requires a different skill set and focus.

Ultimately, the ability to translate data insights into compelling investment narratives and strategic advice is what sets successful investment bankers apart. As the industry evolves, so too must the skills and approaches of those within it, ensuring they remain relevant and valuable to their clients.

PART I: THE CAPITAL MANAGEMENT GAME

Chapter 1: The Capital Management Game: Capital in Search of Arbitrage & Real Returns

In the realm of investment banking and capital management, the process of optimizing capital deployment can be seen as a sophisticated game. The primary objective is to maximize wealth through strategic decision-making. This post explores the personas involved, the rules governing their actions, and the critical role investment bankers play in this complex environment.

Understanding the Players: Strategic, Financial, and Personal Capital

Strategic Capital: This category refers to capital held by corporations and institutions with long-term strategic goals. These entities often seek acquisitions, mergers, or partnerships that align with their overarching business strategies. Their mandate typically involves acquiring assets or businesses that enhance their competitive edge, diversify their portfolio, or enter new markets.

Financial Capital: Managed by private equity firms, hedge funds, and other investment entities, financial capital focuses primarily on generating returns through investments. These entities look for opportunities with a clear path to profitability, often through restructuring, optimization, or eventual resale. The emphasis is on the financial performance of the investments, with a strong focus on exit strategies and timing.

Personal Capital (High Net Worth Individuals - HNWIs):
Individuals with substantial personal wealth who invest in various assets, from real estate to private businesses. Their investment mandates are often more flexible, considering both financial returns and personal interests. These investors may prioritize wealth preservation, income generation, or legacy planning.

The Rules of the Game: Mandates and Strategic Alternatives

Each capital category operates under a set of rules, known as mandates, that dictate their investment strategies. These mandates include the rates at which they are willing to buy or sell assets and outline the criteria for potential investments. Understanding these mandates is crucial as they define the universe of strategic alternatives available under current market conditions.

Strategic Alternatives:

1. **Investment Decisions**: Deciding whether to invest in new opportunities, either through expansion, acquisition, or diversification.
2. **Divestiture**: Identifying non-core assets or underperforming units for sale to streamline operations and focus on core competencies.
3. **Debt Financing**: Leveraging capital through debt issuance to fund growth initiatives or optimize the capital structure.
4. **Equity Financing**: Raising capital by issuing new equity, either to finance new projects or improve liquidity.

The Role of Investment Bankers

Investment bankers are pivotal in this landscape, acting as intermediaries who facilitate the flow of capital and identify arbitrage opportunities. Their roles include:

1. **Origination and Syndication of Deals**: Investment bankers originate deals by identifying potential investment opportunities that align with the mandates of capital holders. They also syndicate these opportunities, bringing together buyers and sellers and arranging necessary financing.
2. **Comprehensive Analysis**: Investment bankers conduct thorough analyses to determine the strength of an investment opportunity. They assess potential returns, quantify risks, and calculate the spread between risk and return, known as alpha. The goal is to find opportunities where the potential return significantly outweighs the associated risks.
3. **Arbitrage Identification**: Bankers seek to identify arbitrage opportunities—situations where there is a chance to earn a risk-free profit due to market inefficiencies. These opportunities are highly sought after, as they provide a clear path to earning returns without corresponding risks.

The Financier's Toolbox

To excel in the capital management game, investment bankers and capital managers utilize a diverse set of tools:

1. **Data Science and Analytics**: Utilizing data analytics to uncover trends, forecast market movements, and identify investment opportunities.
2. **Arbitrage Engineering**: Creating structures that maximize returns and minimize risks, ensuring that capital is deployed efficiently.

Conclusion

The capital management game is a dynamic and intricate process where investment bankers play a crucial role in guiding capital towards the most profitable opportunities. By understanding the mandates of different capital holders and leveraging a comprehensive toolkit, they help maximize wealth and create value in the financial markets. Whether it's strategic, financial, or personal capital, the objective remains the same: achieving the highest and best use of capital through well-informed, strategic decisions.

NOTES:

Arbitrage is getting commitments to buy
1.   Funding the arbitrage
2.   Making the acquisition of the assets to resell immediately to the buyers
3.   This is the arbitrage

The ability to find and syndicate arbitrage opportunities (positive NPV).

Data science approach to investment banking. What insights do we need that inform the investor about the nature of the arbitrage opportunity?

Building the arbitrage:

Researching who has a need or want on the buy side and the need or want quantified (how much they a willing to pay)
Researching who has a product, service or enterprise that they a willing to sell for less than buy side wants (sell side)
Tying up the sell side with option to ourchase

Investment analysis & the analyst:
how close does this resemble an arbitrage?
Capital flows to arbitrage opportunities because returns are linked to the strength of the arbitrage.

Data Science yields a level of confidence in the arbitrage by analyzing analytics related to an investment.

The beginning of becoming a great investor starts with an understanding of arbitrage and what strengthens or weakens it. Thus

will drive returns ex post or ex ante. Porters 5 forces speak to the forces that either strengthen or weaken arbitrage.

We model things to get confidence in the arbitrage by quantifying it with data science and analytics. Knowing that capital flows to arbitrage, how to convey analytics to show you have an arbitrage opportunity. Giving greater confidence to it.

Return is the quantified benefit of the arbitrage.
Risk are factors that weaken the arbitrage strength and certainty.

The ability to assess the arbitrage strength of an opportunity now and in the future.

Understanding the enterprise:

The enterprise:

An intelligent work system dedicated to optimizing the arbitrage in order to maximize return. A system where intelligent actions are taken relative to the data with proper conditional logic in an augmented or automated capacity.

The business of business is arbitrage in order to drive return. An intelligent work system dedicated to arbitrage opportunities. The intelligent work system handles the logistics of the arbitrage. Return & ROI metrics tell us how strongly the enterprise is arbitraging.

Capital flows to those enterprises that demonstrate arbitrage strength now and in the future. Profits flow from arbitrage and return is a function of profits.

We can look at metrics as to whether they strengthen or weaken the arbitrage.

Inventory turn metrics strengthen the arbitrage. Lower days payable strengthen the arbitrage.

Evaluating an enterprise and stock as to its prospects to have access to arbitrage opportunities with current or future products.

Profit as a measure of strength of arbitrage. How strong is the intelligent work system arbitraging?

Capital in search of arbitrage
Arbitrage as a concept and wealth maximization ideal. The paradigm within which to evaluate investments.

The act of business is the act of arbitrage with a superior algorithm (ie solution) which brings customers via positive neuroassociations (ie expected ROI from the solution).

Forces that strengthen or weaken arbitrage.

NPV is the dollar value of the arbitrage in today's dollars.

The transaction is the arbitrage event. Where supply and demand come together to facilitate the arbitrage. A transaction happens when two parties believe they have an arbitrage opportunity.

Understanding human nature:

We all gravitate towards arbitrage opportunities.
People initiate towards arbitrage opportunities.
Natural nature (including the natural ego) works to maximize its arbitrage. This is its mission and purpose. Status is an expression of arbitrage ability and opportunity.

Investment Banking University

Value is the arbitrage perception. That the immediate benefits outweigh the immediate costs. In this way, arbitrage integrates the social and the economic. Using data science to build investment intelligence around a stock or enterprise. Ratios and analytics as decision tools that signal the intelligent action one way or another.

Economics are forces that are acting on the arbitrage of the enterprise. These are cateogirized into forces of supply and forces of demand.

Adam Smith observed that individuals take action to realize arbitrage which gave rise to his "invisible hand" concept.

Developing your arbitrage intelligence.

Investment banking as a data science role to inform investment decisions and facilitate the investment.

Strength of arbitrage is a function of the quality of the algorithm.

Getting into the capital game. Identifying mandates (investment mandates from strategic or financial buyers) and targets (intelligent work systems around an algorithm that arbitrages) and facilitating a match globally. This is the excitement of the game.

Value is the arbitrage opportunity to the customer or market.

The risk reward equation plays into the strength of the arbitrage opportunity. Risk decreases the strength of the arbitrage and reward increases the strength of the arbitrage.

Understanding the History of Enterprise as the History of Better & Better Algorithms:

The history of progress is the history of better and better algorithms & arbitrages as well as the digitization and automation of these algorithms & arbitrages.

The task of the Enterprise is to make the algorithms better and better amd to evolve them (digitize, augment, automate) and build new ones. An algorithm is the product; the solution to a problem.

Capital enables algorithms to be built, commercialized and modernized.

Enter the global capitalist game with Investment Banking University. Become an independent investment banker and discover global capital sources and projects.

A problem as an opportunity means that a problem is an opportunity to build an algorithm to solve that problem. Once verified as having solved the problem, the algorithm can be turned into a modern tool that can solve that problem at scale (ie a software, a product, etc).

This speaks to a product as an algorithm or solution to a problem.

Entrepreneurship as the opportunity for a better, more evolved algorithm in the industry and subindustry. Algorithms as innovations.

Arbitrage and algorithms as the nature of capitalism. The continious innovation of better and new algorithms and the arbitrage they yield is capitalism.

The nature of demand:
Demand is created when someone or an enterprise sees an opportunity for arbitrage. When arbitrage is observed by the arbitraging ego, that person will consume that arbitrage.

The nature of supply:
Algorithms and tools that enable arbitrage.

Arbitrage as the ability to incrementally capture value. Value can be material, social or spiritual. The perception of arbitrage by the arbitraging ego, creates demand to consume that arbitrage.

The history of business is the history of the algorithm and arbitrage and the fortunes made along the way.

The business plan as an algorithm building and arbitrage plan.

Economic cycles are a function of the commercialization of new algorithms and the industries that they build. Going through early adopters through mass adoption.

Technology Entrepreneurship

XYZ is developing to tool to deal with the problem of a manual task or decision by augmenting aspects of it or automating it.

Zero to one means an arbitraging algorithm that can turn into a natural monopoly.

Knowledge and application of algorithms as the basis of skill.

The amount of spontaneous & magical experience for the arbitraging ego is limitless. The amount of positive algorithms to drive these magical experiences is limitless. The amount of wealth driven from algorithms is limitless.

Economic moat is driven by the difficulty to replicate the algorithm and strength of the arbitrage.

Business is the building and running of algorithms to realize an arbitrage.

Contractualize the conditional logic of the work and compensation involved in a project.

The entrepreneur as an enterprise Engineer In charge of the algorithm, the arbitrage, and neuroassociations (leadership).

The investor wants arbitrage strength (durability) of a natural monopoly.

Capital flows to where a clear ROI has been established which is the result of the modeling of it through financial engineering. Hence the importance of financial modeling and valuation (ie financial engineering) skills. Modeling the arbitrage of the running of the algorithm (ie operations). Hence the importance of investment banks in modeling out investments that allow capital to flow to the investment. Modeling the projects of enterprise engineers.

Go to market as neuroassociation engineering (work). Neuroassociative conditioning positive neuroassociations for your enterprise and your products. To build positive neuroassociations, build positive perceptions of value (ie arbitrage strength).

The capitalist economy runs on the egos desire for arbitrage. Always seeking more and larger arbitrages and this is why it is aligned with natural nature.

Computers are the modern factories of the 21st century.

Arbitrage strength as a going forward and current valuation metric.

Vs. P/e multiples that are accounting driven and backwards facing.

Valuation thesis:

Arbitrage strength (strength of neuroassociations of buyers ie demand which is a function of the perceived ROI of the solution & superiority of algorithm of solution which is 10x the value of the next solution in the marketplace which result in a natural monopoly) stocks yield alpha.

Forward looking valuation paradigm rather than backward looking accounting metrics.

The truth is that michael (ie hercustotle) did something that the steve swarzman's of the world did in building AltQuest Group.

Going back to one of the investment themes of our generation, the intelligent enterprise, AI and that which powers it helps enterprises build intelligent workflow automation which is the future of enterprise.

Profit margin is a metric of arbitrage strength.

Building an enterprise with the goal of having your strategic capital compound for you with the growth rate in earnings.

Goal to get the enterprise to a place to unleash the power of compounding for the capital.

Chapter 2: Developing Capital Management Skills

Developing Capital Management Skills: A Comprehensive Guide

In the dynamic field of finance and investment, mastering capital management skills is essential for maximizing returns and minimizing risks. These skills encompass a variety of methodologies and tools that together create a robust framework for making informed financial decisions. This blog post explores key areas crucial for developing effective capital management skills, including portfolio analysis, investment alternative analysis, transaction-specific modeling, valuation techniques, financial statement modeling, accounting principles, corporate finance, and the utilization of Excel.

Portfolio Analysis

What is Portfolio Analysis? Portfolio analysis involves examining a collection of investments to assess their overall performance, risk, and diversification. It helps investors understand the balance of different asset classes within their portfolio and how these can be optimized for better returns.

Key Components:

- **Asset Allocation:** Determining the right mix of asset classes (stocks, bonds, real estate, etc.) based on an investor's risk tolerance and investment goals.
- **Performance Metrics:** Evaluating past performance using metrics such as return on investment (ROI), standard deviation, and beta.
- **Risk Assessment:** Understanding the risk profile of the portfolio, including the correlation between different assets, to minimize potential losses.

Benefits: By analyzing the portfolio, investors can make strategic decisions to rebalance their assets, adjust their exposure to various markets, and align their investments with their long-term financial goals.

Investment Alternative Analysis

Purpose: Investment alternative analysis involves comparing different investment options to identify the most suitable choices. This process considers various factors such as risk, return, liquidity, and market conditions.

Methods:

- **Risk-Return Profile:** Assessing the expected returns relative to the risks involved for each investment option.
- **Liquidity Analysis:** Determining how quickly and easily assets can be converted into cash without significantly affecting their value.
- **Market Trends and Economic Indicators:** Evaluating current market conditions and economic forecasts to inform investment decisions.

Outcome: Investors can select investments that best match their risk tolerance and financial objectives, ensuring a diversified and balanced portfolio.

Transaction-Specific Modeling

Overview: This methodology focuses on analyzing the financial implications of specific investment transactions, such as mergers and acquisitions (M&A), project financing, or new ventures.

Key Elements:

- **Financial Projections:** Creating detailed forecasts of income, expenses, and cash flows.
- **Risk Analysis:** Identifying potential risks and developing mitigation strategies.
- **Scenario Planning:** Exploring different scenarios (e.g., best case, worst case) to understand the potential range of outcomes.

Importance: Transaction-specific modeling helps in determining the viability and profitability of individual investment opportunities, providing a detailed assessment that supports strategic decision-making.

Valuation Techniques

Types of Valuation:

1. **Discounted Cash Flow (DCF) Analysis:** A method that estimates the value of an investment based on its expected future cash flows, discounted to their present value.
2. **Comparative Company Analysis:** Involves comparing a company with similar companies in terms of financial metrics and market multiples to determine its relative value.

3. **Comparative Transactions Analysis:** Examines similar past transactions to estimate the value of an investment.

Application: These techniques help investors and analysts determine the fair value of assets, negotiate purchase prices, and make informed investment decisions.

Financial Statement Modeling

What is Financial Statement Modeling? Financial statement modeling involves creating integrated models that connect a company's income statement, balance sheet, and cash flow statement. This comprehensive modeling approach provides insights into a company's financial health and future performance.

Benefits:

- **Forecasting:** Helps predict future financial performance based on historical data and assumptions.
- **Scenario Analysis:** Allows for the testing of different financial scenarios and their potential impacts on the business.
- **Decision Support:** Informs strategic decisions such as capital allocation, budgeting, and financial planning.

Accounting, Financial Statements, Corporate Finance, and Excel

Core Skills:

- **Accounting Principles:** Understanding fundamental accounting principles is crucial for accurate financial analysis and reporting.
- **Financial Statements Analysis:** Proficiency in reading and interpreting financial statements is essential for assessing a company's performance and financial position.

- **Corporate Finance:** Knowledge of corporate finance concepts, including capital structure, cost of capital, and funding strategies, is vital for effective capital management.

Utilizing Excel: Excel remains a powerful tool for financial modeling, data analysis, and visualization. Its features, such as formulas, pivot tables, and charting, enable analysts to perform complex calculations, model financial scenarios, and present data in an accessible format.

Conclusion

Developing capital management skills requires a comprehensive understanding of various analytical tools and methodologies. From portfolio analysis to financial modeling, these skills equip investors and financial professionals with the necessary expertise to navigate the complexities of financial markets. Mastery of these areas not only enhances the ability to make informed investment decisions but also contributes to achieving long-term financial stability and growth.

NOTES:
Portfolio analysis
Investment alternative analysis
Transaction Specific Modeling
Valuation (DCF, comp companies, comp transactions)
Financial Statement Modeling (integrated financial statements)
Accounting, financial statements, corporate finance, excel

Chapter 3: How Does Wall Street Work?

How Does Wall Street Work? Unveiling the Core of Global Finance

Wall Street, synonymous with the financial epicenter of the world, stands as a symbol of global finance. From the iconic New York Stock Exchange (NYSE) to bustling trading floors, Wall Street encompasses a vast network of financial institutions, investment banks, and trading firms. This post aims to demystify the workings of Wall Street, exploring its core components and the roles various players have in this dynamic ecosystem.

The Financial Capital of the World

Wall Street, located in the heart of New York City, is more than just a physical location; it's a hub where financial markets converge. It houses some of the most influential financial institutions, including major investment banks, hedge funds, and trading firms. These entities are involved in a wide range of activities such as stock trading, bond issuance, mergers and acquisitions (M&A), and asset management. The influence of Wall Street extends globally, impacting markets around the world.

Market Infrastructure

The infrastructure of Wall Street is built around key stock exchanges like the NYSE and NASDAQ. These exchanges are platforms where public companies list their shares, making them available for trading. The process involves a network of brokers, dealers, and market makers who facilitate the buying and selling of securities. With the rise of technology, electronic trading platforms have become integral, allowing for faster and more efficient transactions.

Primary Market vs. Secondary Market:
In the primary market, new securities are issued, allowing companies to raise capital. This involves investment banks that underwrite these new issues. Once these securities are issued, they are traded among investors in the secondary market, where the prices are determined by supply and demand dynamics.

Role of Investment Banks

Investment banks are pivotal on Wall Street. They provide a myriad of services to corporations, governments, and institutional investors. Their roles include:

1. **Capital Raising:** Through IPOs and debt offerings, investment banks help companies raise capital.
2. **Advisory Services:** They advise on M&A transactions, providing valuation and strategic guidance.
3. **Trading and Asset Management:** Engaging in proprietary trading and managing assets for clients are also significant functions.

Key Market Participants

The participants in Wall Street's ecosystem are diverse, including institutional investors like pension funds and mutual funds, hedge funds, retail investors, and high-frequency trading firms. Each group plays a unique role:

- **Institutional Investors:** Manage large pools of capital and are influential in setting market trends.
- **Hedge Funds:** Employ complex strategies to maximize returns, often using leverage.
- **Retail Investors:** Participate via brokerage accounts, their involvement has been democratized through digital platforms.

Regulation and Oversight

Wall Street operates under strict regulatory frameworks to ensure fair and orderly markets. Key regulatory bodies include the Securities and Exchange Commission (SEC) and the Financial Industry Regulatory Authority (FINRA). These entities oversee market activities, enforce compliance with securities laws, and protect investor interests. Their regulations promote transparency, reduce systemic risk, and uphold market integrity.

Divisions within Investment Banks

Investment banks are organized into various divisions, each specializing in different aspects of finance:

- **Mergers & Acquisitions (M&A):** Focuses on corporate restructuring and mergers.
- **Capital Markets:** Deals with raising capital through debt and equity markets.
- **Sales and Trading:** Involves the buying and selling of securities.
- **Research:** Provides analysis and reports on markets and specific companies.
- **Asset Management:** Manages investments for institutions and high-net-worth individuals.

The Impact of Technology

Technological advancements have profoundly transformed Wall Street. High-frequency trading (HFT) firms use algorithms to execute trades at microsecond speeds, capitalizing on minute market movements. Digital platforms have opened the markets to retail investors, enabling greater participation and access to financial information.

Global Influence

Wall Street's reach is global, affecting international financial markets. It serves as a gateway for foreign companies to access U.S. capital, often through listing their shares on American exchanges. The interconnectedness of global economies means that events on Wall Street can ripple through financial markets worldwide, influencing investment strategies and market sentiment.

Challenges and Future Outlook

Despite its dominance, Wall Street faces continuous challenges, including evolving regulations, market volatility, and technological disruptions. The rise of fintech, the application of artificial intelligence, and the increasing emphasis on sustainable investing are reshaping the financial landscape. Adapting to these changes and leveraging new technologies will be crucial for Wall Street's continued relevance and success.

Conclusion

Wall Street is a complex, multifaceted hub that drives global finance. It encompasses a range of institutions and activities, from investment banking to trading, all regulated to ensure market stability. Understanding its workings is essential for anyone looking to navigate the world of finance, whether as a professional or investor. As Wall Street evolves, it will continue to play a critical role in shaping the global financial system.

Chapter 4: Economic Performance Promises through Guidance: The Role of EPS

Economic Performance Promises Through Guidance: The Role of EPS

In the ever-evolving landscape of corporate finance, upper management of corporations frequently communicates with investors by issuing economic performance promises. One key method of delivering these promises is through earnings per share (EPS) guidance. EPS guidance is a critical tool used by companies to set investor expectations, influence market behavior, and direct internal strategic efforts. This blog post explores the intricacies of EPS guidance, its impact on investment decisions, market expectations, and the internal alignment required to meet these promises.

Understanding EPS Guidance

Earnings per Share (EPS) Guidance involves predictions made by a company's upper management about the expected earnings per share for upcoming periods. These projections are crucial because they give investors a glimpse into the company's anticipated financial performance and profitability. Typically, EPS guidance is provided for short-term periods, such as the next fiscal quarter or year, and is often adjusted as new information becomes available. This guidance serves as a form of commitment to shareholders, indicating what they can reasonably expect in terms of returns.

Influence on Investment Decisions

EPS guidance plays a significant role in shaping the decisions of institutional investors, analysts, and individual shareholders. Investors rely heavily on these forecasts to assess potential returns and risks associated with investing in a particular company's stock. A company's ability to meet or exceed its EPS guidance can enhance investor confidence and attract more capital. Conversely, failing to meet expectations can lead to a loss of investor trust and a decline in stock prices. Thus, accurate and reliable EPS guidance is crucial for maintaining investor interest and confidence.

Shaping Market Expectations

The issuance of EPS guidance also significantly shapes market expectations. Analysts and investors use this guidance to update their valuation models and forecasts. When a company releases its EPS guidance, it essentially sets a benchmark against which its future performance will be judged. If actual results fall short of the guidance, it can lead to negative market reactions, such as a drop in stock price. Conversely, exceeding guidance can result in positive market movements. Therefore, companies strive to provide guidance that is both realistic and attainable, to avoid market volatility and manage investor expectations effectively.

Balancing Realism and Optimism

One of the most challenging aspects of providing EPS guidance is finding the right balance between optimism and realism. Management teams must avoid being overly optimistic, as failing to meet high expectations can lead to significant market backlash and damage to the company's credibility. On the other hand, being too conservative might not fully reflect the company's potential, thereby missing opportunities to positively influence investor perception and market valuation. Striking the right balance requires a deep understanding of the company's operational capabilities, market conditions, and potential risks.

Aligning Internal Performance with Guidance

Providing EPS guidance is not merely a public relations exercise; it necessitates meticulous internal alignment and performance management. To achieve the promised economic performance, all departments and business units within the company must work cohesively towards common financial goals. This includes setting specific performance targets, monitoring key performance indicators (KPIs), and making strategic adjustments to ensure operational efficiency and profitability. Effective internal communication and coordination are essential to align the company's actual performance with the promises made through EPS guidance.

Conclusion

In conclusion, EPS guidance serves as a crucial communication tool between corporations and their investors, providing insights into expected financial performance and helping to shape market expectations. The role of investment bankers and corporate finance professionals in crafting and delivering these messages is vital, as they must carefully balance realism with optimism and ensure that internal operations are aligned to meet these promises. Through thoughtful and accurate EPS guidance, companies can build investor trust, stabilize their market position, and ultimately drive long-term value creation.

PART II: WHAT IS INVESTMENT BANKING & WHERE DOES IT FIT INTO THE CAPITAL MANAGEMENT GAME

Chapter 5: What is Investment Banking?

The Comprehensive Guide to Understanding Investment Banking

Investment banking is a critical component of the financial sector, providing essential services that support the flow of capital, the execution of complex financial transactions, and the overall stability of the economy. This blog post aims to offer a thorough understanding of investment banking, detailing its core functions, types of banks, the roles within these institutions, and its broader impact on global finance.

The Core of Investment Banking

At its heart, investment banking involves assisting various entities—such as individuals, corporations, and governments—in raising capital and executing financial transactions. Unlike commercial banks that primarily handle deposits and loans, investment banks specialize in advisory-based services. These services range from underwriting new securities, facilitating mergers and acquisitions (M&A), and providing market-making activities, to proprietary trading and research.

Investment banks essentially serve as intermediaries, connecting those who need capital with those who have capital to invest. They play a pivotal role in ensuring that capital is allocated efficiently, thereby contributing to economic growth and stability.

Key Functions of Investment Banks

1. **Capital Raising:** Investment banks assist clients in raising funds by issuing securities. This can involve Initial Public Offerings (IPOs) for companies looking to go public or the issuance of bonds and other debt instruments. The bank's role includes pricing these securities, underwriting them (assuming the risk of selling them), and managing the entire issuance process.

2. **Mergers and Acquisitions (M&A):** One of the most visible roles of investment banks is advising on M&A transactions. This process involves identifying potential acquisition targets or buyers, conducting detailed financial analyses and due diligence, valuing the companies involved, negotiating terms, and ensuring compliance with all regulatory requirements. Successful M&A deals can lead to significant growth, market expansion, and operational efficiencies for the involved companies.

3. **Sales and Trading:** Investment banks facilitate the buying and selling of securities in the secondary market. They act as market makers by providing liquidity, which is crucial for maintaining market stability. They may also engage in proprietary trading, where they use the bank's capital to trade financial instruments for profit. This activity helps in price discovery and the efficient functioning of markets.

4. **Research:** Another vital function is providing research and analysis on various markets, industries, and companies. Investment banks employ analysts who produce reports that offer insights into market trends, company valuations, and economic forecasts. These reports help investors make

informed decisions, and they are a critical component of the bank's advisory services.

5. **Asset Management:** Many investment banks manage assets on behalf of their clients, including pension funds, endowments, and high-net-worth individuals. Asset management involves creating investment strategies, managing portfolios, and ensuring optimal asset allocation to achieve the clients' financial goals.

6. **Advisory Services:** Beyond M&A, investment banks offer a range of advisory services, including restructuring, capital structure optimization, and risk management. These services help clients navigate complex financial landscapes, make strategic decisions, and enhance their value.

Types of Investment Banks

Investment banks can be categorized based on their size, reach, and areas of specialization:

- **Bulge Bracket Banks:** These are the largest and most globally recognized investment banks, such as Goldman Sachs and JPMorgan Chase. They offer a full spectrum of services and operate on a global scale, handling the largest and most complex financial transactions.
- **Middle Market Banks:** These banks, like Jefferies and Piper Sandler, focus on serving mid-sized companies. They offer similar services as bulge bracket banks but on a smaller scale, often specializing in specific industries or regions.
- **Boutique Banks:** These are smaller, specialized firms that often focus on specific industries or types of transactions, such as M&A. Boutique banks like Lazard and Evercore offer deep expertise in niche markets, providing highly specialized advisory services.

Roles Within Investment Banks

The professionals working in investment banks are responsible for executing various financial transactions and providing advisory services. The roles vary based on experience and responsibility:

1. **Analysts:** Often entry-level positions, analysts are responsible for financial modeling, preparing presentations, and supporting senior bankers in executing deals. This role involves long hours and a steep learning curve, providing a foundational experience in the industry.
2. **Associates:** Typically, associates have a few years of experience or an MBA. They manage analysts, participate in client meetings, and play a more active role in deal-making processes.
3. **Vice Presidents (VPs):** VPs manage teams, maintain client relationships, and oversee the execution of deals. They are involved in strategic decision-making and are responsible for mentoring junior staff.
4. **Directors/Executive Directors:** These professionals focus on high-level client relationships and major transactions. They are instrumental in bringing in new business and executing strategic initiatives.
5. **Managing Directors (MDs):** MDs are senior executives responsible for the overall strategy of the bank, major client relationships, and the largest deals. They play a crucial role in shaping the bank's market presence and profitability.

The Broader Impact of Investment Banking

Investment banking plays a crucial role in the economy by facilitating capital formation, enabling corporate growth through M&A, and ensuring liquidity in financial markets. During economic downturns or financial crises, investment banks help stabilize the economy by restructuring distressed companies, managing public offerings to raise critical capital, and providing market insights.

The industry has evolved significantly, especially in response to challenges like regulatory changes following the 2008 financial crisis and technological advancements such as algorithmic trading and blockchain. Today, investment banks are also focusing on sustainable finance, integrating environmental, social, and governance (ESG) criteria into their investment strategies, reflecting a broader shift towards responsible investing.

Conclusion

Investment banking is a dynamic and essential part of the financial landscape. It encompasses a wide range of activities that not only support corporate growth and market stability but also contribute to the broader economy. Understanding the roles, functions, and impact of investment banking provides valuable insights into the complex world of finance. Whether you're an aspiring professional or simply interested in the financial markets, grasping the fundamentals of investment banking is crucial for navigating the ever-evolving financial environment.

NOTES:
Investment banking is a type of financial service that helps individuals, corporations, and governments raise capital through the issuance and sale of securities. Investment banks act as intermediaries between issuers of securities (sell-side), such as stocks and bonds, and investors who are interested in purchasing those securities (buy-side).

The services provided by investment banks include underwriting, which involves purchasing securities from the issuer and selling them to investors, as well as assisting with mergers and acquisitions, debt and equity offerings, and other financial transactions. Investment banks also provide advice and research to their clients, helping them make informed investment decisions.

The Role of Securitizing Primary Market Investments
Investment bankers securitize primary market investments. Creating the security for the primary market investment that is not currently offered to a secondary market. Typically these are controlling interests and less liquid since they are not available on a secondary marketplace or public exchange. They typically command a higher return as well which is incentive for investors to prefer primary market investments.

Investment bankers can securitize primary market investments by creating and selling financial instruments that are backed by the underlying assets of the investment. This process involves several steps:

Origination: The investment banker works with the issuer of the primary market investment to structure the deal and prepare the underlying assets for securitization.

Pooling: The investment banker groups the underlying assets into a pool, which can be either homogeneous (e.g., a pool of residential mortgages) or heterogeneous (e.g., a pool of commercial loans).

Securitization: The investment banker creates a special purpose vehicle (SPV) to hold the pool of assets and issue securities backed by those assets. The SPV issues different classes of securities, each with a different level of risk and return.

Credit enhancement: To increase the creditworthiness of the securities, the investment banker may add credit enhancements, such as guarantees, insurance, or reserve funds.

Rating: The securities are rated by credit rating agencies based on the creditworthiness of the underlying assets, the credit enhancements, and other factors.

Underwriting and distribution: The securities are sold to investors through an underwriting process, in which investment banks and other financial institutions purchase the securities from the SPV and then sell them to investors.

Servicing: The investment banker or a third-party servicer manages the underlying assets and collects the cash flows, which are then distributed to the investors.

Overall, investment bankers securitize primary market investments by creating securities that are backed by the underlying assets of the investment, and then selling those securities to investors. This process can provide issuers with access to capital and investors with access to new investment opportunities.

Investment Banking as:
1. Generating Strategic Alternatives
2. Pitching Strategic Alternatives
3. Winning the Mandaate to Implement a Strategic Alternative
4. Underwriting & Securitizing the Strategic Alternative

5. Deal-Making to Close on the Strategic Alternative

Chapter 6: What Role Do Investment Bankers Play in the Capital Management Game?

Understanding the Role of Investment Bankers in Capital Management: An In-Depth Exploration

Investment bankers are central figures in the complex and multifaceted world of capital management. Their role is crucial in connecting companies and governments needing capital with investors who have the funds to invest. This post delves into the comprehensive responsibilities and expertise of investment bankers, explaining how they facilitate the efficient flow of capital, drive strategic initiatives, and ultimately create value for all stakeholders involved.

Capital Advisory and Structuring: Crafting the Blueprint for Capital Acquisition

Investment bankers begin their involvement in capital management by offering capital advisory services. This involves assessing a company's financial needs and devising optimal strategies for raising capital. Investment bankers meticulously evaluate different capital sources, including equity, debt, and hybrid instruments, to determine the most suitable option. They consider factors like market conditions, the company's financial health, and strategic objectives.

For example, when a company seeks to raise capital through an Initial Public Offering (IPO), investment bankers guide the process. They assess the company's value, set the price for shares, and coordinate the sale to investors. This process involves not only financial expertise but also a deep understanding of market dynamics to ensure that the company secures the necessary funds at favorable terms.

Facilitating Mergers and Acquisitions (M&A): Navigating Complex Corporate Transactions

One of the most critical roles investment bankers play is in facilitating mergers and acquisitions (M&A). They are integral in helping companies identify potential acquisition targets or suitable merger partners. The process involves comprehensive due diligence to understand the financial health and strategic fit of the companies involved.

Investment bankers use their expertise to conduct thorough financial analyses and valuations, determining the fair value of companies. They craft deal structures that maximize the benefits for their clients, whether it's through cash, stock, or a combination of both. Beyond the numbers, investment bankers are skilled negotiators, working to secure the best possible terms for their clients. They also help navigate regulatory approvals and ensure compliance with legal and financial standards.

For instance, during an acquisition, an investment banker might advise a company on the best way to finance the purchase—whether through debt, issuing new equity, or using cash reserves. They also provide strategic advice on integrating the acquired company's operations, aiming to achieve synergies that enhance the value of the combined entity.

Mastery of Capital Markets: Orchestrating the Symphony of Market Transactions

Investment bankers are experts in capital markets, encompassing a broad range of financial instruments like equities, debt, derivatives, and more. Their role in capital markets is twofold: they help companies raise funds and provide liquidity in the markets.

When companies decide to raise funds through issuing stocks or bonds, investment bankers manage these processes. They assess market conditions to time the issuance, determine the price of securities, and sell them to investors. Their extensive networks with institutional and retail investors are crucial in ensuring the success of these offerings.

Moreover, investment bankers often act as market makers, providing liquidity by buying and selling securities. This activity helps maintain market stability and ensures that there is always a buyer and seller for securities, which is essential for a functioning financial market.

Comprehensive Financial Advisory Services: Beyond Traditional Banking

Investment bankers also provide a range of financial advisory services beyond traditional capital raising and M&A. They assist companies with corporate restructuring, divestitures, spin-offs, and optimizing capital structures. For example, a company facing financial distress might engage investment bankers to help restructure its debt or advise on selling off non-core assets to improve financial stability.

These services are not limited to large corporations. Investment bankers also advise smaller firms and startups, guiding them through complex financial landscapes to achieve their growth objectives. Their advice is grounded in deep industry knowledge, financial expertise, and an understanding of corporate strategy.

Conclusion: The Indispensable Role of Investment Bankers in Capital Management

Investment bankers are indispensable in the realm of capital management. Their extensive knowledge of financial markets, deep analytical skills, and strategic thinking enable them to provide valuable services that facilitate capital flows and support economic growth. By helping companies raise capital, advising on mergers and acquisitions, navigating the complexities of capital markets, and offering comprehensive financial advisory services, investment bankers play a pivotal role in shaping the financial landscape.

In today's dynamic financial environment, the role of investment bankers is more critical than ever. They not only help companies and governments meet their financial needs but also drive innovation and efficiency in the markets. As trusted advisors, investment bankers ensure that capital is allocated effectively, contributing to the overall stability and growth of the global economy.

Chapter 7: Investment Banking as an Intermediary: Bridging the Gap between Sources and Uses of Capital

Investment Banking as an Intermediary: A Deep Dive into Bridging the Gap Between Investors and Issuers

Investment banking plays a fundamental role in the financial ecosystem, acting as a vital intermediary between those who have capital and those who need it. This intermediary function is crucial for the smooth functioning of financial markets and the overall economy. By connecting investors (sources of capital) with issuers (uses of capital), investment banks facilitate the efficient flow of funds, support business growth, and drive economic development. Let's explore in detail how investment banks serve as this essential bridge, their key functions, and the services they offer to both investors and issuers.

The Core Role of Investment Banking

At the heart of investment banking is the provision of various financial services that help entities such as corporations, governments, and other organizations raise capital. Unlike commercial banks, which primarily focus on taking deposits and making loans, investment banks specialize in assisting their clients in raising capital, managing assets, and providing advisory services for complex financial transactions. They act as intermediaries, meaning they stand between the buyers and sellers of securities, ensuring that capital flows smoothly and efficiently from those who have it to those who need it.

Understanding Capital Markets: A Platform for Capital Flows

Investment banks operate within capital markets, which are divided into two main segments:

1. **Primary Markets**: This is where new securities are created and sold for the first time. Investment banks underwrite these new issues, which involves purchasing the securities from the issuer and then selling them to investors. This process is essential for raising new capital, whether through equity offerings like Initial Public Offerings (IPOs) or debt instruments such as bonds.
2. **Secondary Markets**: Once securities are issued, they can be bought and sold among investors in the secondary markets. Investment banks provide the infrastructure and services necessary for these transactions, ensuring liquidity and efficient price discovery. This secondary market activity is crucial as it allows investors to buy and sell securities, thereby maintaining a dynamic and responsive market environment.

Services Provided by Investment Banks to Issuers

For entities looking to raise capital, investment banks offer a comprehensive suite of services:

- **Underwriting Services**: In underwriting, investment banks take on the risk of selling a new issue of securities. They buy these securities from the issuer and sell them to the public or institutional investors. This service is critical during IPOs or when companies issue additional shares or bonds. The bank's role is to ensure the successful sale of these securities, which provides the issuer with the necessary capital.

- **Advisory Services**: Investment banks provide expert advice on a range of strategic financial matters, including mergers and acquisitions (M&A), restructurings, and capital structure optimization. They help clients evaluate potential deals, assess market conditions, and navigate complex regulatory environments. This advisory role is vital in helping companies make informed decisions that align with their strategic goals and enhance shareholder value.

Services Provided by Investment Banks to Investors

Investment banks also play a crucial role in serving the needs of investors, offering a variety of services that help them manage and grow their investments:

- **Market Research and Analysis**: Investment banks employ teams of analysts who conduct in-depth research on markets, industries, and specific companies. They provide valuable insights and recommendations, helping investors make informed decisions. This research covers economic trends, market dynamics, and investment opportunities, offering a comprehensive view of potential risks and rewards.
- **Brokerage Services**: Through their brokerage operations, investment banks facilitate the buying and selling of securities. They execute trades on behalf of clients, whether they are individual investors, institutional investors, or hedge funds. This service is essential for maintaining market liquidity and enabling investors to enter and exit positions efficiently.

Syndication and Distribution of Securities

For large financial transactions, investment banks often collaborate with other financial institutions to form syndicates. This syndication process spreads the risk associated with underwriting large issues of securities and allows investment banks to leverage their collective distribution networks. By doing so, they can reach a broader base of investors, ensuring that the capital-raising effort meets its targets. This collaborative approach is particularly important in large bond issues or international offerings, where the scale and complexity of the transaction require multiple institutions' involvement.

Due Diligence and Risk Assessment

A critical function of investment banks is performing due diligence and risk assessment. Before any transaction, investment banks thoroughly analyze the financial health of the issuer, the market conditions, and the potential risks involved. This due diligence process includes reviewing financial statements, assessing market trends, and evaluating the issuer's business model and management team. By providing this level of scrutiny, investment banks help protect investors and ensure that the securities offered are sound investments.

Investor Relations and Corporate Finance Advisory

Investment banks also assist issuers in managing their relationships with investors. They provide investor relations services, which involve helping companies communicate effectively with their shareholders and the broader investment community. This communication is crucial for maintaining investor confidence and ensuring a transparent flow of information about the company's performance and strategic direction. Additionally, investment banks offer corporate finance advisory services, helping companies optimize their capital structure, plan for future growth, and navigate complex financial challenges.

Global Reach and Cross-Border Transactions

Operating on a global scale, investment banks facilitate cross-border transactions and capital flows. They have the expertise to manage the complexities of international finance, including different regulatory environments, currency risks, and cultural differences. This global reach allows them to connect issuers with a diverse range of investors worldwide, enhancing the ability of companies to raise capital and providing investors with access to international markets.

Promoting Capital Allocation Efficiency

Investment banks play a pivotal role in promoting efficient capital allocation within the economy. By connecting those who need capital with those who have it, they help ensure that resources are directed to their most productive uses. This efficient allocation of capital supports business expansion, innovation, and economic growth. Investment banks also provide liquidity and transparency in financial markets, contributing to market stability and investor confidence.

Conclusion

Investment banks are indispensable in the financial system, acting as intermediaries that bridge the gap between investors and issuers. Through their wide range of services, including underwriting, advisory, research, and brokerage, they facilitate the efficient flow of capital, support business growth, and contribute to the stability and liquidity of financial markets. Their role as intermediaries ensures that capital is allocated efficiently, which is essential for fostering innovation and economic development. As the financial landscape continues to evolve, investment banks will remain key players, adapting to new challenges and opportunities while continuing to drive progress and efficiency in the global economy.

Chapter 8: Types of Issuers that Utilize Investment Banking Services

Understanding the Diverse Range of Issuers That Engage Investment Banking Services

Investment banking is a multifaceted field that plays an essential role in the financial ecosystem. Its services are sought by a wide array of issuers, each with unique needs and objectives. This blog post delves into the various types of issuers that commonly engage investment bankers, illustrating the broad scope of sectors and entities that rely on these financial experts to navigate complex financial landscapes and achieve their capital raising and advisory goals.

Corporations: The Powerhouses of Economic Activity

Corporations, encompassing everything from burgeoning startups to well-established multinational conglomerates, are among the primary users of investment banking services. These businesses often require substantial capital to fund operations, expansion projects, or strategic initiatives like mergers and acquisitions (M&A).

Startups and Early-Stage Companies: For startups, securing seed funding or venture capital is critical for launching and scaling their business. Investment bankers assist in identifying potential investors, structuring equity offerings, and negotiating terms that align with the founders' goals.

Established Corporations: Larger companies might seek capital for a variety of reasons, such as expanding into new markets, investing in research and development, or refinancing existing debt. Investment bankers help these corporations navigate public offerings, private placements, and other financing mechanisms. They provide crucial support in pricing the securities, marketing them to potential investors, and ensuring regulatory compliance throughout the process.

Government Entities: Financing Public Needs

Government entities at the national, state, and local levels frequently utilize investment banking services. These bodies often need to raise capital for public projects and infrastructure development, such as constructing highways, schools, or hospitals.

Municipal Bonds: Investment bankers play a critical role in underwriting municipal bonds, which are a common tool for governments to raise funds for public projects. They help structure these bond offerings, determine the interest rates, and market the bonds to investors. This process ensures that governments can secure the necessary funding while managing their debt levels effectively.

Advisory Services: Beyond capital raising, investment bankers also provide advisory services to governments. This includes advising on debt management strategies, such as when to issue new debt or refinance existing obligations to take advantage of favorable interest rates.

Financial Institutions: Navigating Complex Financial Landscapes

Financial institutions, including banks, insurance companies, and asset management firms, are another significant group of issuers that rely on investment banking services. These institutions often engage in complex transactions that require specialized financial expertise.

Mergers and Acquisitions (M&A): Investment bankers assist financial institutions in M&A transactions, providing valuation analyses, structuring deals, and negotiating terms. These transactions might involve the acquisition of smaller banks, insurance firms, or asset management companies to expand market share or diversify offerings.

Capital Raising: Financial institutions also raise capital by issuing stocks or bonds, and investment bankers help manage these processes. For instance, a bank might issue new equity to strengthen its capital base, or an insurance company might issue bonds to fund new policy offerings.

Nonprofit Organizations: Supporting Mission-Driven Initiatives

Nonprofit organizations, including educational institutions, hospitals, and foundations, often turn to investment bankers for assistance in fundraising and financial management.

Capital Campaigns: For example, universities may undertake capital campaigns to fund new buildings, scholarships, or research programs. Investment bankers help these institutions structure fundraising efforts, which may involve issuing tax-exempt bonds or launching public donation campaigns.

Debt Issuance: Hospitals might issue bonds to finance the construction of new facilities or to purchase advanced medical equipment. Investment bankers ensure these bonds are structured advantageously and marketed to investors who are interested in supporting nonprofit initiatives.

Sovereign Entities and Multilateral Organizations: Complex Financial Transactions

Sovereign entities, such as national governments and central banks, as well as multilateral organizations like the World Bank, often engage investment bankers for their specialized financial needs.

Sovereign Debt Issuances: Investment bankers assist national governments in issuing debt, which can be a critical component of a country's financial strategy. This involves determining the terms of the issuance, marketing the debt to international investors, and managing the sale.

Development Projects: Multilateral organizations may raise funds for large-scale infrastructure or development projects in emerging markets. Investment bankers play a crucial role in structuring these transactions, ensuring that they meet the regulatory requirements of multiple jurisdictions and attract a diverse range of investors.

Conclusion: The Integral Role of Investment Bankers

Investment bankers serve as indispensable intermediaries in the financial ecosystem, connecting a wide range of issuers with investors. Their expertise in capital markets, advisory services, and transaction structuring enables corporations, governments, financial institutions, nonprofits, and sovereign entities to achieve their financial objectives efficiently. By understanding the diverse needs of these issuers, investment bankers help facilitate the flow of capital, drive economic growth, and support the development of critical infrastructure and services worldwide. The breadth and depth of investment banking services underscore the industry's vital role in the global financial landscape.

Chapter 9: Origination of Investment Banking Opportunities from Corporate Issuers

The Detailed Process of Originating Investment Banking Opportunities from Corporate Issuers

Investment banking is a vital sector that connects companies in need of capital with investors looking to allocate funds. One of the critical functions of investment bankers is originating opportunities with corporate issuers, a process that involves several detailed and methodical steps. This blog post will explore the intricacies of this process, emphasizing the various stages that investment bankers go through to identify, cultivate, and execute financial opportunities.

1. Building and Nurturing Relationships

The foundation of originating investment banking opportunities lies in building strong, long-term relationships with corporate decision-makers. Investment bankers actively seek to establish connections with CEOs, CFOs, board members, and other key executives. This is often achieved through a combination of networking events, industry conferences, and one-on-one meetings. The goal is to become a trusted advisor, someone these executives turn to for strategic financial advice.

Investment bankers spend considerable time understanding the company's leadership style, corporate culture, and strategic vision. They may offer insights into market trends, provide valuable connections, or offer preliminary advice on financial matters. This relationship-building phase is crucial as it lays the groundwork for future transactions.

2. In-Depth Market Research and Analysis

Once a relationship is established, investment bankers conduct thorough market research and analysis. This involves studying the industry in which the corporate issuer operates, analyzing competitors, and understanding broader economic and market conditions. Investment bankers also monitor regulatory changes that might impact the company or its industry.

For example, if a company operates in the tech sector, the investment bank would study trends in technology, such as emerging innovations, consumer behavior, and shifts in regulatory landscapes. The analysis also extends to evaluating the financial performance of competitors and potential acquisition targets.

3. Understanding and Identifying Financial Needs

Investment bankers engage in detailed discussions with the company's management to understand their financial objectives. These discussions cover a wide range of topics, including:

- **Expansion Plans**: Whether the company is looking to expand its operations domestically or internationally.
- **Capital Structure**: Assessing whether the company needs to optimize its mix of debt and equity.
- **Mergers and Acquisitions**: Exploring opportunities for growth through acquisitions or divestitures.

- **Operational Improvements**: Identifying areas where the company can improve efficiency or reduce costs.

Through these discussions, investment bankers identify specific financial needs, such as raising capital, restructuring debt, or selling a portion of the business.

4. Providing Strategic Advisory Services

Based on the information gathered, investment bankers provide strategic advisory services tailored to the company's needs. This can include advice on:

- **Capital Raising**: Whether to pursue an initial public offering (IPO), a secondary offering, or a private placement.
- **Mergers and Acquisitions**: Identifying potential targets or buyers, conducting valuations, and advising on deal structures.
- **Restructuring**: Recommending ways to optimize the company's capital structure or improve financial stability.

Investment bankers use their expertise to recommend the best strategies for achieving the company's objectives, considering market conditions and investor sentiment.

5. Structuring and Executing Financial Transactions

Once a strategic plan is in place, investment bankers move to structuring and executing the necessary financial transactions. This involves several key steps:

- **Securities Offerings**: Determining the type, timing, and pricing of securities offerings, whether they are equity or debt instruments.

- **Syndication and Distribution**: For large transactions, investment banks often form syndicates with other banks to share the risk and ensure broad distribution.
- **Underwriting**: Investment banks may underwrite the securities, taking on the risk of selling them to investors.

The execution phase requires meticulous planning and coordination with legal, regulatory, and financial entities to ensure compliance and successful completion.

6. Ongoing Relationship Management and Support

The relationship with corporate issuers doesn't end with the completion of a transaction. Investment bankers provide ongoing support, offering continuous market insights, monitoring the company's financial health, and advising on further strategic initiatives. This ongoing relationship management helps in identifying new opportunities and ensures the investment bank remains a key advisor to the company.

Investment bankers may also assist with investor relations, helping the company communicate effectively with its shareholders and the broader investment community.

Conclusion

The origination of investment banking opportunities from corporate issuers is a multi-faceted process that requires a deep understanding of financial markets, strong relationships, and strategic advisory skills. Investment bankers play a pivotal role in guiding companies through complex financial landscapes, from initial discussions and market research to transaction execution and ongoing support. By doing so, they help corporate issuers achieve their financial goals and contribute to broader economic growth.

Chapter 10: Understanding the Financial Needs of Corporate Issuers

Understanding the Financial Needs of Corporate Issuers

Investment banking is a sophisticated field that requires a deep understanding of corporate issuers' financial needs. This knowledge is crucial for providing effective investment banking services that align with the strategic goals and operational realities of these issuers. Here, we explore the essential aspects of understanding corporate issuers, including their financial positions, growth plans, and capital requirements. By delving into these areas, investment bankers can offer tailored financial solutions that help corporate issuers achieve their objectives.

Assessing Financial Position

The first step in understanding a corporate issuer's financial needs is to thoroughly assess their financial position. Investment bankers begin by analyzing financial statements such as balance sheets, income statements, and cash flow statements. This involves a detailed examination of various financial metrics, including:

- **Liquidity Ratios:** Measures like the current ratio and quick ratio provide insights into the company's ability to meet short-term obligations.

- **Profitability Ratios:** Metrics such as return on equity (ROE), return on assets (ROA), and net profit margin help assess how effectively the company generates profit from its resources.
- **Debt Ratios:** Analyzing the debt-to-equity ratio and interest coverage ratio reveals the company's leverage and ability to service its debt.

By evaluating these and other financial indicators, investment bankers can gauge the issuer's overall financial health, stability, and performance. This assessment helps identify any financial constraints and areas for potential improvement.

Reviewing Historical Performance

Understanding a company's historical financial performance is crucial for predicting future success. Investment bankers review past financial data to identify trends, growth patterns, and key business drivers. This analysis includes:

- **Revenue Growth:** Examining historical revenue trends to understand growth trajectory and market demand.
- **Cost Management:** Analyzing how well the company manages its costs and the impact on profit margins.
- **Profitability Trends:** Assessing the consistency and sustainability of profit margins over time.

Historical performance reviews help investment bankers understand how the company has navigated economic cycles and market conditions. It also highlights the company's resilience and adaptability, which are vital for future financial planning and capital raising initiatives.

Evaluating Growth Plans

Investment bankers need to understand the strategic vision and growth plans of corporate issuers. This involves reviewing business plans, market analyses, and management presentations to grasp the company's expansion strategies, such as:

- **Geographic Expansion:** Plans to enter new markets or regions.
- **Product Development:** Initiatives to launch new products or services.
- **Acquisitions and Mergers:** Strategies to grow through acquiring other businesses or merging with competitors.

By aligning financial solutions with these growth plans, investment bankers can offer advice on financing options and structuring transactions that support the issuer's strategic objectives.

Identifying Capital Requirements

One of the most critical aspects of investment banking is identifying the specific capital requirements of corporate issuers. This involves detailed discussions with company executives to understand their needs for capital, which may include:

- **Project Funding:** Capital needed for new projects or expansions.
- **Working Capital:** Funds required for day-to-day operations and maintaining liquidity.
- **Debt Refinancing:** Capital needed to refinance existing debt to take advantage of better terms or interest rates.
- **Acquisitions:** Funds required for strategic acquisitions or mergers.

By assessing these requirements, investment bankers can propose appropriate financing solutions, such as issuing bonds, equity, or other financial instruments tailored to the issuer's needs.

Considering Industry Dynamics

Investment bankers must also consider the broader industry dynamics that impact corporate issuers. This involves analyzing:

- **Market Trends:** Understanding the current and future trends in the industry.
- **Competitive Landscape:** Evaluating the competition and market position of the issuer.
- **Regulatory Environment:** Assessing the regulatory challenges and compliance requirements specific to the industry.

Understanding these factors is crucial for providing relevant and timely financial advice that helps issuers navigate challenges and capitalize on opportunities within their industry.

Conducting Due Diligence

To gain a comprehensive understanding of a corporate issuer's financial needs, investment bankers conduct thorough due diligence. This process includes:

- **Operational Review:** Evaluating the company's operational efficiency and effectiveness.
- **Financial Analysis:** Conducting a detailed examination of financial statements and metrics.
- **Market Position:** Assessing the company's position within the market and its competitive strengths.
- **Risk Management:** Reviewing the company's risk management practices and potential liabilities.
- **Legal and Regulatory Compliance:** Ensuring the company adheres to relevant laws and regulations.

Due diligence helps identify potential issues or concerns that could impact the issuer's financial health and the feasibility of proposed transactions. It provides a solid foundation for making informed recommendations and structuring appropriate financial solutions.

Conclusion

Understanding the financial needs of corporate issuers is essential for providing effective investment banking services. By assessing financial positions, reviewing historical performance, evaluating growth plans, identifying capital requirements, considering industry dynamics, and conducting due diligence, investment bankers can develop a deep understanding of their clients' needs. This comprehensive approach enables bankers to offer strategic advice, structure tailored financing solutions, and support corporate issuers in achieving their objectives, ultimately driving growth and success in the marketplace.

Chapter 11: Investment Bankers and Strategic Alternatives for Corporate Issuers

Investment bankers are pivotal in helping corporate issuers navigate complex financial landscapes, particularly when exploring strategic alternatives. These alternatives can include mergers and acquisitions (M&A), divestitures, joint ventures, strategic partnerships, and corporate restructuring. Each of these paths presents unique challenges and opportunities, and investment bankers bring their expertise to the table to guide corporate issuers through these processes. This blog post delves into the comprehensive role that investment bankers play in identifying, evaluating, and executing these strategic alternatives, emphasizing the importance of their contributions to maximizing value and achieving successful outcomes.

Identifying Strategic Alternatives

The process begins with identifying potential strategic alternatives. Investment bankers leverage their in-depth industry knowledge, extensive market research, and vast professional networks to uncover opportunities that may not be immediately apparent. This involves a thorough analysis of market trends, competitor activities, and broader industry dynamics. Investment bankers study these factors to spot trends that could influence the corporate issuer's strategic direction, such as emerging market opportunities or technological advancements. They assess the company's strengths, weaknesses, opportunities, and threats (SWOT analysis) to align potential strategies with the issuer's long-term objectives.

Valuation and Financial Analysis

Once potential strategic alternatives are identified, the next crucial step is valuation and financial analysis. Investment bankers utilize various valuation techniques to determine the fair market value of the corporate issuer and any potential acquisition targets or assets. Common methods include:

- **Discounted Cash Flow (DCF) Analysis:** This method estimates the present value of expected future cash flows, adjusted for the time value of money.
- **Comparable Company Analysis (CCA):** This involves comparing the corporate issuer with similar companies in the same industry to derive valuation multiples.
- **Precedent Transactions Analysis:** This looks at similar past transactions to establish benchmarks for valuation.

These analyses are not just about numbers; they involve detailed assessments of the financial health, operational efficiency, and market positioning of the companies involved. Investment bankers also analyze potential synergies that could arise from mergers or acquisitions, such as cost savings or revenue enhancements. This financial scrutiny is critical in determining the feasibility and attractiveness of each strategic alternative.

Facilitating Negotiations

Negotiations are a complex and sensitive aspect of any strategic alternative, and investment bankers play a crucial role in this phase. Acting as intermediaries, they facilitate discussions between the corporate issuer and potential partners or acquirers. Their negotiation skills are invaluable in aligning the interests of different parties, structuring deals that are fair and beneficial, and navigating any conflicts that may arise. Investment bankers bring their deep understanding of market conditions and deal mechanics to the table, helping to set realistic expectations and negotiate terms that reflect the true value of the assets or companies involved.

Due Diligence

The due diligence process is a comprehensive review of all aspects of the entities involved in a potential transaction. Investment bankers coordinate this process, which includes:

- **Financial Due Diligence:** Reviewing financial statements, accounting practices, and financial controls to ensure accuracy and identify any potential financial risks.
- **Legal Due Diligence:** Examining legal agreements, compliance with regulations, and any outstanding litigation or legal issues.
- **Operational Due Diligence:** Assessing the efficiency and effectiveness of operational processes, supply chains, and human resources.

This exhaustive investigation is crucial for identifying any red flags or deal breakers. It helps the corporate issuer make an informed decision, understanding all potential risks and benefits associated with the transaction.

Structuring and Financing

Investment bankers are instrumental in structuring the financial and legal aspects of a deal. They work with legal and financial advisors to craft deal structures that optimize tax efficiency, mitigate risks, and align with corporate governance standards. In terms of financing, they explore various options, including:

- **Debt Financing:** Arranging loans or issuing bonds to raise the necessary capital.
- **Equity Financing:** Issuing new shares of stock to investors.
- **Hybrid Instruments:** Utilizing convertible bonds, preferred shares, or other complex financial instruments.

Investment bankers evaluate the pros and cons of each financing option, considering factors such as cost of capital, dilution of ownership, and market conditions. They also assist in preparing the necessary documentation and disclosures for regulatory compliance.

Managing the Transaction Process

Managing the transaction process is a meticulous task that involves coordinating multiple stakeholders and ensuring that all aspects of the deal are executed smoothly. Investment bankers oversee the preparation of offering memorandums, coordinate with legal teams for due diligence and documentation, and liaise with regulators to secure necessary approvals. They also manage timelines and ensure that all parties meet their obligations, keeping the transaction on track for timely completion.

Post-Transaction Support

The role of investment bankers extends beyond the closure of a deal. They provide ongoing support to ensure that the transaction delivers the expected value. This can include:

- **Post-Merger Integration:** Helping integrate the operations, cultures, and systems of merging companies.
- **Monitoring and Reporting:** Tracking the performance of the new entity and providing regular updates to stakeholders.
- **Strategic Advisory:** Offering continued guidance on optimizing operational efficiency, exploring new growth opportunities, and managing investor relations.

Investment bankers remain engaged to help the corporate issuer navigate any challenges that arise during the integration phase and to ensure that the strategic objectives of the transaction are met.

Conclusion

Investment bankers are indispensable in the world of corporate finance, particularly when it comes to exploring and executing strategic alternatives. Their comprehensive services, from identifying opportunities and conducting rigorous financial analyses to facilitating negotiations and managing the entire transaction process, are crucial for maximizing value and achieving successful outcomes. By leveraging their expertise, market insights, and extensive networks, investment bankers help corporate issuers navigate complex strategic decisions, capitalize on growth opportunities, and drive long-term value creation. Their role is not just to execute transactions but to be trusted advisors who guide companies through the intricacies of the financial markets, ensuring that every strategic move is well-informed and strategically sound.

Chapter 12: The Type of Projects That Get Financed Through Investment Bankers

Investment bankers serve as vital intermediaries in the financial markets, facilitating the flow of capital from investors to projects that require funding. Their expertise and comprehensive services help ensure that a wide range of projects across various sectors receive the necessary financial support to succeed. In this blog post, we will explore in detail the types of projects that typically get financed through investment bankers, highlighting the critical aspects of each sector and the specific contributions of investment bankers.

Infrastructure Projects

Infrastructure projects, such as the construction of highways, bridges, airports, and energy facilities, often require substantial capital investments. These projects are typically long-term and involve significant financial risk due to their scale and complexity. Investment bankers play a crucial role in structuring the financing for these projects. They help secure funding through various instruments, including public-private partnerships (PPPs), municipal bonds, and syndicated loans. By doing so, they ensure that essential public infrastructure projects receive the necessary funds to proceed, contributing to economic growth and public welfare.

Key Aspects:

1. **Risk Management:** Investment bankers assess and mitigate risks associated with construction, operations, and regulatory compliance.
2. **Capital Structuring:** They determine the optimal mix of debt and equity financing to minimize costs and maximize returns.
3. **Market Access:** Investment bankers leverage their networks to attract a broad base of investors, including institutional and retail investors.

Real Estate Development

The real estate sector is another major area where investment bankers provide critical financing. This includes funding for residential, commercial, and mixed-use developments. Real estate projects often require significant upfront capital for land acquisition, construction, and marketing. Investment bankers assist developers in raising funds through various means, such as equity investments, mortgage-backed securities, and Real Estate Investment Trusts (REITs). They also provide valuable market insights and strategic advice, helping developers navigate the complexities of the real estate market.

Key Aspects:

1. **Financing Solutions:** Investment bankers structure financing deals that meet the specific needs of developers, such as bridge loans or construction financing.
2. **Market Analysis:** They provide comprehensive market research and analysis, helping developers make informed decisions.
3. **Investment Opportunities:** Investment bankers create and manage REITs, offering investors a way to invest in real estate without directly owning properties.

Corporate Expansion and Acquisitions

Corporate issuers frequently engage investment bankers to finance expansion strategies, including mergers and acquisitions (M&A). These transactions can be complex and require careful planning and execution. Investment bankers offer a range of services, from advising on deal structure and valuation to securing financing. They help companies raise capital through equity offerings, debt issuances, or a combination of both. Their expertise in navigating regulatory requirements and market conditions is invaluable in ensuring successful transactions.

Key Aspects:

1. **Strategic Advisory:** Investment bankers provide strategic advice on identifying potential acquisition targets, conducting due diligence, and negotiating terms.
2. **Valuation and Structuring:** They perform detailed financial analyses to determine fair valuations and structure deals that optimize financial outcomes.
3. **Capital Raising:** Investment bankers assist in raising the necessary funds, whether through public offerings, private placements, or other financing methods.

Technology and Innovation

The technology sector is characterized by rapid innovation and high growth potential. However, it also comes with significant risks and uncertainties. Investment bankers play a pivotal role in financing technology-driven projects, such as startups, tech companies, and research institutions. They provide venture capital, private equity, and other forms of funding to support research and development, product commercialization, and market expansion. Investment bankers also offer strategic guidance, helping tech companies navigate regulatory challenges and market dynamics.

Key Aspects:

1. **Venture Capital:** Investment bankers help secure venture capital funding for early-stage tech startups, enabling them to develop and scale their products.
2. **Public Offerings:** They assist tech companies in going public through Initial Public Offerings (IPOs), providing access to broader capital markets.
3. **Strategic Partnerships:** Investment bankers facilitate strategic partnerships and alliances, helping tech companies leverage synergies and expand their market reach.

Natural Resources and Energy

Investment bankers are integral to financing projects in the natural resources and energy sectors, including oil and gas exploration, mining, and renewable energy initiatives. These projects often involve significant capital expenditures and long lead times. Investment bankers help structure financing deals that account for the specific risks and opportunities in these sectors. They also assist in raising capital through debt and equity offerings, joint ventures, and other financing structures.

Key Aspects:

1. **Project Finance:** Investment bankers structure project finance deals that allocate risks and rewards among stakeholders.

2. **Regulatory Navigation:** They provide guidance on navigating complex regulatory environments and securing necessary permits and approvals.
3. **Sustainability:** Investment bankers increasingly focus on financing renewable energy projects, aligning with global trends towards sustainability.

Healthcare and Life Sciences

The healthcare and life sciences industries require substantial investment for drug development, clinical trials, medical research, and infrastructure expansion. Investment bankers provide critical funding and advisory services to pharmaceutical companies, biotech firms, and healthcare providers. They assist in raising capital through public and private markets, supporting innovation and development in these vital sectors.

Key Aspects:

1. **Capital Raising:** Investment bankers help healthcare and life sciences companies raise funds through IPOs, secondary offerings, and private placements.
2. **M&A Advisory:** They provide expertise in mergers, acquisitions, and strategic partnerships, helping companies expand and innovate.
3. **Regulatory Expertise:** Investment bankers assist companies in navigating regulatory challenges, ensuring compliance with healthcare laws and regulations.

Capital for Small and Medium Enterprises (SMEs)

Small and medium-sized enterprises (SMEs) often face challenges in accessing capital. Investment bankers provide tailored financing solutions to meet the unique needs of SMEs. This includes debt financing, private placements, and venture capital investments. By supporting SMEs, investment bankers contribute to job creation, innovation, and economic growth.

Key Aspects:

1. **Customized Financing:** Investment bankers design financing packages that address the specific needs and challenges of SMEs.
2. **Growth Capital:** They provide capital for expansion, working capital, and other business needs.
3. **Advisory Services:** Investment bankers offer strategic advice on business growth, market expansion, and financial management.

Public Sector Projects

Investment bankers also play a crucial role in financing public sector projects. This includes infrastructure improvements, educational facilities, and public utilities. They help government entities raise funds through municipal bonds and other financing mechanisms. Investment bankers provide expertise in structuring these deals, ensuring that public projects are funded efficiently and effectively.

Key Aspects:

1. **Municipal Bonds:** Investment bankers assist in issuing municipal bonds, a common tool for funding public sector projects.

2. **Public-Private Partnerships:** They facilitate public-private partnerships (PPPs), leveraging private capital for public infrastructure projects.
3. **Risk Management:** Investment bankers help manage the risks associated with public sector projects, including political, regulatory, and operational risks.

Cross-Border Financing

In an increasingly globalized economy, investment bankers are essential in facilitating cross-border financing. They support multinational corporations in raising capital for international expansion, acquisitions, and joint ventures. This often involves navigating different regulatory environments, managing foreign exchange risks, and understanding cultural nuances. Investment bankers provide the expertise needed to structure and execute these complex transactions, helping companies expand their global footprint.

Key Aspects:

1. **International Expertise:** Investment bankers offer specialized knowledge in international markets, regulations, and cultural differences.
2. **Currency Risk Management:** They help companies manage foreign exchange risks, ensuring stable financial outcomes.
3. **Cross-Border M&A:** Investment bankers facilitate cross-border mergers and acquisitions, enabling companies to enter new markets and achieve global growth.

Impact Investing and Sustainability

There is a growing trend towards financing projects that have a positive social or environmental impact. Investment bankers are increasingly involved in impact investing, supporting projects in areas such as renewable energy, sustainable agriculture, affordable housing, and social enterprises. They help align capital allocation with sustainability goals, catering to investors who prioritize Environmental, Social, and Governance (ESG) criteria. By facilitating the flow of capital into these areas, investment bankers contribute to sustainable development and social good.

Key Aspects:

1. **Sustainable Finance:** Investment bankers support the transition to a low-carbon economy by financing renewable energy projects and other sustainable initiatives.
2. **ESG Criteria:** They incorporate ESG factors into investment decisions, promoting responsible investing practices.
3. **Social Impact:** Investment bankers help channel capital into projects that provide social benefits, such as affordable housing and healthcare.

Conclusion

Investment bankers play an essential role in financing a wide range of projects across various sectors. Their expertise in evaluating project viability, structuring financing options, and navigating complex regulatory environments ensures that capital is allocated efficiently and effectively. From infrastructure and real estate to technology and healthcare, the projects financed through investment banking are critical drivers of economic growth, innovation, and societal progress. Understanding the diverse range of projects that investment bankers finance provides insight into their significant impact on the global economy and the myriad opportunities available in the field of investment banking.

Chapter 13: Generating Strategic Alternatives Consistent with Capital Mandates

Investment bankers serve as pivotal advisors in the financial world, guiding corporate issuers, financial institutions, and high-net-worth individuals through complex capital management decisions. The process of generating strategic alternatives is nuanced and requires a deep understanding of the client's capital mandates, whether they pertain to long-term growth, financial returns, or personal wealth preservation. This blog post delves into the intricate process investment bankers undertake to align strategic alternatives with these capital mandates, ensuring that each decision is not only strategic but also tailored to meet specific financial objectives.

The Bedrock of Capital Mandates

Capital mandates are essentially the guiding principles that dictate how capital should be managed and allocated. These mandates can be broadly classified into three categories:

1. **Strategic Mandates:** Focus on long-term growth, innovation, market expansion, and maintaining a competitive advantage. These mandates often involve decisions related to mergers and

acquisitions (M&A), entering new markets, or developing new product lines.

2. **Financial Mandates:** Aim to maximize returns for investors, manage risks, and ensure regulatory compliance. These are typically concerned with optimizing capital structures, managing debt levels, and ensuring a stable cash flow.

3. **Personal Mandates:** Concern the financial goals of individuals, such as wealth preservation, growth, estate planning, or philanthropy. These mandates may involve structuring investments to minimize tax liabilities, setting up trusts, or planning for retirement.

Understanding these mandates is crucial for investment bankers, as they form the foundation upon which all strategic alternatives are evaluated and developed.

Identifying and Generating Strategic Alternatives

Comprehensive Financial Analysis and Market Research

Investment bankers begin by conducting **in-depth financial analysis** and **market research**. They study the client's financial statements, such as balance sheets, income statements, and cash flow statements, to gain a thorough understanding of the current financial health and performance. They also examine market trends, competitor activities, and industry dynamics to identify potential opportunities and threats.

This analysis helps in pinpointing specific areas where strategic actions can be beneficial. For example, a company with a strong cash position might explore acquisitions, while one with high debt levels might consider restructuring options.

Scenario Planning and Valuation

Once potential opportunities are identified, investment bankers engage in **scenario planning and valuation**. They create financial models to project the outcomes of various strategic alternatives, such as:

- **Mergers and Acquisitions (M&A):** Evaluating potential targets or buyers, estimating synergies, and assessing the financial impact.
- **Divestitures:** Analyzing the benefits of selling off non-core assets to focus on more profitable areas.
- **Capital Raising:** Determining the optimal mix of equity and debt to fund new projects or expansions.

Investment bankers use sophisticated valuation techniques, such as discounted cash flow (DCF) analysis, comparable company analysis, and precedent transactions, to assess the value of different options. These analyses are crucial in providing a clear picture of the potential financial outcomes.

Collaborating with Clients and Crafting Tailored Solutions

Engaging in Deep Consultations

Investment bankers do not work in isolation. They engage in **deep consultations** with their clients to understand their unique goals and constraints. This involves discussing the client's vision, risk tolerance, time horizon, and any specific requirements they might have. For instance, a client with a strategic mandate focused on innovation may be willing to invest in high-risk, high-reward projects, whereas a client with a personal mandate focused on wealth preservation may prefer low-risk investments.

Structuring and Presenting Strategic Alternatives

Based on these consultations, investment bankers **structure and present a range of strategic alternatives**. They prepare detailed presentations that outline the pros and cons of each option, backed by robust financial data and market insights. This helps clients make informed decisions that align with their capital mandates.

For example, if a company is considering an acquisition, the presentation might include an analysis of potential targets, the strategic fit of each, expected synergies, and the financial implications of the acquisition.

Execution and Beyond: Ensuring Successful Outcomes

Transaction Execution and Management

Once a strategic alternative is selected, investment bankers **manage the execution of the transaction**. This includes everything from finalizing deal terms, securing financing, and ensuring compliance with legal and regulatory requirements. They coordinate with various stakeholders, including legal teams, accountants, and regulators, to ensure a smooth process.

Post-Transaction Support and Evaluation

The role of investment bankers extends beyond the transaction. They provide **post-transaction support** to help clients integrate new acquisitions, restructure operations, or manage new investments. They also evaluate the success of the transaction, comparing actual outcomes with projected results and making adjustments as necessary.

Conclusion: The Crucial Role of Investment Bankers in Capital Management

Investment bankers are indispensable in the capital management game, acting as the architects of strategic decisions that align with complex capital mandates. Through meticulous financial analysis, market research, and close collaboration with clients, they generate and execute strategic alternatives that drive growth, maximize returns, and achieve specific financial goals. Their expertise ensures that capital is not only deployed efficiently but also aligned with the long-term objectives of the client, whether they are corporations, financial institutions, or individuals. This comprehensive approach not only facilitates optimal capital management but also fosters sustained success and value creation.

Chapter 14: Aligning Strategic Alternatives to Sponsors

Investment Bankers and the Alignment of Strategic Alternatives with Capital Sponsors

In the intricate world of investment banking, one of the critical responsibilities of investment bankers is to align strategic alternatives with the specific mandates and objectives of capital sponsors. This alignment process is essential in ensuring that the proposed financial strategies not only meet the needs of the corporate issuers but also appeal to potential investors. This blog post will explore the detailed steps involved in understanding, analyzing, and presenting strategic alternatives in a way that aligns with the interests and expectations of capital sponsors.

Understanding Capital Mandates: The Foundation of Alignment

The first and foremost step in this process is understanding the capital mandates of the entities involved. Capital mandates refer to the specific objectives, constraints, and risk appetites of the different personas involved, which can include strategic corporations, financial institutions, and individual investors. Each of these personas has distinct mandates:

1. **Strategic Corporations:** These entities focus on long-term growth, market expansion, and competitive advantage. Their capital mandates often emphasize value creation and sustainable development.
2. **Financial Institutions:** These organizations prioritize generating returns for their investors while managing risks and adhering to regulatory requirements. Their mandates often focus on portfolio diversification and risk management.
3. **Individual Investors:** For personal mandates, the emphasis is usually on wealth preservation, growth, and achieving personal financial goals, such as retirement or estate planning.

Investment bankers must delve deeply into these mandates to comprehend the underlying motivations, constraints, and desired outcomes of each persona. This understanding serves as the foundation for identifying and aligning strategic alternatives.

Capital Mandates as a Guiding Framework for Strategic Alternatives

Once the capital mandates are understood, investment bankers begin the process of identifying and analyzing potential strategic alternatives. This involves:

1. **Thorough Market and Industry Analysis:** Investment bankers conduct in-depth research into market trends, competitive landscapes, and economic conditions. This research helps in identifying opportunities and threats that could impact the strategic alternatives being considered.
2. **Scenario Planning and Financial Modeling:** Using financial models, bankers simulate various scenarios to understand the potential financial impact of different strategies. This includes assessing revenue growth, profitability, cash flow projections, and other key financial metrics.

3. **Risk Assessment:** Identifying potential risks associated with each strategic alternative is crucial. This involves evaluating market risks, operational risks, regulatory risks, and financial risks. The goal is to understand how these risks align with the risk appetite of the capital sponsors.
4. **Valuation Analysis:** Investment bankers employ various valuation methodologies, such as discounted cash flow (DCF) analysis, comparable company analysis, and precedent transaction analysis, to determine the fair value of the assets or companies involved in the strategic alternatives.

Collaborative Development of Strategic Alternatives

With a comprehensive understanding of the mandates and potential strategies, investment bankers work closely with their clients to develop and refine strategic alternatives. This collaborative approach ensures that the proposed strategies align with the long-term goals and risk tolerances of both the corporate issuers and the capital sponsors. This phase includes:

- **Tailoring Solutions:** Crafting specific financial solutions that cater to the unique needs of the stakeholders. For example, structuring an acquisition deal in a way that maximizes tax benefits for the acquirer while minimizing dilution for existing shareholders.
- **Innovative Structuring:** Investment bankers may propose innovative deal structures, such as earn-outs, contingent value rights, or equity-linked securities, to align the interests of all parties and manage risks effectively.

Presentation and Persuasion: Crafting a Compelling Pitch

After developing strategic alternatives, investment bankers prepare detailed presentations to communicate these options to capital sponsors.

The goal is to present a compelling narrative that clearly articulates the benefits, risks, and expected outcomes of the proposed strategies. This presentation typically includes:

- **Comprehensive Analysis:** A thorough explanation of the market opportunity, strategic rationale, and expected financial outcomes. This includes visual aids such as charts, graphs, and financial models to illustrate key points.
- **Addressing Concerns:** Anticipating potential concerns or objections from capital sponsors and providing well-reasoned responses. This might involve discussing contingency plans or risk mitigation strategies.
- **Highlighting Alignment:** Emphasizing how the proposed alternatives align with the capital mandates of the sponsors, showcasing the potential for value creation, risk management, and achieving financial goals.

Execution and Post-Execution Support

Once a strategic alternative is selected, investment bankers play a critical role in the execution of the strategy. This involves:

- **Transaction Management:** Overseeing the entire transaction process, including negotiations, due diligence, regulatory compliance, and finalizing the deal structure.
- **Integration and Post-Transaction Monitoring:** Providing support for the integration of acquired assets or companies, as well as ongoing monitoring of the transaction's performance to ensure that it delivers the anticipated benefits.

Conclusion

Investment bankers are essential in the capital management landscape, serving as the bridge between capital mandates and strategic alternatives. Their role is not only to identify and analyze potential opportunities but also to align these opportunities with the specific needs and objectives of capital sponsors. By understanding the unique mandates of various personas, conducting rigorous analysis, and presenting compelling cases, investment bankers facilitate the successful deployment of capital, driving growth and value creation for all stakeholders involved. Their expertise ensures that the complex process of capital management is navigated smoothly, aligning strategic initiatives with the overarching goals of both issuers and investors.

Chapter 15: What Role Do Investment Bankers Play in Securitizing Primary Market Investments on Wall Street

Securitization has become a fundamental process in modern finance, particularly on Wall Street. It involves transforming illiquid financial assets into tradable securities, thereby enhancing liquidity and providing investors with diverse investment opportunities. Investment bankers play a critical role in this process, acting as key intermediaries between issuers and investors. This blog post explores the multifaceted role of investment bankers in the securitization of primary market investments and the value they add to the financial system.

Understanding Securitization

Securitization is the process of pooling various financial assets, such as mortgages, auto loans, or credit card receivables, and packaging them into securities that can be sold to investors. This process enables the conversion of non-tradable assets into tradable ones, providing liquidity and risk distribution across a broader investor base. Investment bankers are central to this process, leveraging their expertise to structure deals that meet market demands and regulatory standards.

The Intermediary Role of Investment Bankers

Investment bankers act as intermediaries in the securitization process, bridging the gap between issuers (such as banks, corporations, or other entities holding financial assets) and investors (including institutional and retail investors). Their role involves several key functions:

1. **Advisory Services**: Investment bankers provide crucial advice to issuers on the securitization process. They help identify suitable assets for securitization, analyze the financial viability of these assets, and determine the optimal structure for the securities.
2. **Deal Structuring**: One of the primary responsibilities of investment bankers is structuring the securitization deals. This involves determining the appropriate mix of assets, setting up payment structures, and defining the tranching of securities based on risk and return profiles. The goal is to create securities that are attractive to a wide range of investors with varying risk appetites.
3. **Risk Assessment and Due Diligence**: Investment bankers conduct thorough due diligence on the underlying assets. This process includes evaluating the creditworthiness of the assets, assessing potential risks, and ensuring compliance with regulatory requirements. This rigorous analysis helps in accurately pricing the securities and providing investors with reliable investment options.

Origination, Underwriting, and Distribution

Investment bankers are deeply involved in the origination, underwriting, and distribution phases of securitization:

- **Origination**: Investment bankers work with issuers to originate securitized products. This involves the initial pooling of assets and the creation of a legal framework for the securitization.

- **Underwriting**: In the underwriting phase, investment bankers assess the value of the securitized products and determine their pricing. They may also take on the risk of buying the securities from the issuer and selling them to investors, providing a guarantee of sale.
- **Distribution**: Leveraging their extensive networks, investment bankers distribute the securitized products to investors. They market these products, ensuring they reach the appropriate investor base, which can include institutional investors, mutual funds, and individual investors. Their market knowledge and relationships are crucial for effectively placing the securities and achieving successful transactions.

Impact on the Financial System

Investment bankers significantly impact the financial system through their role in securitization. By facilitating the conversion of illiquid assets into tradable securities, they enhance market liquidity and provide investors with new investment opportunities. This process also helps issuers access capital more efficiently and manage their balance sheets.

Challenges and Adaptations

The securitization market is not without challenges. Investment bankers must navigate complex regulatory environments, manage the risks associated with the underlying assets, and adapt to changing market conditions. Recent years have seen increased scrutiny and regulation, particularly following the financial crisis, which highlighted the risks associated with certain securitized products. Investment bankers continue to innovate and adapt, focusing on transparency, risk management, and investor protection.

Conclusion

Investment bankers play a vital role in the securitization of primary market investments on Wall Street. Their expertise in deal structuring, risk assessment, and market distribution is essential for transforming illiquid assets into marketable securities. Through their intermediary role, investment bankers facilitate capital flow, enhance liquidity, and contribute to the overall efficiency and stability of the financial markets. As the market evolves, their role continues to be crucial in navigating the complexities of securitization and ensuring the alignment of interests between issuers and investors.

Chapter 16: What are the Bulge Bracket Investment Banks?

In the world of global finance, a few elite investment banks dominate the landscape, known as "bulge bracket" banks. These institutions are the most prominent and influential players, shaping the financial markets with their vast resources and expertise. Bulge bracket banks provide a comprehensive range of services, from mergers and acquisitions (M&A) advisory to capital raising and securities underwriting. This blog post delves into the role of five major bulge bracket banks—**Goldman Sachs, JPMorgan Chase, Morgan Stanley, Citigroup, and Bank of America Merrill Lynch**—and explores their unique strengths, areas of expertise, and some of their significant recent deals.

1. Introduction to Bulge Bracket Investment Banks

Bulge bracket investment banks are at the top of the financial hierarchy, known for their extensive capabilities and global reach. These banks handle some of the most substantial and complex financial transactions, serving a diverse clientele, including large corporations, governments, institutional investors, and high-net-worth individuals. They are integral to the financial system, providing a wide array of services that facilitate capital flows, economic growth, and market stability.

2. Goldman Sachs

Overview and Global Presence:
Goldman Sachs is a global leader in investment banking, securities, and investment management. With offices in major financial centers worldwide, it caters to a diverse range of clients, including corporations, financial institutions, and governments.

Areas of Expertise:

- **M&A Advisory:** Goldman Sachs is renowned for its expertise in mergers and acquisitions. The firm provides strategic advice and helps clients navigate complex transactions to achieve their growth and restructuring objectives.
- **Capital Raising:** The firm excels in helping clients raise capital through equity and debt offerings. It uses its deep market knowledge and investor relationships to structure and execute successful deals.
- **Securities Underwriting:** Goldman Sachs is a leading underwriter for initial public offerings (IPOs) and other securities offerings, helping clients access public markets.

Recent Major Deals:

- **United Technologies and Raytheon Merger (2020):** Goldman Sachs played a key role in advising United Technologies on its merger with Raytheon, forming one of the largest aerospace and defense companies globally.
- **Uber IPO (2019):** Goldman Sachs was a lead underwriter in Uber's IPO, one of the most anticipated public offerings, raising $8.1 billion.

3. JPMorgan Chase

Overview and Global Presence:
JPMorgan Chase is a financial services powerhouse offering a broad range of services, including investment banking, asset management, and private banking. The firm operates globally, serving a wide array of clients.

Areas of Expertise:

- **Strategic Transactions:** Known for its comprehensive advisory services in strategic transactions, including M&A and capital markets. JPMorgan Chase helps clients achieve their financial goals with innovative solutions.
- **Asset Management:** With a robust asset management division, the firm manages significant assets for both institutional and individual investors.
- **Technology Integration:** JPMorgan Chase leverages advanced technology to enhance client services and streamline its operations.

Recent Major Deals:

- **Amazon Acquisition of Whole Foods (2017):** JPMorgan Chase served as the lead financial advisor to Amazon in its acquisition of Whole Foods, a transformative deal in the retail sector.
- **Qualcomm Acquisition of NXP Semiconductors (2018):** The firm advised Qualcomm in its $44 billion acquisition of NXP Semiconductors, a significant deal in the semiconductor industry.

4. Morgan Stanley

Overview and Global Presence:
Morgan Stanley is a global financial services firm specializing in

wealth management, investment management, and institutional securities. It operates in major financial hubs around the world.

Areas of Expertise:

- **Strategic Advisory:** The firm provides top-tier advisory services for M&A, capital raising, and corporate restructuring, offering clients strategic insights and solutions.
- **Capital Markets:** Morgan Stanley is a leader in facilitating debt and equity offerings, enabling clients to raise capital efficiently.
- **Innovative Technology:** The firm utilizes cutting-edge technology and data analytics to provide innovative financial solutions.

Recent Major Deals:

- **Microsoft Acquisition of LinkedIn (2016):** Morgan Stanley was the lead advisor for Microsoft in its acquisition of LinkedIn, a landmark transaction in the tech sector.
- **Salesforce Acquisition of Tableau (2019):** The firm advised Salesforce in its acquisition of Tableau, enhancing Salesforce's data analytics capabilities.

5. Citigroup

Overview and Global Presence:
Citigroup provides a wide range of financial services, including investment banking, private banking, and asset management. The firm has a significant presence globally, serving clients in various markets and regions.

Areas of Expertise:

- **M&A and Capital Raising:** Citigroup is known for its expertise in advising on M&A transactions and capital raising initiatives, helping clients achieve strategic goals.
- **Global Network:** The firm's extensive global network allows it to provide localized services and insights, catering to diverse client needs.
- **Innovative Solutions:** Citigroup employs innovative strategies and technology to deliver comprehensive financial solutions.

Recent Major Deals:

- **T-Mobile and Sprint Merger (2020):** Citigroup was one of the advisors in the T-Mobile and Sprint merger, a significant transaction in the telecommunications industry.
- **LVMH Acquisition of Tiffany & Co. (2021):** The firm advised LVMH in its acquisition of Tiffany & Co., a major deal in the luxury sector.

6. Bank of America Merrill Lynch

Overview and Global Presence:
Bank of America Merrill Lynch offers a comprehensive range of services, including investment banking, wealth management, and consumer banking. It operates globally with a strong reputation for service excellence.

Areas of Expertise:

- **Strategic Transactions:** The firm excels in providing advisory services for M&A, capital raising, and other strategic transactions.

- **Innovation and Technology:** Bank of America Merrill Lynch focuses on leveraging technology to improve service delivery and client experience.
- **Wealth Management:** The firm offers extensive wealth management services, catering to high-net-worth individuals and institutional clients.

Recent Major Deals:

- **Bristol-Myers Squibb Acquisition of Celgene (2019):** Bank of America Merrill Lynch advised Bristol-Myers Squibb in its acquisition of Celgene, a major transaction in the pharmaceutical industry.
- **Disney Acquisition of 21st Century Fox (2019):** The firm served as a financial advisor to Disney in its acquisition of 21st Century Fox, expanding Disney's entertainment assets significantly.

7. Comparative Analysis and Conclusion

Key Strengths:
While all these banks excel in areas like M&A and capital markets, each has unique strengths. For instance, Goldman Sachs is particularly noted for high-profile M&A deals, while JPMorgan Chase is distinguished for its asset management capabilities.

Technological Innovation:
These banks integrate advanced technology into their operations, enhancing efficiency and client services. For example, Morgan Stanley's data analytics capabilities are highly advanced, while JPMorgan Chase is known for integrating cutting-edge technologies across its services.

Global Influence:
The significant deals handled by these banks have often reshaped entire industries, showcasing their capacity to manage complex transactions. The United Technologies and Raytheon merger, advised by Goldman Sachs, and Amazon's acquisition of Whole Foods, advised by JPMorgan Chase, are prime examples of their impact.

Future Outlook:
Bulge bracket banks are expected to continue driving global finance, focusing on sustainability, technological innovation, and client satisfaction. As they adapt to new challenges and embrace opportunities, they will remain at the forefront of financial markets, influencing the global economy.

Bulge bracket investment banks are the cornerstone of global finance, facilitating major financial transactions and supporting economic growth. Their expertise, market influence, and commitment to excellence make them indispensable in the financial industry. As these banks continue to evolve, they will shape the future of finance, driving innovation and stability in the global economy.

Chapter 17: What are Some Examples of Notable Investment Banking Transactions?

Notable Investment Banking Transactions: Key Deals and Their Execution

Investment banking is characterized by complex, high-stakes transactions that require meticulous planning, strategic foresight, and flawless execution. This blog post delves into several major recent investment banking transactions, exploring the intricacies of how each deal came together. These transactions highlight the pivotal role of investment banks in facilitating mergers, acquisitions, capital raises, and other significant financial events. By examining these deals, we gain insight into the strategic thinking, negotiation processes, and market dynamics that drive successful investment banking.

1. Amazon's Acquisition of Whole Foods

Overview:
In June 2017, Amazon announced its intention to acquire Whole Foods

Market for $13.7 billion. This acquisition marked Amazon's significant foray into the grocery sector, aiming to leverage Whole Foods' physical stores to enhance its distribution network.

Deal Participants:

- **Amazon:** Led by its founder and CEO, Jeff Bezos, Amazon sought to expand its market presence in the grocery industry.
- **Whole Foods Market:** Known for its organic and high-quality food products, Whole Foods was looking for strategic partners to bolster its competitive position.
- **JPMorgan Chase:** Served as the lead financial advisor to Amazon.

Deal Rationale:

- **Expansion into Groceries:** Amazon aimed to disrupt the grocery industry by integrating Whole Foods' physical stores with its online platform.
- **Enhanced Distribution:** The acquisition provided Amazon with a network of physical stores, enhancing its delivery capabilities and market reach.
- **Synergies:** Expected synergies included improved logistics, expanded product offerings, and enhanced customer experience.

How the Deal Came Together:

- **Initial Contact:** Amazon initiated discussions with Whole Foods to explore potential partnerships and acquisitions.
- **Due Diligence:** JPMorgan Chase conducted extensive due diligence, assessing Whole Foods' financial health, market position, and growth prospects.
- **Negotiations:** Negotiations focused on pricing, integration plans, and strategic synergies. Amazon proposed an all-cash

offer of $42 per share, which represented a premium to Whole Foods' stock price.
- **Regulatory Approval:** The deal required regulatory approval, which was obtained without significant hurdles. The acquisition was completed in August 2017, transforming the grocery industry landscape.

2. United Technologies and Raytheon Merger

Overview:
In June 2019, United Technologies (UTC) and Raytheon announced a merger, creating one of the world's largest aerospace and defense companies. The all-stock merger, valued at $121 billion, combined UTC's aerospace businesses with Raytheon's defense operations.

Deal Participants:

- **United Technologies:** An aerospace and building systems conglomerate.
- **Raytheon:** A leading defense contractor specializing in defense and cybersecurity solutions.
- **Goldman Sachs:** Advised United Technologies on the merger.

Deal Rationale:

- **Industry Leadership:** The merger aimed to create a leading aerospace and defense company with a diverse portfolio and enhanced capabilities.
- **Complementary Strengths:** Combining UTC's aerospace expertise with Raytheon's defense solutions promised operational synergies and innovation.
- **Scale and Efficiency:** The merged entity aimed to achieve significant cost savings and operational efficiencies through scale.

How the Deal Came Together:

- **Strategic Discussions:** High-level discussions between the CEOs of both companies identified potential synergies and strategic benefits.
- **Due Diligence:** Comprehensive due diligence was conducted by Goldman Sachs and other advisors, evaluating financials, operations, and potential risks.
- **Merger Agreement:** Negotiations led to an all-stock merger agreement, with UTC shareholders owning 57% and Raytheon shareholders owning 43% of the new entity.
- **Regulatory Approvals:** The deal required approval from various regulatory bodies, including the U.S. Department of Justice and the European Commission. The merger was finalized in April 2020, creating Raytheon Technologies.

3. Bristol-Myers Squibb Acquisition of Celgene

Overview:
In January 2019, Bristol-Myers Squibb (BMS) announced its acquisition of Celgene, a biotechnology company, for $74 billion. This acquisition aimed to create a premier biopharma company with a leading oncology portfolio.

Deal Participants:

- **Bristol-Myers Squibb:** A global biopharmaceutical company focused on oncology, immunology, and cardiovascular diseases.
- **Celgene:** A biotechnology company specializing in cancer and inflammatory disorders treatments.
- **Bank of America Merrill Lynch:** Served as the lead financial advisor to Bristol-Myers Squibb.

Deal Rationale:

- **Enhanced Oncology Portfolio:** The acquisition bolstered BMS's oncology pipeline with Celgene's leading cancer therapies.
- **Revenue Diversification:** The deal provided BMS with diversified revenue streams from Celgene's portfolio.
- **Innovation and Growth:** Combining R&D capabilities aimed to accelerate the development of innovative therapies.

How the Deal Came Together:

- **Initial Outreach:** BMS approached Celgene to discuss potential strategic collaborations, which evolved into acquisition talks.
- **Valuation and Due Diligence:** Bank of America Merrill Lynch conducted thorough valuation and due diligence, assessing Celgene's financials, pipeline, and market potential.
- **Negotiations:** The negotiation process focused on deal structure, price, and strategic fit. BMS proposed a cash-and-stock deal valuing Celgene at $74 billion.
- **Regulatory Approvals:** The acquisition required regulatory approvals from multiple jurisdictions. The deal was completed in November 2019, significantly enhancing BMS's product portfolio and market position.

4. Microsoft Acquisition of LinkedIn

Overview:
In June 2016, Microsoft announced its acquisition of LinkedIn for $26.2 billion, marking one of the largest technology deals in history. The acquisition aimed to integrate LinkedIn's professional network with Microsoft's productivity tools.

Deal Participants:

- **Microsoft:** A global technology leader known for its software, hardware, and cloud services.
- **LinkedIn:** The world's largest professional networking site.
- **Morgan Stanley:** Served as the lead financial advisor to Microsoft.

Deal Rationale:

- **Professional Network Integration:** Microsoft aimed to integrate LinkedIn's network with its Office suite and cloud services to enhance productivity tools.
- **Data and Analytics:** The acquisition provided Microsoft with valuable data and insights from LinkedIn's user base.
- **Growth Opportunities:** Leveraging LinkedIn's platform for advertising and new product development.

How the Deal Came Together:

- **Strategic Vision:** Microsoft's CEO, Satya Nadella, and LinkedIn's CEO, Jeff Weiner, envisioned the strategic integration of their platforms.
- **Due Diligence:** Morgan Stanley conducted extensive due diligence, evaluating LinkedIn's user data, financial performance, and market position.
- **Negotiations:** Negotiations centered on valuation, integration plans, and future growth strategies. Microsoft offered $196 per share in an all-cash transaction.
- **Regulatory Approvals:** The deal required antitrust approvals from various jurisdictions. The acquisition was completed in December 2016, enhancing Microsoft's position in the enterprise social networking space.

5. T-Mobile and Sprint Merger

Overview:
In April 2018, T-Mobile and Sprint announced a merger valued at $26 billion, aiming to create a stronger competitor in the U.S. telecommunications market. The merger combined T-Mobile's aggressive growth strategy with Sprint's extensive spectrum assets.

Deal Participants:

- **T-Mobile:** A major U.S. wireless carrier known for its disruptive market strategies.
- **Sprint:** A telecommunications company with significant spectrum holdings.
- **Citigroup:** One of the financial advisors to T-Mobile.

Deal Rationale:

- **Market Competitiveness:** The merger aimed to create a more competitive player in the U.S. telecom market, challenging AT&T and Verizon.
- **Network Synergies:** Combining networks to improve coverage, capacity, and service quality.
- **Innovation and Growth:** Leveraging combined resources to accelerate the deployment of 5G technology.

How the Deal Came Together:

- **Strategic Discussions:** Leadership from both companies engaged in discussions to explore the strategic benefits of a merger.
- **Due Diligence:** Citigroup conducted comprehensive due diligence, assessing the financial health, spectrum assets, and operational capabilities of both companies.

- **Merger Agreement:** Negotiations led to a merger agreement with an all-stock transaction structure, valuing Sprint at $26 billion.
- **Regulatory Approvals:** The merger required approvals from the Federal Communications Commission (FCC) and the Department of Justice (DOJ). The deal closed in April 2020, creating a stronger, more competitive telecom company.

Chapter 18: What are the Different Types of Investment Banks?

Different Types of Investment Banks and Their Specializations

Investment banks are integral to the global financial system, offering a variety of services that support the flow of capital, facilitate complex transactions, and drive economic growth. However, not all investment banks are created equal. They can be broadly categorized based on their size, scope of services, client focus, and industry specialization. This blog post delves into the various types of investment banks, elaborating on their distinct roles, the kinds of deals they typically handle, and examples of major players in each category.

1. Bulge Bracket Investment Banks

Overview

Bulge bracket investment banks are the titans of the financial world. These large, multinational institutions offer a full spectrum of financial services, including mergers and acquisitions (M&A) advisory, capital raising, securities underwriting, asset management, and wealth management. They operate globally and have a significant influence on both financial markets and the global economy.

Key Players

- **Goldman Sachs**
- **JPMorgan Chase**
- **Morgan Stanley**
- **Citigroup**
- **Bank of America Merrill Lynch**

Types of Deals

- **Mergers and Acquisitions (M&A)**: Bulge bracket banks often handle the most complex and high-profile M&A transactions. They provide comprehensive advisory services, from strategy development to execution. For example, **Goldman Sachs** played a crucial role in the $121 billion merger between United Technologies and Raytheon, advising on valuation, negotiations, and integration strategies.
- **Initial Public Offerings (IPOs)**: These banks are the go-to institutions for companies seeking to go public. They manage the entire IPO process, including underwriting, pricing, and marketing shares. **Morgan Stanley** was instrumental in Uber's $8.1 billion IPO, coordinating one of the largest tech IPOs in history.
- **Debt Issuances**: Bulge bracket banks assist companies in raising capital through debt instruments like bonds. They structure and underwrite these securities, ensuring the issuer secures favorable terms. For instance, **JPMorgan Chase** has been involved in numerous significant corporate bond issues, providing capital for expansion and other corporate needs.
- **Equity Offerings**: Apart from IPOs, these banks manage secondary offerings and private placements, helping

companies raise equity capital. **Bank of America Merrill Lynch** has managed several secondary equity offerings for major tech companies, providing critical funding for growth.

- **Strategic Advisory**: Bulge bracket banks offer strategic advisory services, including restructuring, divestitures, and corporate governance. **Citigroup**, for example, provided advisory services in the $26 billion T-Mobile and Sprint merger, a deal that reshaped the U.S. telecom industry.

2. Middle Market Investment Banks

Overview

Middle market investment banks cater to mid-sized companies, providing a range of financial services similar to bulge bracket banks but on a smaller scale. They typically focus on deals that are significant yet not as large as those handled by bulge bracket institutions.

Key Players

- **Jefferies**
- **Piper Sandler**
- **William Blair**
- **Houlihan Lokey**

Types of Deals

- **Mergers and Acquisitions (M&A)**: These banks are adept at handling M&A transactions for mid-sized firms, offering tailored advisory services. **Jefferies**, for instance, advised on a $500 million healthcare sector acquisition, guiding the client through the entire deal process.
- **Private Placements**: Middle market banks frequently assist companies in raising capital through private placements of

equity or debt. **Piper Sandler** facilitated a $200 million private equity placement for a technology startup, matching the firm with suitable investors.

- **Debt and Equity Offerings**: These banks manage debt and equity offerings, helping mid-sized companies access the capital markets. **William Blair** managed a $150 million bond issuance for a manufacturing firm, supporting its expansion plans.
- **Restructuring and Recapitalization**: Middle market banks often provide advisory services for companies undergoing financial restructuring or recapitalization. **Houlihan Lokey** has a strong reputation in this area, advising numerous companies on restructuring their debt and equity structures.

3. Boutique Investment Banks

Overview

Boutique investment banks specialize in specific industries, types of transactions, or regions. They are often smaller than bulge bracket and middle market banks but provide highly specialized services, leveraging deep expertise in their niche areas.

Key Players

- **Lazard**
- **Evercore**
- **Moelis & Company**
- **Centerview Partners**

Types of Deals

- **Mergers and Acquisitions (M&A)**: Boutique banks frequently specialize in M&A advisory, providing detailed, sector-specific advice. **Evercore** advised on a $2 billion pharmaceutical industry acquisition, leveraging its expertise in the healthcare sector.

- **Financial Restructuring**: These banks often assist companies in distress, providing financial restructuring services. **Lazard** managed the restructuring of a major airline's debt, helping the company navigate a challenging financial landscape.
- **Strategic Advisory**: Boutique banks offer advisory services for strategic initiatives like spin-offs, joint ventures, and corporate governance. **Moelis & Company** provided strategic advisory services for a significant media company's spin-off, guiding them through the complex process.
- **Capital Raising**: They also assist in raising capital through private equity and venture capital placements. **Centerview Partners** facilitated a $100 million venture capital round for a fintech startup, connecting the firm with investors aligned with its growth strategy.

4. Regional Investment Banks

Overview

Regional investment banks operate primarily within specific geographic areas, focusing on clients and transactions in those regions. They provide a range of services tailored to the unique needs of local businesses and investors.

Key Players

- **Baird**
- **Raymond James**
- **Stephens Inc.**
- **Stifel Financial Corp.**

Types of Deals

- **Local Mergers and Acquisitions (M&A)**: These banks advise on M&A transactions within their geographic regions. **Raymond James** advised on a $300 million acquisition in the Southeastern U.S., providing local market insights and expertise.
- **Debt and Equity Offerings**: Regional banks help companies raise capital through debt and equity offerings. **Baird** managed a $50 million bond issuance for a manufacturing firm in the Midwest, facilitating its expansion.
- **Private Placements**: They assist local businesses in raising capital through private placements. **Stephens Inc.** facilitated a $30 million private placement for a regional healthcare provider, ensuring the funding aligned with the company's growth plans.
- **Advisory Services**: These banks offer advisory services, including valuations and financial planning. **Stifel Financial** advised a regional bank on its strategic growth plan, leveraging its local market knowledge.

5. Elite Boutique Investment Banks

Overview

Elite boutique investment banks are specialized firms that provide high-end advisory services, similar to bulge bracket banks but typically do not engage in capital markets or trading. They are known for their expertise in handling complex, high-value transactions.

Key Players

- **Perella Weinberg Partners**
- **PJT Partners**

- **LionTree Advisors**
- **Greenhill & Co.**

Types of Deals

- **Mergers and Acquisitions (M&A)**: These banks focus on high-value M&A transactions, offering top-tier advisory services. **PJT Partners** advised on a $10 billion acquisition in the tech sector, providing in-depth strategic advice.
- **Restructuring Advisory**: Elite boutiques are often involved in complex restructuring deals. **Perella Weinberg** managed the restructuring of a large energy company's debt, navigating the company through financial challenges.
- **Strategic Advisory**: They offer strategic advisory services for corporate actions like divestitures and spin-offs. **Greenhill & Co.** advised on a consumer goods company's spin-off, ensuring a smooth and successful separation.
- **Fairness Opinions and Valuations**: These banks provide fairness opinions and valuations for significant transactions. **LionTree Advisors** offered valuation services for a large media merger, ensuring the transaction was fair and equitable for all parties involved.

Conclusion

Investment banks are diverse entities, each specializing in different areas and serving distinct market segments. From the global giants of the bulge bracket banks to the specialized niche players of the boutique firms, each type of investment bank plays a crucial role in the financial ecosystem. Understanding the unique functions and strengths of these institutions helps clients and stakeholders navigate the complex landscape of investment banking, ensuring they find the right partner for their financial needs. Whether a company seeks to go public, raise capital, acquire another business, or restructure its finances, there is an investment bank with the expertise and resources to assist them.

Chapter 19: What is the Average Compensation in Investment Banking?

Understanding Average Compensation in Investment Banking: A Comprehensive Breakdown

Investment banking is known for its lucrative compensation packages, which typically consist of a base salary supplemented by significant bonuses. The total compensation varies widely depending on the role, experience level, and performance of both the individual and the firm. Let's delve into the average compensation figures across different levels within the investment banking hierarchy.

Analyst Level

Role and Responsibilities:
Analysts are typically entry-level professionals, often recent college graduates, who perform research, financial modeling, and support senior bankers.

Average Compensation:

- **Base Salary:** Around $85,000 per year
- **Bonuses:** Ranging from $50,000 to $100,000 or more, depending on individual and firm performance

- **Total Compensation:** Typically ranges from $135,000 to $185,000 annually

Associate Level

Role and Responsibilities:
Associates are usually more experienced professionals, often with an MBA or other advanced degrees. They manage analysts, handle client communications, and contribute to deal execution.

Average Compensation:

- **Base Salary:** Between $120,000 and $150,000 per year
- **Bonuses:** Can range from $100,000 to $300,000 or more
- **Total Compensation:** Generally ranges from $220,000 to $450,000 annually

Vice President (VP)

Role and Responsibilities:
Vice Presidents are mid-senior level employees who manage client relationships, oversee the execution of transactions, and play a pivotal role in deal origination and strategy.

Average Compensation:

- **Base Salary:** Approximately $200,000 to $250,000 per year
- **Bonuses:** Can range from $200,000 to $500,000 or more
- **Total Compensation:** Typically ranges from $400,000 to $750,000 annually

Director/Executive Director

Role and Responsibilities:
Directors and Executive Directors are senior-level professionals responsible for managing large teams and complex deals. They play a critical role in business development and maintaining client relationships.

Average Compensation:

- **Base Salary:** Ranges from $300,000 to $400,000 per year
- **Bonuses:** Can range from $400,000 to $1 million or more
- **Total Compensation:** Generally ranges from $700,000 to $1.4 million annually

Managing Director (MD)

Role and Responsibilities:
Managing Directors are the top-tier professionals in investment banking, overseeing major divisions or the entire firm. They are key decision-makers, responsible for driving the firm's strategic direction and large-scale transactions.

Average Compensation:

- **Base Salary:** Between $500,000 and $1 million per year
- **Bonuses:** Can range from $1 million to $10 million or more
- **Total Compensation:** Typically ranges from $1.5 million to $11 million annually

Key Factors Influencing Compensation

1. **Firm Performance:** The overall profitability and performance of the firm significantly impact bonuses.
2. **Individual Performance:** Personal achievements and contributions to revenue generation play a crucial role.

3. **Market Conditions:** The economic and market environment can influence compensation trends, especially bonuses.
4. **Experience and Expertise:** More experienced bankers typically command higher compensation packages.

Conclusion

Investment banking offers substantial financial rewards, but the compensation packages vary significantly based on the role, experience, and performance metrics. While the base salary provides a steady income, the bonuses—often comprising a large portion of the total compensation—are closely tied to the individual's and firm's success. This structure incentivizes high performance and aligns the interests of the employees with those of the firm.

These figures provide a general overview and can vary depending on the firm, geographic location, and market conditions. Nonetheless, investment banking remains one of the most financially rewarding careers in the finance industry.

Chapter 20: How Did Wall Street Come Into Existence?

The Birth and Evolution of Wall Street: From Colonial Outpost to Global Financial Powerhouse

Introduction

Wall Street, often considered the epicenter of global finance, has a rich history that spans several centuries. Its evolution from a simple colonial trading post to a complex and influential financial hub reflects the broader development of the American economy. This blog post will provide a detailed exploration of Wall Street's origins, its transformation through various historical events, and its current status as a pivotal player in global finance. Understanding this history offers valuable insights into how Wall Street became synonymous with economic power and innovation.

Early Beginnings: The Dutch Settlement and the Wall

The history of Wall Street begins in the early 17th century, during the era of Dutch colonization. In 1624, Dutch settlers established the colony of New Amsterdam at the southern tip of what is now Manhattan Island. The area served as a trading post due to its strategic location by the East River, facilitating commerce with Europe and other colonies.

To protect the settlement from potential invasions by the British and attacks by Native American tribes, the Dutch constructed a wooden wall in 1653 along the northern boundary of the colony. This defensive barrier was erected along what is today known as Wall Street. Although the wall was dismantled in 1699 after the British took control of the colony and renamed it New York, the name "Wall Street" persisted.

Colonial Commerce and the Buttonwood Agreement

Under British rule, New York quickly became a bustling center for commerce and trade. Wall Street, in particular, emerged as a focal point for business activities. Merchants, traders, and brokers gathered under a buttonwood tree at 68 Wall Street to trade securities, a practice that laid the groundwork for the organized financial markets we see today.

A significant milestone in Wall Street's history was the signing of the Buttonwood Agreement in 1792 by 24 brokers and merchants. This agreement established a formalized securities market, setting rules for trading and fixing a commission rate. The Buttonwood Agreement is considered the foundation of what would eventually become the New York Stock Exchange (NYSE).

The Formation and Growth of the NYSE

The NYSE was formally established in 1817, originally called the New York Stock & Exchange Board. It provided a structured and regulated environment for securities trading, which was essential for maintaining investor confidence and market integrity. The exchange operated from various rented spaces before moving to its iconic location at 11 Wall Street in 1865.

The NYSE played a crucial role in financing America's rapid industrialization during the 19th century. It facilitated the capital raising necessary for building infrastructure, expanding manufacturing, and supporting other industries. The exchange became a cornerstone of the American financial system, helping businesses grow and innovate.

The Rise of Investment Banking

As the U.S. economy expanded, the role of investment banks became increasingly important. Investment banks, such as J.P. Morgan & Co., emerged as key players in underwriting securities, advising on mergers and acquisitions, and providing financial advisory services. These institutions were instrumental in raising capital for companies and managing complex financial transactions.

J.P. Morgan, a leading financier, played a pivotal role in consolidating industries and stabilizing financial markets during times of crisis. For instance, during the Panic of 1907, J.P. Morgan intervened to stabilize the banking system, highlighting the need for a central banking authority. This crisis led to the creation of the Federal Reserve System in 1913, which provided a more structured and secure financial system.

20th Century: Regulation and Innovation

The 20th century brought significant challenges and regulatory changes to Wall Street. The stock market crash of 1929 and the subsequent Great Depression exposed weaknesses in the financial system, leading to the introduction of stringent regulations. The Securities Act of 1933 and the Securities Exchange Act of 1934 established the Securities and Exchange Commission (SEC) to oversee and regulate the securities markets, ensuring transparency and protecting investors.

Post-World War II, Wall Street experienced substantial growth and innovation. The economic boom of the post-war era, coupled with advancements in technology, transformed the financial industry. The development of new financial instruments, such as derivatives and high-yield bonds, allowed for more sophisticated investment strategies and risk management techniques.

The 21st Century: Navigating Crises and Embracing Innovation

The 21st century has been marked by significant financial crises, including the dot-com bubble burst in 2000 and the global financial crisis of 2008. The latter, triggered by the collapse of the subprime mortgage market, had profound implications for the global economy. It led to massive government interventions and the implementation of the Dodd-Frank Wall Street Reform and Consumer Protection Act in 2010. This legislation aimed to reduce systemic risks, increase transparency, and protect consumers.

Despite these challenges, Wall Street has continued to innovate and adapt. The rise of fintech, blockchain technology, and algorithmic trading has transformed how financial transactions are conducted. These innovations have made financial services more efficient and accessible but have also introduced new regulatory and ethical considerations.

Conclusion

The evolution of Wall Street from a simple trading post to a global financial powerhouse is a testament to its resilience and adaptability. Throughout its history, Wall Street has played a central role in shaping the American and global economies. Its development reflects broader economic trends and innovations, from the establishment of organized securities markets to the rise of investment banking and modern financial technologies.

Today, Wall Street remains a symbol of financial power and innovation, continuing to influence global markets and economies. As it navigates new challenges and opportunities, Wall Street will undoubtedly continue to evolve, maintaining its status as a pivotal player in the world of finance. Understanding its history provides valuable context for its current role and future trajectory in the global financial system.

PART II: DEVELOPING A BUY-SIDE PERSPECTIVE

Chapter 21: How Investment Bankers Play the Capital Management Game

How Investment Bankers Master the Art of Capital Management

Investment bankers play a pivotal role in the intricate world of capital management, guiding organizations and individuals through the complex processes of allocating and deploying capital. This game of capital management involves different objectives, strategies, and rules depending on whether the focus is on strategic, financial, or personal capital management. Understanding these nuances is crucial for making informed investment decisions that maximize returns and align with specific mandates.

The Different Games in Capital Management

Strategic Capital Management: Strategic capital management is all about optimizing resources to achieve long-term growth, profitability, and a competitive edge. Investment bankers assist corporations in identifying and seizing opportunities for mergers and acquisitions, capital investments, and strategic partnerships. These decisions are made with the intent of enhancing a company's market position and operational efficiency.

Financial Capital Management: In financial capital management, the emphasis is on generating returns for investors while managing risks and ensuring liquidity. This involves a range of activities such as asset allocation, portfolio management, and trading. Investment bankers help clients navigate financial markets, structure investments, and optimize the mix of debt and equity financing to achieve the best possible financial outcomes.

Personal Capital Management: Personal capital management is tailored to the needs of high-net-worth individuals and families. The primary objectives here are wealth preservation, growth, and the achievement of specific financial goals, such as retirement planning, estate planning, and philanthropy. Investment bankers provide personalized advice on asset diversification, tax optimization, and investment strategies that align with the client's risk tolerance and financial aspirations.

Capital Mandates: The Guiding Principles

Capital mandates are the foundational rules that guide how capital is allocated and utilized. These mandates differ depending on the focus area:

- **Strategic Capital Mandates**: These mandates prioritize long-term value creation and strategic goals. Investment bankers help organizations explore options like mergers and acquisitions, capital projects, and new market entries.
- **Financial Capital Mandates**: These focus on delivering competitive returns while managing risk. Investment bankers assist in constructing investment portfolios, trading strategies, and financial instruments to optimize returns.
- **Personal Capital Mandates**: These are concerned with preserving and growing wealth according to personal goals

and risk preferences. This involves estate planning, tax strategies, and investment in various asset classes.

Exploring Strategic Alternatives

Once the capital mandates are clear, investment bankers work with clients to explore strategic alternatives. This process involves:

1. **Identifying Opportunities**: Scanning the market for potential acquisitions, partnerships, or investment opportunities that align with the client's objectives.
2. **Due Diligence**: Conducting thorough research and analysis to assess the viability and potential risks associated with each opportunity.
3. **Valuation and Financial Modeling**: Using various valuation techniques and financial models to estimate the potential returns and impact on the client's portfolio or business.
4. **Negotiation and Structuring**: Assisting in negotiations and structuring deals in a way that maximizes benefits and minimizes risks.

Roles of Investment Bankers in Capital Management

Investment bankers serve as crucial intermediaries in the capital management game. They offer a range of services that are tailored to meet the specific needs of their clients:

- **Advisory Services**: Providing expert advice on mergers, acquisitions, divestitures, and other strategic transactions. They help clients navigate complex regulatory environments and market conditions.
- **Underwriting**: Assisting in the issuance of securities, such as stocks and bonds, to raise capital. Investment bankers ensure

that these securities are properly priced and marketed to investors.

- **Risk Management**: Identifying and mitigating potential risks associated with investments and financial transactions. This includes assessing market, credit, and operational risks.
- **Wealth Management**: Offering personalized financial planning and investment management services to high-net-worth individuals, helping them achieve their financial goals.

Conclusion

Investment bankers are essential players in the capital management game, offering expertise and strategic guidance to help clients make informed decisions. Whether the focus is on strategic, financial, or personal capital management, understanding the specific capital mandates and exploring the appropriate strategic alternatives are crucial steps in optimizing capital deployment. Investment bankers not only facilitate transactions but also provide valuable insights that drive long-term value creation and financial success. Their role is indispensable in ensuring that capital is used effectively, whether for growing a business, achieving financial returns, or preserving personal wealth.

Universe of strategic alternatives and strategic alternative generation
Strategic alternative pitching
Strategic alternative quantification
Strategic alternative mandate
Strategic alternative implementation

Chapter 22: Developing a Buy-Side Perspective

Developing a Comprehensive Buy-Side Perspective in Investment Banking

In the intricate world of finance, the **buy-side** plays a pivotal role, representing the entities and investors that purchase securities and other investment assets. Unlike the sell-side, which primarily focuses on creating, promoting, and selling investment products, the buy-side is concerned with **managing portfolios** to maximize returns. Understanding the buy-side's perspective is crucial for anyone involved in finance, as it directly influences investment strategies, risk management, and portfolio construction. This blog post delves into the diverse types of buy-side investors, the importance of investment mandates, and the detailed process of performing investment analysis in accordance with these mandates.

The Diverse Landscape of Buy-Side Investors

Buy-side investors encompass a broad spectrum of entities, each with unique goals, strategies, and risk tolerances. Here's a closer look at the key players in this segment:

1. **Asset Management Firms**:

- ○ **Role**: Manage a wide array of investment portfolios, including mutual funds, pension funds, and endowments.
- ○ **Focus**: Diversification across various asset classes like equities, bonds, and alternative investments.
- ○ **Objective**: Achieve steady returns while managing risk for their clients.

2. **Hedge Funds**:
   - ○ **Role**: Engage in active management strategies to achieve high returns, often taking on significant risk.
   - ○ **Strategies**: Include long-short equity, global macro, event-driven, and more.
   - ○ **Objective**: Generate alpha (excess returns) above market benchmarks through complex trading strategies.

3. **Private Equity Firms**:
   - ○ **Role**: Invest in private companies with the aim of increasing their value and eventually exiting through a sale or IPO.
   - ○ **Focus**: Restructuring, operational improvements, and strategic guidance.
   - ○ **Objective**: Achieve substantial returns over a longer investment horizon.

4. **Sovereign Wealth Funds**:
   - ○ **Role**: Government-owned investment funds that manage a nation's wealth.
   - ○ **Assets**: Include real estate, infrastructure, public and private equity.
   - ○ **Objective**: Preserve and grow the wealth of the nation, often with a long-term focus.

5. **Insurance Companies**:
   - ○ **Role**: Invest premiums collected from policyholders to cover future claims.

- **Focus**: Income-generating investments to match future liabilities.
- **Objective**: Achieve stable returns while maintaining a conservative risk profile.

6. **Family Offices**:
   - **Role**: Manage the wealth of high-net-worth families.
   - **Services**: Include investment management, estate planning, and philanthropy.
   - **Objective**: Preserve and grow family wealth across generations.

7. **Retail Investors**:
   - **Role**: Individual investors who manage their own portfolios.
   - **Channels**: Use brokerage accounts, mutual funds, ETFs, and other platforms.
   - **Objective**: Varies widely, from growth to income to preservation of capital.

The Role of Investment Mandates

An **investment mandate** is a crucial component in the buy-side landscape. It serves as a set of guidelines or instructions that dictate how an investment manager should allocate and manage funds. Here's a detailed look at what an investment mandate typically includes:

1. **Investment Objectives**:
   - Specifies the primary goals, such as capital growth, income generation, or capital preservation.
   - Examples: A mandate might prioritize dividend income for retirees or aggressive growth for younger investors.

2. **Risk Tolerance**:
   - Defines the acceptable level of risk, including market, credit, and liquidity risks.

- Examples: A conservative mandate may focus on investment-grade bonds, while an aggressive mandate may allow for higher equity exposure.
3. **Asset Allocation**:
    - Outlines the preferred distribution of assets across different classes like equities, bonds, real estate, and alternatives.
    - Examples: A balanced portfolio might include a mix of 60% equities and 40% bonds.
4. **Restrictions and Constraints**:
    - Specifies any restrictions on certain types of investments, industries, or geographies.
    - Examples: Prohibitions on investing in tobacco companies or foreign securities.
5. **Performance Benchmarks**:
    - Sets the standard for evaluating the performance of the portfolio.
    - Examples: Comparing returns to a benchmark index like the S&P 500.

Performing Investment Analysis

Investment analysis on the buy-side is a meticulous process aimed at aligning investment decisions with the investment mandate. Here's a breakdown of this process:

1. **Identifying Investment Opportunities**:
    - **Screening**: Use criteria like industry sector, market cap, financial health, and growth potential to identify suitable investments.
    - **Tools**: Utilize databases, financial news, and industry reports to gather data.
2. **Fundamental Analysis**:

- Financial Health: Review balance sheets, income
    statements, and cash flow statements.
- Qualitative Factors: Assess management quality,
    market position, competitive landscape, and business
    model.
3. **Quantitative Analysis**:
    - **Financial Metrics**: Calculate ratios like P/E, P/B,
      ROE, and others to evaluate valuation and
      profitability.
    - **Forecasting**: Use models to project future earnings,
      revenue, and cash flows.
4. **Portfolio Fit and Risk Assessment**:
    - **Diversification**: Ensure the new investment
      complements the existing portfolio, reducing overall
      risk.
    - **Correlation Analysis**: Assess how the new asset
      correlates with current holdings.
5. **Ongoing Monitoring and Rebalancing**:
    - **Performance Review**: Regularly compare the
      portfolio's performance against benchmarks and
      mandates.
    - **Adjustments**: Make necessary changes to maintain
      alignment with the investment mandate.

Conclusion

Understanding the buy-side perspective involves a deep dive into the
various types of investors, the nuances of investment mandates, and the
rigorous process of investment analysis. By aligning their strategies
with specific mandates, buy-side professionals can effectively manage
portfolios, optimize returns, and navigate the complexities of the
financial markets. Whether dealing with institutional investors,
high-net-worth individuals, or retail clients, the principles of

disciplined investment analysis and adherence to mandates are fundamental to achieving long-term success in capital management.

NOTES:

Investment Analysis
Investment science is all about how to properly analyze return vehicles. We analyze benefit streams in order of priority (dividend then free cash flow, then EBITDA, then earnings, then revenues) and compare return vehicles relative to the ideal ones in the marketplace. Our goal is to pick best of breed, not dinosaurs or dogs.

Key Takeaway: The most tenured investors pursue a real return strategy which is the pinnacle of investing strategies. The highest quality of return is a real return driven from a dividend benefit stream. Going down the spectrum of quality of return leads you to speculation.

Quality of Returns: Real Dividend Driven Return vs. Speculative Share Price Driven Return
The most seasoned investors build a portfolio starting with real quality returns to acheive the income needs of the limited partners and then work their way down the quality of return spectrum towards speculative share price driven return looking for more growth.

When analyzing investments and building a portfolio, start with the ideal financial perpetuities in the marketplace relative to a real return strategy (the optimal strategy).

Once the LPs income needs are met, the investment professional can then build the rest of their portfolio for capital appreciation in the share price working your way down the quality of return spectrum towards speculation.

Key Takeaway: Buy the financial perpetuity quality rather than the story of the stock. Evaluate it for the real returns it gives you and then the speculative (share price driven) returns that it gives you second. We are analyzing return vehicles rather than buying into the story.

Key Takeaway: The purpose of investing is to aquire return vehicles that provide a real return that meets the financial expenses of the limited partner (LP) and allows them to obtain financial freedom (investment income equal to or more than annual expenses). An investment strategy needs to be align to this realization.

Chapter 23: Who Are the Biggest Private Equity Firms?

The Titans of Private Equity: A Deep Dive into the Biggest Firms and Their Monumental Deals

Private equity (PE) firms are powerhouse entities in the financial world, known for their ability to acquire, manage, and restructure companies with the goal of generating substantial returns. These firms typically buy private companies or take public companies private, improve their operations, and eventually exit the investments through sales or initial public offerings (IPOs). This blog post provides an in-depth exploration of the largest private equity firms, their specializations, and notable transactions that have marked their influence in the industry.

1. Blackstone Group

Overview:

- **Founded:** 1985 by Stephen A. Schwarzman and Peter G. Peterson.
- **Assets Under Management (AUM):** Over $600 billion.
- **Specializations:** Leveraged buyouts (LBOs), real estate, hedge fund management, and credit.

Core Services:

- **Leveraged Buyouts (LBOs):** Blackstone excels in acquiring companies by utilizing borrowed capital, making it a leader in this strategy. LBOs involve significant debt, which is used to finance the acquisition of a company. The acquired company's cash flows typically repay the debt.
- **Real Estate Investments:** With a vast portfolio, Blackstone invests in commercial properties, hotels, and residential complexes. Their real estate arm is one of the largest in the world.
- **Strategic Acquisitions and Restructuring:** They focus on operational improvements and financial restructuring to enhance the value of their portfolio companies.

Notable Deals:

- **Hilton Worldwide Holdings (2007):** Acquired for $26 billion, one of the largest LBOs in history. Blackstone restructured Hilton, optimizing operations, and successfully took it public in 2013.
- **Refinitiv (2018):** Acquired a majority stake in this financial data provider for $20 billion. Later, it was sold to London Stock Exchange Group for $27 billion in 2019, demonstrating Blackstone's strategic buy-and-build approach.

2. The Carlyle Group

Overview:

- **Founded:** 1987 by William E. Conway Jr., Daniel A. D'Aniello, and David M. Rubenstein.
- **AUM:** Over $260 billion.
- **Specializations:** Corporate private equity, real assets, global credit, and investment solutions.

Core Services:

- **Corporate Buyouts:** Carlyle is known for buying companies across diverse sectors such as aerospace, defense, healthcare, and technology.
- **Growth Capital:** They provide capital to companies to facilitate expansion, development of new products, or market entry.
- **Infrastructure Investments:** Carlyle invests in long-term infrastructure projects, including energy and utilities.

Notable Deals:

- **United Defense Industries (1997):** Acquired for $850 million and later sold to BAE Systems for $4.2 billion. This deal exemplifies Carlyle's ability to enhance value through strategic acquisitions.
- **ZoomInfo (2019):** Invested in this business data provider, which later went public in 2020, raising $935 million, marking one of the most successful tech IPOs of that year.

3. Kohlberg Kravis Roberts (KKR)

Overview:

- **Founded:** 1976 by Henry Kravis, George R. Roberts, and Jerome Kohlberg.
- **AUM:** Over $230 billion.
- **Specializations:** Private equity, energy, infrastructure, real estate, credit, hedge funds.

Core Services:

- **Leveraged Buyouts (LBOs):** Pioneers in the LBO market, KKR focuses on companies with significant potential for operational improvements.
- **Growth Equity:** Invests in companies that need capital to scale and expand.
- **Infrastructure and Real Assets:** Investments include energy, transportation, and real estate projects.

Notable Deals:

- **RJR Nabisco (1988):** This $31.1 billion acquisition is one of the most famous LBOs, chronicled in the book "Barbarians at the Gate." It highlighted the complexity and risks of large-scale buyouts.
- **First Data (2007):** Acquired for $29 billion, showcasing KKR's capability in handling large-scale buyouts and enhancing company value.

4. Apollo Global Management

Overview:

- **Founded:** 1990 by Leon Black, Joshua Harris, and Marc Rowan.
- **AUM:** Over $450 billion.
- **Specializations:** Private equity, credit, real estate.

Core Services:

- **Distressed Assets:** Known for investing in and revitalizing distressed companies, turning them into profitable ventures.
- **Leveraged Buyouts (LBOs):** Apollo's strategic use of debt in acquisitions has been a hallmark of its investment strategy.

- **Debt Investments:** Involvement in distressed debt and high-yield bonds.

Notable Deals:

- **LyondellBasell (2010):** Invested in the bankrupt chemical company, helping it emerge from bankruptcy and grow into a $30 billion enterprise.
- **ADT Inc. (2016):** Acquired for $15 billion, focusing on improving the company's technology and market reach.

5. TPG Capital

Overview:

- **Founded:** 1992 by David Bonderman and James Coulter.
- **AUM:** Over $100 billion.
- **Specializations:** Private equity, growth capital, real estate, impact investing.

Core Services:

- **Corporate Buyouts:** Acquiring companies in technology, healthcare, and consumer goods.
- **Growth Equity:** Capital investment in high-growth companies.
- **Impact Investing:** Investments that aim to generate social and environmental impact alongside financial returns.

Notable Deals:

- **Airbnb (2014):** Investment that supported Airbnb's growth into a global hospitality leader.

- **Creative Artists Agency (CAA) (2010):** Acquired a majority stake, helping expand its market position and service offerings.

Conclusion

The world's largest private equity firms, including Blackstone, The Carlyle Group, KKR, Apollo Global Management, and TPG Capital, are pivotal in shaping the global economy. They engage in a variety of transactions ranging from leveraged buyouts to growth equity investments, each tailored to maximize value and achieve substantial returns. These firms not only manage vast amounts of capital but also play a crucial role in transforming companies and industries. Understanding their operations and notable transactions provides a window into the strategic complexities and significant influence these entities wield in the financial world.

Chapter 24: How Does Private Equity Work?

How Private Equity Works: An In-Depth Exploration

Private equity (PE) is a vital segment of the financial industry, focusing on investing in companies that are not publicly traded. This field offers investors the opportunity to potentially earn substantial returns by investing in private companies or by taking public companies private. The goal is to enhance the value of these companies through various strategies and eventually exit the investment at a profit. This blog post will delve into the comprehensive process of how private equity works, detailing each stage from fundraising to exit strategies, while highlighting the roles of key players involved.

What is Private Equity?

Private equity involves investing in privately-held companies or acquiring public companies to take them private. The primary purpose is to improve the company's value over time through operational improvements, strategic initiatives, and financial restructuring. The end goal is to sell the company at a profit through various exit strategies, such as initial public offerings (IPOs), trade sales, or secondary buyouts.

Types of Private Equity

1. **Venture Capital:** Focuses on early-stage companies with high growth potential. These investments are typically high-risk but can yield significant returns if the companies succeed.

2. **Growth Capital:** Involves investing in mature companies that need capital to expand or restructure operations, enter new markets, or finance significant acquisitions.
3. **Leveraged Buyouts (LBOs):** A common strategy where a PE firm uses borrowed funds to acquire a company, with the acquired company's assets often used as collateral for the loans.
4. **Distressed Investments:** Targets companies that are struggling financially. PE firms buy these companies at a lower price with the intention of turning them around.
5. **Mezzanine Financing:** A hybrid form of financing that combines elements of debt and equity, often used to finance the expansion of existing companies.

The Private Equity Process

1. Fundraising

The journey begins with fundraising. PE firms raise capital from institutional investors, high-net-worth individuals, pension funds, endowments, and sovereign wealth funds. These investors become limited partners (LPs) in the PE fund. The capital committed by LPs is not immediately invested but is drawn down over time as the firm identifies investment opportunities.

2. Sourcing Deals

PE firms source potential investment opportunities through a variety of channels, including:

- **Industry Networks:** Utilizing extensive contacts within specific industries to identify promising companies.
- **Financial Markets:** Analyzing market trends and economic indicators to spot undervalued or high-potential sectors.

- **Direct Outreach:** Engaging directly with companies that meet the investment criteria.

Due diligence is a critical part of this process, where PE firms conduct thorough assessments of the target company's financial health, market position, competitive landscape, and growth potential. This evaluation helps in determining whether the company aligns with the fund's investment mandate and goals.

3. Investment and Acquisition

Once a suitable target is identified, the PE firm proceeds with the acquisition. The acquisition process typically involves:

- **Valuation and Negotiation:** Determining the value of the company and negotiating the terms of purchase.
- **Leveraged Buyouts (LBOs):** In many cases, PE firms use LBOs, which involve significant borrowing to finance the purchase. The borrowed funds are secured against the assets of the acquired company, allowing the PE firm to minimize its capital investment.

Example: In 2007, KKR and TPG Capital executed a leveraged buyout of Texas-based Energy Future Holdings for $45 billion, largely financed through debt.

4. Value Creation and Management

After acquiring a company, PE firms focus on enhancing its value. This is done through several means:

- **Operational Improvements:** Streamlining operations, cutting unnecessary costs, and improving efficiency. This may involve changing management, optimizing supply chains, and entering new markets.

- **Strategic Initiatives:** Introducing new product lines, expanding geographically, or restructuring the company's operations to better align with market demands.

PE firms closely monitor the performance of their portfolio companies, using key performance indicators (KPIs) to track progress and make necessary adjustments.

Example: 3G Capital, after acquiring Kraft Foods, implemented significant cost-cutting measures, boosting the company's profitability.

5. Exit Strategies

The ultimate goal of private equity is to exit the investment profitably. Common exit strategies include:

- **Initial Public Offerings (IPOs):** Taking the company public, allowing the PE firm to sell shares in the open market.
- **Trade Sales:** Selling the company to another company, often a strategic buyer who can derive synergies from the acquisition.
- **Secondary Buyouts:** Selling the company to another PE firm.
- **Recapitalization:** Restructuring the company's capital structure, often involving refinancing to return capital to investors while retaining some ownership.

Example: Blackstone's sale of Refinitiv to the London Stock Exchange Group for $27 billion is a notable instance of a successful exit strategy.

Key Players in Private Equity

1. General Partners (GPs)

- **Role:** GPs are the PE firm managers responsible for raising the fund, sourcing deals, managing portfolio companies, and executing exit strategies.

- **Compensation:** GPs typically earn a management fee (around 2% of assets under management) and a performance fee known as carried interest (usually 20% of the profits).

2. Limited Partners (LPs)

- **Role:** LPs are the investors who provide the capital for the PE fund. They include institutional investors, such as pension funds and endowments, as well as high-net-worth individuals and family offices.
- **Involvement:** LPs typically do not have a say in the day-to-day operations of the PE firm but expect returns on their investments.

Conclusion

Private equity is a sophisticated and powerful form of investment that plays a significant role in the financial markets. It involves a systematic process of fundraising, deal sourcing, acquisition, value creation, and exit. Through this process, private equity firms can significantly enhance the value of their portfolio companies, delivering substantial returns to their investors. Understanding the intricacies of how private equity works is crucial for anyone interested in the world of high finance, corporate restructuring, and investment strategy. This complex yet rewarding field continues to evolve, adapting to market conditions and economic trends, making it a dynamic and integral part of the global financial landscape.

Chapter 25: What Types of IRRs Are Expected by Private Equity & Corporate M&A Departments

Deep Dive into Expected and Realized IRRs in Private Equity and Corporate M&A

What is IRR?

Definition and Importance:

- **Internal Rate of Return (IRR)**: IRR is a key financial metric used to assess the profitability of potential investments. It represents the annualized effective compounded return rate that makes the net present value (NPV) of all cash flows from an investment equal to zero. Essentially, IRR helps investors understand the efficiency and potential profitability of an investment over time.
- **Importance**: IRR is crucial for both private equity (PE) firms and corporate M&A departments. It allows them to compare different investment opportunities on a standardized basis and make informed decisions about where to allocate capital. A

higher IRR indicates a more profitable investment, assuming the associated risks are manageable.

Expected IRRs in Private Equity

Private Equity IRR Benchmarks:

- **General Expectations**: PE firms typically aim for high IRRs due to the higher risk and the active role they play in managing portfolio companies. The expected IRRs can vary significantly depending on the type of investment and market conditions. Generally, PE firms look for IRRs in the range of 20% to 30% or more.
- **Venture Capital**: Investments in early-stage companies are high-risk but can offer high rewards, with expected IRRs often ranging from 25% to 35%. The high failure rate of startups is offset by the potential for exceptional returns from successful investments.
- **Growth Equity**: For companies that are more established but still expanding, expected IRRs are usually in the 20% to 25% range. These companies typically have proven business models but need capital for scaling.
- **Leveraged Buyouts (LBOs)**: In LBOs, PE firms use a mix of equity and significant debt to acquire a company. Expected IRRs generally range from 20% to 30%. The use of leverage can amplify returns, but it also increases financial risk.
- **Distressed Investments**: These involve investing in struggling companies with the potential for turnaround. Expected IRRs can exceed 30%, reflecting the higher risk and the need for significant operational and financial restructuring.

Examples of Realized IRRs in Private Equity:

1. **Blackstone and Hilton Worldwide:**

- Acquisition (2007): Blackstone acquired Hilton Worldwide for $26 billion.
  - **Restructuring**: Implemented cost efficiencies and global expansion strategies.
  - **Exit (2013)**: IPO and subsequent gradual sell-down.
  - **Realized IRR**: Approximately 20% annualized return, demonstrating a successful turnaround and value creation strategy.

2. **KKR and Dollar General:**
   - **Acquisition (2007)**: KKR acquired Dollar General for $7.3 billion.
   - **Operational Improvements**: Focused on optimizing store operations and expanding the store count.
   - **Exit (2009)**: Took the company public again via IPO.
   - **Realized IRR**: Around 30% annualized return, illustrating effective operational enhancement and market positioning.

Expected IRRs in Corporate M&A

Corporate M&A IRR Benchmarks:

- **Strategic Acquisitions**: Corporations typically seek IRRs in the range of 12% to 20%. These investments are often aimed at achieving strategic objectives such as market expansion, technological advancement, or synergy realization.
- **Synergy Realization**: Higher expected IRRs are anticipated when acquisitions are expected to generate significant cost savings or revenue enhancements.
- **Industry Variations**: The expected IRRs can vary significantly depending on the industry:
  - **Technology**: Higher expected IRRs (15%-25%) due to rapid innovation, scalability, and high growth potential.

- Consumer Goods: Moderate expected IRRs (10%-15%) due to more stable cash flows and established market positions.

Examples of Realized IRRs in Corporate M&A:

1. **Amazon and Whole Foods:**
   - **Acquisition (2017)**: Amazon acquired Whole Foods Market for $13.7 billion.
   - **Strategic Integration**: Leveraged Whole Foods' physical stores for enhancing Amazon's grocery delivery and distribution network.
   - **Synergies**: Combined digital and physical retail capabilities.
   - **Realized IRR**: Estimated around 15%, showcasing strategic alignment and operational synergy.
2. **Disney and Pixar:**
   - **Acquisition (2006)**: Disney acquired Pixar for $7.4 billion.
   - **Creative and Operational Integration**: Enhanced Disney's animation capabilities and content library.
   - **Content Expansion**: Generated significant box office and merchandise revenue.
   - **Realized IRR**: Estimated over 20%, demonstrating successful creative integration and significant financial returns.

Factors Influencing Expected and Realized IRRs

Private Equity Factors:

- **Entry Valuation**: Lower entry valuations provide a greater potential for value appreciation, positively impacting IRRs.

- **Operational Improvements**: Effective management can lead to improved profitability and operational efficiency, enhancing IRR.
- **Leverage**: While debt can boost returns, it also adds financial risk, which can affect the IRR.
- **Exit Strategy**: The timing and method of exit (IPO, sale to a strategic buyer, or secondary buyout) are critical in realizing the targeted IRR.

Corporate M&A Factors:

- **Strategic Fit**: The degree to which the acquisition aligns with the company's long-term strategic goals and the potential for synergy realization.
- **Integration Success**: The smooth integration of the acquired company's operations, culture, and systems is vital for achieving the expected IRR.
- **Market Conditions**: Economic and market conditions can influence the performance of the acquired company and the overall IRR.
- **Regulatory Environment**: Regulatory approvals and compliance can impact the timeline and success of M&A deals, affecting the realized IRR.

Conclusion

Understanding the expected and realized IRRs in private equity and corporate M&A is essential for investors, managers, and stakeholders. These metrics not only provide a benchmark for assessing potential investments but also help in evaluating the success of completed deals. Private equity firms generally aim for higher IRRs due to the high-risk, high-reward nature of their investments. In contrast, corporate M&A departments often have more moderate IRR targets, reflecting a balance between strategic objectives and financial returns. By analyzing notable transactions and the factors that influence IRRs, we gain a deeper understanding of the complexities and dynamics of the investment landscape, ultimately guiding more informed and strategic decision-making.

Chapter 26: What are Strategic & Financial Buyers?

Understanding Strategic and Financial Buyers in Investment Banking: A Deep Dive

In the intricate world of mergers and acquisitions (M&A), **strategic** and **financial buyers** are two distinct types of acquirers, each with unique motivations, goals, and approaches to transactions. These differences significantly impact the strategies employed in negotiations, deal structures, and the post-acquisition integration process. This blog post provides a comprehensive exploration of who these buyers are, what drives them, and how they operate within the M&A landscape, supported by real-world examples.

Defining Strategic and Financial Buyers

Strategic Buyers are typically existing companies looking to acquire other businesses that align with their long-term business strategies. These acquisitions are driven by the desire to create synergies—whether through cost reduction, revenue enhancement, market expansion, or technological advancement.

Financial Buyers, on the other hand, are primarily investment firms like private equity (PE) firms, hedge funds, and venture capitalists. Their primary objective is financial gain, often achieved by buying undervalued or underperforming companies, improving them, and then selling them at a profit.

Motivations Behind Strategic Buyers

1. **Synergies**:
   - **Revenue Synergies**: By acquiring another company, a strategic buyer can expand its product offerings, enter new markets, or cross-sell to an expanded customer base. For example, **Amazon's acquisition of Whole Foods** allowed Amazon to enter the grocery market, leveraging Whole Foods' physical store presence with Amazon's distribution capabilities.
   - **Cost Synergies**: Strategic buyers often look to reduce operational costs by eliminating redundancies and achieving economies of scale. For instance, **Disney's acquisition of Pixar** not only enriched Disney's animation portfolio but also provided opportunities to streamline operations and combine creative resources.
2. **Market Expansion**:
   - Strategic buyers may acquire companies to gain access to new geographic markets or demographic segments. For example, **Walmart's acquisition of Flipkart** was driven by Walmart's desire to enter the Indian e-commerce market.
3. **Technological Advancements**:
   - Acquiring companies with superior technology or unique capabilities can provide a competitive edge. **Google's acquisition of YouTube** is a classic example, where Google saw an opportunity to dominate the online video market.
4. **Competitive Positioning**:
   - Sometimes, acquisitions are made to eliminate competition or to gain strategic assets that competitors lack. This defensive strategy ensures that the acquirer strengthens its market position.

Motivations Behind Financial Buyers

1. **Return on Investment (ROI)**:
   - Financial buyers focus on acquiring companies that offer the potential for substantial financial returns. They seek to buy low, improve the business, and sell high. The expected IRRs (Internal Rate of Return) for these buyers typically range from 20% to 30% or more.

2. **Value Creation**:
   - Financial buyers often target underperforming companies with the potential for operational improvements. By implementing better management practices, restructuring debt, or optimizing operations, they aim to increase the company's value.

3. **Leverage**:
   - Many financial buyers use leveraged buyouts (LBOs) as a key strategy, where they use a mix of equity and borrowed funds to finance acquisitions. The use of leverage amplifies potential returns but also increases risk.

4. **Exit Strategies**:
   - Unlike strategic buyers, financial buyers plan their exit strategies from the outset. Common exits include selling the company to another firm, taking it public through an IPO, or selling it to another private equity firm.

Key Differences Between Strategic and Financial Buyers

1. **Objectives**:
   - **Strategic Buyers**: Focus on long-term integration and operational synergies.

- Financial Buyers: Primarily interested in financial returns and typically have a shorter investment horizon.

2. **Approach to Valuation**:
   - Strategic Buyers: May be willing to pay a premium for strategic assets due to potential synergies.
   - Financial Buyers: More focused on the intrinsic value of the company and potential for value enhancement.

3. **Integration and Management**:
   - Strategic Buyers: Often integrate the acquired company into their existing operations, focusing on achieving synergies.
   - Financial Buyers: May restructure the company, implement new management, and improve efficiencies.

4. **Exit Strategy**:
   - Strategic Buyers: Generally, have a long-term perspective, focusing on integrating the acquisition into their broader strategy.
   - Financial Buyers: Aim for a clear exit, often within 3-7 years, through IPOs, secondary sales, or strategic sales.

Illustrative Examples

1. **Amazon's Acquisition of Whole Foods**:
   - Type: Strategic Buyer
   - Objective: Expand into the grocery sector, enhance logistics, and integrate physical and digital retail.

2. **KKR's Acquisition of Dollar General**:
   - Type: Financial Buyer

- **Objective**: Improve operational efficiency, expand store footprint, and eventually exit through a public offering.
3. **Disney's Acquisition of Pixar**:
    - **Type**: Strategic Buyer
    - **Objective**: Strengthen Disney's animation capabilities and content library.
4. **Blackstone's Acquisition of Hilton Worldwide**:
    - **Type**: Financial Buyer
    - **Objective**: Enhance value through restructuring and eventually exit via IPO.

Conclusion

Strategic and financial buyers play distinct roles in the M&A landscape, each bringing unique strengths and strategies to the table. **Strategic buyers** focus on achieving long-term operational synergies and market expansion, while **financial buyers** aim for high returns through strategic management and timely exits. Understanding the differences between these two types of buyers is crucial for businesses considering M&A activities, as it helps in aligning transaction strategies with the right type of buyer to achieve the desired outcomes. By analyzing motivations, approaches, and real-world examples, businesses can better navigate the complexities of the M&A process and make informed decisions.

Chapter 27: What Does an Ideal LBO Candidate Look Like?

What Does an Ideal LBO Candidate Look Like?

In private equity, leveraged buyouts (LBOs) are a popular method for acquiring companies. This process involves using a combination of equity and significant debt to finance the acquisition. The acquired company's assets and cash flows typically serve as collateral for the borrowed money. The aim is to improve the company's financial performance and profitability, eventually selling it at a profit or taking it public. Identifying the right candidate for an LBO is critical for success. This blog post explores the characteristics that make a company an ideal candidate for an LBO, explaining each trait in detail and providing real-world examples.

Key Characteristics of an Ideal LBO Candidate

1. **Strong and Predictable Cash Flows**
    Importance: Reliable and consistent cash flows are essential because they ensure that the company can meet the debt obligations incurred during the buyout. Cash flow stability reduces the risk of financial distress and helps manage the interest payments on the debt.

Example: Companies in non-cyclical industries like utilities, consumer goods, and healthcare often exhibit stable cash flows. For instance, RJR Nabisco, acquired by KKR in 1989, had robust cash flows from its tobacco and food businesses, making it a prime LBO target.

2. **Low Existing Debt Levels**
   Importance: Companies with low levels of existing debt are more attractive because they can take on additional leverage without becoming overburdened. High debt levels can limit the company's ability to secure new loans and increase financial risk.
   Example: When KKR acquired Dollar General in 2007, the company had low debt, allowing KKR to leverage additional financing for the acquisition.

3. **Strong Market Position**
   Importance: A company with a dominant or strong market position often enjoys competitive advantages such as brand recognition, economies of scale, or proprietary technology. These factors can help sustain profitability and growth.
   Example: The acquisition of Kraft Foods by 3G Capital and Berkshire Hathaway in 2015 was driven by Kraft's strong market position and well-known brands.

4. **Experienced Management Team**
   Importance: A capable and experienced management team is crucial for executing the necessary changes post-acquisition. Their expertise can help drive operational improvements, manage the transition, and achieve the strategic objectives of the buyout.
   Example: The 2005 buyout of Toys "R" Us by Bain Capital, KKR, and Vornado Realty Trust relied on the existing management team's experience to navigate the complexities of the retail industry.

5. **Opportunities for Operational Improvements**
   Importance: Companies with clear opportunities for

operational enhancements—such as cost reductions, efficiency improvements, or revenue growth—are particularly attractive. These improvements can significantly boost profitability and, consequently, the value of the company.

Example: The acquisition of Hertz by Clayton, Dubilier & Rice and The Carlyle Group in 2005 focused on implementing operational improvements and cost-cutting measures, leading to a successful IPO.

6. **Non-Cyclical Industry**

    Importance: Companies in industries less affected by economic downturns provide more stable cash flows, reducing the risk associated with high debt levels. Non-cyclical industries, such as healthcare, consumer staples, and utilities, often exhibit stable demand regardless of economic conditions.

    Example: The buyout of HCA Healthcare by Bain Capital, KKR, and Merrill Lynch Global Private Equity in 2006 leveraged the stability of the healthcare industry, ensuring consistent cash flow and profitability.

7. **Assets That Can Serve as Collateral**

    Importance: Tangible assets such as real estate, machinery, or inventory can be used as collateral to secure the debt financing required in an LBO. Collateral provides lenders with security, potentially lowering borrowing costs.

    Example: In the 2007 buyout of Energy Future Holdings by KKR, TPG Capital, and Goldman Sachs, the company's substantial energy infrastructure assets were used as collateral for the debt.

8. **Potential for Strategic Divestitures**

    Importance: The ability to sell non-core assets can provide additional cash flow to pay down debt and focus the company on its core business. Divestitures can streamline operations and improve financial health.

    Example: The acquisition of Albertsons by Cerberus Capital

Management in 2013 included the sale of non-core stores, which helped optimize the company's operations and improve profitability.

Real-World Examples of Successful LBOs

RJR Nabisco by KKR (1989)

- **Overview**: KKR's $25 billion buyout of RJR Nabisco is one of the most well-known LBOs.
- **Outcome**: Despite the high leverage, KKR enhanced operational efficiency and eventually divested parts of the business profitably.

Dollar General by KKR (2007)

- **Overview**: KKR acquired Dollar General for $7.3 billion, focusing on expansion and operational improvements.
- **Outcome**: The firm successfully brought Dollar General to an IPO in 2009, demonstrating significant value creation.

Hertz by Clayton, Dubilier & Rice and The Carlyle Group (2005)

- **Overview**: The $15 billion buyout of Hertz aimed at restructuring and operational enhancement.
- **Outcome**: The acquisition led to substantial cost savings and operational improvements, culminating in a successful IPO in 2006.

HCA Healthcare by Bain Capital, KKR, and Merrill Lynch Global Private Equity (2006)

- **Overview**: The $33 billion buyout was based on the stability and growth potential of the healthcare industry.

- **Outcome**: The strategic growth and operational improvements post-acquisition led to a successful IPO in 2011.

Conclusion

An ideal LBO candidate possesses a combination of strong and predictable cash flows, low existing debt, a solid market position, an experienced management team, and clear opportunities for operational improvements. Additionally, being in a non-cyclical industry, having tangible assets for collateral, and the potential for strategic divestitures are critical factors that make a company suitable for an LBO. These attributes help private equity firms identify and acquire companies that can be transformed into profitable investments, resulting in significant returns.

Through real-world examples, we can see how these characteristics play out in actual transactions, underscoring the complexity and potential of LBOs in the investment landscape. Understanding what makes an ideal LBO candidate is crucial for investment professionals looking to navigate the intricacies of leveraged buyouts and achieve successful outcomes.

Chapter 28: What Does an Investment Mandate Look Like?

Crafting Investment Mandates: A Deep Dive for Strategic and Financial Sponsors

Investment mandates serve as a comprehensive guide for making investment decisions, outlining the objectives, risk tolerance, and strategies that shape how capital is allocated and managed. They are essential tools for both strategic and financial sponsors, ensuring that investments align with broader goals and provide a structured framework for evaluating opportunities. In this detailed exploration, we'll dive into the components of investment mandates, the distinctions between those for strategic and financial sponsors, and real-world examples to illustrate these principles.

What is an Investment Mandate?

An investment mandate is a formalized set of guidelines that specifies the criteria for investing capital. It defines the investment objectives, risk appetite, asset allocation preferences, and performance benchmarks. These mandates are crucial for maintaining a disciplined investment approach, ensuring consistency in decision-making, and aligning with the sponsor's overarching goals.

Importance of Investment Mandates:

- **Consistency:** Provides a consistent approach to evaluating and selecting investments, reducing subjectivity and ad-hoc decision-making.
- **Risk Management:** Helps manage and mitigate risks by setting clear boundaries and criteria for investments.
- **Performance Monitoring:** Establishes benchmarks and metrics to evaluate the success of investments over time.

Strategic Sponsors: Defining Investment Mandates

Who They Are:
Strategic sponsors are typically corporations or businesses investing in companies, technologies, or assets that complement their core operations. Their primary goal is not just financial return but also enhancing their business capabilities and market position.

Key Components of Strategic Investment Mandates:

1. **Strategic Alignment:**
   - **Objective:** Investments must align with the company's long-term business strategy. This includes expanding into new markets, acquiring new technologies, or securing critical resources.
   - **Detail:** For example, a technology firm may prioritize investments in AI startups to integrate advanced technologies into its product line, enhancing its competitive edge.
2. **Market Position and Synergies:**
   - **Objective:** Target acquisitions should offer synergies that can enhance market share, improve operational efficiency, or create new product opportunities.

- o **Detail:** A pharmaceutical company might seek to acquire smaller biotech firms with promising drug pipelines that complement its existing portfolio.
3. **Risk Management:**
    - o **Objective:** The mandate outlines acceptable levels of financial and operational risk. It may include guidelines on debt levels, market volatility, and geopolitical risks.
    - o **Detail:** A consumer goods company may avoid high-risk markets with unstable political climates to protect its brand reputation and market stability.
4. **Integration and Execution Plan:**
    - o **Objective:** There must be a clear plan for integrating new acquisitions into the existing business structure, including considerations for cultural fit and operational alignment.
    - o **Detail:** For instance, a global retail chain acquiring a local brand must ensure that the integration plan addresses supply chain management and brand positioning in the new market.

Financial Sponsors: Crafting Investment Mandates

Who They Are:
Financial sponsors, such as private equity firms, venture capitalists, and hedge funds, focus on achieving high financial returns through strategic investments. Their primary concern is the financial performance of the portfolio companies and the exit strategy.

Key Components of Financial Investment Mandates:

1. **Target Return on Investment (ROI):**

- **Objective:** Establish specific return thresholds, such as a minimum internal rate of return (IRR) or multiple on invested capital (MOIC).
- **Detail:** A private equity firm might set a minimum IRR of 20%, aiming for substantial returns within a specified timeframe.

2. **Risk-Adjusted Returns:**
   - **Objective:** Balance potential returns with associated risks, ensuring a diversified portfolio to mitigate risk.
   - **Detail:** A hedge fund may use complex financial instruments like derivatives to hedge against market downturns while targeting high-growth opportunities.

3. **Investment Horizon:**
   - **Objective:** Define the expected duration of investments, often ranging from 3 to 7 years, with planned exits through IPOs or sales.
   - **Detail:** Venture capital firms might focus on startups with high growth potential, planning exits as these companies mature and scale.

4. **Value Creation Strategy:**
   - **Objective:** Identify strategies for increasing the value of portfolio companies, such as through operational improvements, restructuring, or strategic add-ons.
   - **Detail:** A private equity firm might acquire a manufacturing company, implement cost-saving measures, and expand into new markets to enhance profitability.

Differences Between Strategic and Financial Investment Mandates

Primary Objectives:

- **Strategic Sponsors:** Focus on achieving long-term business goals, such as market expansion and operational synergies.
- **Financial Sponsors:** Aim for high financial returns, focusing on exit strategies and maximizing investment value.

Approach to Risk:

- **Strategic Sponsors:** May accept higher operational risks if they align with strategic goals.
- **Financial Sponsors:** Prioritize managing financial risks, often using diversification and hedging strategies.

Investment Horizon:

- **Strategic Sponsors:** Often have a longer-term perspective, integrating acquisitions into core operations.
- **Financial Sponsors:** Have defined exit timelines, typically planning exits within 3-7 years.

Integration and Value Creation:

- **Strategic Sponsors:** Focus on seamless integration and leveraging synergies.
- **Financial Sponsors:** Concentrate on restructuring, cost-cutting, and operational efficiencies.

Real-World Examples

Amazon's Acquisition of Whole Foods (Strategic Sponsor):
Amazon acquired Whole Foods to enhance its grocery delivery capabilities, integrate physical stores with its e-commerce platform, and expand its market reach. The investment mandate likely focused on synergies between Whole Foods' retail expertise and Amazon's distribution network.

Blackstone's Acquisition of Hilton Worldwide (Financial Sponsor):
Blackstone's acquisition of Hilton Worldwide involved restructuring the company, improving operational efficiencies, and expanding its global footprint. The firm focused on achieving a high IRR through operational improvements and a strategic exit via IPO.

Conclusion

Investment mandates are essential tools for guiding investment decisions, whether for strategic sponsors looking to enhance business capabilities or financial sponsors seeking high returns. By understanding and clearly defining these mandates, investors can make informed decisions, align investments with broader objectives, and effectively manage risks. As the investment landscape evolves, both strategic and financial sponsors must continuously refine their mandates to adapt to changing market conditions, technological advancements, and emerging opportunities.

PART III: FRONT OFFICE INVESTMENT BANKING PROCESS

Chapter 29: Front Office Investment Banking Process

A Detailed Overview of the Front Office Investment Banking Process

Front office investment banking is the epicenter of client interactions and the execution of financial transactions. It encompasses a wide array of activities crucial to the revenue generation and strategic development of investment banks. This article offers a comprehensive, step-by-step explanation of the front office investment banking process, highlighting its complexity and the critical role it plays in the financial industry.

What is Front Office Investment Banking?

Definition and Core Responsibilities

Front Office Investment Banking refers to the division of an investment bank that deals directly with clients. It is primarily involved in generating business, managing client relationships, and executing deals. The front office is responsible for:

1. **Client Engagement:** Engaging with clients, including corporations, governments, and institutional investors, to understand their needs and offer tailored financial solutions.

2. **Deal Origination:** Identifying and creating business opportunities, such as mergers and acquisitions (M&A), capital raising, and other financial transactions.
3. **Strategic Advisory:** Providing expert advice on various financial strategies, including market positioning, corporate restructuring, and investment decisions.

These activities are crucial for securing mandates, driving business development, and generating revenue for the bank.

Key Processes in Front Office Investment Banking

1. Coverage

Coverage involves analyzing specific industries or market segments to identify trends, opportunities, and key players. This foundational work is essential for effective client interactions and deal origination.

Key Steps:

- **Selecting Industries:** Bankers focus on industries or sectors based on market trends, expertise, and potential client interest.
- **Vertical and Subvertical Analysis:** This involves deep dives into specific sectors to understand the nuances and dynamics, which helps in identifying key companies and market trends.
- **Index Building:** Creating a comprehensive database of companies within the selected industries helps track market movements and potential opportunities.
- **Developing Marketing Materials:** Crafting presentations, reports, and pitch books that highlight market insights and strategic opportunities for clients.

Example: A banker covering the technology sector may focus on sub-sectors like fintech or cybersecurity, providing insights into key trends and emerging companies.

2. Matching Mandates with Targets

Objective: Align the investment criteria of strategic and financial sponsors with potential acquisition targets.

Key Steps:

- **Understanding Buyer Profiles:** Detailed knowledge of the investment preferences and objectives of both strategic and financial sponsors.
- **Mandate Acquisition:** Securing formal agreements from sponsors that outline their investment criteria, such as target industries, deal size, and strategic goals.
- **Target Identification:** Using industry knowledge and networks to find companies that meet the mandates' criteria.

Example: A private equity firm may have a mandate to invest in mid-sized manufacturing companies with strong cash flows and low debt.

3. Origination and Pitching

Objective: Generate and present business opportunities to potential clients, maintaining a continuous pipeline of deals.

Key Steps:

- **Identifying Key Decision Makers:** Building relationships with individuals who have decision-making power within target companies.

- **Origination Process:** This involves continuously identifying new opportunities and reaching out to potential clients to discuss these opportunities.
- **Pitch Preparation:** Developing detailed pitches that outline the strategic alternatives and benefits for the client.
- **Delivering the Pitch:** Presenting these opportunities to clients to secure engagement and mandate.

Example: An investment bank might pitch an M&A deal to a large corporation looking to expand its market share in a specific region.

4. Fee Structuring and Engagement Letters

Objective: Establish financial terms and formalize the client engagement.

Key Steps:

- **Determining the Fee Structure:** Deciding on the appropriate fee arrangement (e.g., retainer, success fee) based on the deal's complexity and expected value.
- **Negotiating Fees:** Discussing and finalizing the fee amount with the client, ensuring it reflects the work and value provided by the bank.
- **Engagement Letter:** Drafting a legal agreement that outlines the scope of services, fee structure, and other terms of the engagement.

Example: A bank might charge a retainer fee plus a success fee based on the completion and size of the transaction.

5. Underwriting and Valuation

Objective: Accurately assess the value of the target company using various methodologies and ensure appropriate pricing for the transaction.

Key Steps:

- **Collecting Financial Data:** Gathering detailed financial statements and performance metrics of the target company.
- **Building Financial Models:** Creating financial models to project future earnings, cash flows, and valuation.
- **Applying Valuation Techniques:** Using methods such as Discounted Cash Flow (DCF), Comparable Company Analysis, and Precedent Transactions to determine the company's worth.
- **Valuation Presentation:** Presenting a valuation "football field" that visually represents the valuation range based on different methodologies.

Example: For an M&A deal, the bank may determine a valuation range for the target company, helping to set a realistic price expectation for the negotiation.

6. Marketing and Deal Execution

Objective: Market the investment opportunity and manage the deal's execution process.

Key Steps:

- **Creating Marketing Materials:** Developing teasers and Confidential Information Memoranda (CIM) that provide essential details about the investment opportunity.
- **Buyer List Development:** Identifying and reaching out to potential buyers, whether they are strategic or financial sponsors.

- **Deal Structuring:** Negotiating and finalizing deal terms, including payment structures, contingencies, and legal covenants.
- **Managing the M&A Process:** Overseeing due diligence, finalizing the purchase agreement, and ensuring a smooth closing process.

Example: The bank may create a CIM for a company looking to sell a business unit, detailing the unit's operations, financial performance, and strategic value.

Conclusion

The front office investment banking process is a multifaceted journey involving detailed industry analysis, strategic client engagement, meticulous deal structuring, and effective execution. Each step, from initial client contact to final deal closure, requires a blend of analytical skills, market knowledge, and relationship-building expertise. Mastering these processes is crucial for anyone aspiring to succeed in investment banking, as it not only drives the bank's revenue but also enhances the client's strategic objectives and financial performance. Understanding this comprehensive process provides a foundation for navigating the complexities of the investment banking landscape and achieving long-term success.

Chapter 30: Front Office Investment Banking Process: Deep Dive

Front Office Investment Banking: A Comprehensive and Detailed Exploration

Investment banking is a multifaceted industry, with the "front office" serving as the crucial interface between the bank and its clients. This role involves a variety of tasks, from building relationships to executing deals, all of which are vital for the bank's success. This blog post will thoroughly explore the front office investment banking process, breaking down each stage and explaining its significance with detailed content.

What is Front Office Investment Banking?

Front Office Investment Banking is the client-facing segment of investment banks. It involves interacting with clients, originating deals, and ensuring the execution of transactions. The primary goal is to generate revenue and provide value through various financial services. The front office encompasses several key functions, each crucial for maintaining the bank's competitive edge and financial health.

Key Functions:

1. **Client Engagement:**
   - **Building Relationships:** The foundation of front office activities lies in establishing strong, trusting relationships with clients. This involves understanding clients' industries, challenges, and strategic goals. Senior bankers engage with CEOs, CFOs, and other key decision-makers to align the bank's offerings with the clients' needs.
     - *Example:* A senior banker at a global investment bank might spend months nurturing a relationship with a Fortune 500 company's CFO, understanding their expansion plans, and positioning the bank as a partner for potential capital raising or M&A activities.
   - **Maintaining Relationships:** Relationship management doesn't end after the initial contact. Continuous engagement through regular updates, market insights, and strategic discussions helps maintain a strong connection. This ongoing interaction ensures the banker stays top-of-mind for future transactions.
     - *Example:* Regular check-ins and updates about market trends can keep the banker relevant and aware of any new opportunities, such as the client considering an acquisition or needing advice on a new market entry.
2. **Deal Origination:**
   - **Identifying Opportunities:** This involves proactively scouting for potential deals by monitoring market trends, economic indicators, and industry developments. Bankers must be well-versed in their

sectors to spot opportunities that align with their clients' strategic goals.

- *Example:* A banker specializing in the technology sector might identify a trend towards consolidation in cloud computing services, prompting outreach to clients about potential mergers or acquisitions.

  o **Initiating Deals:** Once an opportunity is identified, bankers pitch the idea to clients, outlining potential benefits, strategic fit, and financial implications. This stage is crucial as it transforms abstract opportunities into concrete business discussions.

- *Example:* Presenting a detailed analysis to a client about the benefits of acquiring a competitor, including potential market share growth and cost synergies.

3. **Strategic Advisory:**
   o **Providing Advice:** Beyond transactions, bankers offer ongoing strategic advice, helping clients navigate complex financial landscapes. This can include advising on capital structure, market entry strategies, or divestitures.

- *Example:* Advising a manufacturing company on optimizing its capital structure to lower its cost of capital and improve financial flexibility.

   o **Tailored Solutions:** Each client's situation is unique, requiring customized solutions. Bankers must consider the client's specific financial health, market position, and strategic objectives when crafting their advice.

- *Example:* Crafting a bespoke solution for a multinational corporation to spin off a non-core division while ensuring minimal disruption to its main operations.

Front Office vs. Deal Support

Front Office: This is the public-facing, revenue-generating side of investment banking. Bankers here are responsible for cultivating client relationships, identifying and initiating deals, and providing strategic advice. They are the primary point of contact for clients and lead the execution of deals.

Deal Support: Consists of analysts and associates who work behind the scenes. They provide the essential analytical support required for deals, including financial modeling, preparing presentations, and conducting detailed market research. While they don't usually interact with clients directly, their work is critical to the success of the front office.

Importance of Front Office Experience: Experience in the front office is invaluable for anyone looking to build a career in investment banking. It provides direct exposure to deal-making, client management, and strategic decision-making, all of which are essential skills for senior roles within the industry.

The Methodology of Front Office Investment Banking

A successful career in investment banking hinges on mastering the front office process. This methodology comprises several critical stages, each essential for executing successful transactions.

1. Coverage

Coverage refers to the specialization in specific industries or market segments. It involves a detailed understanding of the chosen sectors, which is foundational for client engagement and deal origination.

Steps in the Coverage Process:

- **Choosing Coverage Areas:** Bankers select industries or sectors to focus on based on market potential, their own expertise, and strategic alignment with the bank's strengths. This choice dictates the banker's market positioning and the types of clients they will target.
  - *Example:* A banker with a background in pharmaceuticals may focus on biotech companies, leveraging their knowledge of drug development and regulatory environments.
- **Vertical & Subvertical Analysis:** This involves breaking down industries into specific niches to better understand the dynamics at play, including competitive landscapes, key players, and growth prospects.
  - *Example:* In the renewable energy sector, analyzing subverticals like solar, wind, and bioenergy to identify emerging technologies and investment opportunities.
- **Index Building:** Compiling a comprehensive list of companies within the selected sectors, including key financial metrics and business details. This index serves as a reference for tracking potential deals and industry trends.
  - *Example:* An index of fintech companies, detailing their market capitalization, revenue growth, and technological innovations.
- **Developing Marketing Materials:** Creating detailed documents that communicate insights and opportunities to clients. This includes industry reports, pitch books, and

presentations that highlight the bank's capabilities and market expertise.

- ○ *Example:* A pitch book showcasing recent M&A trends in the tech sector, complete with case studies and market analysis.

2. Mandate/Target Matching & Generating Strategic Alternatives

After establishing coverage, the next step is matching client mandates with potential targets, identifying opportunities that align with client strategies.

Steps in the Mandate/Target Matching Process:

- **Identifying Strategic & Financial Buyers:** Understanding the distinct needs of different buyers, whether they are strategic companies looking for synergies or financial investors seeking returns.
  - ○ *Example:* Identifying a private equity firm interested in acquiring underperforming companies with turnaround potential.
- **Securing Investment Mandates:** Formalizing client intentions with written mandates, which outline specific criteria and objectives for potential investments.
  - ○ *Example:* An investment mandate from a strategic buyer specifying interest in acquiring companies with established customer bases in Asia.
- **Identifying Suitable Targets:** Using the mandate as a guideline to find companies that meet the criteria, leveraging industry knowledge and market insights.
  - ○ *Example:* Finding a mid-sized technology firm with a strong R&D pipeline that matches a strategic buyer's mandate for innovative tech acquisitions.

3. Origination & Pitching Strategic Alternatives

Origination involves generating a pipeline of potential deals, while pitching involves presenting these opportunities to clients.

Steps in the Origination Process:

- **Identifying Key Decision Makers:** Recognizing who within an organization has the authority to make decisions about potential deals.
  - *Example:* Targeting the head of corporate development at a multinational company when proposing a strategic acquisition.
- **The Cycle of Origination:** A continuous process of identifying, contacting, and engaging potential clients. This requires persistence and a proactive approach to uncovering new opportunities.
  - *Example:* Regularly attending industry conferences to network and identify potential clients and partners.
- **Preparing for the Pitch:** Crafting a persuasive presentation that clearly outlines the proposed deal's benefits, supported by thorough research and analysis.
  - *Example:* A comprehensive pitch book detailing the financial and strategic rationale for a proposed merger between two companies.
- **Pitching to Clients:** Delivering the pitch effectively, addressing client concerns, and highlighting the unique value proposition of the proposed deal.
  - *Example:* Presenting a merger scenario that showcases potential market share growth and cost-saving synergies.

4. Fee Structuring & Winning Mandates

To formalize an engagement, the bank and client must agree on a fee structure and secure a mandate.

Key Considerations:

- **Types of Fees:** Determining the fee structure, which could include retainer fees, success fees, or a combination.
  - *Example:* A retainer fee paid upfront for advisory services, plus a success fee contingent on the deal's completion.
- **Negotiating Fee Size:** The size of the fee is negotiated based on the deal's complexity, size, and potential value to the client.
  - *Example:* Higher fees for larger deals with complex structures due to the extensive work and risk involved.
- **Engagement Letter:** This formal agreement outlines the terms of the engagement, including the scope of work, fee structure, and confidentiality provisions.
  - *Example:* An engagement letter for a buy-side advisory detailing the services provided, the expected timeline, and the agreed fees.

5. Underwriting the Strategic Alternative (Continued)

Steps in the Underwriting Process:

- **Collecting Historical Financials:** Gathering comprehensive financial data to evaluate the company's past performance.
- *Example:* Analyzing income statements, balance sheets, and cash flow statements from the past five years.
- **Building Financial Models:** Developing detailed models that forecast future performance, incorporating different assumptions and market conditions.

- *Example:* Creating a discounted cash flow (DCF) model to estimate the present value of future cash flows, adjusting for risk and growth prospects.
- **Valuation Techniques:** Applying multiple valuation methods to derive a fair value range for the target company.
- *Example:* Using Comparable Company Analysis to benchmark the target against similar companies and derive valuation multiples.
- **Valuation Football Field:** Creating a graphical representation of the valuation range using different methodologies provides a visual overview of the potential value of the target company. This helps in understanding the variance in valuations based on different approaches.
  - *Example:* A chart showing valuation ranges derived from Discounted Cash Flow (DCF), Comparable Company Analysis, and Precedent Transactions, highlighting how different assumptions can lead to different valuation outcomes.
- **Customizing Financial Models:** Tailoring the financial models to reflect specific transaction scenarios, such as potential synergies in an acquisition or cost-cutting measures in a restructuring. This customization is critical for accurate valuation and strategic planning.
  - *Example:* Adjusting a financial model to include projected cost savings from merging two companies' supply chains.

6. Packaging & Securitizing the Strategic Alternative

After underwriting, the next step involves creating detailed marketing materials to present the investment opportunity to potential buyers or investors.

Key Elements:

- **Teaser Creation:** A teaser is a brief document that provides a high-level overview of the investment opportunity without revealing the company's identity. It includes key financial metrics, market position, and strategic highlights to attract interest.
  - *Example:* A teaser for a retail company might mention its strong brand, revenue growth, and market presence without disclosing the company's name.
- **Confidential Information Memorandum (CIM):** The CIM is a comprehensive document that provides in-depth information about the target company, including detailed financial statements, business operations, market analysis, and strategic rationale. It is shared with serious buyers under a confidentiality agreement.
  - *Example:* A CIM for a potential acquisition in the automotive sector might include details about the company's manufacturing capabilities, distribution network, and future growth plans.

7. Buyer List Development and Deal Structuring

Once the marketing materials are ready, the next steps involve identifying potential buyers and structuring the deal.

Steps in the Process:

- **Developing a Buyer List:** This involves compiling a list of potential buyers who may have a strategic or financial interest in the acquisition. The list typically includes both strategic buyers, who may benefit from synergies, and financial buyers, such as private equity firms looking for investment opportunities.

- - *Example:* A buyer list for a software company might include major tech firms, private equity firms specializing in technology, and venture capitalists.
- **Initial Outreach:** Contacting potential buyers to gauge their interest in the opportunity. This step is critical for generating competitive tension and maximizing the sale price.
  - *Example:* Reaching out to the corporate development teams of potential acquirers to discuss the investment opportunity and assess their level of interest.

8. Deal Structuring

Deal structuring involves negotiating the terms of the transaction, including valuation, payment structure, and other critical elements.

Steps in the Deal Structuring Process:

- **Valuation Range:** Establishing a range within which the deal is expected to be valued. This range is informed by the underwriting process and market conditions. It provides a basis for negotiations between the buyer and seller.
  - *Example:* Negotiating a valuation range of $100 million to $120 million for a mid-sized manufacturing company based on its financial performance and market potential.
- **Deal Terms:** Finalizing the terms of the transaction, including the payment structure (cash, stock, or a combination), conditions precedent, representations and warranties, and covenants. This stage is crucial for ensuring both parties are clear on the expectations and protections in the transaction.
  - *Example:* Agreeing on an earn-out clause where the final payment depends on the acquired company's performance post-transaction.

9. The M&A Process

The final stage involves completing the transaction through a structured M&A process.

Steps in the M&A Process:

- **IOI From Buyer:** An Indication of Interest (IOI) is a non-binding offer from a potential buyer outlining their initial valuation and deal terms. This document signals serious interest and initiates more detailed negotiations.
    - *Example:* A private equity firm submitting an IOI proposing an acquisition price of $80 million with a mix of cash and equity.
- **Buyer-Seller Meetings:** These meetings are crucial for discussing the deal terms in detail, addressing any concerns, and building rapport between the parties. They often include presentations, Q&A sessions, and site visits.
    - *Example:* An in-person meeting between the management teams of the acquiring company and the target, discussing integration plans and strategic visions.
- **Purchase Agreement:** Drafting and negotiating the definitive purchase agreement, which legally binds the terms of the transaction. This document includes detailed terms and conditions, representations and warranties, and indemnities.
    - *Example:* A purchase agreement outlining the agreed purchase price, conditions for closing, and post-closing adjustments.
- **Due Diligence:** A thorough review by the buyer of the target company's legal, financial, and operational aspects. This step ensures that all material information has been disclosed and that there are no hidden risks.

- *Example:* A legal team conducting due diligence on potential litigation risks and contract obligations of the target company.
- **Complete Due Diligence:** Finalizing the due diligence process and confirming that all conditions precedent have been met. Any issues discovered during due diligence are resolved or negotiated.
  - *Example:* Addressing concerns raised during due diligence, such as outstanding legal disputes or financial irregularities.
- **Closing & Flow of Funds:** The final step involves completing the transaction, which includes signing the final agreements, transferring ownership, and disbursing the agreed-upon funds. This marks the official change of ownership.
  - *Example:* On the closing date, the buyer transfers the purchase price to the seller, and the seller transfers the shares or assets of the company to the buyer.

NOTES:

What is Front Office Investment Banking?

Front office investment banking speaks to the process and role of the senior banker, the one responsible for landing the engagements with clients and being a dealmaker. The front office investment banker spends their time building and maintaining relationships within their coverage area and for their specific financial product. Ultimately the senior banker explores strategic alternatives with their clients in order to win mandates to implement the strategic alternative and generate fees for the investment bank.

Front Office vs. Deal Support

The front office is referred to as 'client-facing' while deal support (analysts & associates) does the work to create the deliverables for the marketing materials and deal materials. If you want a long and successful career in investment banking, it makes sense to get front office investment banking experience even if it is in the lower middle market and middle market.

Front Office Investment Banking Methodology

In order to build a career in investment banking, it is essential to know and practice the Front Office Investment Banking Process. Whether one's career track is in a bulge bracket investment bank, middle market M&A group, or as a lower middle market M&A advisor, it is crucial to know the primary process of the investment banker.

1) **Coverage** – Coverage gives us the basis for research and marketing material that we use in origination and other forms of marketing/analysis. The Coverage Process is the following:
   a) Choosing Coverage
   b) Vertical & Subvertical Coverage
   c) Index Building
   d) Metrics
   e) Benchmarking

Investment Banking University

f) Marketing Material

2) **Mandate/Target Matching & Generating Strategic Alternatives** – After building out one's coverage, the investment banker can then begin matching the investment mandates of strategic & financial buyers to potential targets within their coverage. The Mandate/Target Matching Process is the following:
   a) Identifying Strategic & Financial Buyers
   b) Obtaining Investment Mandates
   c) Structuring Buy Side Engagements
   d) Identifying Targets

3) **Origination & Pitching Strategic Alternatives** – Once we have built out buy side relationships within our coverage area, we can then begin outreach to targets for our buy side partners. Origination is the primary work of the investment banker in order to keep the pipeline of deals full. The Origination Process is the following:
   a) Identifying Decision Makers
   b) The Cycle of Origination
   c) Initial Outreach
   d) Preparing for the Pitch
   e) Pitching

4) **Fee Structuring & Winning Mandate to Implement Strategic Alternative** – In order to get paid, the investment banker has to land the engagement. Once the fee is agreed upon, the investment banker puts the fee structure in something called an engagement letter. The Fee Structuring & Winning the Mandate Process is the following:
   a) Type of Fee
   b) Size of Fee
   c) Sell Side & Buy Side Representation?

    d)   M&A Engagement Letter

5) **Underwriting the Strategic Alternative** – Underwriting aids us in understanding the intrinsic value of the target company and pricing the company under various scenarios & methodologies. The Underwriting Process in the following:
   a) Gathering Historical Financials
   b) Building the Financial Statement Model
   c) Finding Adjusted EBITDA
   d) Deriving Valuation from the Three Methodologies
   e) Building the Valuation Football Field
   f) Customizing the Financial Statement Model for Specific Transactions

6) **Packaging & Securitizing the Strategic Alternative** – After underwriting the financial product (ex. M&A), we can move forward with packaging in the form of various marketing material including a teaser & Confidential Information Memorandum (CIM). The Packaging Process is the following:
   a) Teaser Creation
   b) Confidential Information Memorandum (CIM)

7) **Buyer List** – After landing the M&A engagement, the investment banker will need to build a buyer list and then begin outreach to the buyer list to generate interest. The Buyer List Process is the following:
   a) Database Utilization
   b) Strategic Buyers
   c) Financial Buyers
   d) Initial Outreach

8) **Deal Structuring** - After building & executing on a buyer list, it is up to the investment banker to work with the buyer and seller to structure a deal. This means negotiating the valuation

range and deal terms. The Deal Structuring Process is as follows:

    a) Valuation Range
    b) Deal Terms

9) **M&A Process** - Once agreeing on a valuation range and deal terms, legal is brought into the deal to consummate the transaction. The M&A process is as follows:

    a) IOI From Buyer
    b) Buyer Seller Meeting
    c) Purchase Agreement Given to Seller
    d) Signed Purchase Agreement with Different Terms
    e) Enter Due Diligence
    f) Complete Due Diligence
    g) Closing & Flow of Funds

Chapter 31: Getting Started in M&A

Getting Started in M&A: A Comprehensive Guide for Aspiring Investment Bankers

Embarking on a career in mergers and acquisitions (M&A) within the investment banking sector, especially focusing on the lower middle market, requires a combination of education, practical skills, networking, and strategic thinking. This detailed guide will walk you through the essential steps and considerations for starting your journey in this dynamic field.

Laying the Educational Foundation

Relevant Education and Coursework

A robust educational background in finance, economics, or business administration forms the cornerstone of a successful career in M&A. Pursuing a bachelor's degree in one of these disciplines equips you with the fundamental concepts of financial analysis, accounting, and valuation techniques. Advanced courses in corporate finance, mergers and acquisitions, investment analysis, and strategic management are particularly beneficial. These courses offer deep dives into complex financial structures, deal mechanics, and strategic considerations, providing the theoretical underpinnings necessary for practical application.

Continuous Learning and Market Awareness

The world of M&A is constantly evolving, driven by market trends, regulatory changes, and economic shifts. Staying updated with the latest developments is crucial. This involves subscribing to industry publications like *The Wall Street Journal*, *Financial Times*, and *Bloomberg*, which provide insights into current market trends and major deals. Additionally, attending industry conferences and webinars offers opportunities to learn from experts and stay abreast of the latest best practices and innovations.

Developing Essential Financial Modeling Skills

Mastering Financial Models

Financial modeling is a critical skill in M&A, as it enables you to project a company's future financial performance and assess its value. Begin by mastering the basics of Excel, including advanced functions and financial formulas. Progress to building comprehensive financial models that include income statements, balance sheets, and cash flow statements. Understanding how to model different scenarios, such as base, upside, and downside cases, is essential for assessing various outcomes and risks associated with potential deals.

Practical Application and Case Studies

Practice is key to honing your financial modeling skills. Work on case studies that simulate real-world scenarios, allowing you to apply theoretical knowledge to practical situations. For instance, analyze past mergers or acquisitions, reconstruct the financial models, and evaluate the outcomes. This hands-on experience is invaluable for understanding the intricacies of deal structures and valuation methodologies.

Identifying and Sourcing Deal Opportunities

Building a Deal Pipeline

Finding potential M&A opportunities involves a proactive and systematic approach. Begin by conducting thorough market research to identify industries with high growth potential or those undergoing consolidation. Utilize online platforms like *PitchBook* and *CapIQ* to gather data on potential targets. Attending industry-specific events and trade shows can also provide insights into companies looking to expand, divest, or acquire.

Leveraging Your Network

Networking is an essential component of deal sourcing. Cultivate relationships with business owners, industry experts, and other professionals who may have insider knowledge of potential transactions. Join professional organizations such as the *Association for Corporate Growth (ACG)* or local business chambers. Active participation in these communities can provide access to off-market deals and exclusive opportunities.

Crafting a Compelling Pitch

Tailoring Your Presentation

Once you've identified a potential deal, crafting a compelling pitch is crucial. Your pitch should be tailored to the specific needs and goals of the target company or entrepreneur. Begin with a concise executive summary that highlights the strategic rationale for the deal. Follow with detailed financial projections, valuation analysis, and potential synergies. Address potential concerns and outline a clear path to achieving the transaction's objectives.

Building Credibility and Trust

Building trust with potential clients is vital. Demonstrate your expertise by providing well-researched, data-driven insights. Use case studies of similar transactions to showcase your track record and ability to deliver value. Be transparent about your fees, process, and any risks involved in the transaction. A well-prepared pitch not only showcases your technical skills but also establishes you as a credible and reliable partner.

Collaborating with Industry Experts

Assembling a Strong Team

M&A transactions often require expertise in various areas, including legal, accounting, tax, and regulatory compliance. Assemble a team of specialists who can provide comprehensive support throughout the deal process. This may include lawyers who specialize in M&A law, accountants for financial due diligence, and tax advisors to optimize the transaction structure.

Navigating Complex Transactions

Working with experts ensures that all aspects of the transaction are thoroughly evaluated and executed. For instance, legal advisors can help navigate complex regulatory requirements, while accountants can uncover potential financial risks. Collaborating with these professionals not only enhances the quality of your work but also provides clients with confidence in your ability to manage complex transactions.

Continuous Learning and Adaptation

Keeping Up with Industry Trends

The M&A landscape is constantly changing, influenced by economic cycles, technological advancements, and regulatory shifts. Stay informed about these changes through continuous education and professional development. Attend advanced courses, obtain relevant certifications such as the Chartered Financial Analyst (CFA) designation, and participate in industry seminars.

Seeking Mentorship and Feedback

Mentorship is invaluable in the early stages of your career. Seek out experienced professionals who can provide guidance, share their experiences, and offer constructive feedback. Regularly review your work with mentors and peers to identify areas for improvement and refine your skills.

Conclusion

Starting a career in M&A investment banking, particularly in the lower middle market, requires a multifaceted approach. By building a strong educational foundation, mastering financial modeling, actively sourcing deals, crafting compelling pitches, collaborating with experts, and continuously learning, you can establish yourself in this competitive field. The journey demands dedication, adaptability, and a relentless pursuit of excellence, but the rewards in terms of career growth and financial success can be substantial. As you navigate this path, remember that each deal is an opportunity to learn, grow, and make a meaningful impact in the world of business and finance.

NOTES:
Getting Started in M&A:
For those just getting started in investment banking, it is preferable to start with the SMB & lower middle market building relationships with financial and strategic buyers as well as potential targets. This means building your rolodex. Obtain the investment mandates from the strategic and financial buyers and establish a fee arrangement for buy-side deals. This will most likely end up being the Lehman scale for the fee on the buy-side.

For example, with AltQuest Group, I chose to cover manufacturing. If you are starting in the lower middle market, the goal is to get 10 sell side engagements at any given time. It took me one year to get 10 sell side engagements working 40 hours per week and not on weekends. Further, it is going to take you 6 months to one year to close a deal so stay proactive with origination and mandate/target matching.

As you get better and establish a process, your email conversion rates will go up and you will be pitching more and your ability to win sell side engagements will go up. I am at the point now that if a seller is interested in selling, I will either win the sell side mandate or I will structure it as a buy side deal and receive the fee from the strategic/financial buyer.

Chapter 32: M&A as a Product

M&A as a Comprehensive Product in Investment Banking

Mergers and acquisitions (M&A) represent a cornerstone of the services provided by investment banks. These transactions, which involve the merging or acquisition of companies, are complex and multifaceted, requiring a deep understanding of both financial and strategic considerations. Investment banks play an essential role in guiding clients through the entire M&A process, offering expertise and facilitating successful deals. This blog post provides an in-depth look at the stages of M&A, highlighting the critical functions and value investment banks bring to the table.

The Initial Phase: Identifying Potential Targets

The M&A process often begins with the identification of potential acquisition targets. Investment bankers leverage their industry knowledge, analytical skills, and extensive networks to identify companies that align with their clients' strategic goals. This phase is crucial as it sets the stage for the entire transaction.

- **Strategic Goal Alignment:** Investment banks work closely with their clients to understand their long-term objectives, such as entering new markets, acquiring innovative technologies, or expanding product lines. For example, Microsoft's acquisition of LinkedIn aimed to bolster its

presence in the professional networking and social media space, integrating LinkedIn's platform with Microsoft's cloud services to create a more comprehensive offering.
- **Market Research and Analysis:** Investment bankers conduct thorough market research to identify targets that meet these strategic objectives. This involves analyzing market trends, competitor landscapes, and potential growth areas. They look for companies with complementary strengths that can create synergies post-acquisition.

Developing a Strategic Rationale and Valuation

Once a potential target is identified, investment banks help develop a clear strategic rationale for the acquisition. This involves a detailed analysis of how the target aligns with the client's business strategy and the benefits the acquisition will bring.

- **Financial Analysis:** A comprehensive financial assessment of the target company is conducted. This includes evaluating historical financial performance, current financial health, and future growth prospects. For example, Disney's acquisition of Pixar not only aimed to enhance Disney's creative capabilities but also to leverage Pixar's advanced animation technology, thus expanding Disney's competitive edge in animated films.
- **Valuation Techniques:** Investment banks use various valuation methods to determine the fair value of the target. These methods include discounted cash flow analysis, comparable company analysis, and precedent transactions. The goal is to arrive at a valuation that reflects the intrinsic worth of the company while considering market conditions and potential synergies.

Structuring the Deal and Negotiation

After establishing the strategic rationale and valuation, the next step is structuring the deal and negotiating terms. This stage is critical as it determines the transaction's financial and operational aspects.

- **Deal Structure:** Investment banks design the transaction structure, including the mix of cash, stock, or other securities used as payment. They consider the tax implications, regulatory requirements, and financial impact on the client. For instance, Amazon's acquisition of Whole Foods involved a strategic use of cash reserves to fund the purchase, allowing Amazon to expand its physical retail presence.
- **Negotiation and Bridging Gaps:** Investment bankers act as intermediaries during negotiations, helping to bridge any differences between the buyer and seller. They work to align the interests of both parties, ensuring that the deal terms are acceptable and beneficial. Key terms negotiated include the purchase price, representations and warranties, and conditions for closing.

Executing the Transaction and Integration

Once the deal terms are agreed upon, the focus shifts to executing the transaction and integrating the acquired company. This phase is crucial for realizing the anticipated benefits and ensuring a smooth transition.

- **Due Diligence:** Investment banks coordinate a thorough due diligence process, examining all aspects of the target company, including financials, legal matters, operations, and market position. Due diligence helps identify any potential risks or liabilities and confirms the accuracy of the information provided by the seller.
- **Legal Documentation and Financing:** The transaction requires meticulous legal documentation to formalize the terms and conditions. Investment banks work with legal teams

to draft and review the necessary contracts. They also assist in arranging the financing for the deal, whether through debt, equity, or a combination of both.

- **Post-Transaction Integration:** Successful integration is critical to achieving the strategic goals of the acquisition. Investment banks often play an advisory role in the integration process, helping to align business processes, merge corporate cultures, and implement operational improvements. For example, Pfizer's acquisition of Warner-Lambert involved a comprehensive integration plan to merge their product lines and streamline operations, creating a more efficient and profitable pharmaceutical giant.

Conclusion

M&A as a product in investment banking is a highly specialized service that requires a blend of financial expertise, strategic insight, and negotiation skills. Investment banks facilitate the entire M&A process, from identifying potential targets to executing transactions and ensuring successful integrations. By providing comprehensive support and guidance, they help companies achieve their strategic objectives, whether it's expanding into new markets, acquiring new technologies, or enhancing their competitive position.

Understanding the detailed processes and roles investment banks play in M&A provides valuable insights into how these complex transactions are orchestrated. As companies continue to seek growth and innovation through M&A, the expertise of investment banks remains indispensable in navigating the challenges and maximizing the benefits of these strategic moves.

NOTES:
Since M&A (Mergers & Acquisitions) is the core product of investment banking, discussions around investment banking typically relate to M&A. M&A is the selling of a minority or controlling interest in company.

Financial and strategic buyers have what is known as investment/corporate M&A mandates which detail the size and industry of prospective targets for acquisition. The investment banker takes these mandates and matches them with targets and takes a fee for doing so. Investment bankers typically focus on one industry and provide what is known as coverage by building an index of public companies and tracking changes in targets relative to the index in terms of:

- Revenue
- EBITDA
- Multiples

The investment banker monitors trends in these variables and determines the optimal time to sell (when multiples are strong) or acquire (when multiples are weak) and advises target management accordingly. When a target agrees to sell via an investment banker, this relationship is known as a sell-side mandate and an M&A process will be led by the investment banker.

During the M&A process, there are definite steps and deliverables including a teaser, CIM, and management presentation. The M&A process can include many prospective buyers (broad auction) or few prospective buyers (targeted or negotiated sale).

The real work of M&A is origination, mandate/target matching and deal-structuring. Financial modeling and valuation is merely for decision support and deals often get done simply based upon precedent transactions analysis. Thus, the priority of the investment bankers is to obtain a base level understanding of financial modeling & valuation but then to immediately start originating sell side and buy side mandates.

Investment bankers explore strategic alternatives (value creation opportunities) with corporation's CEO's/owners according the company's strategic priorities. Questions like:

- What businesses should we be in? (Answer: where multiples are higher and/or will be increasing in the future)
- What businesses should we not be in anymore? (Answer: where multiples are lower and/or will be decreasing in the future)
- Should we buy or build to enter those markets? (Answer: the result of a buy vs. build analysis)
- If we should buy, what are some acquisition targets in order to buy our way in?
- If we should sell, what are some reasonable acquirers?

Chapter 33: Investment Banking in Practice

Investment Banking in Practice: A Detailed Exploration of Key Functions and Processes

Investment banking encompasses a wide array of activities, all aimed at facilitating capital flow and enhancing financial outcomes for clients. The practical aspect of investment banking revolves around four primary capabilities: research and hypothesis generation, partnering with sources of capital, collaborating with users of capital, and pricing and securitizing investment opportunities. Each of these capabilities plays a crucial role in the complex ecosystem of investment banking, ensuring the effective execution of financial transactions.

1. Research and Hypothesis Generation

Objective: Establishing a strong research foundation is the cornerstone of effective investment banking. This involves developing a comprehensive understanding of market dynamics, industry trends, and company-specific factors that influence valuations and potential returns.

Key Components:

- **Sector and Subsector Analysis:** Investment bankers specialize in specific sectors (e.g., technology, healthcare) and subsectors (e.g., biotech, fintech). They conduct detailed research to understand the unique characteristics, growth drivers, and challenges within these areas.
  - *Example:* An analyst specializing in renewable energy might track advancements in solar technology, government regulations, and competitive landscapes to identify investment opportunities.
- **Trend Analysis and Forecasting:** Analysts examine both macroeconomic trends (like interest rates, inflation) and microeconomic trends (such as consumer behavior, technological innovation). They assess how these trends impact financial metrics like revenue growth and profit margins, influencing the overall valuation of companies.
  - *Example:* A shift toward remote work could increase demand for cloud computing services, potentially boosting the valuations of tech companies in that space.
- **Valuation Techniques:** Investment bankers use various methods, including discounted cash flow (DCF), comparable company analysis, and precedent transactions, to estimate the value of companies. They consider future benefit streams and apply appropriate multiples to forecast potential market value.
  - *Example:* In evaluating a tech startup, an analyst might forecast future earnings and apply a growth-stage multiple to determine a valuation.

2. Partnering with Sources of Capital

Objective: To align with sources of capital, investment bankers secure mandates and referral fee agreements with investors who provide the necessary funding for various transactions.

Key Components:

- **Investment Mandates:** These are agreements that outline the specific investment criteria and objectives of investors, which can be strategic (corporate investors looking for synergies) or financial (private equity firms seeking returns).
  - *Example:* A private equity firm might have a mandate to invest in mid-sized companies in the healthcare sector with a focus on turnaround opportunities.
- **Relationship Building:** Investment bankers cultivate relationships with institutional investors, family offices, venture capitalists, and hedge funds. These relationships are crucial for accessing capital and understanding investor preferences.
  - *Example:* A banker working with a sovereign wealth fund might regularly update them on potential infrastructure investment opportunities.

3. Collaborating with Users of Capital

Objective: Investment bankers work with companies (users of capital) that require funding for growth, acquisitions, or other strategic initiatives. These partnerships can lead to advisory roles or formal sell-side mandates.

Key Components:

- **Identifying Positive NPV Projects:** Bankers identify projects that are expected to generate a positive net present value (NPV), indicating profitability and value creation. They work with companies to assess the feasibility and financial viability of these projects.

- *Example:* A manufacturing company looking to expand its production capacity may seek advisory services to raise capital through a new bond issuance.
- **Structuring and Securing Funding:** Once a project is identified, bankers assist in structuring the deal, choosing the right mix of debt and equity, and preparing the company for fundraising. This includes creating financial models, drafting offering documents, and setting up roadshows for potential investors.
  - *Example:* An investment banker might help a tech company secure venture capital funding by preparing a detailed pitch deck and financial model.

4. Pricing and Securitizing Investment Opportunities

Objective: After identifying and structuring an investment opportunity, the next step is to price and package it into a marketable security. This involves detailed financial analysis, risk assessment, and the creation of marketing materials.

Key Components:

- **Underwriting:** Investment bankers assess the financial health and potential risks associated with a project or company. This process includes conducting due diligence, adjusting financials for non-recurring items, and ensuring accurate financial projections.
  - *Example:* Before launching an IPO, bankers will thoroughly vet the company's financials, ensuring all disclosures are accurate and comprehensive.
- **Securitization and Marketing:** The investment is packaged into a security, such as stocks, bonds, or other financial instruments. Bankers create detailed marketing materials,

including a teaser document and a Confidential Information Memorandum (CIM), to present the investment opportunity to potential buyers.

- ○ *Example:* For a public offering, the CIM might include the company's business model, competitive analysis, financial projections, and risk factors.

Building a Market: Bankers then engage with potential investors, presenting the investment opportunity and negotiating terms. They utilize their networks and market knowledge to attract suitable investors and secure commitments.

Conclusion

Investment banking is a dynamic and intricate field that demands a deep understanding of finance, strategic acumen, and excellent relationship-building skills. The practice of investment banking involves a series of interconnected processes—from conducting in-depth research and fostering relationships with capital providers to advising companies and securitizing investment opportunities. By mastering these capabilities, investment bankers can effectively facilitate capital flows, support corporate growth, and contribute to economic development. Understanding the nuances of these processes provides valuable insights into the world of finance and the critical role that investment bankers play in shaping the financial landscape.

PART IV: COVERAGE

Chapter 34: Coverage

The Role of Sector Indices in Investment Banking

In the investment banking industry, sector indices are vital tools used to monitor and analyze the performance and trends of specific industries. These indices aggregate the stock prices of companies within a particular sector, offering a comprehensive view of the sector's overall market sentiment, trends, and financial health. Investment bankers rely heavily on sector indices to inform their strategic decision-making, provide insights into market dynamics, and benchmark the performance of individual companies against the broader market. Let's delve deeper into how these indices work, their significance, and how investment bankers use them to guide their activities.

What Are Sector Indices?

Sector indices are specialized indices that represent a specific industry or sector in the stock market. They include a collection of companies that operate within the same industry, such as technology, healthcare, energy, or consumer goods. For example, the **S&P 500 Energy Index** tracks companies within the energy sector, while the **NASDAQ Biotechnology Index** focuses on biotech firms. These indices provide a snapshot of the sector's overall performance, reflecting changes in stock prices, market capitalization, and investor sentiment.

Key Components of Sector Indices:

- **Companies:** Firms operating within the same industry, selected based on market capitalization and other criteria.
- **Weights:** The influence of each company within the index, often determined by market capitalization.
- **Benchmarks:** Metrics used to compare the performance of companies within the index.

Tracking Performance and Relative Strength

Sector indices are crucial for tracking the relative performance of a sector compared to the broader market. Investment bankers use these indices to gauge whether a sector is performing above or below market expectations. For instance, if the **S&P 500 Technology Index** is outperforming the **S&P 500 Index**, it indicates that technology companies are doing well relative to the overall market.

How Bankers Use This Information:

- **Performance Analysis:** Assessing whether a sector is gaining or losing investor interest.
- **Investment Decisions:** Allocating resources to sectors showing strong performance.
- **Risk Assessment:** Identifying sectors that may be at risk due to underperformance.

Identifying Sector-Specific Trends

Sector indices help investment bankers identify emerging trends within a specific industry. By analyzing the index components, bankers can discern patterns such as:

- **Growth Trends:** Sectors experiencing rapid growth due to technological advancements or increased consumer demand.
- **Declining Trends:** Industries facing challenges due to regulatory changes, market saturation, or declining demand.

- **Shifts in Market Sentiment:** Changes in investor behavior, such as increasing or decreasing investment in a particular sector.

Examples of Identifiable Trends:

- **Technological Innovation:** For instance, a rise in the NASDAQ Biotechnology Index may indicate growing interest in biotech innovations and advancements.
- **Regulatory Impact:** A decline in the S&P 500 Financials Index might reflect concerns over new financial regulations impacting bank profits.

Informing Investment Strategies

Investment bankers use the data from sector indices to inform their investment strategies. By understanding which sectors are performing well, they can guide clients in making informed investment decisions. For example, if the **Dow Jones U.S. Real Estate Index** shows strong performance, bankers might recommend investing in real estate-related assets.

Strategic Applications:

- **Sector Allocation:** Deciding how much to invest in different sectors based on performance and potential.
- **Timing of Investments:** Choosing optimal times to enter or exit investments based on sector trends.
- **Diversification:** Balancing portfolios across various sectors to manage risk.

Benchmarks for Performance Evaluation

Sector indices serve as benchmarks for evaluating the performance of individual companies and investment portfolios. By comparing a company's stock performance to its sector index, bankers can determine whether the company is outperforming or underperforming its peers.

Benchmarking Uses:

- **Performance Measurement:** Assessing the success of investment strategies and individual investments.
- **Portfolio Analysis:** Determining the relative performance of portfolio holdings within a sector.

Conclusion

Sector indices are indispensable tools in investment banking, providing critical insights into market trends, sector performance, and investor sentiment. They enable investment bankers to make data-driven decisions, offer strategic advice to clients, and evaluate the performance of investments. By closely monitoring these indices, bankers can stay ahead of market trends, identify lucrative opportunities, and effectively manage risk, thereby ensuring the successful execution of investment strategies. Understanding and utilizing sector indices is a fundamental aspect of investment banking practice, crucial for achieving superior investment outcomes.

NOTES:

Coverage Process
1. Choosing Coverage
2. Vertical & Subvertical Coverage
3. Index Building
4. Metrics
5. Benchmarking
6. Marketing Material

Investment Banking University
All Rights Reserved

Chapter 35: How to Choose Coverage

How to Choose Coverage in Investment Banking

Choosing the right coverage area is a pivotal decision for investment bankers, influencing their career trajectory, the clients they work with, and the nature of transactions they manage. This decision involves several critical considerations, including the size of companies to focus on, the specific industries or sectors (verticals), and potentially more specialized sub-sectors (subverticals). Additionally, geographic considerations play a crucial role in defining the market focus. Here's an in-depth guide on how to choose your coverage in investment banking, including key factors and detailed content for each aspect.

1. Choosing the Size of Companies

Public Companies:

- **Overview:** These are large corporations whose shares are publicly traded on stock exchanges. They often have complex structures and are subject to strict regulatory requirements.
- **Advantages:** Working with public companies offers the potential for large-scale transactions, significant fees, and high

visibility within the industry. The transactions can include public offerings, mergers, and large-scale acquisitions.
- **Challenges:** The competition to secure deals with public companies is intense. Additionally, bankers must navigate a complex regulatory environment, including securities laws and public disclosure requirements. The deals are often highly scrutinized by analysts and the public, adding pressure to ensure accuracy and success.

Middle Market Companies:

- **Overview:** Typically, these companies have revenues ranging from $50 million to $1 billion. They are often privately held or family-owned businesses looking for growth, restructuring, or exit strategies.
- **Advantages:** The middle market offers a balance between large public companies and smaller businesses, with substantial deal flow across various industries. Investment bankers can work on a range of transactions, including mergers, acquisitions, and capital raises.
- **Challenges:** Transactions in this segment often require specialized knowledge of different industries. Middle market companies may not have the same level of financial sophistication as large public firms, requiring more hands-on advisory services.

Lower Middle Market Companies:

- **Overview:** These firms typically generate revenues between $5 million and $50 million. They may be emerging businesses with significant growth potential or established companies looking to expand or streamline operations.
- **Advantages:** Lower competition compared to larger segments, coupled with opportunities to work closely with

business owners and management teams. There is a high potential for growth and value creation, as these companies often have untapped markets or operational inefficiencies.

- **Challenges:** Lower middle market companies may have less experienced management teams and limited financial resources. Investment bankers may need to assist more comprehensively with strategy, financial planning, and market positioning.

Small and Medium-Sized Businesses (SMBs):

- **Overview:** Typically, these businesses have revenues under $5 million and are often privately held. SMBs can include startups, local businesses, and niche market players.
- **Advantages:** Working with SMBs offers a chance to build foundational skills in investment banking. The deal sizes are smaller, but the volume of potential transactions can be high, providing numerous learning opportunities.
- **Challenges:** SMBs often face higher risks of business failure and financial instability. The deal sizes are smaller, which can mean lower fees. There may also be a greater need for advisory services, as these companies often lack sophisticated financial and operational infrastructures.

2. Vertical and Subvertical Coverage

Vertical Coverage:

- **Definition:** Focusing on a specific industry, such as healthcare, technology, energy, or consumer goods. This choice is often influenced by personal experience, market interest, and perceived growth potential.
- **Benefits:** Specializing in a vertical allows investment bankers to develop deep expertise and understanding of

industry-specific trends, regulations, and business dynamics. This expertise helps in building credibility with clients and identifying unique opportunities within the industry.

- **Considerations:** When choosing a vertical, consider your background and interests. For example, a background in biotechnology might naturally lead to a focus on the healthcare sector. The vertical should also have a robust deal flow and potential for growth to ensure long-term career prospects.

Subvertical Coverage:

- **Definition:** Within a chosen vertical, subverticals represent more specialized areas of focus. For example, within the technology vertical, subverticals could include software, hardware, and IT services.
- **Benefits:** Subvertical specialization allows for even greater expertise. It enables bankers to become experts in niche markets, which can be a significant differentiator in a competitive landscape. This specialization can also lead to more targeted networking and marketing efforts, enhancing deal origination capabilities.
- **Considerations:** When selecting a subvertical, assess the market size, growth prospects, and level of competition. Specializing in a growing subvertical with limited competition can provide a competitive edge and increase your value to clients.

3. Geographic Considerations

Local Market Focus:

- **Advantages:** Starting with a local focus helps build a strong network and deep understanding of the regional market. It reduces travel costs and logistical complexities, making it easier to meet clients and manage relationships.

- **Approach:** Begin by targeting businesses in your immediate geographic area, such as your city or metropolitan region. Engage with local business communities, attend regional conferences, and leverage local professional associations.

Expanding Geographically:

- **Expansion Strategy:** Once a solid local foundation is established, consider expanding to broader geographic regions, such as state-wide or national markets. Ultimately, expansion can extend to international markets, depending on your firm's reach and capabilities.
- **Tools and Techniques:** Utilize digital tools like CRM systems to manage client relationships across geographies. Virtual meetings and online research platforms can help maintain and build relationships with clients in distant locations.

4. Building Credibility in Your Chosen Coverage

Staying Informed:

- **Importance:** Staying current with industry trends, market developments, and regulatory changes is crucial for providing relevant advice to clients.
- **Methods:** Regularly read industry-specific publications, subscribe to relevant newsletters, and participate in webinars and industry conferences.

Networking:

- **Importance:** Building a strong network of industry contacts is essential for deal origination and gaining market insights.

- **Methods:** Engage with professionals at industry events, join relevant trade associations, and connect with key stakeholders on professional networking platforms.

Understanding Industry Metrics:

- **Importance:** Knowing the key performance indicators (KPIs) and financial metrics relevant to your chosen industry allows for better analysis and advisory services.
- **Methods:** Learn about the typical financial metrics used in the industry, such as EBITDA margins, revenue growth rates, and return on assets. Understand how these metrics impact valuation and investment decisions.

Conclusion

Selecting the right coverage area in investment banking is a strategic decision that requires careful consideration of your skills, interests, and market conditions. Start with a focus on SMBs or middle market companies to build foundational skills, then gradually scale up to larger companies as you gain experience. Choose verticals and subverticals that align with your background and interests, and consider the growth potential and competitive landscape of each sector. Finally, build credibility by staying informed, networking, and mastering industry-specific metrics. By following these guidelines, you can position yourself for success in the dynamic and competitive world of investment banking.

Chapter 36: The Lower Middle Market & Middle Market

Navigating the Lower Middle Market & Middle Market in Investment Banking

The lower middle market (LMM) and middle market (MM) are significant sectors in the investment banking landscape, offering abundant opportunities for mergers and acquisitions (M&A), capital raising, and advisory services. These markets, comprising small to mid-sized companies, are where most investment banking activities occur. Understanding the characteristics, nuances, and distinctions within these markets is crucial for investment bankers aiming to navigate and succeed in this space.

Overview of the Lower Middle Market & Middle Market

The LMM and MM consist of a wide range of companies, from small businesses to substantial enterprises. These markets are vital as they encompass the majority of corporate entities and a significant portion of economic activities. Investment bankers in these markets often engage in a variety of transactions, from M&A deals to capital-raising initiatives, making these sectors a key area of focus for building a career in investment banking.

Breaking Down the M&A Market

1. Small and Medium-Sized Businesses (SMBs): Companies with Revenue Less Than $5 Million

- **Characteristics:** Typically local and often family-owned, SMBs operate on a smaller scale with limited growth potential and resources.
- **Transactions:** Involves straightforward deals such as local acquisitions, small-scale capital raises, and family business successions. The focus is often on helping these businesses scale up or transition ownership.

2. Lower Middle Market: Companies with $5 Million to $50 Million in Revenue

- **Characteristics:** Companies in this bracket may have established operations but often seek further growth. They generally have EBITDA (Earnings Before Interest, Taxes, Depreciation, and Amortization) below $10 million.
- **Transactions:** Investment bankers work on transactions involving growth capital, strategic acquisitions, and sometimes succession planning. These businesses are ripe for investment as they have proven models but need capital to scale.

3. Middle Market: Companies with $50 Million to $500 Million in Revenue

- **Characteristics:** These companies are more established with broader market reach and operational complexities. EBITDA typically ranges from $10 million to $75 million.
- **Transactions:** This market involves more sophisticated M&A activities, including private equity investments, strategic buyouts, and comprehensive capital market activities.

4. Upper Middle Market: Companies with $500 Million to $1 Billion in Revenue

- **Characteristics:** These are often well-established businesses with significant market influence. They are usually publicly held or backed by private equity firms.
- **Transactions:** The transactions are often complex, involving strategic consolidations, large-scale buyouts, and sometimes cross-border M&A deals.

Further Defining the Middle Market

The middle market can be more precisely defined using total enterprise value (TEV), a comprehensive measure that includes equity value, debt, and cash. According to sources like PitchBook:

- **Middle Market Definition:** Companies with TEV between $25 million and $1 billion.
- **Core Middle Market:** Companies with TEV between $100 million and $500 million.

This distinction helps investment bankers focus their services and expertise on companies of a particular scale and complexity, enabling them to provide more tailored advice and execution.

Significance in Investment Banking

The LMM and MM are vital for several reasons:

- **Volume of Transactions:** These segments see a high volume of M&A deals, providing a consistent stream of opportunities for investment bankers.
- **Diverse Client Needs:** Companies in these markets have varied needs, such as accessing growth capital, pursuing strategic acquisitions, or planning for ownership transitions.

This diversity allows investment bankers to offer a wide range of services.

- **Growth Potential:** LMM companies often look to scale, while MM firms may seek to consolidate their market positions, presenting significant opportunities for value creation.
- **Career Development:** Engaging with these markets allows bankers to gain diverse experience across different types of deals and industries, building a robust skill set and career foundation.

Conclusion

The lower middle market and middle market are essential territories for investment bankers. These markets offer a rich array of opportunities, from straightforward transactions with SMBs to complex deals with upper middle market firms. Understanding the unique characteristics and needs of companies within these segments is crucial for providing effective advisory services, facilitating successful transactions, and building a successful career in investment banking. As these companies grow and evolve, so too do the opportunities for investment bankers to create value and drive economic growth.

Chapter 37: Index Building

Building an Effective Sector Index in Investment Banking

In the complex world of investment banking, constructing a sector index requires meticulous selection of public comparable companies, commonly referred to as "public comps." These comps serve as benchmarks for valuation, performance analysis, and comparative studies within a specific industry sector. This blog post delves into the intricate methodologies and considerations that investment bankers employ to select relevant public comps, thereby building a comprehensive and representative sector index.

Understanding the Sector and Industry Dynamics

Foundational Research and Analysis:

The initial phase involves a deep dive into the sector's unique characteristics, growth drivers, and competitive landscape. This includes examining:

- **Market Trends:** Investment bankers analyze current and historical market trends to identify emerging opportunities and challenges within the sector. This includes technological

advancements, shifts in consumer behavior, and regulatory changes.
- **Key Performance Drivers:** Understanding what drives performance in the sector—such as cost structures, pricing power, or supply chain dynamics—is crucial. For example, in the technology sector, innovation and intellectual property might be key drivers, whereas, in consumer goods, brand loyalty and distribution channels may play a larger role.

Strategic Objectives:

Bankers must align their sector analysis with the strategic objectives of their firm or clients. This involves understanding whether the focus is on growth sectors, stability, or sectors undergoing significant transformation. This strategic alignment helps in narrowing down the selection of public comps.

Establishing Selection Criteria

Defining Clear Parameters:

To ensure that the selected public comps accurately represent the sector, investment bankers set specific criteria, including:

- **Market Capitalization:** Companies are categorized into large-cap, mid-cap, and small-cap to capture a range of enterprise sizes. This diversity helps in understanding how different segments of the sector perform under varying market conditions.
- **Revenue Size and Growth Rates:** Consistent revenue growth is a positive indicator. Investment bankers look at historical data to assess whether companies have stable and increasing revenue streams.

- **Profitability and Margins:** Metrics such as EBITDA margins and net profit margins are scrutinized to gauge operational efficiency and profitability. High profitability can indicate strong market positioning and effective cost management.
- **Geographic Presence and Product Offerings:** Companies operating in similar geographic regions or offering comparable products/services are preferred. This ensures that the index reflects the global or regional nature of the sector.

Analyzing Financial Metrics and Ratios

Detailed Financial Analysis:

Investment bankers conduct thorough financial analysis using various metrics and ratios. These include:

- **Price-to-Earnings (P/E) Ratio:** Indicates how much investors are willing to pay per dollar of earnings, providing insights into market sentiment and valuation.
- **Price-to-Sales (P/S) Ratio:** Offers a view of how the market values the company's revenue. It is particularly useful for companies with high growth but low earnings.
- **Return on Equity (ROE):** Measures the profitability relative to shareholders' equity, indicating how effectively a company uses its capital.

Comparative Analysis:

By comparing these metrics across potential comps, investment bankers can identify outliers and align the selection with companies that best represent the sector's financial health and growth potential.

Conducting Peer Group Analysis

Creating Peer Groups:

Peer group analysis involves assembling a group of companies within the sector that share similar characteristics, such as size, growth potential, and business models. This helps in:

- **Benchmarking Performance:** Comparing key financial and operational metrics to understand how a company performs relative to its peers.
- **Identifying Industry Leaders and Laggards:** Recognizing companies that are outperforming or underperforming can provide insights into best practices and potential risks.

Sector-Specific Considerations:

For instance, in the energy sector, peer groups might include companies with similar production volumes, reserve sizes, or technological capabilities. In contrast, in the retail sector, factors such as brand strength, store footprint, and online presence might be more relevant.

Incorporating Market Capitalization Ranges

Ensuring Comprehensive Representation:

Including companies with a wide range of market capitalizations ensures that the sector index provides a balanced view of the industry. This approach considers:

- **Large-Cap Companies:** Typically well-established, with significant market influence. They often set the tone for the sector's overall performance.
- **Mid-Cap Companies:** Represent growth opportunities and often serve as acquisition targets for larger firms.

- **Small-Cap Companies:** May offer high growth potential but come with higher risk. They can provide insights into emerging trends and innovations.

Considering Geographic and Operational Factors

Global vs. Regional Focus:

Geographic considerations are crucial, especially for sectors with global operations. Investment bankers consider:

- **Regional Economic Conditions:** Companies operating in regions with strong economic growth may present better investment opportunities.
- **Regulatory Environment:** Understanding the regulatory landscape is vital, as it can significantly impact a company's operations and profitability.

Operational Similarities:

Companies with similar operational models, such as supply chain logistics, production processes, or customer service approaches, are compared. This ensures that the index reflects a cohesive group of companies facing similar operational challenges and opportunities.

Regular Review and Reassessment

Dynamic Nature of Sector Indices:

The business environment is ever-changing, and so should be the sector index. Investment bankers regularly review and update their list of public comps to:

- **Incorporate New Market Entrants:** Adding new public companies or removing those that no longer fit the criteria ensures the index remains current.
- **Reflect Changes in Market Conditions:** Adjusting for shifts in economic conditions, consumer preferences, or technological advancements keeps the index relevant.
- **Account for Corporate Actions:** Mergers, acquisitions, and divestitures can significantly alter the composition and focus of companies, requiring adjustments to the index.

Ongoing Analysis and Communication:

Maintaining open communication with industry analysts, staying updated on market news, and continually reassessing the chosen public comps are essential for an accurate and effective sector index.

Conclusion

Building a sector index in investment banking is a meticulous and ongoing process that requires deep industry knowledge, analytical rigor, and strategic foresight. By understanding sector dynamics, establishing robust selection criteria, analyzing financial metrics, and regularly updating the index, investment bankers can provide valuable insights and guidance to clients. This process not only aids in accurate valuation and investment decision-making but also enhances the overall understanding of industry trends and company performance.

NOTES:

Index Building
After choosing your coverage, the investment banker is then to build an index for each of the verticals and sub-verticals made up with the public comps. The index and the changes in the index are going to provide a measuring stick within which to evaluate targets against.

For example, the vertical may be manufacturing and the sub-vertical could be healthcare.

Metrics
Regarding the vertical index and sub-vertical index, the investment banker ultimately tracks trends in:

- Growth rates
- Margins
- Multiples
- Industry specific drivers

Changes in these metrics (expanding or contracting) lead to changes in the behavior of firms when it comes to capital raising & M&A.

Benchmarking
The investment banker takes the index and establishes tiers which turn into peer groups. This is why we pull comps, to build an index and benchmark against the comps. The indexing and benchmarking that is done for a target company is going to serve as the basis for advising on strategic alternatives. One should build indexes at the vertical level, then sub-vertical level and finally sub-vertical by product level.

Chapter 38: Coverage Reports & Marketing Material

Crafting Comprehensive Coverage Reports & Marketing Materials in Investment Banking

In the competitive field of investment banking, effectively created coverage reports and marketing materials are invaluable. They serve multiple functions, including showcasing the banker's expertise, keeping clients informed, and facilitating new business acquisitions. This blog post will delve into the methodologies and strategies used to produce these essential documents, detailing each step and its significance in the broader scope of investment banking.

1. Mastering Coverage Methodology

Coverage Methodology is a systematic approach to monitoring and analyzing specific industries and sectors. This approach helps investment bankers maintain a robust understanding of market dynamics and develop tailored insights for clients.

- **Industry Macroeconomics**:
    - **Detailed Analysis**: This involves a thorough examination of broad economic indicators that affect

an entire industry, such as GDP growth, inflation, and employment trends.

- ○ **Significance**: Understanding these factors is crucial as they influence market conditions, consumer behavior, and ultimately, the financial performance of companies within the sector. For example, a downturn in GDP may signal reduced consumer spending, impacting retail sectors adversely.
- **Industry Spending**:
  - ○ **Tracking Investment Trends**: Investment bankers monitor capital expenditures, R&D investments, and operational costs to understand where companies allocate resources.
  - ○ **Importance**: This data provides insight into growth areas within an industry. For instance, an increase in R&D spending may indicate a focus on innovation, suggesting potential future market leaders.
- **Sub-Sector Spending**:
  - ○ **Focused Analysis**: Diving deeper into specific segments of an industry to identify where investments are being made.
  - ○ **Value**: Helps pinpoint specific growth opportunities within a broader industry. For example, within the tech sector, significant spending on cloud computing services could highlight a growing trend.
- **Stock Market Performance**:
  - ○ **Market Sentiment Analysis**: Assessing stock price trends, market capitalization, and trading volumes of companies within the sector.
  - ○ **Insight**: This indicates investor confidence and market sentiment. Rising stock prices in a particular sub-sector may reflect strong earnings or positive market outlooks.
- **Public Sub-Sector Financial and Valuation Performance**:

- ○ **Benchmarking**: Comparing financial health, such as revenue, profit margins, and market value, across companies within the sub-sector.
- ○ **Purpose**: Establishes benchmarks for performance, helping in valuation assessments and identifying overvalued or undervalued stocks.
- **Sub-Sector Index**:
  - ○ **Index Construction**: Creating an index to track the financial performance and valuation metrics of companies within a sub-sector.
  - ○ **Utility**: This index provides a quick reference for comparing companies and assessing the overall health and trends within a sub-sector.

2. Keeping Clients Informed with Industry M&A Market Updates

Regular updates on M&A activities are vital for client engagement and strategic planning:

- **Deal Volume and Spending**:
  - ○ **Quantitative Tracking**: Monitoring the number and value of M&A transactions within an industry.
  - ○ **Relevance**: This data helps gauge the level of activity and investor interest in the sector. For instance, a surge in deal volume may indicate a consolidating industry.
- **Exit Multiples**:
  - ○ **Valuation Metrics**: Analyzing the multiples at which companies are being acquired (e.g., EBITDA multiples).
  - ○ **Application**: Helps in understanding the current valuation landscape, crucial for both buyers and sellers in setting expectations.

- **Sub-Sector M&A Activity**:
  - **Detailed Breakdown**: Providing granular data on M&A activities within specific sub-sectors.
  - **Importance**: Highlights areas of high transactional activity, which may indicate lucrative opportunities or emerging trends.
- **M&A Deal Volume by Product Category**:
  - **Categorization**: Breaking down deal volume by different product categories within sub-sectors.
  - **Benefit**: Allows for a more nuanced understanding of where the market is headed and which segments are attracting investments.
- **Exit Multiples by Product Category**:
  - **Detailed Valuation Insights**: Providing exit multiples categorized by product type.
  - **Insight**: This offers a finer analysis of valuation trends across various product lines, aiding in strategic decision-making.

3. Deep Dive: Appendix and Key Metrics

The appendix in coverage reports often contains vital, detailed metrics and additional insights:

- **Sub-Sector Index Key Metrics**:
  - **Comprehensive Metrics**: Key financial and operational metrics such as revenue growth rates, EBITDA margins, and capital expenditure trends.
  - **Purpose**: These metrics provide a holistic view of the sub-sector's performance and are critical for deep financial analysis.
- **Most Active Buyers**:

- - **Tracking Acquirers**: Identifying companies or entities that are most active in acquiring within the sector.
  - **Strategic Insight**: Understanding who is actively buying provides insights into market strategies and potential future moves.
- **Key Metrics by Product Category**:
  - **In-depth Analysis**: Breaking down performance metrics by specific product categories within the sub-sector.
  - **Utility**: This granularity helps in comparing and contrasting the performance and valuation of different product lines.

4. Building a Robust Contact Network (Rolodex Building)

Building a comprehensive and accurate contact list is crucial for deal origination:

- **Company Information**:
  - **Details Gathering**: Collecting detailed information about companies, including key personnel, contact details, and company size.
  - **Importance**: Ensures effective and targeted communication, critical for business development and maintaining relationships.
- **Initial Contact Records**:
  - **Engagement Tracking**: Documenting responses from initial outreach efforts, including interest levels and timelines for follow-up.
  - **Purpose**: Helps manage client engagement and ensures timely follow-ups, maintaining a strong client relationship.

- **Strategic Inquiry**:
  - ○ **Regular Check-ins**: Periodically asking companies about their openness to strategic alternatives, such as mergers or acquisitions.
  - ○ **Relevance**: Keeps the lines of communication open and helps identify potential opportunities early.
- **Coverage Updates**:
  - ○ **Ongoing Communication**: Regular updates on sector and sub-sector performance.
  - ○ **Benefit**: Keeps clients informed and engaged, reinforcing the banker's role as a trusted advisor.

5. Creating and Utilizing Marketing Materials

Marketing materials are crucial for showcasing expertise and maintaining client engagement:

- **Monthly/Quarterly Newsletters**:
  - ○ **Regular Updates**: Brief updates on market trends, sector performance, and notable events.
  - ○ **Function**: Maintains regular contact with clients and keeps them informed about relevant developments.
- **Industry/Sector Reports**:
  - ○ **In-Depth Analysis**: Comprehensive reports that delve into market trends, financial metrics, and future outlooks.
  - ○ **Purpose**: Used for substantial client engagement, demonstrating deep expertise and providing strategic insights.
- **Pitchbooks**:
  - ○ **Tailored Presentations**: Custom presentations designed for specific client engagements, detailing market trends, strategic alternatives, and the bank's capabilities.

- Importance: Essential for winning mandates by showcasing the bank's expertise and proposed strategies.

6. Strategic Vertical & Geographic Coverage

Effective coverage requires a strategic focus on specific verticals and geographic areas:

- **Verticals**:
  - **Industry Focus**: Choosing a specific industry or vertical to develop deep expertise, such as technology, healthcare, or finance.
  - **Importance**: Allows investment bankers to become industry specialists, enhancing credibility and client trust.
- **Geographic Focus**:
  - **Regional Specialization**: Starting with a local focus before expanding regionally or nationally.
  - **Strategy**: Building a strong local presence before expanding helps in understanding regional market dynamics and building a reliable network.
- **Database Utilization**:
  - **Tools and Resources**: Using platforms like RocketReach to compile comprehensive contact lists.
  - **Advantage**: Ensures thorough market coverage and effective client outreach.
- **Firm Count**:
  - **Target Goals**: Aiming to cover a substantial number of firms within the chosen vertical and geographic area.
  - **Objective**: Ensures a broad market presence and maximizes potential deal opportunities.

Conclusion

Coverage reports and marketing materials are not just routine tasks but are critical components of the investment banking process. They provide the necessary insights to clients, help maintain and build relationships, and are instrumental in securing new business. By meticulously applying coverage methodologies, producing insightful reports, and maintaining robust client communication, investment bankers can navigate the complex M&A landscape effectively. Regular updates and continuous refinement of these materials are essential to staying relevant and impactful in a rapidly changing market.

Chapter 39: Financial Data Sources

Comprehensive Guide to Financial Data Sources in Investment Banking

Investment banking relies heavily on accurate, timely, and comprehensive financial data to make informed decisions, conduct analyses, and advise clients. Three primary financial data sources—Capital IQ, Bloomberg, and FactSet—are essential tools that investment bankers use to access a wide range of financial information. This blog post will delve into each of these platforms, explaining their features, tools, and how they are applied in the day-to-day activities of investment bankers.

Capital IQ: A Deep Dive into Comprehensive Financial Data

Overview: Capital IQ, a product of S&P Global, is renowned for its extensive coverage of financial information, including detailed company financials, market data, news, and research reports. It serves as a critical resource for investment bankers, providing the data necessary for in-depth financial analysis and benchmarking.

Key Features and Tools:

1. **Company Financials:**
   - **Detail:** Capital IQ provides access to detailed financial statements, including income statements, balance sheets, and cash flow statements for companies globally. This data is critical for evaluating a company's financial health and comparing it with industry peers.
   - **Use Case:** Investment bankers use this data to assess profitability, liquidity, and financial stability, which are essential for valuation and investment decisions.
2. **Market Data:**
   - **Detail:** Includes real-time and historical data on stock prices, trading volumes, indices, and more.
   - **Use Case:** Helps bankers monitor market trends, understand market sentiment, and analyze stock performance over time.
3. **News and Events:**
   - **Detail:** Aggregates news and key events impacting companies and markets.
   - **Use Case:** Keeps bankers updated on significant developments that could affect investment decisions, such as mergers, acquisitions, or regulatory changes.
4. **Research Reports:**
   - **Detail:** Offers access to analyst reports, market research, and industry analysis.
   - **Use Case:** Provides deeper insights into market trends, competitive landscapes, and emerging opportunities.

Applications in Investment Banking:

- **Financial Analysis:** Essential for conducting comparative analyses, valuation modeling, and financial due diligence.

- **Financial Modeling:** Supports the creation of detailed models to forecast financial performance and evaluate potential investments.
- **Screening and Filtering:** Allows bankers to screen companies based on various financial metrics, aiding in the identification of investment opportunities.

Bloomberg: Real-Time Data and Analytics Powerhouse

Overview: Bloomberg is a leading platform known for its real-time financial news, comprehensive market data, and advanced analytical tools. It is a staple in the financial industry, used extensively by investment bankers for its robust data and analytics capabilities.

Key Features and Tools:

1. **Real-Time Financial News:**
   - ○ **Detail:** Bloomberg provides live updates and in-depth coverage of global financial markets.
   - ○ **Use Case:** Critical for making timely investment decisions and staying ahead of market developments.
2. **Market Data and Analytics:**
   - ○ **Detail:** Offers detailed data on equities, fixed income, commodities, currencies, and more.
   - ○ **Use Case:** Helps bankers track and analyze financial instruments, assess market conditions, and identify investment opportunities.
3. **Data Visualization:**
   - ○ **Detail:** Includes tools for creating charts, graphs, and other visual representations of data.
   - ○ **Use Case:** Visual tools aid in interpreting complex data and presenting findings to clients in an understandable manner.
4. **Economic Indicators:**

- **Detail:** Provides data on key economic indicators, such as GDP, inflation rates, and employment figures.
- **Use Case:** Essential for macroeconomic analysis and understanding the broader economic context.

Applications in Investment Banking:

- **Market Monitoring:** Used to track daily market movements, news, and economic data.
- **Financial Analysis:** Supports detailed analysis of financial instruments and market trends.
- **Client Presentations:** Utilized to create compelling visuals for client meetings and presentations.

FactSet: Integrated Data and Custom Analytics

Overview: FactSet integrates data from various sources, providing a holistic view of the financial markets. It is widely used for financial analysis, market research, and portfolio management, offering comprehensive tools and data to support investment decisions.

Key Features and Tools:

1. **Comprehensive Financial Data:**
   - **Detail:** FactSet offers detailed data on company financials, market data, and economic indicators, integrating information from multiple sources.
   - **Use Case:** Enables thorough analysis and comparison across companies and industries.
2. **Data Integration:**
   - **Detail:** Allows users to combine and analyze data from different sources seamlessly.
   - **Use Case:** Facilitates a more comprehensive understanding of market conditions and trends.

3. **Customizable Dashboards:**
   - ○ **Detail:** Users can create personalized dashboards to display relevant data and metrics.
   - ○ **Use Case:** Customization helps focus on specific areas of interest and streamline analysis.
4. **Reporting Tools:**
   - ○ **Detail:** Includes tools for generating detailed reports, which can be customized and shared with clients.
   - ○ **Use Case:** Essential for creating professional and detailed reports for client communication.

Applications in Investment Banking:

- **Financial Analysis and Modeling:** FactSet's data and tools are crucial for developing detailed financial models and conducting in-depth analysis.
- **Market Research:** The platform's comprehensive data helps in staying informed about market trends and developments.
- **Client Reporting:** Customizable reporting tools enable the creation of clear and informative reports for clients.

Conclusion

Capital IQ, Bloomberg, and FactSet are indispensable resources in investment banking, each offering unique capabilities and features that support the complex tasks of financial analysis, market research, and client engagement. Mastery of these platforms allows investment bankers to provide insightful analysis, make informed investment decisions, and communicate effectively with clients. Understanding and effectively utilizing these data sources is a key component of success in the fast-paced and competitive field of investment banking.

NOTES:

If you are at a larger investment bank, you will have various paid data sources at your disposal. These include:

- Bloomberg
- CapitalIQ
- FactSet

For those that are not at a larger bank, one can use the free sources of financial data including:

- Yahoo Finance
- Google Finance

Yahoo Finance and Google Finance get their EBITDA numbers from CapitalIQ and their analyst EPS consensus estimates from there as well.

Investment banks typically do not want you to use the EBITDA from CapitalIQ, Bloomberg, FactSet and would prefer that you spread the comps individually to get to EBITDA.

We are ultimately using the financial data sources to build and maintain our various indices associated with our coverage group.

Chapter 40: The Different Types of Filings Used in Investment Banking

Understanding Public Filings in Investment Banking: An In-Depth Guide

Public filings are foundational documents in the world of investment banking, serving as essential tools for compliance, transparency, and informed decision-making. These filings, required by the Securities and Exchange Commission (SEC), provide a detailed snapshot of a company's financial health, business operations, and governance practices. Investment bankers rely on these documents not only to guide their transactions but also to provide critical insights to clients and investors. This blog post explores the various types of public filings, their purposes, contents, and the role of investment bankers in their preparation and analysis.

1. Registration Statement (Form S-1)

Purpose and Importance:
Form S-1 is the gateway for companies planning to go public through an Initial Public Offering (IPO). This registration statement is a comprehensive document that lays out all the necessary information about a company's business, financials, and risks, providing potential investors with the data they need to make informed investment decisions.

Key Contents:

- **Business Overview:** This section provides a thorough description of the company's business model, products or services, market position, and competitive landscape. It is designed to give potential investors a clear understanding of what the company does and where it stands in the market.
- **Financial Information:** Detailed financial statements are included, covering past performance and future projections. This section typically includes income statements, balance sheets, cash flow statements, and notes to the financial statements, all crucial for assessing the company's financial health.
- **Management Details:** Information about the company's leadership, including biographies of key executives and directors, is provided. This helps investors evaluate the management team's experience and qualifications.
- **Risk Factors:** A detailed list of risks associated with investing in the company, covering industry-specific risks, market conditions, regulatory issues, and any other factors that might affect the company's performance.

Role of Investment Bankers:
Investment bankers play a pivotal role in preparing the Form S-1. They assist in drafting the document, ensuring that all information is accurate and compliant with SEC regulations. They also help position the

company's story compellingly to attract potential investors. Investment bankers are deeply involved in setting the IPO price and structuring the securities being offered, balancing the company's need to raise capital with investor expectations for returns.

2. Quarterly Report (Form 10-Q)

Purpose and Importance:
Form 10-Q is a quarterly report that provides an update on a company's financial performance and operations. It is less comprehensive than the annual report but offers a timely view of the company's condition, helping investors track performance throughout the year.

Key Contents:

- **Financial Statements:** This includes unaudited financial statements for the quarter, such as income statements, balance sheets, and cash flow statements. These documents provide a snapshot of the company's financial health over the short term.
- **Management's Discussion and Analysis (MD&A):** This narrative section offers insights into the company's financial results, explaining significant changes and developments. It includes a discussion of market conditions, operational shifts, and future outlook.
- **Disclosures:** Updates on any major events, legal proceedings, or changes in accounting policies are included here, providing transparency about factors that might affect the company's financial standing.

Role of Investment Bankers:
While the preparation of Form 10-Q is primarily the responsibility of the company's financial team, investment bankers may provide guidance, especially during periods of significant transactions or

market shifts. They ensure that all disclosures align with the strategic narrative of the company and support ongoing investor relations efforts.

3. Annual Report (Form 10-K)

Purpose and Importance:
Form 10-K is a comprehensive annual report that provides a detailed overview of the company's business, financial condition, and governance. It includes audited financial statements and is a key resource for investors seeking a thorough understanding of a company's annual performance and long-term strategy.

Key Contents:

- **Business Overview:** This section expands on the information provided in the S-1, including a more detailed look at the company's business strategy, market position, and industry trends.
- **Audited Financial Statements:** These include the income statement, balance sheet, cash flow statement, and statement of shareholders' equity, along with notes explaining accounting policies and other details.
- **MD&A:** An in-depth analysis of the financial results, including comparisons with previous years, explanations of significant changes, and a discussion of future prospects and risks.
- **Corporate Governance:** Information about the board of directors, executive compensation, and corporate governance policies is detailed, providing insights into how the company is managed and controlled.

Role of Investment Bankers:
Investment bankers may assist in the preparation of the 10-K,

especially if the company is undergoing significant transactions, such as mergers or acquisitions. They help ensure that the financial statements and narratives accurately reflect the company's situation and align with market expectations.

4. Proxy Statement (Form DEF 14A)

Purpose and Importance:

The proxy statement, filed as Form DEF 14A, is used when a company seeks shareholder votes on important issues, such as electing directors or approving executive compensation plans. It provides detailed information to shareholders so they can make informed decisions on these matters.

Key Contents:

- **Meeting Agenda:** Outlines the items to be voted on at the shareholder meeting, including detailed descriptions and rationales for each proposal.
- **Board of Directors:** Information on board nominees, including their qualifications, past experience, and other board memberships.
- **Executive Compensation:** A breakdown of executive pay, including salaries, bonuses, stock options, and other forms of compensation, along with a discussion of the company's compensation philosophy.
- **Corporate Actions:** Information on any proposed mergers, acquisitions, or other significant corporate actions requiring shareholder approval.

Role of Investment Bankers:

Investment bankers often play a critical role in preparing proxy statements, particularly in situations involving significant corporate actions like mergers or major strategic shifts. They help craft the messaging and ensure that the document clearly communicates the benefits of the proposed actions, thereby facilitating shareholder approval.

Conclusion

Public filings such as the Form S-1, 10-Q, 10-K, and DEF 14A are integral to maintaining transparency and compliance in the financial markets. They provide essential information to investors, regulators, and other stakeholders. Investment bankers are crucial in the preparation and presentation of these filings, ensuring accuracy, compliance, and strategic alignment. By mastering the nuances of these documents, investment bankers can effectively guide their clients through complex financial transactions and enhance investor confidence in the capital markets.

PART VI: MANDATE/TARGET MATCHING & GENERATING STRATEGIC ALTERNATIVES

Chapter 41: Mandate/Target Matching & Generating Strategic Alternatives

The Comprehensive Guide to Mandate/Target Matching & Generating Strategic Alternatives in Investment Banking

Investment banking is a complex and nuanced field where precision and expertise are crucial, especially in mergers and acquisitions (M&A). One of the core functions investment bankers perform is matching investment mandates of strategic and financial buyers with appropriate target companies. This process, known as mandate/target matching, is vital for ensuring that the strategic and financial objectives of buyers align with the potential opportunities presented by target companies. This comprehensive guide delves into why mandate/target matching is essential, the detailed steps involved, and the methodologies investment bankers employ to achieve successful matches.

Why Mandate/Target Matching is Crucial

1. Aligning Strategic Objectives

Investment bankers must ensure that potential acquisition targets align with the strategic goals of the buyers. This alignment is crucial for achieving objectives such as expanding market share, acquiring new technologies, entering new markets, or diversifying product offerings. For instance, a tech company might be looking to acquire a startup with innovative AI capabilities to enhance its product suite. The strategic alignment ensures that the acquisition contributes meaningfully to the buyer's long-term goals.

2. Ensuring Financial Viability

Financial viability is another critical aspect. Investment bankers need to match buyers with targets that fit their financial criteria, such as specific revenue thresholds, EBITDA margins, and acceptable risk levels. This matching ensures that the acquisition is financially sound and that the target company can provide the desired return on investment. It involves a deep analysis of the target's financial health, including profitability, cash flow stability, and growth potential.

3. Streamlining the Acquisition Process

By narrowing down the list of potential targets to those that meet the buyers' criteria, investment bankers streamline the M&A process. This efficiency saves time and resources, allowing for a more focused and expedited negotiation and due diligence process. It also reduces the likelihood of pursuing unsuitable targets, which can lead to wasted efforts and potential deal failure.

4. Maximizing Value Creation

Effective mandate/target matching facilitates transactions that create value for both the buyer and the seller. It enables buyers to acquire assets that are not only strategically beneficial but also enhance financial performance. For sellers, being matched with the right buyer ensures that their business is valued appropriately and that they can secure favorable deal terms.

The Mandate/Target Matching Process

The process of matching mandates with targets is intricate and requires a meticulous approach. Below are the detailed steps that investment bankers follow:

1. Identifying Strategic & Financial Buyers

Strategic Buyers:

- **Definition:** Companies looking to acquire others to enhance their business operations, such as through vertical or horizontal integration.
- **Objectives:** Typically seek synergies like cost reductions, revenue growth, or technological advancements.
- **Example:** A pharmaceutical company acquiring a biotech firm for its drug pipeline.

Financial Buyers:

- **Definition:** Investors such as private equity firms and venture capitalists focused on acquiring companies for financial gains.
- **Objectives:** Often interested in restructuring, improving profitability, and eventually selling the company for a profit.
- **Example:** A private equity firm buying a manufacturing company to streamline operations and sell it at a higher valuation.

Process:

- Conduct extensive market research to identify potential buyers, including analyzing industry reports and financial statements.
- Create detailed profiles of these buyers, including their acquisition history, financial health, and strategic goals.

2. Obtaining Investment Mandates

An investment mandate is a detailed outline provided by the buyer that specifies the criteria for potential acquisitions.

Contents of Investment Mandates:

- **Strategic Objectives:** Goals such as market expansion, acquisition of complementary technologies, or geographic diversification.
- **Financial Criteria:** Includes target revenue, EBITDA, acceptable valuation multiples, and investment horizon.
- **Operational Preferences:** Desires for management team capabilities, operational efficiency, and scalability.
- **Risk Tolerance:** Level of acceptable risk, including market, operational, and financial risks.

Process:

- Engage in detailed discussions with potential buyers to understand their strategic and financial goals.
- Document these goals and criteria in a formal investment mandate, which serves as a blueprint for identifying suitable targets.

3. Structuring Buy-Side Engagements

Tailoring a specific approach for each buyer ensures that the search for potential targets aligns with their unique needs.

Key Components:

- **Customized Search Strategies:** Develop strategies based on the buyer's specific criteria, focusing on industry, geography, and company size.
- **Engagement Letters:** Formal agreements that outline the scope of services, confidentiality terms, and fee structures.

Process:

- Develop a comprehensive search strategy and outline it in an engagement letter.
- Negotiate the terms of the engagement with the buyer, ensuring clarity and mutual agreement.

4. Identifying Suitable Targets

Market Research:

- Conduct thorough market research to identify potential target companies. This includes analyzing industry reports, financial statements, and market trends to shortlist companies that fit the buyer's criteria.

Financial Analysis:

- Perform an in-depth financial analysis to evaluate the target's financial health. This involves reviewing key metrics such as revenue growth, profit margins, and cash flow stability.

Strategic Evaluation:

- Assess the strategic fit of potential targets by considering factors such as market position, competitive advantages, and potential synergies. For instance, a company with a strong distribution network may be highly attractive to a buyer looking to expand its market reach.

Initial Contact:

- Once potential targets are identified, initiate contact to gauge their interest in a potential transaction. This step involves gathering additional information and assessing the target's willingness to engage in further discussions.

Conclusion

Mandate/target matching is a cornerstone of successful investment banking, especially in the M&A domain. By meticulously aligning the investment mandates of strategic and financial buyers with suitable targets, investment bankers facilitate transactions that drive growth, enhance value, and fulfill the strategic and financial objectives of all parties involved. This process requires a deep understanding of market dynamics, a thorough analysis of both buyers and targets, and the ability to build and maintain strong relationships.

Effective mandate/target matching not only ensures successful transactions but also contributes significantly to the broader economic landscape by enabling companies to achieve their growth and operational goals. As such, it is a critical skill for any investment banker aspiring to excel in the field of M&A.

Chapter 42: Identifying Strategic & Financial Buyers

Comprehensive Guide to Identifying Strategic & Financial Buyers in Investment Banking

In the intricate world of investment banking, identifying the right buyers for mergers and acquisitions (M&A) is a foundational skill. This involves understanding and pinpointing both strategic and financial buyers who have the interest and capacity to engage in transactions. The process of identifying these buyers is a blend of industry knowledge, analytical skills, and strategic outreach. This blog post delves into the detailed methodologies and processes used by investment bankers to identify and engage potential buyers, tailored to align with the defined coverage area and specific investment mandates.

Defining the Coverage Area

Importance of Industry and Sector Focus

Defining the coverage area involves selecting specific industries or sub-verticals within which the investment banker operates. This focus allows bankers to specialize, gaining deep insights into the nuances of particular sectors. By concentrating on certain industries, investment bankers can build specialized knowledge, develop key contacts, and understand market dynamics, which are crucial for identifying relevant buyers.

For example, an investment banker specializing in the healthcare sector might focus on sub-verticals like medical devices, pharmaceuticals, or healthcare IT. This specialization enables the banker to understand the specific needs and trends within these sub-sectors, making it easier to identify potential buyers.

Identifying Strategic and Financial Buyers

Strategic Buyers: Characteristics and Identification

Strategic buyers are typically corporations looking to make acquisitions that align with their long-term business strategies. These buyers are interested in acquiring companies that can help them achieve goals such as entering new markets, acquiring innovative technologies, or gaining competitive advantages. For instance, a large tech company may seek to acquire a startup with cutting-edge AI capabilities to enhance its product offerings.

Key Characteristics:

- **Long-term Focus**: Interested in acquisitions that provide lasting strategic benefits.
- **Synergy Potential**: Looking for opportunities to integrate new capabilities or markets with their existing operations.
- **Operational Integration**: Often have dedicated teams to ensure smooth integration of acquired companies.

Identification Process:

1. **Industry Research**: Conducting detailed research on industry trends and identifying companies with active M&A strategies.
2. **Analyzing Corporate Announcements**: Monitoring press releases, annual reports, and investor presentations for insights into strategic priorities.
3. **Networking**: Leveraging industry contacts and attending sector-specific conferences and events.

Financial Buyers: Characteristics and Identification

Financial buyers include entities such as private equity firms, hedge funds, and venture capitalists. Unlike strategic buyers, financial buyers primarily focus on the financial returns of an acquisition. They often seek to improve the acquired company's performance and sell it at a profit within a few years.

Key Characteristics:

- **Short to Mid-term Focus**: Typically plan to hold investments for 3-7 years before exiting.
- **Value Creation**: Focus on improving operational efficiencies, expanding market share, or financial restructuring.
- **Exit Strategy**: Aim to sell the acquired company through secondary sales, IPOs, or mergers.

Identification Process:

1. **Database Utilization**: Using databases like Capital IQ, Bloomberg, and FactSet to identify private equity firms and other financial buyers active in specific industries.
2. **Investment Mandates**: Analyzing investment criteria, such as target company size, preferred sectors, and geographic focus.
3. **Deal Tracking**: Monitoring past transactions to understand the types of deals these buyers are interested in.

Obtaining Investment Mandates

Understanding and Formalizing Investment Criteria

An **investment mandate** outlines the specific acquisition criteria of a buyer. This document serves as a guideline for identifying suitable acquisition targets. It includes various criteria, such as:

- **Geographic Preferences**: Specific regions or countries where the buyer is interested in acquiring companies.
- **Revenue Size**: Target range for the annual revenue of potential acquisitions.
- **EBITDA and Profitability Metrics**: Desired earnings and profitability characteristics.
- **Sector and Sub-Sector Focus**: Specific industries or market segments of interest.

Engaging with Buyers

Investment bankers engage with potential buyers to discuss and clarify their investment mandates. This involves:

1. **Direct Meetings**: Setting up meetings to discuss strategic goals and specific investment criteria.
2. **Questionnaires and Surveys**: Sending detailed questionnaires to potential buyers to gather information on their acquisition preferences.
3. **Ongoing Communication**: Maintaining regular contact to update and refine mandates as market conditions or strategic priorities change.

Structuring Buy-Side Engagements

Formalizing the Relationship

Once the investment mandates are obtained, the relationship between the investment banker and the buyer is formalized through a **buy-side engagement agreement**. This agreement defines the scope of the services provided, the expectations from both parties, and the compensation structure.

Key Components:

- **Scope of Services**: Detailed description of the advisory services, including target identification, valuation, and negotiation support.
- **Expectations and Responsibilities**: Clear delineation of the responsibilities of both the investment banker and the buyer.
- **Compensation Structure**: Details of the fees, which may include retainer fees, success fees, and other performance-based incentives.

Sourcing Potential Targets

With clear mandates, investment bankers begin the process of identifying potential targets. This involves:

1. **Market Research**: Using industry reports, market analyses, and news sources to find potential acquisition targets.
2. **Financial Analysis**: Evaluating the financial health and performance metrics of potential targets.
3. **Strategic Evaluation**: Assessing how well potential targets align with the buyer's strategic goals and criteria.

Facilitating the Deal Process

Initial Contact and Engagement

Investment bankers initiate contact with potential targets to assess their interest in a potential transaction. This step involves:

- **Confidential Outreach**: Discreetly approaching potential targets without revealing the buyer's identity.
- **Preliminary Discussions**: Engaging in initial discussions to gauge interest and gather preliminary information.

Due Diligence and Negotiations

If a target expresses interest, the investment banker coordinates the due diligence process, ensuring a thorough evaluation of the target's operations, financials, and strategic fit. This phase includes:

- **Financial and Operational Due Diligence**: Detailed review of financial statements, operational processes, and key metrics.
- **Legal Due Diligence**: Examination of legal matters, including contracts, liabilities, and compliance issues.

- **Negotiation of Terms**: Assisting in the negotiation of key deal terms, such as purchase price, payment structure, and post-acquisition plans.

Conclusion

The process of identifying and engaging strategic and financial buyers is a critical component of investment banking. It requires a deep understanding of industry dynamics, meticulous research, and strategic communication. By effectively matching investment mandates with suitable targets, investment bankers facilitate transactions that align with the strategic and financial goals of their clients, ultimately driving successful outcomes and creating value for all parties involved.

NOTES:
Now that we have defined our coverage, we can go about identifying strategic & financial buyers consistent with that coverage.

We can use various database services and platforms to screen for these buyers which will end up being corporate M&A departments (strategics) or financial buyers (private equity).

Obtaining Investment Mandates
Strategic and financial buyers will have criterion within which they invest. For example, they have certain industries and sub-verticals that they focus on.

Criterion will specify:
- Geography
- Revenue
- EBITDA
- Vertical & sub-vertical

Structuring Buy Side Engagements
After obtaining the investment mandates and discussing with strategic and financial buyers, most of them will have some sort of boilerplate agreement to source deals for them in a buy side capacity.

Chapter 43: Identifying Targets

Identifying M&A Targets: An In-Depth Guide

Identifying suitable targets for mergers and acquisitions (M&A) is a crucial function in investment banking. This process involves a thorough understanding of the client's strategic goals, detailed market research, and a comprehensive evaluation of potential targets. In this post, we'll explore the extensive methodologies investment bankers use to identify and select M&A targets, ensuring a high likelihood of successful transactions.

1. Understanding Client Objectives

Engaging with the Client

The first and most fundamental step in identifying M&A targets is a deep understanding of the client's objectives. This involves:

- **In-Depth Discussions:** Engaging in detailed conversations with the client to ascertain their strategic motivations. For example, determining whether the client is aiming for market expansion, acquiring cutting-edge technology, or diversifying their product portfolio. These discussions help in setting clear acquisition criteria, such as desired market entry or synergies.
- **Defining Specific Goals:** These can include entering new markets, boosting technological capabilities, or consolidating market positions. For instance, if a client in the healthcare sector wants to expand into telemedicine, this goal will shape the search for companies specializing in digital health platforms.

Aligning with Strategic Priorities

Aligning potential acquisitions with the client's broader strategic priorities is crucial:

- **Criteria Development:** Establishing detailed criteria that align with the client's long-term goals. For example, focusing on targets that offer complementary technologies or products.
- **Strategic Mapping:** Creating a strategic map that aligns potential acquisitions with the client's long-term vision, ensuring all identified targets fit into a larger growth strategy.

2. Conducting Comprehensive Industry Research

Analyzing Market Trends

To identify potential targets, investment bankers must have a solid grasp of the industry landscape:

- **Market Dynamics:** Analyzing factors such as technological advancements, regulatory changes, and economic conditions that influence the industry. For example, understanding how changes in healthcare regulations can open up new opportunities in medical technology.
- **Identifying Growth Segments:** Pinpointing emerging sectors or niches within the industry that present growth opportunities. For example, identifying a growing trend in sustainable packaging within the manufacturing sector.

Understanding Industry Dynamics

A deep understanding of the competitive landscape helps in identifying viable targets:

- **Competitive Analysis:** Assessing the market share, key players, and competitive pressures within the industry. For example, analyzing the market share of top companies in the renewable energy sector.
- **Subsector Specialization:** Focusing on specific subsectors that align with the client's interests, such as fintech within the broader financial services industry.

Identifying Complementary Offerings

Identifying companies that offer complementary products or services can enhance the client's existing operations:

- **Operational Synergies:** Looking for targets that can provide operational efficiencies, such as cost savings or enhanced distribution networks.
- **Product and Service Fit:** Ensuring that the target's offerings align with the client's existing products and services, which can facilitate integration and expansion.

3. Leveraging Market Intelligence and Data Sources

Monitoring Industry News and Reports

Staying updated with the latest industry developments is crucial for identifying potential targets:

- **Industry Publications:** Regularly reviewing industry-specific publications, financial news outlets, and market research reports. This helps in staying abreast of new developments and identifying emerging companies.
- **Case Studies and Previous Transactions:** Learning from previous M&A transactions to understand successful strategies and common pitfalls.

Accessing Financial Databases

Investment bankers use financial databases to gather detailed information about potential targets:

- **Comprehensive Data Access:** Utilizing platforms like Capital IQ, Bloomberg, and FactSet for access to financial data, historical performance, and market metrics.
- **Advanced Screening:** Employing screening tools to filter companies based on various financial metrics, such as revenue, EBITDA, and market capitalization.

Leveraging Professional Networks

Industry contacts and professional networks can provide valuable insights and access to potential targets:

- **Networking and Events:** Attending industry conferences, networking events, and engaging with industry insiders to discover potential acquisition targets that may not be widely known.
- **Referrals and Introductions:** Utilizing professional networks to get introductions to potential targets or gather insider information.

4. Evaluating Financial Performance

Analyzing Financial Indicators

A thorough financial analysis is essential to understand the target's viability:

- **Key Financial Metrics:** Assessing metrics such as revenue growth, profit margins, cash flow stability, and debt levels to gauge financial health.
- **Historical Performance Analysis:** Reviewing historical financial performance to understand the target's business trends and potential future performance.

Conducting Due Diligence

Due diligence is a critical step in the target identification process:

- **Financial Due Diligence:** In-depth examination of financial statements, tax records, and audit reports to uncover any financial risks.
- **Legal and Regulatory Compliance:** Ensuring that the target is compliant with relevant laws and regulations, which could affect the transaction's feasibility.

5. Assessing Strategic Fit

Cultural Compatibility

Assessing the cultural fit between the client and the target is crucial for post-acquisition integration:

- **Cultural Assessment:** Analyzing corporate cultures, management styles, and company values to ensure a smooth integration.
- **Integration Planning:** Developing a comprehensive plan for integrating the target's operations, personnel, and corporate culture with the client's.

Management Capabilities

The quality and experience of the target's management team can significantly impact the acquisition's success:

- **Leadership Evaluation:** Reviewing the backgrounds and track records of the target's management team to ensure they have the necessary skills and experience.
- **Retention Strategies:** Considering strategies to retain key management and employees post-acquisition.

Operational Synergies

Identifying and quantifying potential operational synergies can add significant value:

- **Cost Reduction Opportunities:** Analyzing potential areas for cost savings, such as consolidated operations or shared services.
- **Revenue Growth Potential:** Exploring opportunities for revenue enhancement through cross-selling, market expansion, or new product development.

6. Evaluating Transaction Potential

Regulatory Environment

Understanding the regulatory implications of the transaction is vital:

- **Compliance and Legal Review:** Ensuring the transaction complies with antitrust laws and other regulatory requirements.
- **Regulatory Approval Process:** Assessing the likelihood of obtaining necessary regulatory approvals and potential challenges.

Competition for the Target

Understanding the competitive landscape for acquiring the target is crucial:

- **Interest from Other Buyers:** Analyzing the level of interest from other potential buyers, which could influence the negotiation process and final acquisition price.
- **Negotiation Strategy:** Developing a strategy for negotiating with the target and other interested parties.

7. Presenting to the Client

Developing Pitch Materials

Creating compelling pitch materials is essential for presenting potential targets to the client:

- **Comprehensive Documentation:** Preparing detailed documents that include financial analysis, strategic fit assessments, potential synergies, and risk analysis.
- **Visual Presentation:** Utilizing visual aids like charts, graphs, and infographics to clearly convey key information and recommendations.

Communicating Benefits and Risks

Providing a balanced view of the potential acquisition is critical:

- **Highlighting Strategic Benefits:** Clearly articulating the strategic benefits of the acquisition, such as market expansion or technology acquisition.
- **Addressing Potential Risks:** Transparently discussing potential risks, such as cultural misalignment or regulatory hurdles, and proposed mitigation strategies.

Conclusion

Identifying suitable M&A targets involves a complex and comprehensive process that requires a deep understanding of the client's strategic objectives, thorough industry research, and detailed financial analysis. By following a structured approach, investment bankers can effectively identify and present acquisition opportunities that align with the client's goals, ensuring successful and value-creating transactions. This process not only enhances the likelihood of deal success but also strengthens client relationships and trust.

NOTES:
Identifying Targets
Now that we have investment mandates from strategic & financial buyers, we can go about screening for targets from databases such as Salesgenie.

After pulling the list of potential targets we then need to go in and analyze further each of the potential targets.

Applying the Mandate/Target Matching Methodology
The Mandate/Target Matching Methodology is the following:

1. Build relationships with strategic and financial buyers in a given industry sector or subsector (Use Mergr.com as a database within which to understand investment mandates and contact information)
2. Indicate your interest in sourcing deals on their behalf and obtain their investment mandate. This will usually be detailed in a one-page teaser or presentation that they will send to you
3. Screen for companies that match the mandate(s) in Salesgenie.com and obtain CEO/owner emails and phone numbers
4. Begin emailing and calling CEO/owners and soliciting interest in exploring strategic alternatives
5. Structure as a sell-side engagement or a buy-side engagement depending on CEO/owner's level of interest in buying/selling
6. Collect historical financial data for the last three years
7. Introduce the financial and/or strategic buyer to the opportunity with the summary financial information and have them sign an NDA
8. Have a call with the financial and/or strategic buyer and then make the formal introduction to the CEO/owner and have a buyer/seller meeting

Chapter 44: Understanding the Strategic Capital Management Process

Understanding the Strategic Capital Management Process in Corporate Finance

In the intricate world of corporate finance, strategic capital management plays a pivotal role in determining the success and sustainability of large corporations. This process involves a series of carefully planned steps that help organizations allocate resources efficiently, evaluate potential investments, and ultimately maximize shareholder value. This blog post delves into the key components of the strategic capital management process, focusing on the crucial roles of top management, the importance of thorough financial analysis, effective project evaluation, capital budgeting, and ongoing performance monitoring.

The Role of Top Management in Strategic Capital Management

1. Setting Financial Strategic Direction

The journey of strategic capital management begins with the CEO and executive team. These leaders are responsible for setting the financial strategic direction of the company. This involves defining the long-term financial goals, such as profitability targets, market expansion plans, or diversification strategies. The clarity and foresight provided by top management in this phase ensure that all subsequent investment decisions are aligned with the overarching corporate vision.

2. Defining Investment Criteria

Top management must establish specific investment criteria, which act as a filter for evaluating potential projects. These criteria typically include the required return on investment (ROI), acceptable levels of risk, and the strategic fit of the project within the company's broader objectives. For instance, a technology company may prioritize investments in innovative software solutions that promise high returns and align with its mission of technological leadership.

3. Resource Allocation

Deciding how to allocate financial resources among various projects is a critical responsibility of top management. They must balance between investing in high-growth opportunities and maintaining sufficient reserves for operational needs or unforeseen expenses. This careful allocation ensures that the company can pursue strategic initiatives while maintaining financial stability.

4. Oversight and Governance

Once projects are underway, top management's role extends to oversight and governance. This includes monitoring project progress, ensuring adherence to budgetary constraints, and making course corrections when necessary. Effective oversight helps mitigate risks and ensures that projects contribute positively to the company's financial health.

5. Promoting Financial Discipline

Promoting a culture of financial discipline is essential for sustainable growth. Top management must instill a mindset of prudent financial management across all levels of the organization, ensuring that all investments are scrutinized and only those that meet rigorous standards are approved.

Financial Analysis and Project Evaluation

1. Initial Project Screening

The strategic capital management process begins with an initial screening of potential projects. This step involves assessing each project against the pre-established investment criteria. Projects that do not meet the basic requirements for ROI, strategic fit, or risk tolerance are filtered out early, allowing the company to focus on more promising opportunities.

2. Detailed Financial Analysis

For projects that pass the initial screening, a more detailed financial analysis is conducted. This involves forecasting future cash flows, calculating key financial metrics such as net present value (NPV), internal rate of return (IRR), and payback period. These metrics help determine the financial viability of each project and its potential to generate value for the company.

3. Risk Assessment

A thorough risk assessment is crucial to understanding the potential challenges and uncertainties associated with each project. This includes evaluating market risks, operational risks, and financial risks. For instance, a project involving the launch of a new product line may carry significant market risk if consumer demand is uncertain.

4. Scenario Analysis

Scenario analysis involves creating multiple projections based on different market conditions—such as best-case, worst-case, and most-likely scenarios. This analysis helps the company understand how each project might perform under various circumstances, providing a more comprehensive view of potential outcomes.

5. Strategic Fit Assessment

In addition to financial metrics, it's essential to evaluate how well each project aligns with the company's strategic objectives. Projects that enhance the company's competitive position, expand its market presence, or introduce innovative technologies are often prioritized, as they contribute to long-term strategic goals.

Capital Budgeting

1. Capital Budgeting Process

Capital budgeting is the process of planning and managing a company's long-term investments. It involves identifying potential investment opportunities, evaluating their financial and strategic viability, and selecting the projects that offer the highest value. This process ensures that the company's limited resources are allocated to the most promising initiatives.

2. Project Prioritization

After evaluating potential projects, the next step is prioritizing them based on their expected returns and strategic importance. This prioritization helps ensure that the most valuable projects receive the necessary funding and attention. For example, projects with a high NPV and strong alignment with strategic goals may be prioritized over others with lower financial returns.

3. Budget Allocation

Once projects are prioritized, capital is allocated accordingly. This step involves determining the funding sources for each project, whether through internal cash flows, debt financing, or equity financing. The chosen funding method depends on the company's financial strategy and risk tolerance.

4. Approval Process

A formal approval process is established to ensure that all investment decisions are thoroughly vetted. This process typically involves multiple levels of review and approval, from departmental managers to senior executives and the board of directors. The approval process ensures that investments are well-considered and aligned with corporate objectives.

Strategy Implementation

1. Translating Plans into Action

The implementation phase involves turning strategic plans into actionable steps. This requires detailed planning, clear timelines, and assigned responsibilities. For instance, if the company decides to acquire a new technology, the implementation plan would include steps for integrating the technology, training staff, and marketing the new capabilities.

2. Resource Allocation

Efficient resource allocation is critical during the implementation phase. This involves distributing financial, human, and technological resources to ensure that all projects receive the support they need to succeed.

3. Organizational Structures

Creating or adjusting organizational structures may be necessary to support the implementation of strategic initiatives. This could involve forming new departments, creating cross-functional teams, or appointing project managers to oversee key initiatives.

4. Establishing Performance Metrics

Defining clear performance metrics and KPIs helps track the progress and success of strategic initiatives. These metrics provide a quantitative way to measure performance, making it easier to identify areas for improvement.

5. Aligning Processes and Systems

To support the execution of strategic plans, it may be necessary to adjust existing processes and systems. This alignment ensures that all parts of the organization work together towards common goals.

6. Effective Communication

Clear and consistent communication is essential for the successful implementation of strategies. This ensures that all stakeholders understand the strategic goals, their roles, and the expected outcomes.

7. Change Management and Employee Engagement

Implementing strategic initiatives often involves significant change. Effective change management practices, including regular communication and employee engagement, are crucial for managing transitions smoothly and maintaining morale.

Monitoring and Evaluation

1. Tracking Progress

Ongoing monitoring of the implementation process is essential for ensuring that projects stay on track. This involves regular reviews of progress against plans, identifying any deviations, and taking corrective actions as needed.

2. Performance Measurement

Using KPIs and other metrics, companies can measure the effectiveness of their strategic initiatives. This performance measurement helps in identifying successful projects and those that may need adjustments.

3. Regular Reporting and Reviews

Regular performance reviews and strategic meetings provide a forum for discussing progress, addressing issues, and making informed decisions. These reviews are critical for maintaining focus and ensuring that the company remains on course.

4. Adjustments and Course Corrections

Based on performance data and changing business conditions, companies may need to adjust their strategies. This flexibility allows organizations to respond to new opportunities or challenges effectively.

5. Ensuring Strategic Alignment

Finally, it's important to ensure that all strategies remain aligned with the company's overarching objectives and market conditions. This alignment helps maintain focus and achieve desired outcomes.

Challenges in Strategic Capital Management

1. Managing Complexity and Scale

Large corporations often deal with complex and large-scale operations, making strategic capital management challenging. This complexity requires effective coordination and management across multiple departments and business units.

2. Alignment Across Business Units

Ensuring that diverse business units and functions are aligned with the overall corporate strategy is crucial. This involves promoting coherence and consistency across the organization.

3. Balancing Innovation and Efficiency

Fostering innovation while maintaining operational efficiency and cost-effectiveness is a key challenge. This balance is essential for achieving long-term success.

4. Adapting to Market Dynamics

Quickly adapting to rapidly changing market conditions and customer preferences is essential for maintaining competitiveness. This requires agility and flexibility in strategic capital management.

5. Overcoming Cultural Resistance

Addressing cultural resistance to change and fostering a culture that embraces strategic initiatives is important for successful implementation.

6. Effective Communication and Coordination

Ensuring effective communication and coordination across geographically dispersed units is essential for maintaining alignment and achieving strategic goals.

Best Practices in Strategic Capital Management

1. Promoting a Strategic Mindset

Encouraging a strategic mindset throughout the organization helps in fostering a culture of strategic thinking and innovation.

2. Fostering Collaboration

Promoting collaboration and cross-functional integration leverages diverse perspectives and expertise, enhancing strategic decision-making.

3. Leveraging Technology and Data Analytics

Using technology and data analytics to gain strategic insights and make informed decisions helps in identifying opportunities and addressing challenges.

4. Nurturing a Learning Culture

Cultivating a culture that embraces learning, experimentation, and risk-taking encourages innovation and continuous improvement.

5. Ensuring Strategic and Cultural Alignment

Aligning strategic initiatives with the organizational culture ensures smooth implementation and employee engagement.

6. Continuous Monitoring and Adaptation

Continuously monitoring strategies and adapting them based on feedback and changing conditions ensures relevance and effectiveness.

Conclusion

The strategic capital management process in corporate finance is a dynamic and multi-faceted endeavor that requires meticulous planning, robust financial analysis, and strategic foresight. Top management plays a critical role inThe strategic capital management process in corporate finance is a dynamic and multi-faceted endeavor that requires meticulous planning, robust financial analysis, and strategic foresight. Top management plays a critical role in setting the financial strategic direction, defining investment criteria, and overseeing the efficient allocation of resources to ensure the company's long-term growth and financial health. By leveraging a systematic approach that includes understanding client objectives, conducting thorough industry research, utilizing market intelligence, evaluating financial performance, assessing strategic fit, and monitoring performance, large corporations can navigate the complexities of strategic capital management and achieve sustainable growth and success.

In summary, the strategic capital management process involves several key steps:

1. **Role of Top Management**:
   - **Setting Financial Strategic Direction**: Defining long-term financial goals and investment criteria.
   - **Resource Allocation**: Efficient distribution of financial resources among projects.
   - **Oversight and Governance**: Monitoring project progress and promoting financial discipline.
2. **Financial Analysis and Project Evaluation**:
   - **Initial Project Screening**: Assessing projects against investment criteria.
   - **Detailed Financial Analysis**: Forecasting cash flows and evaluating key financial metrics.
   - **Risk Assessment**: Identifying potential challenges and uncertainties.
3. **Capital Budgeting**:

- Capital Budgeting Process: Planning and managing long-term investments.
- Project Prioritization: Prioritizing projects based on expected returns and strategic importance.
- Budget Allocation: Allocating capital to selected projects.

4. **Strategy Implementation**:
   - **Translating Plans into Action**: Converting strategic plans into actionable steps.
   - **Resource Allocation**: Efficient distribution of resources.
   - **Effective Communication and Change Management**: Promoting clear communication and managing change.

5. **Monitoring and Evaluation**:
   - **Tracking Progress**: Monitoring the implementation process.
   - **Performance Measurement**: Using KPIs to measure success.
   - **Adjustments and Course Corrections**: Making necessary adjustments to strategies.

6. **Challenges in Strategic Capital Management**:
   - **Managing Complexity and Scale**: Dealing with complex and large-scale operations.
   - **Balancing Innovation and Efficiency**: Fostering innovation while maintaining operational efficiency.

7. **Best Practices in Strategic Capital Management**:
   - **Promoting a Strategic Mindset**: Encouraging strategic thinking and innovation.
   - **Fostering Collaboration**: Promoting cross-functional integration.
   - **Leveraging Technology and Data Analytics**: Using technology and data analytics for strategic insights.

Through diligent research, strategic planning, and effective execution, corporations can effectively manage their capital, ensure alignment with strategic goals, and create long-term value for shareholders. The key to success lies in maintaining flexibility, continuously monitoring progress, and being willing to adapt to changing market conditions and opportunities. By adopting these practices, companies can navigate the complexities of strategic capital management and drive sustained success.

Chapter 45: The Role That Investment Bankers Play in the Strategic Management Process

The Role of Investment Bankers in Strategic Management: An In-Depth Exploration

Investment bankers play a multifaceted and pivotal role in the strategic management processes of corporations. They bring a wealth of expertise in financial markets, industry knowledge, and transactional experience, making them indispensable partners in both formulating and executing strategic initiatives. This blog post provides an in-depth exploration of the various roles that investment bankers fulfill, from strategic planning to value creation and capital markets expertise.

Strategic Planning: Crafting the Vision

Collaboration with Corporate Leadership

Investment bankers work closely with corporate executives and board members to craft the strategic vision of the company. This collaboration involves a comprehensive analysis of the current market environment, competitive landscape, and potential growth opportunities. By leveraging their deep understanding of industry trends and market dynamics, investment bankers help leadership teams define clear, actionable strategic objectives. These may include market expansion, diversification, acquisition of new technologies, or enhancing operational efficiencies.

Insight into Industry Trends and Market Dynamics

Investment bankers are adept at identifying key industry trends that could impact the company's future. They provide insights into emerging markets, technological innovations, and potential threats from competitors. This foresight enables companies to anticipate changes in the market and position themselves advantageously. For example, an investment banker might advise a technology company to pivot towards artificial intelligence and machine learning, recognizing the growing demand and future potential in these fields.

Strategic Partnerships and Acquisitions

Investment bankers often identify and recommend potential strategic partnerships or acquisitions that align with the company's long-term goals. This could involve scouting for companies with complementary technologies or market reach. For instance, they might suggest a merger with a firm that has a strong foothold in a desired geographic region, thereby facilitating market entry and expansion.

Financial Analysis: The Backbone of Decision-Making

In-Depth Financial Statement Analysis

A critical function of investment bankers in strategic management is conducting thorough financial analyses. They scrutinize financial statements, including income statements, balance sheets, and cash flow statements, to assess the company's financial health. This analysis helps in identifying strengths, such as strong cash flows, and weaknesses, like high debt levels, which could impact the company's strategic decisions.

Valuation and Forecasting

Investment bankers use various valuation techniques to assess the value of the company or potential acquisition targets. These techniques include discounted cash flow (DCF) analysis, comparable company analysis, and precedent transactions. Through these methods, they estimate the intrinsic value of a business, allowing the company to make informed decisions about mergers, acquisitions, or divestitures.

Risk Assessment and Scenario Analysis

Another vital component of financial analysis is assessing the risks associated with potential strategies. Investment bankers conduct scenario analyses to model the potential impact of different strategic choices under various economic conditions. This might involve creating best-case, worst-case, and most-likely financial scenarios to evaluate the robustness of a proposed strategy.

Transaction Advisory: Navigating Complex Deals

Identifying Suitable Targets

Investment bankers are instrumental in identifying potential M&A targets that align with a company's strategic objectives. This involves extensive market research and due diligence to ensure that the target companies are financially sound and strategically beneficial. For example, they might target companies with innovative products or strong intellectual property that can provide a competitive edge.

Deal Structuring and Negotiation

Once suitable targets are identified, investment bankers assist in structuring and negotiating the terms of the deal. They work to ensure that the deal structure maximizes value for the company, whether through share swaps, cash transactions, or a combination of both. They also negotiate terms that protect the company's interests, such as warranties and indemnities in the purchase agreement.

Regulatory and Compliance Guidance

Investment bankers provide essential guidance on navigating the regulatory landscape. This includes understanding antitrust laws, foreign investment restrictions, and other regulatory requirements that could impact the transaction. Their expertise ensures that the deal complies with all relevant laws and regulations, minimizing the risk of legal issues post-transaction.

Capital Markets Expertise: Accessing Financial Resources

Raising Capital

Investment bankers assist companies in raising capital through debt or equity offerings. They provide advice on the most appropriate financing mix based on the company's financial strategy, market conditions, and the cost of capital. For instance, they might recommend an initial public offering (IPO) to raise equity capital or suggest issuing corporate bonds for debt financing.

Pricing and Market Timing

Determining the right time to enter the market and the appropriate pricing of securities are crucial elements of capital raising. Investment bankers use their market expertise to advise on the timing and pricing of IPOs, secondary offerings, or bond issues. Their goal is to maximize the capital raised while minimizing the cost of issuance.

Investor Relations and Communication

Post-offering, investment bankers play a key role in managing investor relations. They help the company communicate effectively with investors, ensuring transparency and maintaining a positive market perception. This involves crafting messages that highlight the company's strategic vision, financial performance, and future prospects.

Value Creation: Enhancing Shareholder Wealth

Optimizing Capital Structure

Investment bankers provide advice on optimizing the company's capital structure to enhance shareholder value. This might involve restructuring debt, repurchasing shares, or adjusting the mix of debt and equity. The goal is to achieve a capital structure that minimizes the cost of capital while providing financial flexibility.

Identifying Cost Savings and Synergies

In the context of mergers and acquisitions, investment bankers identify potential cost savings and synergies that can be realized post-transaction. This might include integrating supply chains, consolidating operations, or leveraging combined marketing efforts. They also help in developing integration plans that ensure a smooth transition and the realization of projected synergies.

Strategic Divestitures

In some cases, value creation involves divesting non-core assets or underperforming business units. Investment bankers assist in identifying these divestitures and executing the sale process. By shedding non-core assets, the company can focus on its core competencies and invest in areas with higher growth potential.

Industry Knowledge and Network: Leveraging Expertise and Connections

Deep Industry Insight

Investment bankers possess deep knowledge of the industries they cover. This includes understanding the key players, competitive dynamics, regulatory environment, and technological trends. Their insights are invaluable for companies looking to make strategic moves within their industry.

Extensive Network of Contacts

The network of contacts that investment bankers maintain is another critical asset. This network includes potential investors, strategic partners, industry experts, and regulatory authorities. By leveraging these connections, investment bankers can facilitate introductions, gather market intelligence, and expedite deal-making processes.

Conclusion: The Strategic Advantage of Investment Bankers

Investment bankers are invaluable partners in the strategic management process for corporations. Their expertise in strategic planning, financial analysis, transaction advisory, capital markets, and value creation enables companies to navigate complex challenges and capitalize on opportunities. By leveraging their deep industry knowledge and extensive networks, investment bankers help corporations enhance shareholder value, achieve strategic objectives, and sustain competitive advantage. Whether through guiding strategic decisions, raising capital, or facilitating mergers and acquisitions, investment bankers play a critical role in shaping the future of businesses in today's dynamic and competitive marketplace.

Chapter 46: The Role of Investment Bankers in Finding the Lowest Cost of Capital Alternative for Corporate Issuers

The Role of Investment Bankers in Finding the Lowest Cost of Capital Alternative for Corporate Issuers

Finding the lowest cost of capital is a crucial endeavor for corporate issuers as it directly influences their financial efficiency and profitability. Investment bankers are key players in this process, leveraging their expertise in financial markets, negotiation skills, and strategic insights to secure the most favorable financing options. This blog post explores the detailed and multifaceted role that investment bankers play in helping corporate issuers find the lowest cost of capital alternatives. We will delve into capital structure assessment, financing options analysis, market research and investor outreach, negotiation and structuring, and ongoing monitoring and risk management.

Capital Structure Assessment: Laying the Groundwork

1. Evaluating the Debt and Equity Mix Investment bankers begin by analyzing the issuer's existing capital structure, which involves a careful review of the current mix of debt and equity. This assessment helps identify the balance between these two components and determines whether the current structure is optimal or if adjustments are necessary. A balanced capital structure is crucial for minimizing the overall cost of capital while maintaining financial flexibility and stability.

2. Analyzing Costs and Terms A comprehensive analysis of the costs associated with current financing arrangements is conducted. This includes evaluating the interest rates on debt, the cost of equity (including dividend expectations and dilution effects), and any associated fees. Investment bankers also scrutinize the terms and conditions of existing debt, such as covenants and maturity schedules, to understand the issuer's obligations and potential refinancing opportunities.

3. Identifying Optimization Opportunities By benchmarking the issuer's capital structure against industry norms and best practices, investment bankers identify areas for potential improvement. This could involve recommending a shift towards a more debt-heavy structure if the company has underutilized debt capacity, thereby benefiting from tax shields. Conversely, if the company is highly leveraged, bankers might suggest equity financing to strengthen the balance sheet.

Financing Options Analysis: Exploring the Best Fit

1. Debt Financing Investment bankers evaluate various debt instruments, including bonds, syndicated loans, and credit facilities. They assess these options based on interest rates, term length, covenants, and the overall cost of borrowing. The goal is to identify the most cost-effective debt financing option that aligns with the company's strategic objectives and financial health.

2. Equity Financing When considering equity financing, investment bankers analyze the potential impact on existing shareholders, including dilution and changes in control. They evaluate the current market conditions to determine the best timing for issuing new shares. Bankers also advise on the type of equity to issue, whether common stock, preferred shares, or convertible securities, depending on the company's needs and market appetite.

3. Convertible and Hybrid Instruments Convertible securities, which can be converted into equity, offer a blend of debt and equity characteristics. These instruments can provide lower initial costs compared to pure equity and offer flexibility for both issuers and investors. Investment bankers analyze the terms of convertibles, such as conversion ratios and pricing, to ensure they are advantageous for the issuer.

4. Scenario Analysis and Financial Modeling Investment bankers utilize advanced financial models to simulate various scenarios and outcomes. These models help forecast cash flows, assess the impact on earnings per share (EPS), and evaluate the potential changes in the company's financial ratios. By doing so, they can compare the costs and benefits of different financing options under various market conditions.

Investment Banking University
All Rights Reserved

Market Research and Investor Outreach: Connecting with the Right Partners

1. Analyzing Market Conditions Investment bankers continuously monitor economic indicators, interest rate trends, and market sentiment. This real-time analysis helps in identifying the best windows for capital raising activities. For instance, in a low-interest-rate environment, it may be advantageous to issue debt, while a bullish equity market may present a favorable environment for stock offerings.

2. Identifying Investor Preferences Understanding what different types of investors seek—such as risk tolerance, yield requirements, and investment horizons—is crucial. Investment bankers tailor their financing proposals to align with these preferences, enhancing the likelihood of successful transactions. For example, long-term institutional investors may prefer stable, high-quality debt, while hedge funds might seek higher returns through more speculative investments.

3. Engaging a Broad Network Investment bankers leverage their extensive networks to reach out to a diverse pool of potential investors, including institutional investors, private equity firms, venture capitalists, and banks. They solicit multiple offers to ensure a competitive process, which helps secure the most favorable terms for the issuer.

Negotiation and Structuring: Securing the Best Deal

1. Negotiating Interest Rates and Fees One of the core functions of investment bankers is negotiating the terms of financing, including interest rates, underwriting fees, and other associated costs. Their deep market knowledge and negotiation expertise are critical in securing the lowest possible costs and favorable terms for their clients.

2. Structuring the Deal Investment bankers play a crucial role in structuring financing deals to align with the corporate issuer's strategic goals. This includes setting covenants, determining repayment schedules, and ensuring flexibility in terms of prepayment or refinancing. The structure must also be attractive to investors while being sustainable for the issuer.

3. Ensuring Flexibility and Alignment A key aspect of structuring is ensuring that the financing arrangement provides sufficient flexibility for the issuer to manage its financial operations. This includes provisions for additional funding, refinancing options, and other terms that allow the company to adapt to changing market conditions.

Ongoing Monitoring and Risk Management: Maintaining Financial Health

1. Assessing and Mitigating Risks Investment bankers continuously assess the risks associated with different financing structures, including interest rate risk, credit risk, and market volatility. They develop strategies to mitigate these risks, such as interest rate swaps, credit default swaps, and other hedging instruments.

2. Monitoring Market Conditions After the capital has been raised, investment bankers continue to monitor the market for potential refinancing opportunities or new capital raising. They provide ongoing advice on market conditions, helping issuers capitalize on favorable shifts in the market to lower their cost of capital further.

3. Regular Communication and Reporting Investment bankers maintain regular communication with the corporate issuer, providing updates on market conditions, the performance of financial instruments, and potential strategic moves. This continuous engagement ensures that the issuer remains well-informed and can make timely decisions.

Conclusion: The Strategic Advantage of Investment Bankers in Capital Management

Investment bankers are indispensable in helping corporate issuers navigate the complexities of finding the lowest cost of capital. Through meticulous capital structure assessments, comprehensive analysis of financing options, strategic market research, and skillful negotiation, they ensure that corporate issuers secure the most cost-effective and strategic financing solutions. Their role extends beyond initial capital raising to ongoing monitoring and risk management, providing corporate issuers with the expertise and insights needed to maintain financial health and support long-term growth. By partnering with investment bankers, corporations can optimize their capital structure, reduce costs, and achieve their strategic objectives with confidence.

Chapter 47: The Role of Investment Bankers in Sourcing High Return Opportunities for Strategic and Financial Investors

The Role of Investment Bankers in Sourcing High Return Opportunities for Strategic and Financial Investors

In the complex landscape of investment banking, the ability to source high return opportunities is vital for both strategic and financial investors. Investment bankers are key players in this process, leveraging their extensive market knowledge, industry relationships, and analytical prowess to connect investors with lucrative opportunities. This post explores the multifaceted role investment bankers play in identifying, evaluating, and facilitating these opportunities, focusing on deal origination, due diligence, valuation analysis, transaction execution, market insights, and post-investment support.

Deal Origination: The Starting Point of High Return Opportunities

Building and Leveraging Industry Networks

Investment bankers cultivate and maintain vast networks across various industries. These networks include relationships with corporate executives, industry experts, entrepreneurs, and other stakeholders. By engaging with these individuals, investment bankers gain insider knowledge about companies that may be seeking strategic alternatives, such as mergers, acquisitions, or capital raising. For instance, they might learn about a tech startup looking for growth capital or a manufacturing firm seeking to divest a non-core division.

Example: An investment banker might have a long-standing relationship with a CEO in the healthcare sector. When this CEO decides to sell a division, the banker is among the first to know, giving them a head start in finding a suitable buyer.

Utilizing Market Intelligence and Research

Investment bankers use advanced tools and resources to conduct market research. They analyze industry reports, financial databases, and proprietary analytics to identify trends, emerging markets, and potential investment opportunities. This research is crucial for understanding the dynamics of specific sectors and pinpointing companies with high growth potential.

Example: By analyzing market data, investment bankers might identify a surge in demand for renewable energy solutions, prompting them to seek out companies in that space that are poised for growth.

Proactive Outreach and Engagement

Beyond waiting for opportunities to present themselves, investment bankers proactively reach out to companies that fit the profile of potential investment targets. This involves cold-calling, attending industry conferences, and setting up meetings to discuss potential strategic options. This proactive approach helps uncover opportunities that may not be publicly advertised.

Example: An investment banker contacts a promising mid-sized logistics company to explore the possibility of an acquisition, even if the company isn't actively looking to sell. This direct engagement can sometimes reveal willingness to negotiate that wouldn't otherwise be apparent.

Due Diligence: Ensuring Viable and Secure Investments

Conducting Comprehensive Financial Analysis

Due diligence is a critical phase where investment bankers scrutinize a target company's financial health. They delve into financial statements to assess revenue trends, profitability, cash flow, and debt levels. This analysis helps determine whether the company is financially sound and if it can meet investors' return expectations.

Example: Analyzing the financials of a target company reveals that while it has strong revenue growth, its margins are thin due to high operational costs. This insight helps investors understand the true financial condition of the business.

Assessing Market Position and Growth Potential

Investment bankers evaluate a company's market position, including its market share, competitive advantages, and growth prospects. This involves understanding the competitive landscape, identifying key competitors, and assessing the company's ability to expand into new markets or innovate.

Example: A company that holds a significant market share in a niche segment with few competitors might be considered a strong investment due to its defensible position and growth potential.

Evaluating Management and Operational Efficiency

The quality of a company's management team and operational efficiency are critical factors in investment decisions. Investment bankers assess the experience, track record, and capabilities of the management team. They also evaluate the company's operational processes, scalability, and efficiency.

Example: A seasoned management team with a proven track record of navigating industry challenges might make a company a more attractive investment despite current financial difficulties.

Identifying and Mitigating Risks

Investment bankers identify potential risks associated with the investment, including market, regulatory, and operational risks. They assess how these risks might impact the investment and develop strategies to mitigate them.

Example: If a target company operates in a highly regulated industry, investment bankers might consider potential regulatory changes and their impact on the business's operations and profitability.

Valuation Analysis: Determining the Worth of Investment Opportunities

Building Financial Models

Investment bankers build detailed financial models to estimate a company's valuation. These models incorporate various methodologies, including discounted cash flow (DCF) analysis, comparable company analysis, and precedent transaction analysis. These approaches provide a range of valuations that help in assessing the company's worth.

Example: Using DCF analysis, investment bankers can estimate the present value of a company's future cash flows, providing a benchmark for its intrinsic value.

Assessing Revenue Growth and Profitability

A thorough assessment of a company's revenue growth and profitability is crucial. Investment bankers analyze historical data and forecast future performance based on market conditions and company-specific factors.

Example: If a company has consistently grown its revenues by 15% annually and has plans to expand into new markets, this growth trajectory is factored into the valuation.

Evaluating Market Potential and Competitive Edge

Investment bankers consider a company's market potential and competitive advantages. They assess factors like intellectual property, brand strength, and customer loyalty, which can significantly impact the company's valuation.

Example: A biotech company with a strong patent portfolio and a promising pipeline of new drugs may receive a higher valuation due to its potential for future growth and revenue generation.

Transaction Execution: Facilitating Smooth and Successful Deals

Creating Investment Memorandums and Pitch Materials

Investment bankers prepare comprehensive documents, including investment memorandums and pitch decks, to present the investment opportunity to potential investors. These documents provide detailed information about the target company, including its financials, market position, and strategic rationale for the investment.

Example: A well-crafted investment memorandum might include detailed financial projections, an analysis of market trends, and a discussion of the potential synergies the acquisition could bring.

Negotiating Terms and Structuring Deals

Investment bankers are instrumental in negotiating the terms of the deal, ensuring that the structure is beneficial for both the investor and the target company. This includes negotiating the purchase price, payment structure, and other critical terms.

Example: In a leveraged buyout (LBO), investment bankers might negotiate favorable debt financing terms to reduce the overall cost of capital for the acquisition.

Overseeing the Closing Process

Investment bankers manage the entire closing process, coordinating with legal, financial, and regulatory teams to ensure that all aspects of the deal are completed smoothly. This includes finalizing agreements, transferring funds, and ensuring compliance with all legal requirements.

Example: Ensuring that all necessary regulatory approvals are obtained and that the terms of the sale are clearly defined and agreed upon by all parties.

Market Insight and Timing: Enhancing Investment Returns

Providing Market Trends and Economic Analysis

Investment bankers provide ongoing market insights, keeping investors informed about economic indicators, market trends, and industry-specific developments. This information is crucial for making informed decisions about the timing of investments.

Example: Advising on the best time to enter the market based on current economic conditions and market sentiment, such as waiting for a downturn to acquire assets at a lower price.

Developing Entry and Exit Strategies

Investment bankers help investors develop strategies for both entering and exiting investments. They analyze market conditions, competitive dynamics, and valuation trends to identify optimal entry and exit points.

Example: Recommending a strategic acquisition during a market dip and planning an exit through an IPO during a market upswing.

Performance Monitoring and Exit Planning

Post-investment, investment bankers continue to provide support by monitoring the performance of the investment and assisting with exit planning. They track key performance indicators and advise on the best exit strategy, whether through a sale, IPO, or other means.

Example: Monitoring a company's progress and advising on an exit strategy when the company reaches a certain valuation or market condition.

Post-Investment Support: Ensuring Continued Success

Ongoing Market Updates and Performance Monitoring

Investment bankers keep investors updated with regular market reports and performance analysis, helping them stay informed about their investment's progress and market conditions.

Example: Providing quarterly reports that include financial performance, market analysis, and updates on strategic initiatives.

Identifying Value Creation Opportunities

Investment bankers help identify opportunities to create additional value within the portfolio company. This can include identifying operational improvements, exploring new markets, or pursuing further acquisitions.

Example: Suggesting ways to improve operational efficiency, such as streamlining supply chain processes or investing in new technologies.

Planning and Executing Exits

Investment bankers assist in planning and executing exit strategies, ensuring that investors can realize their returns. They help prepare the company for sale, including optimizing its financial performance and positioning it attractively to potential buyers.

Example: Preparing a company for an IPO by improving financial transparency, strengthening corporate governance, and building a compelling growth story.

Conclusion

Investment bankers are integral to sourcing high return opportunities for strategic and financial investors. They provide a comprehensive suite of services, from deal origination and due diligence to valuation, transaction execution, and post-investment support. Their expertise in market analysis, financial modeling, and negotiation ensures that investors can access the best opportunities and maximize their returns. Through their continued engagement, investment bankers help investors navigate the complexities of the market, manage risks, and achieve their investment objectives.

PART VII: ORIGINATION & PITCHING STRATEGIC ALTERNATIVES

Chapter 48: Origination & Pitching Strategic Alternatives

Origination & Pitching Strategic Alternatives in Investment Banking: A Detailed Guide

Origination is a core function in investment banking that involves sourcing and identifying potential opportunities for transactions, whether for buy-side engagements or structuring sell-side engagements. This blog post delves into the intricacies of origination in investment banking, focusing on the processes, strategies, and methodologies involved. It covers building buy-side relationships, identifying buy-side opportunities, structuring sell-side engagements, maintaining a deal pipeline, leveraging networks and market intelligence, customizing solutions for clients, and continuous monitoring and evaluation.

Building Buy-Side Relationships

Establishing Connections

Investment bankers start by establishing connections with potential buy-side partners, such as private equity firms, strategic buyers, and other institutional investors. This involves understanding their investment criteria, such as preferred industries, company sizes, and geographic focus.

- **Investment Criteria**: For instance, a private equity firm may focus on technology companies with revenues between $50 million and $200 million. Understanding these specifics helps bankers target the right opportunities.
- **Strategic Goals**: Some buyers may look for market expansion, while others may seek to acquire innovative technologies.

Engagement Activities

Regular engagement activities are crucial for maintaining strong relationships. This includes attending industry conferences, hosting meetings, and participating in networking events. Such interactions help bankers stay updated on the evolving investment strategies and preferences of their partners.

- **Industry Conferences**: Events like industry summits provide an opportunity for bankers to connect with multiple potential buyers in a focused setting.

- **Networking**: Maintaining a presence in relevant professional circles allows bankers to stay informed about market trends and potential deals.

Valuable Insights

These engagements provide bankers with valuable insights into the investment strategies of their partners. This knowledge enables them to align their origination efforts with the specific needs and interests of their clients, making it easier to match buyers with suitable opportunities.

- **Example**: Knowing that a particular private equity firm is interested in companies focused on sustainable technologies can guide bankers to prioritize deals in that sector.

Identifying Buy-Side Opportunities

Proactive Sourcing

Origination requires proactive sourcing of opportunities. Investment bankers must continuously identify potential acquisition targets that align with the investment mandates of their buy-side partners.

- **Market Analysis**: Regular analysis of market trends, industry reports, and financial statements helps identify potential targets.
- **Company Screening**: Screening for companies based on financial performance, market positioning, and growth potential is a critical step.

Research and Analysis

Comprehensive research and analysis are necessary to evaluate potential targets. This includes financial performance reviews, growth potential assessments, and competitive landscape analysis.

- **Financial Metrics**: Key metrics like EBITDA, revenue growth, and profit margins are analyzed to gauge the financial health of a target company.
- **Strategic Fit**: Bankers also assess how well a target fits with the buyer's strategic goals, such as market expansion or technology acquisition.

Target Evaluation

Evaluating potential targets involves using various tools and methodologies to assess their viability. This may include financial modeling, valuation analysis, and due diligence.

- **Valuation Methods**: Techniques like discounted cash flow (DCF) analysis, comparable company analysis, and precedent transactions help determine the target's value.
- **Due Diligence**: Thorough investigation into a company's operations, financials, and legal standing is essential to identify any potential risks.

Structuring Sell-Side Engagements

Assessing Suitability

For sell-side engagements, investment bankers assess whether a company is ready for sale. They consider factors such as the company's financial health, market conditions, and strategic objectives of the owners.

- **Financial Health**: Reviewing the company's financial statements, cash flow, and debt levels to assess stability.
- **Market Timing**: Evaluating whether the current market conditions are favorable for a sale.

Positioning for Sale

Once a company is identified as a suitable sell-side candidate, bankers work on positioning it for sale. This includes preparing marketing materials, conducting valuations, and identifying potential buyers.

- **Information Memorandums**: Detailed documents that provide comprehensive information about the company, including its financial performance, market position, and growth prospects.
- **Buyer Identification**: Identifying and reaching out to potential buyers who would be interested in the company's assets or market position.

Marketing the Deal

Creating compelling marketing materials is crucial. These materials must highlight the company's strengths, market position, and future potential to attract potential buyers.

- **Pitch Books**: Customized presentations that include key financials, market analysis, and strategic opportunities.
- **Narrative Development**: Crafting a compelling story around the company's value proposition.

Maintaining a Full Deal Pipeline

Consistent Deal Flow

Maintaining a robust deal pipeline ensures a consistent flow of potential transactions. Investment bankers must continuously source and evaluate new opportunities to keep the pipeline full.

- **Active Sourcing**: Continuously looking for new opportunities in the market to add to the pipeline.
- **Pipeline Management**: Regularly reviewing the pipeline to prioritize the most promising deals.

Increasing Success Rates

A well-managed deal pipeline increases the likelihood of successful transactions. It allows bankers to focus on high-quality opportunities and ensures they are prepared to act quickly when opportunities arise.

- **Deal Prioritization**: Focusing on deals with the highest potential for success.
- **Responsive Strategy**: Quickly adjusting strategies based on market conditions and client needs.

Leveraging Networks and Market Intelligence

Building Strong Networks

Building and maintaining strong networks with industry insiders, entrepreneurs, and other intermediaries is essential. These networks can provide access to off-market deals and exclusive opportunities.

- **Industry Contacts**: Leveraging relationships with key industry players to gain insights into potential deals.

- **Confidentiality and Trust**: Maintaining the trust of these contacts is crucial for accessing sensitive information.

Market Insights

Staying informed about market trends and insights is critical. This includes understanding economic indicators, regulatory changes, and industry shifts.

- **Economic Analysis**: Monitoring macroeconomic trends that could impact market conditions.
- **Regulatory Environment**: Keeping abreast of changes in regulations that could affect the feasibility of transactions.

Proprietary Deals

Access to proprietary deals provides a competitive advantage. These deals are often not widely known and can offer more favorable terms.

- **Exclusive Opportunities**: Deals that are not publicly advertised and are accessible only through direct relationships.
- **Lower Competition**: Less competition for these deals can result in better terms and valuations.

Customizing Solutions for Clients

Tailoring Solutions

Investment bankers must customize solutions to meet the unique needs of their clients. This involves developing creative deal structures and financial strategies that align with the client's objectives.

- **Customized Financial Structures**: Creating tailored financial structures, such as hybrid financing or leveraged buyouts, to meet specific client needs.
- **Strategic Alignment**: Ensuring that the proposed solutions align with the client's strategic goals, whether it's expansion, diversification, or consolidation.

Synergistic Acquisitions

Identifying acquisition targets that provide synergies is key. This includes looking for companies that can offer operational efficiencies, market expansion, or technological advancements.

- **Operational Synergies**: Opportunities to reduce costs or improve efficiency through integration.
- **Market Synergies**: Expanding the client's market reach or customer base.

Exploring Divestitures

Investment bankers also assist clients in exploring divestiture opportunities. This involves identifying non-core assets that can be sold to streamline operations and focus on core competencies.

- **Asset Valuation**: Assessing the value of non-core assets to determine the potential proceeds from a sale.
- **Strategic Divestment**: Identifying the best timing and method for divestment to maximize value.

Strategic Partnerships

Facilitating strategic partnerships, such as joint ventures or alliances, is another way to add value. These partnerships can provide access to new markets, technologies, or expertise.

- **Partnership Structuring**: Structuring partnerships that align with both parties' strategic goals and provide mutual benefits.
- **Negotiation and Agreement**: Facilitating negotiations and drafting agreements to formalize the partnership.

Continuous Monitoring and Evaluation

Ongoing Process

Origination is a continuous process that requires constant monitoring and evaluation. Investment bankers must stay vigilant to changing market conditions and client needs.

- **Market Monitoring**: Regularly updating market analysis and financial models based on the latest data.
- **Client Needs Assessment**: Continuously assessing client needs and adjusting strategies accordingly.

Performance Tracking

Tracking the performance of deals and client portfolios is essential. This involves monitoring the progress of ongoing transactions and evaluating the outcomes of completed deals.

- **KPI Monitoring**: Tracking key performance indicators to assess the success of transactions.
- **Client Reporting**: Providing clients with regular updates and insights into the performance of their investments.

Adaptive Strategies

Investment bankers must adapt their strategies in response to market changes and client feedback. This flexibility ensures that they remain relevant and effective in delivering value.

- **Strategy Adjustment**: Modifying origination strategies to align with new market conditions or emerging trends.
- **Feedback Incorporation**: Incorporating client feedback to improve service delivery and client satisfaction.

Conclusion

Origination and pitching strategic alternatives are vital functions in investment banking. They involve a complex blend of relationship-building, market analysis, financial acumen, and strategic insight. Investment bankers play a critical role in creating value for their clients by identifying and executing high-quality opportunities. By maintaining a robust deal pipeline, leveraging extensive networks, and continuously adapting to market conditions, they ensure that their clients have access to the best possible strategic alternatives. This ongoing effort not only drives successful transactions but also fosters long-term client relationships and sustained growth in the competitive world of investment banking.

NOTES:

Why Origination?

Once we have built out buy side relationships within our coverage area, we then begin to source targets for our buy side partners. Origination is the primary work of the investment banker in order to keep the pipeline of deals full.

We can source targets for buy side engagements or structure a sell side engagement if appropriate.

Origination Process

1. Identifying Decision Makers
2. The Cycle of Origination
3. Initial Outreach
4. Preparing for the Pitch
5. Pitching

Chapter 49: Identifying Decision Makers

Identifying Decision Makers in Investment Banking: A Comprehensive Guide

Identifying the key decision-makers within target companies is a critical aspect of investment banking, especially when exploring strategic alternatives such as mergers, acquisitions, or partnerships. This process requires a deep understanding of the company's ownership structure, management team, and internal governance. This blog post delves into the methodologies and importance of accurately identifying decision-makers, distinguishing between owners and management, and effectively engaging with the appropriate stakeholders.

Analyzing Ownership Structure

Importance of Understanding Ownership

Analyzing the ownership structure of a target company is fundamental to understanding the distribution of power and influence. This analysis provides insights into who holds significant sway over major strategic decisions, which is crucial for effectively navigating discussions about potential deals.

Types of Ownership Structures

1. **Family-Owned Businesses**:
   - **Decision-Making Dynamics**: In family-owned businesses, decision-making often rests with a few key family members. Understanding these family dynamics is crucial for identifying who truly controls the company's strategic direction.
   - **Strategic Considerations**: Family businesses may prioritize legacy and long-term stability over short-term profits, influencing their openness to strategic alternatives.
2. **Publicly Traded Companies**:
   - **Complex Governance**: These companies have a more complex governance structure involving boards of directors, institutional investors, and sometimes activist shareholders.
   - **Identifying Influencers**: Major shareholders, including institutional investors, often hold significant voting power and can influence major decisions like mergers or acquisitions.
3. **Private Equity-Backed Firms**:
   - **Dual Influences**: Decision-making is typically shared between the management team and private equity investors. The investors' priorities often include achieving high returns within a specific timeframe, which can drive strategic decisions.
   - **Key Players**: Understanding the private equity firm's investment thesis and exit strategy is essential for aligning proposals with their goals.

4. **Closely Held Corporations**:
   - ○ **Direct Involvement**: A small group of shareholders who are actively involved in the business often make major strategic decisions. These individuals may be founders or long-term employees with deep ties to the company.

Methodology for Analyzing Ownership

- **Review Public Filings**: Documents like SEC filings, annual reports, and proxy statements can reveal ownership stakes and the identity of significant shareholders.
- **Use Industry Databases**: Tools such as Capital IQ, Bloomberg, and FactSet provide detailed ownership and historical information.
- **Understand Company History**: Examining past ownership changes and strategic shifts can offer insights into current power dynamics.

Identifying Owners

Importance of Identifying Owners

Owners often have the final say in strategic decisions. Engaging directly with them can accelerate the decision-making process and provide a clear understanding of the company's strategic priorities.

Steps to Identify Owners

1. **In-Depth Research**:
   - ○ **Data Sources**: Use SEC filings, private company databases, and industry reports to identify major shareholders and their influence on the company.
2. **Shareholder Registers**:

- Detailed Information: Shareholder registers provide
  contact information and the extent of ownership,
  crucial for understanding who holds power.
3. **Institutional Investors**:
  - **Strategic Influence**: These investors often have
    significant influence and can drive or block strategic
    decisions based on their investment strategies.

Engagement Strategy

- **Direct Communication Channels**: Establishing direct lines
  of communication with owners is crucial. Tailoring
  communication to address their specific interests and concerns
  helps build rapport and trust.
- **Customized Messaging**: Communication should be
  personalized, highlighting how proposed strategic alternatives
  align with the owners' goals and values.

Mapping the Management Team

Importance of the Management Team

The management team, especially the CEO, CFO, and other senior
executives, plays a vital role in the company's strategic direction and
operational management. Understanding their roles and influence helps
in targeting the right individuals for discussions about strategic
alternatives.

Steps to Map the Management Team

1. **Identify Key Executives**:
  - **Key Figures**: Focus on top executives who are likely
    to have a significant impact on strategic decisions.

Gather detailed information about their backgrounds, responsibilities, and influence within the company.

2. **Understand Roles and Responsibilities**:
   - **Detailed Profiles**: Understanding each executive's specific role helps tailor engagement strategies. For example, the CFO's approval may be crucial for financial aspects of a deal, while the COO may provide insights into operational implications.

3. **Use Public Sources**:
   - **Gather Information**: Utilize company websites, press releases, LinkedIn profiles, and industry publications to collect comprehensive data on the management team.

Engagement Strategy

- **Personalized Communication**: Develop communication strategies that cater to the interests and responsibilities of each executive.
- **Initial Meetings**: Arrange introductory meetings to discuss potential opportunities and gauge the management team's interest and openness to strategic changes.

Leveraging Industry Networks and Contacts

Benefits of Industry Networks

Utilizing industry networks and contacts is invaluable for gathering insider information and facilitating introductions to key decision-makers. These networks can provide access to exclusive deal flow and confidential insights.

Approach

1. **Networking Events**:
   - ○ **Opportunities for Engagement**: Attending industry-specific events can provide opportunities to meet potential contacts and discuss market trends and potential deals.
2. **Industry Associations**:
   - ○ **Active Participation**: Joining relevant industry associations can help build relationships and gain access to exclusive reports and events.
3. **Professional Networks**:
   - ○ **Leveraging LinkedIn**: Using professional networking platforms like LinkedIn can help connect with industry professionals, engage in discussions, and stay updated on relevant news and trends.

Strategy

- **Building Relationships**: Cultivating and maintaining relationships within the industry is essential for gaining introductions to key decision-makers.
- **Gaining Referrals**: Personal recommendations from trusted contacts can facilitate introductions and establish credibility with potential targets.

Engaging in Preliminary Outreach

Purpose of Initial Outreach

Initial outreach is crucial for setting the stage for deeper engagement and discussion. It serves to establish initial contact, express interest, and lay the groundwork for future discussions.

Approach

1. **Crafting Messages**:
   - **Targeted Communication**: Develop messages that are specifically tailored to the interests and concerns of each decision-maker.
2. **Introductory Emails**:
   - **Concise and Compelling**: Emails should clearly state the purpose of the outreach, the potential benefits of engaging, and a call to action for further discussion.
3. **Follow-Up Calls**:
   - **Personal Connection**: Follow-up calls can reinforce the initial message and help establish a personal connection.
4. **Face-to-Face Meetings**:
   - **Building Rapport**: In-person meetings, where possible, help build stronger relationships and facilitate more detailed discussions.

Best Practices

- **Highlighting Expertise**: Demonstrating a deep understanding of the target company's industry and challenges can build credibility.
- **Articulating Value**: Clearly outlining the potential benefits of engaging in strategic discussions helps capture the interest of decision-makers.

Conclusion

Summary: Identifying the right decision-makers within target companies is a critical step in engaging effectively about strategic alternatives. This involves a comprehensive understanding of the ownership structure, mapping the management team, leveraging industry networks, and crafting targeted communication strategies.

Value Creation: Effective engagement with the correct stakeholders can lead to successful transactions, alignment of strategic interests, and value creation for all parties involved. By following these detailed methodologies, investment bankers can enhance their effectiveness in facilitating strategic discussions and transactions.

NOTES:
Identifying Decision Makers
After pulling a list of target companies within our coverage area consistent with buy side mandates, we need to get an understanding of the ownership structure of the target companies:
Owner vs. Management team

Owner vs. Management team
Obtaining contact information for the appropriate decision makers:
1. Rocketreach
2. Salesgenie
3. FastPeopleSearch or PeopleSearchNow

Chapter 50: The Cycle of Origination

The Comprehensive Cycle of Origination in Investment Banking

Origination in investment banking is a multifaceted and continuous process that involves establishing, nurturing, and maintaining relationships with clients and prospects. It is crucial for sourcing deals, pitching strategic alternatives, and managing transactions. This blog post provides an in-depth look into each phase of the origination cycle, detailing the methodologies and activities involved, and highlighting their significance in the investment banking landscape.

1. Establishing Sell-Side Relationships

Initial Outreach

Objective:
The initial step in the origination process is to establish contact with potential clients. The primary objective is to explore possible collaboration opportunities and set the groundwork for a strong professional relationship.

Market Updates:
Investment bankers initiate contact by providing potential clients with market updates. These updates cover essential information on the current state of mergers and acquisitions (M&A), capital markets, and industry-specific trends. For example, an investment banker might present a comprehensive report on recent M&A activity in the technology sector, highlighting key transactions and emerging trends that could influence the client's strategic decisions.

Demonstrating Expertise:
Sharing detailed market analyses demonstrates the investment banker's expertise and understanding of the market. By providing insights into recent transactions, regulatory changes, and economic conditions, bankers establish themselves as knowledgeable advisors who can add value to the client's decision-making process.

Building Credibility

Regular Communication:
Maintaining consistent and proactive communication with potential clients is crucial. This includes sending regular newsletters, market reports, and updates that keep the client informed about the latest trends and opportunities. For example, a quarterly newsletter might cover the impact of macroeconomic changes on industry valuations and the potential implications for strategic planning.

Engagement:
Investment bankers engage in active dialogue with potential clients through meetings, conference calls, and presentations. These engagements allow bankers to discuss market developments and how they might affect the client's business, further establishing trust and rapport.

2. Providing Market Insights

Ongoing Relationship Development

Continuous Updates:
Investment bankers must provide continuous updates on market trends and developments. This involves sharing insights into market dynamics, such as shifts in consumer preferences, technological advancements, and competitive pressures.

Insightful Reports:
Regularly providing insightful reports, such as industry overviews or market forecasts, helps the client stay informed and make strategic decisions. For example, an investment banker might deliver a detailed report on the healthcare industry, highlighting key growth areas and potential risks.

Positioning as Advisors:
By consistently delivering valuable insights and strategic advice, investment bankers position themselves as trusted advisors. This ongoing advisory role helps in building a strong, long-term relationship with the client.

Establishing Trust

Thought Leadership:
Investment bankers establish themselves as thought leaders by publishing whitepapers, research articles, and analysis pieces that provide deep insights into industry trends and strategic considerations.

Tailored Insights:
Customizing insights to address the specific challenges and goals of the client enhances the relevance and impact of the advice provided. This could involve tailored reports that assess the potential impact of regulatory changes on the client's business operations.

3. Pitching Strategic Alternatives

Tailored Pitches

Opportunity Identification:
Once a relationship is established, investment bankers begin identifying and pitching strategic alternatives. This involves understanding the client's strategic objectives and identifying opportunities that align with these goals.

In-Depth Analysis:
Bankers conduct thorough analyses, including financial modeling, SWOT analysis, and valuation assessments, to build a compelling case for the proposed strategic alternatives. For instance, a banker might develop a detailed model demonstrating the financial benefits of a potential merger.

Customized Presentations:
The presentations are tailored to the specific needs and objectives of the client, ensuring that the proposed alternatives are relevant and actionable. For example, a customized presentation for a retail company might focus on the benefits of acquiring a complementary e-commerce business.

Building a Case

Strategic Alignment:
Demonstrating how the proposed alternatives align with the client's long-term strategic goals is crucial. This involves clearly articulating how the proposed transaction can enhance market position, improve operational efficiency, or unlock new revenue streams.

Risk and Reward Analysis:
Providing a balanced analysis of the potential risks and rewards

associated with each alternative helps the client understand the implications of each option and make informed decisions.

4. Relationship Building Activities

Fostering Connections

Informal Gatherings:
Investment bankers often engage with clients in informal settings, such as lunches, dinners, or industry events. These interactions provide an opportunity to discuss business in a more relaxed environment and strengthen personal relationships.

Understanding Needs:
Informal gatherings allow bankers to gain deeper insights into the client's business, challenges, and strategic priorities. This understanding is critical for tailoring advice and recommendations.

Commitment:
Regular, meaningful interactions demonstrate the banker's commitment to understanding the client's business and long-term goals, further solidifying the relationship.

5. Navigating Due Diligence

Thorough Evaluation

Due Diligence Phase:
If the client expresses interest in a proposed strategic alternative, the process moves into due diligence. This phase involves a comprehensive evaluation of the target company's financial health, market position, operational capabilities, and legal standing.

Collaborative Effort:
Investment bankers work closely with the client's management team and external advisors to conduct thorough due diligence, identifying any potential issues that could impact the transaction.

Identifying Obstacles:
The due diligence process helps identify potential obstacles or risks, allowing the banker to address these issues proactively and ensure a smooth transaction process.

Guidance and Support

Addressing Concerns:
Investment bankers provide guidance and support throughout the due diligence process, helping the client navigate any challenges and make informed decisions.

Detailed Analysis:
Conducting a detailed analysis ensures that all aspects of the target's operations and market position are thoroughly evaluated.

6. Negotiating and Executing the Transaction

Deal Structuring

Negotiation Phase:
Following due diligence, bankers play a key role in negotiating the transaction terms. This includes finalizing the deal structure, determining the purchase price, and establishing payment terms.

Preparation:
Bankers prepare detailed financial models and valuation analyses to support the negotiation process, ensuring that the deal terms are fair and favorable.

Transaction Terms:
Negotiating transaction terms involves working closely with both parties to reach an agreement that aligns with their respective objectives.

Transaction Management

Coordination:
Investment bankers coordinate with legal, tax, and other advisors to ensure that all aspects of the transaction are addressed and that regulatory requirements are met.

Smooth Execution:
Managing the transaction process involves overseeing timelines, ensuring that all documentation is completed accurately, and maintaining clear communication with all stakeholders.

7. Maintaining Post-Transaction Relationships

Ongoing Engagement

Post-Transaction Phase:
Maintaining relationships post-transaction is crucial for future engagements. Investment bankers continue to provide market updates, strategic advice, and support as the client integrates the new assets or business.

Regular Communication:
Providing ongoing updates and staying engaged with the client ensures that the relationship remains strong and that the banker remains a trusted advisor.

Building Long-Term Partnerships:
By continuing to offer valuable insights and support, bankers position

themselves as long-term partners, paving the way for future transactions and collaborations.

Future Opportunities

Continued Support:
Investment bankers offer ongoing strategic advice and support, helping clients identify new growth opportunities or further strategic initiatives.

Client Retention:
Strong post-transaction relationships often lead to future engagements and referrals, contributing to the banker's reputation and success.

Conclusion

The cycle of origination in investment banking is a continuous process that involves building relationships, providing market insights, pitching strategic alternatives, and managing transactions. Each phase is critical for establishing trust, demonstrating expertise, and ensuring successful outcomes. Investment bankers play a pivotal role in guiding clients through the complexities of the financial markets, providing tailored advice and solutions that align with their strategic goals. Through consistent engagement and a deep understanding of their clients' needs, investment bankers build long-lasting relationships that drive success and create value.

NOTES:
The Cycle of Origination
In order to properly originate deals, we need to establish sell side relationships by giving market updates to executives, telling them what is going on in the M&A and capital markets. As the relationship is established, you can then pitch them strategic alternatives including selling their company.

Throughout the relationship building process, there will be lunches and dinners to catch up on what the target has been doing and their strategic plans.

Initial Outreach
1. Email origination strategy
2. Open to exploring strategic alternatives?
3. Exploratory Call
4. Introduction
5. Explaining coverage & buy side relationships
6. Timeline for an exit
7. Exploring strategic alternatives
8. Target valuation

Chapter 51: Pitching Strategic Alternatives

Pitching Strategic Alternatives: A Detailed Guide

Introduction: The Importance of Pitching Strategic Alternatives

Pitching strategic alternatives is a critical function in investment banking. This process involves presenting potential pathways to clients that can enhance their business's value, achieve growth objectives, or address specific challenges. Investment bankers use their expertise to propose well-considered options, backed by thorough analysis and market insights. The goal is to guide clients toward making informed strategic decisions that align with their long-term goals.

1. Establishing a Strong Rapport with the Client

Initial Engagement: Building a Foundation

- **Listening and Understanding**: The first step in any pitch meeting is to deeply understand the client's business, challenges, and goals. This involves active listening, where bankers not only hear but also comprehend the client's vision and concerns.
- **Setting the Tone**: By starting the meeting with questions that invite the client to share their thoughts, bankers create a collaborative atmosphere. This sets the stage for a productive dialogue where the client feels valued and understood.

Demonstrating Empathy: Recognizing Client Challenges

- **Acknowledging Challenges**: Investment bankers acknowledge the specific challenges faced by the client, whether these are market competition, regulatory hurdles, or internal operational issues. This acknowledgment shows that the banker has done their homework and is genuinely concerned with finding solutions.
- **Expressing Commitment**: Expressing a strong commitment to helping the client overcome these challenges reinforces the banker's role as a trusted advisor. For example, a banker might say, "We understand that navigating regulatory complexities can be daunting. Our team is here to guide you through these intricacies."

2. Detailed Analysis of Industry and Market Dynamics

Industry Assessment: Laying the Groundwork

- **In-Depth Analysis**: Investment bankers provide a thorough overview of the industry, including current trends, competitive dynamics, and regulatory environments. This assessment helps the client see where their company stands relative to the market.
- **Future Outlook**: Discussing the potential future scenarios in the industry helps the client understand how external factors might impact their business. For example, an analysis of upcoming regulatory changes could indicate potential challenges or opportunities.

*Market Dynamics and Competitive Landscape:**

- **Market Trends**: Identifying and explaining key trends, such as technological advancements or changes in consumer behavior, provides context for the strategic alternatives being proposed.

- **Competitive Positioning**: Analyzing the client's competitive position involves examining their market share, strengths, and weaknesses compared to competitors. This helps in identifying areas where the client can leverage their advantages or mitigate vulnerabilities.

3. Proposing Strategic Alternatives: Crafting the Proposal

*Identifying and Explaining Alternatives:**

- **Range of Options**: Presenting a range of strategic alternatives, from organic growth opportunities to potential acquisitions or mergers, provides the client with a spectrum of possibilities. Each option should be clearly defined, with a thorough explanation of how it aligns with the client's goals.
- **Strategic Fit**: For each alternative, bankers explain how it fits into the client's overall strategy. For example, if the client aims to expand into new markets, the banker might suggest an acquisition of a company with a strong presence in the desired region.

*Supporting Data and Evidence:**

- **Financial Projections**: Detailed financial models and projections are used to illustrate the potential outcomes of each alternative. These models include assumptions, expected cash flows, and valuation impacts.
- **Case Studies and Market Research**: Presenting case studies of similar companies that have successfully implemented similar strategies can help illustrate potential outcomes. Additionally, market research provides quantitative support for the proposed alternatives.

4. Addressing Concerns and Mitigating Risks: Transparent Communication

Identifying Risks and Challenges:*

- **Comprehensive Risk Analysis**: For each proposed alternative, bankers conduct a thorough risk assessment, identifying potential pitfalls such as market volatility, integration challenges, or financial risks.
- **Open Discussion**: Encouraging an open discussion about these risks allows the client to voice their concerns. This transparency helps build trust and shows that the banker is not only interested in pitching a deal but also in safeguarding the client's interests.

Mitigation Strategies:*

- **Proactive Solutions**: Bankers propose concrete strategies to mitigate identified risks. For example, they might suggest hedging strategies to protect against market volatility or phased integration plans to manage the complexities of mergers.
- **Contingency Planning**: Developing contingency plans for various scenarios ensures that the client is prepared for unexpected challenges. This proactive approach helps the client feel more secure about making a strategic move.

5. Emphasizing Long-Term Partnership and Support

Ongoing Advisory Role:*

- **Beyond the Transaction**: Investment bankers emphasize their role as long-term partners, offering ongoing support and advisory services. This includes regular updates on market conditions, continued financial analysis, and strategic advice.

- **Access to Resources**: Bankers also highlight their ability to connect clients with valuable resources, such as potential partners, investors, or specialized consultants.

*Commitment to Client Success:**

- **Demonstrating Value**: By showing a commitment to the client's long-term success, bankers position themselves as indispensable advisors. This commitment is demonstrated through continuous engagement, tailored advice, and a genuine interest in helping the client achieve their strategic objectives.

Conclusion: Guiding Strategic Decisions

Investment bankers play a critical role in guiding clients through complex strategic decisions. By thoroughly analyzing the market, presenting well-researched alternatives, and addressing potential risks, they help clients make informed choices that align with their long-term goals. The process of pitching strategic alternatives is not just about closing a deal but about building a lasting partnership based on trust, expertise, and mutual success. Through a comprehensive and empathetic approach, investment bankers ensure that their clients are well-prepared to navigate the complexities of strategic decision-making and achieve their desired outcomes.

Preparing for the Pitch

From the initial exploratory call we are going to gather information at a high level in order to prepare a formal presentation exploring their strategic alternatives and what the sell side process would look like. Preparing the pitchbook occurs here as well.

Pitching

Walking the DMs through the pitchbook in order to explore what a sell side process would look like:

1. Timeline
2. Likely buyers
3. M&A landscape
4. Valuation

Investment Banking University
All Rights Reserved

Chapter 52: Strategic Management & the Investment Banker

Pitching Strategic Alternatives in Investment Banking

Pitching strategic alternatives is a fundamental aspect of investment banking, where bankers present various strategic options to their clients, typically companies looking to achieve growth, optimize operations, or enhance shareholder value. This process is comprehensive and involves several key steps, each requiring careful consideration and detailed analysis. In this blog post, we will delve into the nuanced process of pitching strategic alternatives, focusing on the preparation, presentation, and follow-up stages.

Building the Foundation: Understanding Client Needs

Initial Client Engagement

Listening to Understand: The process begins with an in-depth understanding of the client's needs, goals, and current challenges. Investment bankers start by engaging in conversations with the client's management team to gain insights into their strategic objectives. This involves asking detailed questions about their long-term vision, short-term goals, and specific issues they are facing. For example, a company may be looking to expand into new markets, improve profitability, or exit a non-core business segment.

Demonstrating Empathy and Expertise: During these discussions, investment bankers demonstrate their understanding of the client's business and industry. They acknowledge the client's challenges and convey their expertise in navigating similar situations. This establishes the banker's credibility and positions them as a trusted advisor. For instance, a banker might reference past experience in handling similar transactions in the same industry, showcasing their knowledge and reassuring the client of their capability.

Detailed Analysis and Market Assessment

Comprehensive Industry Analysis

Market Dynamics and Trends: Investment bankers conduct a thorough analysis of the industry in which the client operates. This includes examining market trends, regulatory changes, competitive dynamics, and technological advancements. For example, in the healthcare industry, bankers might analyze trends in telemedicine adoption, regulatory shifts affecting pharmaceutical pricing, and the competitive landscape of healthcare providers.

Competitive Landscape and Positioning: Understanding the client's position relative to its competitors is crucial. Investment bankers assess the strengths and weaknesses of the client's competitors, their market share, and recent strategic moves. This information helps in identifying areas where the client can gain a competitive advantage. For instance, if competitors are investing heavily in digital transformation, the client may need to consider similar investments to remain competitive.

Financial Analysis and Modeling

Valuation and Financial Health: Bankers perform a detailed financial analysis, including valuation assessments, profitability analysis, and financial health checks. This involves creating financial models that project future revenues, expenses, and cash flows based on different scenarios. They also evaluate key financial metrics such as EBITDA margins, return on equity, and debt-to-equity ratios. For example, they might analyze how a potential acquisition could impact the client's financial position and shareholder value.

Scenario Analysis: Scenario analysis is a critical component of the financial assessment. Investment bankers model various scenarios, such as the impact of economic downturns, changes in consumer behavior, or competitive actions. This helps in understanding the potential risks and rewards associated with each strategic alternative. For instance, they may project the financial outcomes of expanding into a new geographic market versus launching a new product line.

Crafting the Pitch: Presenting Strategic Alternatives

Identifying and Proposing Alternatives

Strategic Options: Based on the analysis, investment bankers identify a range of strategic alternatives that align with the client's goals. These can include organic growth strategies like expanding product lines or geographic markets, and inorganic strategies such as mergers, acquisitions, joint ventures, or divestitures. For instance, a technology company might be presented with options to acquire a smaller competitor, enter a new international market, or form a strategic partnership for product development.

Rationale and Justification: Each strategic alternative is presented with a clear rationale. Bankers explain why a particular strategy is recommended, supported by data and analysis. They discuss how the alternative aligns with the client's strategic goals, such as enhancing market share, diversifying revenue streams, or improving operational efficiency. For example, if the recommendation is to acquire a competitor, bankers might highlight potential cost synergies, expanded customer base, and enhanced technological capabilities.

Supporting the Pitch with Evidence

Data-Driven Insights

Financial Projections and Case Studies: To substantiate their recommendations, bankers provide detailed financial projections, supported by market research and case studies. These projections illustrate potential revenue growth, cost savings, and profitability improvements. Case studies from similar transactions are used to demonstrate potential outcomes and reassure the client of the feasibility of the proposed strategies. For example, a case study might show how a previous client successfully integrated an acquisition, achieving significant cost reductions and market expansion.

Risk Assessment and Mitigation Strategies: Investment bankers also address potential risks associated with each strategic alternative. They discuss possible financial, operational, and market risks, and propose mitigation strategies. This includes identifying key risk factors and providing contingency plans to manage them. For instance, they might discuss the risks of entering a new market, such as regulatory hurdles and cultural differences, and suggest ways to navigate these challenges.

Engaging in Dialogue: Addressing Client Concerns

Interactive Discussion

Open Communication: During the pitch, bankers encourage open dialogue, inviting the client to ask questions and express concerns. This interactive approach helps clarify any uncertainties and provides an opportunity for the bankers to further explain their recommendations. For example, if the client is concerned about the integration challenges of an acquisition, bankers can discuss their experience in managing post-merger integration and outline a detailed plan.

Customization and Flexibility: Investment bankers are prepared to customize their recommendations based on the client's feedback. They show flexibility in their approach, offering tailored solutions that best meet the client's unique needs and preferences. For example, if the client prefers a less aggressive growth strategy, bankers might shift the focus from acquisitions to organic growth initiatives.

Concluding the Pitch: Emphasizing Long-Term Partnership

Long-Term Advisory Role

Commitment to Ongoing Support: Investment bankers emphasize their commitment to supporting the client beyond the immediate transaction. They position themselves as long-term partners, offering ongoing advisory services, market insights, and strategic guidance. This commitment reassures the client of continued support in implementing the chosen strategic alternative and adapting to future challenges.

Building a Partnership: The relationship does not end with the pitch. Bankers continue to provide valuable insights and support, helping clients navigate the complexities of executing the chosen strategies. This includes assisting with negotiations, securing financing, and managing post-transaction integration. For example, bankers might help the client negotiate terms with potential partners or investors and oversee the integration process after a merger.

Conclusion: Inspiring Confidence and Driving Strategic Decisions

Inspiring Confidence

Data-Driven and Well-Researched: By presenting well-researched and data-driven strategic alternatives, investment bankers inspire confidence in their clients. They demonstrate a deep understanding of the client's business and the market, providing clear and actionable recommendations. This builds trust and positions the bankers as trusted advisors who can help the client navigate complex strategic decisions.

Guiding Strategic Path: Ultimately, the goal is to guide the client toward a strategic path that aligns with their goals and enhances shareholder value. Through a comprehensive and thoughtful approach, investment bankers provide the insights and support needed to make informed decisions. They help clients identify the best opportunities, mitigate risks, and execute strategies that drive long-term success.

By following this detailed and methodical approach, investment bankers can effectively pitch strategic alternatives, build strong client relationships, and contribute to their clients' strategic growth and success.

NOTES:
Consulting, KPIs & ROI

Consultants try to determine which KPIs are most connected to ROI (value drivers) and then make recommendations for turning the dial on those KPIs to drive ROI.

Chapter 53: Aligning Strategic Alternatives to C-Level & Board Level Priorities aka Executive Alignment

Pitching Strategic Alternatives: A Comprehensive Guide

When investment bankers pitch strategic alternatives, they undertake a thorough and nuanced process to guide clients toward optimal business decisions. This process involves a series of well-structured steps, from building rapport to presenting data-driven insights and addressing potential concerns. Here's an in-depth look at how investment bankers conduct these pitches effectively, with each phase explored in detail.

Establishing a Strong Rapport

Initial Engagement:

1. **Listening to the Client:** The first step in any meeting is active listening. Investment bankers engage the client in discussions about their current challenges, business goals, and long-term aspirations. By asking thoughtful, open-ended questions, they encourage the client to share detailed information about their strategic concerns and vision for the future.

2. **Demonstrating Empathy:** Acknowledging the client's specific issues and market conditions is crucial. Investment bankers show that they understand the unique aspects of the client's business environment. For instance, they might say, "Given the recent regulatory changes in your sector, we understand your concern about potential impacts on market positioning."
3. **Building Trust:** This is done by aligning with the client's perspective and showing genuine interest in their success. Investment bankers communicate their dedication to finding the best possible outcomes, thus positioning themselves as trusted advisors rather than mere service providers.

Detailed Analysis of Industry and Market Dynamics

Industry Assessment:

1. **Understanding the Industry:** Investment bankers provide a comprehensive overview of the industry in which the client operates. This includes analyzing macroeconomic trends, regulatory landscapes, and technological advancements. They discuss how these factors influence the industry and could impact the client's strategic decisions.
2. **Market Dynamics:** Detailed insights into market trends, such as consumer behavior changes or shifts in competitive dynamics, are crucial. Bankers might highlight trends like the digital transformation in retail or the shift towards renewable energy in utilities, explaining how these trends create opportunities or threats.
3. **Competitive Landscape:** Bankers assess the strengths and weaknesses of the client's competitors, providing a comparative analysis. They might discuss market share data, recent strategic moves by competitors, and the client's relative positioning.

Proposing Strategic Alternatives

Identifying Alternatives:

1. **Organic Growth Strategies:** Investment bankers propose strategies such as expanding product lines, entering new geographic markets, or optimizing existing operations. For example, they might suggest the client consider entering an emerging market where demand for their products is growing.
2. **Inorganic Growth Strategies:** They also consider mergers, acquisitions, joint ventures, and alliances. For instance, a banker might recommend acquiring a competitor to quickly gain market share or access new technology.

Explaining the Rationale:

Investment bankers provide a clear rationale for each proposed alternative, connecting them to the client's business goals. They explain how these strategies can address specific challenges or leverage opportunities, such as reducing costs through operational synergies or expanding market reach.

Providing Evidence and Data-Driven Insights

Financial Projections:

1. **Illustrating Potential Outcomes:** Detailed financial models are presented, showing projected revenues, costs, and profitability under each strategic alternative. These projections are based on robust data and assumptions about future market conditions.
2. **Market Research:** Data on market size, growth rates, and customer segments are provided to validate the feasibility of the proposed strategies. For example, if expanding into a new market, they present demographic data and consumer spending patterns.
3. **Case Studies:** Investment bankers present case studies of similar companies that have successfully implemented comparable strategies. These examples help clients see potential paths forward and the possible benefits.

Addressing Concerns and Mitigating Risks

Open Discussions:

1. **Engaging with the Client:** During the presentation, investment bankers actively engage the client in discussions about potential risks and challenges. They encourage clients to voice concerns and ask questions, ensuring a transparent dialogue.
2. **Risk Analysis:** A comprehensive risk assessment is provided for each strategic alternative. This includes financial risks, market risks, and operational risks. For example, they might discuss the volatility of currency exchange rates if the strategy involves international expansion.
3. **Mitigation Strategies:** Solutions to mitigate identified risks are proposed. For instance, if the client is concerned about market volatility, the bankers might suggest hedging strategies or diversifying investments.

Emphasizing Long-Term Partnership and Support

Ongoing Advisory Services:

1. **Commitment to Client Success:** Investment bankers emphasize their role as long-term partners. They offer ongoing advisory services, such as market monitoring, financial analysis, and strategic planning.
2. **Access to Networks:** They highlight their ability to connect the client with potential partners, investors, or acquirers. These connections can facilitate future strategic initiatives.
3. **Trusted Advisors:** Investment bankers assure clients of their continued support throughout the implementation of the chosen strategy. They position themselves as an integral part of the client's strategic journey, offering expertise and resources whenever needed.

Inspiring Confidence and Guiding Strategic Decisions

Building Confidence:

1. **Presenting Well-Researched Alternatives:** By providing well-researched and thoroughly analyzed strategic alternatives, investment bankers build confidence in their recommendations. They

ensure that every suggestion is backed by data and aligns with the client's goals.

2. **Addressing Concerns Thoughtfully:** By addressing concerns and discussing risks candidly, bankers help the client feel more secure in their decisions. They provide a balanced view, acknowledging potential downsides while emphasizing the strategic benefits.

3. **Tailoring Recommendations:** Investment bankers customize their recommendations to align perfectly with the client's specific needs and circumstances. This bespoke approach ensures that the client receives advice that is not only relevant but also actionable and practical.

By meticulously following these steps, investment bankers can effectively pitch strategic alternatives, helping clients navigate complex decisions and achieve their long-term business objectives. The process is not just about presenting options but also about building a partnership based on trust, expertise, and mutual success.

Chapter 54: What Are the Most Important Strategic Alternatives for a Company to Consider?

The Comprehensive Guide to Pitching Strategic Alternatives in Investment Banking

Pitching strategic alternatives is a crucial aspect of investment banking, involving the presentation of potential paths a client can take to achieve their business objectives. This process requires a deep understanding of the client's needs, thorough market analysis, and the ability to communicate complex financial strategies clearly. Let's delve into the detailed and explanatory aspects of this process, ensuring a thorough understanding of each step involved.

Building a Strong Foundation of Trust and Understanding

1. Initial Engagement:

- **Objective:** The first goal in any client meeting is to establish a strong rapport. This involves creating a comfortable environment where the client feels understood and valued.
- **Active Listening:** Investment bankers start by asking open-ended questions and actively listening to the client's responses. They focus on understanding the client's current challenges, long-term goals, and immediate concerns. For instance, if a client is concerned about market volatility, the banker might ask, "How have recent market fluctuations affected your business strategy?"
- **Empathy and Assurance:** Demonstrating empathy involves acknowledging the client's challenges and expressing a genuine

interest in finding solutions. For example, if a client is facing increased competition, the banker might say, "I understand that increased competition is a significant concern. Let's explore how we can position your company to maintain a competitive edge."

In-Depth Market and Industry Analysis

2. Comprehensive Market Dynamics Assessment:

- **Industry Overview:** Investment bankers provide a thorough overview of the industry in which the client operates. This includes discussing key trends, such as technological advancements, regulatory changes, and consumer behavior shifts. For example, in the healthcare sector, bankers might highlight trends like the rise of telemedicine and its implications.
- **Competitive Landscape:** Analyzing the competitive landscape involves identifying key players, their market share, and recent strategic moves. Bankers assess competitors' strengths and weaknesses to identify potential opportunities and threats. For instance, they might analyze a competitor's recent acquisition and its impact on the market dynamics.

3. Detailed Analysis of Strategic Alternatives:

- **Organic Growth Options:** These include strategies that leverage the client's existing resources. For example, expanding into new geographic markets or launching new products. The banker would provide data on market size, growth rates, and potential customer segments in these new markets.
- **Inorganic Growth Options:** These involve external growth strategies like mergers, acquisitions, or joint ventures. The banker might present several potential acquisition targets, detailing how each could complement the client's existing business. For instance, acquiring a competitor could provide immediate market share growth, while a partnership with a tech company could bring in innovative capabilities.

Presenting Data-Driven Insights and Evidence

4. Financial Analysis and Projections:

- **Detailed Financial Models:** Investment bankers create comprehensive financial models to project the financial outcomes of each strategic alternative. This includes revenue forecasts, cost implications, and profitability estimates. For instance, they might show how a merger could lead to economies of scale and cost savings.
- **Market Research Data:** They back their recommendations with robust market research, providing evidence for the viability of each option. This could include data on market trends, customer demand, and competitive analysis.

5. Case Studies and Historical Precedents:

- **Learning from Past Successes:** Bankers often present case studies of similar companies that have successfully implemented comparable strategies. This helps to illustrate the potential benefits and pitfalls of each option. For instance, they might highlight a case where a company successfully entered a new market through a strategic partnership, demonstrating the potential for similar success.

Navigating Client Concerns and Risk Mitigation

6. Open Discussion of Risks and Challenges:

- **Risk Identification:** It's crucial to address potential risks associated with each strategic alternative, such as regulatory hurdles, integration challenges, or market entry barriers. For example, a merger might come with risks related to cultural integration or antitrust concerns.
- **Mitigation Strategies:** For each identified risk, investment bankers propose specific mitigation strategies. For instance, they might suggest a phased market entry approach to manage the risk of expanding into a new geographic region.

Conclusion and Commitment to Long-Term Partnership

7. Long-Term Partnership and Continuous Support:

- **Ongoing Advisory Services:** Investment bankers emphasize their commitment to providing ongoing support beyond the initial pitch. This includes helping with the implementation of the chosen strategy, monitoring market conditions, and adjusting strategies as needed.
- **Building a Relationship of Trust:** The goal is to establish a long-term relationship where the banker acts as a trusted advisor, consistently offering valuable insights and recommendations. This ongoing partnership ensures that the client feels supported and confident in their strategic decisions.

By meticulously following these steps, investment bankers can deliver compelling and well-substantiated pitches that resonate with their clients' strategic objectives. This comprehensive approach not only helps in winning client mandates but also fosters long-term partnerships built on trust and mutual success.

PART VIII: FEE STRUCTURING & WINNING THE MANDATE TO IMPLEMENT THE STRATEGIC ALTERNATIVE

Chapter 55: Fee Structuring & Winning the Mandate to Implement the Strategic Alternative

Fee Structuring & Winning the Mandate to Implement the Strategic Alternative

Fee structuring and winning the mandate are pivotal steps in investment banking, ensuring that the services provided are appropriately valued and that both the banker and client are aligned in their objectives. This process involves not only setting fees but also demonstrating the banker's expertise, understanding the client's needs, and formalizing the relationship through an engagement letter. Let's delve into the detailed steps involved in these critical aspects of investment banking.

Importance of Fee Structuring

Defining Fee Structuring and Its Objectives: Fee structuring is the process of determining the compensation investment bankers will receive for their advisory and transactional services. It is a crucial step because it ensures that the investment bank's incentives align with the client's goals, fostering a mutually beneficial relationship. Properly structured fees can motivate bankers to work diligently towards a successful transaction, as their compensation often depends on the deal's outcome.

Alignment of Incentives: By tying compensation to the success of the transaction, fee structures help align the banker's interests with those of the client. This means that the banker's earnings are contingent upon achieving the client's objectives, such as successfully selling a business or raising capital.

Fair Compensation: The fees should reflect the complexity, risk, and potential value creation of the transaction. This ensures that investment bankers are adequately rewarded for their expertise, effort, and the resources they commit.

Facilitating Long-Term Relationships: Transparent and fair fee structures contribute to building trust and long-term relationships with clients. When clients feel they are paying a fair price for valuable services, they are more likely to return for future transactions.

Engaging in Mandate Acquisition

Winning the Mandate: Securing the mandate is a crucial step where the client formally engages the investment bank's services. This involves:

1. **Demonstrating Expertise:** Investment bankers must present their credentials, including a track record of successful deals, industry-specific knowledge, and specialized skills. This might involve presenting detailed case studies, client testimonials, and success stories that highlight their ability to deliver results.

2. **Building Credibility:** Establishing credibility involves demonstrating an in-depth understanding of the client's industry and specific challenges. This can be achieved through regular market updates, insightful analysis, and sharing thought leadership materials that showcase the banker's knowledge and insights.
3. **Preparing a Compelling Pitch:** The pitch should include a comprehensive market analysis, strategic recommendations, and a clear value proposition. It should highlight unique selling points, such as access to proprietary research, specialized teams, and extensive networks.
4. **Engaging with Clients:** Maintaining active engagement through regular communication, meetings, and consultations is essential. Investment bankers should respond promptly to inquiries and provide tailored insights to demonstrate their commitment and reliability.

Types of Fee Structures

Success Fee Basis: This structure involves payment contingent on the successful completion of the transaction. It is commonly used in M&A transactions, especially when the outcome is uncertain, aligning the interests of both the banker and the client.

Retainer Fees: A retainer fee is a fixed payment made periodically, regardless of the transaction's success. This fee covers the initial costs and time investment, providing the banker with financial stability during the engagement. It is often used in complex or long-term transactions.

Flat Fees: Flat fees are predetermined and fixed, agreed upon at the engagement's outset. This structure offers simplicity and predictability, making it suitable for well-defined transactions.

Combination Fees: This hybrid model combines elements of success fees, retainers, and flat fees. It provides flexibility to adjust the fee structure based on the transaction's complexity, risk, and duration.

Determining the Size of the Fee

Assessing Deal Complexity: The size and complexity of the deal often dictate the fee structure. Larger and more complex transactions generally involve more work and justify higher fees, especially if they require specialized knowledge and extensive resources.

Market Conditions: Market dynamics, such as competition among investment banks and economic conditions, can influence fee structures. In highly competitive markets, banks may offer more competitive fees, while favorable economic conditions might allow for higher fees.

Value Delivered: Fees should reflect the potential benefits and value created for the client through the transaction. Higher fees may be justified for transactions that significantly enhance the client's value.

M&A Engagement Letter

Formal Agreement: The engagement letter formalizes the agreement between the investment bank and the client, detailing the scope of services, fee structure, payment terms, and other conditions. It ensures clarity and transparency, setting expectations for both parties.

Scope of Services and Confidentiality Provisions: The letter outlines the specific services provided and includes clauses to protect confidential information shared during the engagement.

Other Terms and Conditions: This section may cover termination clauses, indemnities, and exclusivity agreements, providing a comprehensive framework for the engagement.

Sell Side and Buy Side Representation

Sell Side Representation: In sell-side engagements, the investment banker advises the company or owner looking to sell their business. The banker prepares the business for sale, markets it to potential buyers, and negotiates the sale terms.

Buy Side Representation: For buy-side engagements, the banker works with acquirers or investors seeking suitable acquisition targets. This includes identifying targets, conducting due diligence, and negotiating acquisition terms.

Tailoring Fees to Engagement: The fee structure may vary depending on whether the banker represents the buy side or sell side, reflecting the engagement's complexity and value.

Conclusion

Recap of Key Points: Effective fee structuring and mandate acquisition are crucial for successful investment banking engagements. They ensure fair compensation, align incentives, and foster long-term relationships with clients.

Final Thoughts: By understanding and effectively managing these processes, investment bankers can secure mandates, deliver value to clients, and achieve success in their transactions. Transparent and fair fee structures, coupled with a demonstrated commitment to the client's success, are key to building lasting partnerships and securing future business opportunities.

NOTES:

Why Fee Structuring & Winning the Mandate?

In order to get paid, investment bankers have to land the engagement. Once the fee is agreed upon, the investment banker puts fee structure in something called an engagement letter. In the lower middle market to middle market, most investment bankers work on a success fee basis meaning that they only receive compensation on a deal when it actually goes through and closes.

Fee Structuring & Winning the Mandate Process

1. Type of Fee
2. Size of Fee
3. Sell Side & Buy Side Representation?
4. M&A Engagement Letter

Chapter 56: M&A Fee Structure

Pitching Strategic Alternatives in Investment Banking: A Comprehensive Guide

Pitching strategic alternatives is a pivotal activity in investment banking, where bankers present tailored strategic options to their clients. These alternatives can range from mergers and acquisitions (M&A) to divestitures, capital raising, and more. The process involves a structured approach, detailed analysis, and effective communication. Here's an in-depth look at how investment bankers effectively pitch these alternatives to clients.

1. Establishing a Strong Rapport

Initial Engagement:

- **Listening to the Client:** The first step involves understanding the client's unique needs, challenges, and long-term goals. Investment bankers start by asking open-ended questions, allowing clients to express their strategic objectives and concerns. This deep dive into the client's business environment helps bankers tailor their pitch.
- **Demonstrating Empathy:** Bankers acknowledge the client's current situation, challenges, and aspirations, demonstrating a thorough understanding of the business's nuances. This

acknowledgment shows the client that the bankers are attuned to their specific circumstances.

- **Building Trust:** Establishing a foundation of trust is crucial. Investment bankers do this by showing a genuine commitment to the client's success, ensuring that all recommendations are aligned with the client's best interests.

2. Detailed Analysis of Industry and Market Dynamics

Industry Assessment:

- **Market Dynamics and Trends:** Bankers conduct a comprehensive analysis of the client's industry, highlighting key trends, regulatory changes, and market dynamics. This includes understanding factors such as technological advancements, shifts in consumer preferences, and economic indicators that may affect the industry.
- **Competitive Landscape:** The competitive landscape analysis involves assessing the strengths, weaknesses, opportunities, and threats (SWOT analysis) of the client's competitors. Bankers evaluate market share, product positioning, and recent strategic initiatives of these competitors.

Providing Evidence and Data-Driven Insights:

- **Financial Projections:** Bankers provide detailed financial projections, including revenue forecasts, cost savings, and potential profitability from each strategic alternative. These projections are based on rigorous financial modeling, taking into account various scenarios and assumptions.
- **Market Research and Data:** Investment bankers present comprehensive market research data, including industry reports, market size, growth rates, and customer

demographics. This data supports the feasibility and potential success of the proposed strategies.

- **Case Studies and Benchmarking:** To build a compelling case, bankers often use case studies of similar companies that have successfully implemented comparable strategies. These case studies provide real-world evidence of the benefits and challenges associated with the proposed alternatives.

3. Proposing Strategic Alternatives

Identifying Alternatives:

- **Organic Growth Strategies:** These include initiatives such as expanding into new geographic markets, launching new products, or enhancing operational efficiency. Bankers highlight the potential for the client to grow using its existing resources and capabilities.
- **Inorganic Growth Strategies:** This category includes M&A, joint ventures, and strategic partnerships. Investment bankers identify potential targets for acquisition or merger, presenting detailed analysis on how these actions could create synergies and enhance the client's market position.

Explaining the Rationale:

- **Alignment with Client Goals:** Each alternative is linked to the client's specific strategic objectives, whether it's market expansion, diversification, or cost reduction. Bankers explain how each option aligns with the client's long-term vision and the potential benefits.

4. Addressing Concerns and Mitigating Risks

Open Discussions:

- **Engaging with the Client:** Bankers encourage open dialogue, inviting the client to voice any concerns or questions. This collaborative approach ensures that all parties are on the same page.
- **Risk Analysis:** A thorough risk assessment is conducted for each strategic alternative. Bankers identify potential financial, operational, and market risks, providing a balanced view of the opportunities and challenges.
- **Mitigation Strategies:** For each identified risk, bankers propose specific mitigation strategies. For example, if market volatility is a concern, bankers might suggest hedging strategies or diversifying the investment.

5. Emphasizing Long-Term Partnership and Support

Ongoing Advisory Services:

- **Commitment to Client Success:** Investment bankers emphasize their commitment to providing continuous support, not just during the transaction but also post-deal. This includes offering strategic advice, market insights, and operational support as needed.
- **Access to Networks:** Bankers leverage their extensive networks to provide the client with access to potential partners, investors, or buyers, facilitating future growth opportunities.

6. Inspiring Confidence and Guiding Strategic Decisions

Building Confidence:

- **Presenting Well-Researched Alternatives:** The presentation of strategic alternatives is thorough and well-supported by data and analysis, helping to build the client's confidence in the proposed strategies.

- **Tailoring Recommendations:** Recommendations are customized to fit the client's specific situation, demonstrating the bankers' deep understanding of the client's business and market environment.

Conclusion

Pitching strategic alternatives requires a combination of industry expertise, financial acumen, and strong communication skills. Investment bankers play a crucial role in guiding clients through complex strategic decisions, offering insights and solutions that align with the client's goals. By following a structured approach and building strong relationships, bankers can effectively present and implement strategic alternatives that drive long-term value for their clients.

NOTES:

M&A Fee Structure:

Regarding fees, here is a simplified understanding of fee structure for sell side engagements. The key to remember here is that you do not make your money when you quote your fee, you make your money when you close the deal. The point is that I would rather win an engagement and give up 1% to 2% of the fee than have the seller think that I am not being fair. The Lehman scale simplifies this a bit but often times the seller will want to know the exact % that they will be paying you.

- Large cap – Lehman scale
- Mid cap – Lehman scale
- Small cap – Lehman scale
- Middle market – Double Lehman structure
- Lower middle market – 3% to 10%
- SMB: 10% to 12%

Investment Banking University
All Rights Reserved

Chapter 57: Structuring the Fee

Understanding the Art of Pitching Strategic Alternatives in Investment Banking

In the world of investment banking, pitching strategic alternatives is a sophisticated and methodical process. It's not merely about presenting options but about deeply understanding the client's business, the industry, and market conditions, and then crafting a compelling narrative that aligns with the client's goals. Let's dive into the detailed steps involved in this process, highlighting the nuances that make a pitch successful.

1. Establishing a Strong Rapport and Understanding Client Needs

Initial Engagement: The first step in any pitch is establishing a rapport with the client. Investment bankers begin by listening intently to the client's needs, challenges, and strategic objectives. This phase is crucial as it sets the tone for a collaborative relationship. It's not just about hearing but about truly understanding the client's business landscape, concerns, and aspirations.

- **Example:** If a client is a tech startup looking to scale, the banker might inquire about their growth challenges, funding needs, and long-term vision.

Demonstrating Empathy: Empathy goes beyond understanding; it's about relating to the client's situation. Investment bankers often share similar past experiences with other clients or sectors, illustrating that they comprehend the client's unique position.

- **Example:** A banker could mention, "We've seen similar challenges with other tech startups and successfully guided them through strategic partnerships and funding rounds."

Building Trust: This phase involves more than just establishing credentials. Bankers must position themselves as trusted advisors committed to the client's success. This is achieved through transparency, reliability, and demonstrating a genuine interest in the client's business.

2. Providing a Thorough Analysis of Industry and Market Dynamics

Industry Assessment: Investment bankers conduct a deep dive into the client's industry, examining market trends, regulatory changes, and competitive landscapes. This analysis includes both qualitative insights and quantitative data, such as market share statistics and growth forecasts.

- **Example:** For a client in renewable energy, the banker would analyze trends in solar and wind energy adoption, regulatory incentives, and technological advancements.

Market Dynamics and Competitive Landscape: Understanding market dynamics involves looking at supply and demand, price fluctuations, and customer preferences. The competitive landscape analysis includes identifying key competitors, their market positions, and strategic moves.

- **Example:** In the context of a pharmaceutical company, this might involve analyzing the pipeline of competing drugs, patent expirations, and emerging biotechnologies.

3. Crafting and Pitching Strategic Alternatives

Identifying Alternatives: Based on the gathered information, bankers propose a range of strategic alternatives. These could include organic growth strategies like expanding product lines or geographic reach, or inorganic options such as mergers, acquisitions, and joint ventures.

- **Example:** For a retail client, strategic alternatives could include expanding into e-commerce, acquiring a competitor, or diversifying product offerings.

Explaining the Rationale: Each proposed alternative comes with a detailed explanation of its rationale, supported by data and analysis. Investment bankers outline how each option aligns with the client's strategic goals, providing a clear path to achieving these objectives.

- **Example:** The banker might explain how an acquisition could provide immediate access to new markets and customer bases, justifying the recommendation with market data and financial projections.

4. Supporting the Pitch with Data-Driven Insights

Financial Projections and Market Research: Investment bankers present comprehensive financial models projecting potential outcomes for each strategic alternative. These models include revenue forecasts, cost structures, and profitability analyses. Market research supports these projections, providing a foundation of evidence for the proposed strategies.

- **Example:** For an acquisition proposal, the banker might present a detailed cash flow analysis showing potential cost synergies and revenue enhancements post-merger.

Case Studies: To bolster their recommendations, bankers often present case studies of similar companies that have successfully implemented comparable strategies. These real-world examples help clients envision the potential success of the proposed alternatives.

- **Example:** A case study of a successful merger in the same industry could illustrate the potential benefits and lessons learned.

5. Addressing Concerns and Mitigating Risks

Risk Analysis and Mitigation Strategies: Investment bankers are thorough in identifying potential risks associated with each alternative. They discuss these openly with the client, providing mitigation strategies and contingency plans to address these risks.

- **Example:** If entering a new market, the banker might highlight potential regulatory risks and suggest strategies like securing local partnerships to navigate these challenges.

6. Emphasizing Long-Term Partnership and Support

Ongoing Advisory Services and Networks: Bankers emphasize their role as long-term partners, offering continuous support beyond the initial transaction. They provide access to their networks, which can be invaluable for strategic partnerships, additional funding, or future transactions.

- **Example:** A banker might offer to introduce the client to potential joint venture partners or investors from their network.

Building Confidence and Guiding Strategic Decisions: The ultimate goal is to inspire confidence in the client. By thoroughly explaining each alternative, addressing concerns, and providing a clear action plan, investment bankers guide clients toward the most strategic and beneficial decision.

Conclusion

Pitching strategic alternatives is a comprehensive process that requires a deep understanding of the client's business, industry dynamics, and strategic objectives. Investment bankers act as trusted advisors, providing tailored, data-driven recommendations and ongoing support. Their role is crucial in helping clients navigate complex strategic decisions and achieve long-term success. Through meticulous preparation, empathetic engagement, and expert guidance, investment bankers build strong relationships and deliver value that extends beyond the pitch room.

Chapter 58: The Engagement Letter

Crafting a Comprehensive Pitch: Investment Bankers and Strategic Alternatives

In the world of investment banking, pitching strategic alternatives is a sophisticated and multifaceted process. It involves a combination of relationship-building, meticulous analysis, persuasive communication, and continuous support. This blog post dives deep into the elaborate process that investment bankers follow to pitch strategic alternatives to clients, ensuring they make informed, strategic decisions.

1. Building Strong Foundations: Establishing Rapport and Understanding Client Needs

Initial Engagement and Listening: Investment bankers begin by engaging with the client in a manner that emphasizes understanding and empathy. They ask open-ended questions and listen carefully to the client's challenges, goals, and aspirations. This step is crucial for setting a cooperative tone and establishing the banker as a reliable partner who is genuinely interested in the client's success.

Demonstrating Expertise and Empathy: Bankers acknowledge the client's unique challenges and opportunities, which helps in building trust. For example, they might discuss industry-specific challenges, such as regulatory changes or competitive pressures, and offer initial thoughts on how these could be navigated.

Commitment to Client Success: Expressing a clear commitment to the client's long-term success is vital. Investment bankers make it clear that their goal is to assist the client in achieving their strategic objectives, not just to close a deal.

2. In-Depth Market and Industry Analysis

Industry Assessment: Investment bankers provide a comprehensive overview of the client's industry. This includes an analysis of current market trends, regulatory factors, and competitive dynamics. By doing so, they set the stage for discussing potential strategic moves.

Market Dynamics and Trends: They delve into specific trends affecting the market, such as technological innovations, shifts in consumer behavior, or changes in supply chain dynamics. This information is crucial for understanding the broader context in which the client operates.

Competitive Landscape: A detailed analysis of competitors is presented, including their market positions, recent strategic moves, and strengths and weaknesses. This helps the client understand where they stand in relation to their competitors and what opportunities or threats exist.

3. Proposing Strategic Alternatives: A Tailored Approach

Identifying and Categorizing Alternatives: Investment bankers identify a range of strategic alternatives, which can be broadly categorized into organic and inorganic growth strategies.

- **Organic Growth Strategies:** These include expanding existing product lines, entering new markets, or enhancing operational efficiencies. For example, a banker might suggest developing a new product line to tap into an emerging market trend.
- **Inorganic Growth Strategies:** These involve mergers, acquisitions, joint ventures, or strategic partnerships. For instance, acquiring a competitor or a complementary business to gain market share or new capabilities.

Rationale and Justification: For each proposed alternative, investment bankers provide a thorough explanation of the rationale behind it. They connect the proposed strategies with the client's overarching goals and market realities, ensuring the client understands the potential benefits.

Case Studies and Success Stories: To lend credibility to their recommendations, bankers often present case studies of similar companies that successfully implemented comparable strategies. These real-world examples provide a tangible demonstration of the potential benefits.

4. Data-Driven Insights and Financial Projections

Financial Analysis: Investment bankers present detailed financial projections for each strategic alternative. This includes revenue forecasts, cost implications, potential returns, and break-even analysis. These projections are backed by thorough financial modeling and market research.

Market Research: They provide data on market size, growth rates, customer demographics, and other relevant factors. This research supports the feasibility and attractiveness of the proposed strategies.

Scenario Analysis: Bankers may also conduct scenario analysis to present different outcomes based on varying market conditions, helping the client understand the range of possible results.

5. Addressing Risks and Mitigation Strategies

Open Discussion of Risks: Investment bankers encourage an open discussion about potential risks associated with each alternative. This includes financial, operational, and market risks.

Risk Mitigation Strategies: They propose practical strategies to mitigate these risks, such as diversifying investments, hedging against market fluctuations, or implementing phased rollouts of new initiatives.

Transparent Communication: Throughout the discussion, bankers maintain transparency, ensuring the client fully understands the risks and the measures in place to address them.

6. Post-Pitch: Continuous Support and Partnership

Ongoing Advisory Role: After the initial pitch, investment bankers continue to support the client by providing ongoing advisory services. This includes regular updates on market conditions, further refinement of strategies, and assistance with implementation.

Leveraging Networks: Bankers leverage their extensive networks to connect the client with potential partners, investors, or buyers, facilitating additional strategic opportunities.

Long-Term Relationship Building: The relationship doesn't end with the pitch. Investment bankers aim to build long-term partnerships, positioning themselves as trusted advisors who can provide value across multiple strategic initiatives over time.

Conclusion: A Holistic Approach to Strategic Advisory

The process of pitching strategic alternatives is not just about presenting options; it's about deeply understanding the client's needs, providing comprehensive and data-driven recommendations, addressing risks transparently, and offering continuous support. By following this holistic approach, investment bankers can help their clients navigate complex market landscapes and make informed, strategic decisions that drive long-term success.

NOTES:

The M&A Engagement Letter

In order to get paid, investment bankers have to land the engagement. Once the fee is agreed upon, the investment banker puts the fee in writing in something called an engagement letter.

M&A engagement letter structure

The typical M&A engagement letter structure outlines the following:

- Term
- Exclusivity
- Size
- Other services
- Valuation

PART VIII: UNDERWRITING THE STRATEGIC ALTERNATIVE

Chapter 59: Financial Modeling & Valuation Framework

Financial Modeling & Valuation Framework: A Comprehensive Guide

In investment banking, financial modeling and valuation are core skills that enable professionals to analyze the financial health of companies, determine their intrinsic value, and structure strategic transactions. This guide explores the essential components of financial modeling and valuation, detailing the processes involved in creating models, valuing companies, and capturing value through transactions.

Understanding Financial Modeling

Financial modeling is the process of building a structured representation of a company's financial performance. This model helps predict future financial outcomes and assess various business scenarios. The following components are crucial in financial modeling:

Financial Accounting and Statements

1. **Income Statement**:

- **Purpose**: Provides a summary of the company's revenues, expenses, and net profit over a specific period.
- **Key Elements**: Includes revenue streams, cost of goods sold (COGS), gross profit, operating expenses (such as salaries, rent, and utilities), and net income.
- **Usage**: Helps in understanding the profitability of the company and is a starting point for cash flow analysis.

2. **Balance Sheet**:
   - **Purpose**: Offers a snapshot of the company's financial position at a given moment, showing what it owns and owes.
   - **Key Elements**: Includes assets (current and non-current), liabilities (short-term and long-term), and shareholders' equity.
   - **Usage**: Essential for assessing the company's financial stability and solvency.

3. **Cash Flow Statement**:
   - **Purpose**: Tracks the cash generated and spent over a period, divided into operating, investing, and financing activities.
   - **Key Elements**: Shows cash flows from core business operations, capital expenditures, and financing activities like issuing debt or equity.
   - **Usage**: Critical for understanding the liquidity position and cash management efficiency of the company.

Excel as a Tool

- **Excel** is the preferred tool for financial modeling due to its flexibility and powerful computational capabilities. It allows investment bankers to build dynamic models that can handle complex calculations, scenario analyses, and data visualization.

- **Applications**: Bankers use Excel to create integrated models that seamlessly link the income statement, balance sheet, and cash flow statement. This integration helps in accurately projecting future financial performance and assessing the impact of various strategic decisions.

Financial Statement Analysis

- **Reviewing Historical Financials**: Involves analyzing past financial statements to identify trends and patterns. This analysis helps in establishing a baseline for forecasting future performance.
- **Ratio Analysis**: Bankers use ratios like return on equity (ROE), debt-to-equity ratio, and current ratio to evaluate the company's profitability, leverage, and liquidity.
- **Trend Analysis**: This involves looking at financial data over several periods to identify trends in revenue growth, expense management, and profitability.

Valuation Techniques

Valuation is the process of determining the present value of a company or its assets. Investment bankers use various methods to value companies, each providing different perspectives:

Comparable Companies Analysis (Comp Companies)

- **Method**: Involves comparing the target company with similar publicly traded companies to determine its value.
- **Key Metrics**: Utilizes multiples like price-to-earnings (P/E) and enterprise value-to-EBITDA (EV/EBITDA).

- **Purpose**: Provides a market-based valuation, helping to establish a benchmark for the target company's value.

Precedent Transactions Analysis

- **Method**: Values a company based on the multiples paid in similar past transactions.
- **Key Metrics**: Similar to comparable companies but focuses on historical acquisition prices.
- **Purpose**: Offers a benchmark based on actual transaction data, reflecting what buyers have been willing to pay.

Discounted Cash Flow (DCF) Analysis

- **Method**: Values a company by calculating the present value of its expected future free cash flows.
- **Key Steps**:
    1. **Forecasting Free Cash Flows**: Based on assumptions about revenue growth, costs, capital expenditures, and working capital.
    2. **Calculating Terminal Value**: Estimates the value of the business beyond the explicit forecast period.
    3. **Discounting Cash Flows**: Uses the weighted average cost of capital (WACC) to discount future cash flows to their present value.
- **Purpose**: Provides an intrinsic valuation based on the company's fundamentals.

Transaction-Specific Modeling

For specific transactions, investment bankers develop specialized financial models:

Merger Models

- **Purpose**: Analyze the financial impact of merging two companies, focusing on whether the merger will be accretive or dilutive to the acquirer's earnings per share (EPS).
- **Components**: Include pro forma financial statements, synergy analysis, and accretion/dilution analysis.

Leveraged Buyout (LBO) Models

- **Purpose**: Evaluate the feasibility and potential returns of acquiring a company using a significant amount of debt.
- **Key Metrics**: Focus on the internal rate of return (IRR) and the company's ability to service debt.
- **Structure**: Involves modeling cash flows, debt repayment schedules, and equity returns.

Capturing Value Through Transactions

Investment bankers use financial models and valuation analyses to advise on and structure transactions that maximize shareholder value:

Deal Structuring

- **Components**: Involves determining the appropriate mix of debt, equity, and other financial instruments to finance a transaction.
- **Considerations**: Focuses on optimizing the capital structure to minimize costs and maximize flexibility.

Negotiation and Execution

- **Role**: Investment bankers play a critical role in negotiating deal terms, including price, payment structure, and conditions.
- **Execution**: Ensures that all aspects of the transaction align with the strategic goals of the involved parties.

Post-Transaction Integration

- **Activities**: Investment bankers may assist in the integration process to realize synergies and ensure the smooth combination of businesses.
- **Focus**: Includes aligning organizational structures, harmonizing systems, and integrating operations to maximize value.

Conclusion

Financial modeling and valuation are foundational skills in investment banking, providing the analytical basis for strategic decision-making and transaction execution. Mastery of these techniques enables investment bankers to effectively advise clients, assess investment opportunities, and drive successful outcomes. Understanding these frameworks is crucial for professionals in corporate finance and investment banking, as they provide the tools needed to navigate complex financial landscapes and deliver value to stakeholders.

Chapter 60: Underwriting the Strategic Alternative

The Importance of Underwriting in Investment Banking

In investment banking, underwriting is a critical process that involves assessing the intrinsic value of a target company and determining its appropriate price under various market scenarios. This comprehensive analysis involves multiple valuation methodologies and is essential for making informed investment decisions. Here's a detailed breakdown of the underwriting process and its importance in investment banking.

Why Underwriting Matters

Understanding Intrinsic Value: Underwriting allows investment bankers to delve deep into a company's financial health, operational efficiency, market positioning, and future growth prospects. By evaluating these factors, bankers can establish the company's true worth, independent of market sentiments. This assessment is crucial for investors to avoid overpaying for an acquisition or missing valuable opportunities due to undervaluation. For instance, a company with strong cash flows but operating in a volatile market may be undervalued by the market, presenting a strategic investment opportunity.

Pricing Under Various Scenarios: Investment bankers employ underwriting to explore multiple scenarios, such as economic upturns, downturns, or sector-specific changes. They use various valuation methods, including comparable company analysis, precedent transactions, and discounted cash flow (DCF) analysis. This comprehensive approach provides a range of potential values for a company, aiding in negotiations and strategic planning. For example, during an economic downturn, a DCF analysis might reveal that the company's future cash flows are more resilient than competitors, justifying a higher valuation.

The Underwriting Process

1. Gathering Historical Financials

Importance: The foundation of the underwriting process is the thorough collection and analysis of a company's past financial performance. This data provides insight into the company's revenue trends, cost structures, profitability, and cash flow patterns.

Process: Investment bankers gather audited financial statements and other relevant documents, scrutinizing them for accuracy and reliability. This step ensures that all subsequent analyses are based on a solid foundation. For example, reviewing a company's historical income statements can reveal consistent revenue growth, indicating strong market demand.

2. Building the Financial Statement Model

Income Statement Forecasting: Bankers project future revenues and expenses, considering factors like market growth rates and cost trends. This forecast helps estimate the company's future profitability.

Balance Sheet Forecasting: They estimate future assets, liabilities, and equity, assessing the company's financial stability and capital structure.

Cash Flow Forecasting: Investment bankers predict future cash inflows and outflows, crucial for evaluating liquidity and the company's ability to finance its operations and investments.

For instance, in forecasting the income statement, bankers might project increased costs due to rising raw material prices, affecting the company's profit margins.

3. Finding Adjusted EBITDA

Definition: Adjusted EBITDA (Earnings Before Interest, Taxes, Depreciation, and Amortization) provides a clearer picture of a company's operational performance by excluding non-recurring, irregular, and non-cash items.

Calculation: Bankers start with the standard EBITDA and adjust for items like one-time legal expenses, restructuring costs, or gains/losses from asset sales. This adjusted figure offers a more accurate representation of ongoing business profitability.

For example, if a company incurred significant legal fees from a one-time lawsuit, these would be excluded from the adjusted EBITDA to prevent distorting the company's operational efficiency.

4. Deriving Valuation from Multiple Methodologies

Comparable Companies Analysis: This method involves comparing the target company with similar publicly traded companies using valuation multiples like P/E (Price-to-Earnings) ratio.

Precedent Transactions Analysis: This approach uses multiples from past transactions involving similar companies to estimate the target's value.

Discounted Cash Flow (DCF) Analysis: DCF calculates the present value of the company's expected future cash flows, discounted back at the company's cost of capital.

For instance, in a DCF analysis, if a company is expected to generate increasing cash flows due to market expansion, this would be reflected in a higher present value.

Building the Valuation Football Field

Purpose: The valuation football field visually represents a range of values derived from different methodologies. It shows the low, median, and high values, providing a comprehensive view of the company's potential valuation.

For example, if the DCF analysis suggests a high valuation while comparable company analysis suggests a lower value, the football field can illustrate this range, aiding in setting realistic expectations.

Customizing the Financial Statement Model

Purpose: Customizing the model involves adjusting for specific transaction scenarios, such as mergers, acquisitions, or leveraged buyouts (LBOs). This helps in understanding the financial implications of these transactions.

Process: Bankers adjust for factors like financing structure, expected synergies, or integration costs. For instance, in an LBO scenario, they model the debt repayment schedule and interest expenses to assess the transaction's feasibility and impact on the company's cash flows.

Conclusion

Summary: Underwriting is a vital component of investment banking, involving thorough financial analysis and valuation. It helps determine a company's intrinsic value and appropriate pricing under various scenarios. By leveraging multiple valuation methodologies and customizing financial models, investment bankers provide critical insights and recommendations, ensuring that investments align with clients' strategic objectives and financial goals.

Investment bankers' meticulous underwriting process not only informs sound investment decisions but also facilitates successful negotiations and transaction executions, ultimately leading to value creation and sustainable growth for all stakeholders involved.

Chapter 61: The Relationship Between Data Science & Finance/Investment Banking

The Symbiosis of Data Science and Investment Banking: Unlocking Value through Data-Driven Decisions

Introduction

In the realm of investment banking, data has always been a cornerstone for decision-making. The integration of data science into this field has significantly enhanced the precision, efficiency, and scope of financial analysis and transaction facilitation. This blog post delves into the pivotal relationship between data science and finance, particularly within the context of investment banking, and explores how leveraging advanced data science techniques can optimize investment strategies and outcomes.

The Integral Role of Data Science in Finance

Data science acts as the backbone for financial analysis in investment banking. It encompasses various methodologies and tools to process, analyze, and interpret vast amounts of financial data, enabling bankers to make informed decisions.

1. Financial Data Compilation and Structuring:

- **Accounting Foundations:** Investment banking relies on detailed financial statements—balance sheets, income statements, and cash flow statements. These documents, meticulously compiled through accounting processes, form the fundamental dataset for further analysis.
- **Data Structuring:** Proper structuring of this financial data allows for standardized evaluation across different companies and industries, making it easier to compare and contrast performance metrics.

2. Advanced Analytics Applied to Financial Data:

- **Descriptive Analytics:** This involves summarizing historical financial data to understand past performance. Key financial ratios and metrics are calculated to assess a company's operational efficiency and profitability.
- **Predictive Analytics:** Utilizing historical data, predictive models such as regression analysis and machine learning algorithms forecast future financial outcomes. For instance, revenue projections and risk assessments are derived from these models.
- **Prescriptive Analytics:** Beyond forecasting, prescriptive analytics suggests optimal strategies based on predictive insights. This includes recommending investment decisions or financial restructuring to maximize returns.

3. Data Visualization:

- Transforming complex data sets into visual formats like dashboards, charts, and graphs helps stakeholders quickly grasp essential insights. For example, visualizations can highlight trends in revenue growth or market share shifts, aiding in strategic planning.

The Core Objective of Investment Banking: Facilitating Informed Transactions

Investment banking's primary goal is to facilitate transactions that are beneficial to clients, whether through mergers, acquisitions, capital raising, or restructuring. **Data science** enhances this process by providing a solid data foundation for decision-making.

1. Data Integrity and Reliability:

- Ensuring data accuracy and relevance is crucial, as flawed data can lead to poor investment decisions. Data science methodologies help in cleansing and validating data, thus enhancing its reliability.

2. Comprehensive Analytical Framework:

- Through data science, investment bankers can conduct in-depth analyses that include historical performance, future projections, and scenario planning. This comprehensive approach allows for a holistic view of potential investment opportunities.

3. Delivering Actionable Insights:

- The insights generated must be actionable and clear. Investment bankers use these insights to craft detailed reports and presentations, helping clients understand the strategic value of potential transactions.

The Mathematical Foundations of Data Science in Finance

Mathematics underpins both data science and finance, offering a quantitative lens through which financial phenomena are analyzed.

1. Quantitative Analysis:

- Mathematics enables the quantitative analysis of financial data, essential for tasks such as valuation, risk assessment, and portfolio optimization. Techniques like statistics, calculus, and linear algebra are fundamental in this analysis.

2. Financial Modeling:

- Mathematical models are used to represent financial scenarios, providing a framework for forecasting and decision-making. These models help in understanding the potential impact of various financial strategies and market conditions.

Conclusion

The integration of data science into investment banking has revolutionized the industry, providing a deeper, data-driven understanding of market dynamics and investment opportunities. By leveraging advanced analytics, data visualization, and mathematical models, investment bankers can offer more accurate and insightful advice, ultimately facilitating better investment decisions and transactions. As the field continues to evolve, the symbiosis between data science and finance will only grow stronger, underscoring the importance of data literacy and analytical skills in the modern financial landscape.

NOTES:

The Most Recent Data Set as a Print:
The print is the most recent set of data to come out for either the fiscal
year month quarter, so we referred to the print as the most recent data.

Analyzing the most recent data to come out of it to allow us to make
inferences (insights that drive decision making).

Investment Banking University
All Rights Reserved

Chapter 62: How Financial Models Are Structured

The Symbiosis of Data Science and Investment Banking: Unlocking Value through Data-Driven Decisions

Introduction

In the realm of investment banking, data has always been a cornerstone for decision-making. The integration of data science into this field has significantly enhanced the precision, efficiency, and scope of financial analysis and transaction facilitation. This blog post delves into the pivotal relationship between data science and finance, particularly within the context of investment banking, and explores how leveraging advanced data science techniques can optimize investment strategies and outcomes.

The Integral Role of Data Science in Finance

Data science acts as the backbone for financial analysis in investment banking. It encompasses various methodologies and tools to process, analyze, and interpret vast amounts of financial data, enabling bankers to make informed decisions.

1. Financial Data Compilation and Structuring:

- **Accounting Foundations:** Investment banking relies on detailed financial statements—balance sheets, income statements, and cash flow statements. These documents, meticulously compiled through accounting processes, form the fundamental dataset for further analysis.
- **Data Structuring:** Proper structuring of this financial data allows for standardized evaluation across different companies and industries, making it easier to compare and contrast performance metrics.

2. Advanced Analytics Applied to Financial Data:

- **Descriptive Analytics:** This involves summarizing historical financial data to understand past performance. Key financial ratios and metrics are calculated to assess a company's operational efficiency and profitability.
- **Predictive Analytics:** Utilizing historical data, predictive models such as regression analysis and machine learning algorithms forecast future financial outcomes. For instance, revenue projections and risk assessments are derived from these models.
- **Prescriptive Analytics:** Beyond forecasting, prescriptive analytics suggests optimal strategies based on predictive insights. This includes recommending investment decisions or financial restructuring to maximize returns.

3. Data Visualization:

- Transforming complex data sets into visual formats like dashboards, charts, and graphs helps stakeholders quickly grasp essential insights. For example, visualizations can highlight trends in revenue growth or market share shifts, aiding in strategic planning.

The Core Objective of Investment Banking: Facilitating Informed Transactions

Investment banking's primary goal is to facilitate transactions that are beneficial to clients, whether through mergers, acquisitions, capital raising, or restructuring. **Data science** enhances this process by providing a solid data foundation for decision-making.

1. Data Integrity and Reliability:

- Ensuring data accuracy and relevance is crucial, as flawed data can lead to poor investment decisions. Data science methodologies help in cleansing and validating data, thus enhancing its reliability.

2. Comprehensive Analytical Framework:

- Through data science, investment bankers can conduct in-depth analyses that include historical performance, future projections, and scenario planning. This comprehensive approach allows for a holistic view of potential investment opportunities.

3. Delivering Actionable Insights:

- The insights generated must be actionable and clear. Investment bankers use these insights to craft detailed reports and presentations, helping clients understand the strategic value of potential transactions.

The Mathematical Foundations of Data Science in Finance

Mathematics underpins both data science and finance, offering a quantitative lens through which financial phenomena are analyzed.

1. Quantitative Analysis:

- Mathematics enables the quantitative analysis of financial data, essential for tasks such as valuation, risk assessment, and portfolio optimization. Techniques like statistics, calculus, and linear algebra are fundamental in this analysis.

2. Financial Modeling:

- Mathematical models are used to represent financial scenarios, providing a framework for forecasting and decision-making. These models help in understanding the potential impact of various financial strategies and market conditions.

Conclusion

The integration of data science into investment banking has revolutionized the industry, providing a deeper, data-driven understanding of market dynamics and investment opportunities. By leveraging advanced analytics, data visualization, and mathematical models, investment bankers can offer more accurate and insightful advice, ultimately facilitating better investment decisions and transactions. As the field continues to evolve, the symbiosis between data science and finance will only grow stronger, underscoring the importance of data literacy and analytical skills in the modern financial landscape.

Chapter 63: The Role of Financial Modeling & Valuation in Strategic Alternative Analysis & Deal Structuring

The Role of Financial Modeling & Valuation in Strategic Alternative Analysis & Deal Structuring

In investment banking, **financial modeling and valuation** are indispensable tools that enable bankers to evaluate strategic alternatives and craft effective deal structures. These techniques provide a comprehensive analysis of a company's financial health and market value, crucial for making informed decisions about mergers, acquisitions, divestitures, and other corporate actions. This post delves into the importance of these skills in the context of strategic alternative analysis and deal structuring, exploring their applications, methodologies, and significance in the investment banking process.

Financial Modeling: Analyzing and Predicting Financial Performance

Definition and Purpose: Financial modeling involves constructing a detailed, quantitative representation of a company's financial situation. This model is based on historical data, projections, and assumptions, allowing investment bankers to predict future financial outcomes and assess the impact of various strategic decisions.

Key Components:

1. **Historical Data Analysis:** Investment bankers start by gathering historical financial data, such as income statements, balance sheets, and cash flow statements. Analyzing past performance helps identify trends and provides a foundation for future projections. For instance, examining a company's historical revenue growth can reveal patterns that inform future forecasts.
2. **Projections and Assumptions:**
   - **Revenue Forecasting:** Estimating future sales based on market trends, competitive analysis, and internal growth strategies.
   - **Expense Forecasting:** Projecting future costs, including cost of goods sold (COGS), operating expenses, and capital expenditures. Assumptions about inflation, cost efficiencies, and other factors play a critical role here.
3. **Key Financial Metrics:**
   - **Revenue Growth:** Understanding trends in sales performance over time.
   - **Profitability Ratios:** Including gross margin, operating margin, and net profit margin.
   - **Cash Flow Analysis:** Forecasting cash inflows and outflows to assess liquidity and operational efficiency.
   - **Return on Investment (ROI):** Evaluating the potential profitability of investments or new projects.

Applications in Strategic Analysis:

1. **Scenario Analysis:** Investment bankers use financial models to create various business scenarios (e.g., best-case, worst-case) and evaluate their impact on financial performance. This approach helps in understanding the potential outcomes and preparing for different market conditions.
2. **Sensitivity Analysis:** By adjusting key assumptions like sales growth rates or cost changes, bankers can assess how sensitive a company's financial health is to these variables. For example, they may evaluate how a change in raw material prices could impact profitability.
3. **Monte Carlo Simulations:** These simulations use random variables to predict a range of possible outcomes, providing a probabilistic assessment of potential risks and returns.

Valuation: Determining Fair Market Value

Definition and Importance: Valuation is the process of estimating the worth of a company or its assets. This is crucial for pricing transactions accurately, whether in mergers, acquisitions, or sales. Accurate valuation ensures that all parties in a transaction receive fair consideration, fostering trust and facilitating smoother negotiations.

Valuation Techniques:

1. **Discounted Cash Flow (DCF) Analysis:**
    o   **Definition:** This method calculates the present value of expected future cash flows, discounted by the company's cost of capital. It provides a direct measure of an investment's value based on its projected cash flows.

- **Process:** Includes projecting cash flows, estimating terminal value, and discounting these to the present value using the weighted average cost of capital (WACC).
2. **Comparable Company Analysis (Comps):**
   - **Definition:** This technique involves valuing a company by comparing it to similar publicly traded companies. The comparison is based on financial ratios such as P/E, EV/EBITDA, and others.
   - **Process:** Identify peers, calculate multiples, and apply these multiples to the target company's financial metrics.
3. **Precedent Transactions Analysis:**
   - **Definition:** This method involves analyzing past transactions of similar companies to determine a valuation benchmark. It provides insight into market conditions and investor sentiment at the time of the transaction.
   - **Process:** Identify relevant transactions, calculate valuation multiples from these deals, and apply them to the target.

Deal Structuring: Crafting the Optimal Deal Framework

Definition and Process: Deal structuring involves determining the best way to finance a transaction, whether through cash, stock, debt, or a combination thereof. It also includes negotiating terms that protect both parties and ensure the deal's success.

Key Considerations:

1. **Financing Structures:** Determining the optimal mix of cash, equity, and debt based on the company's financial strategy and market conditions.

2. **Synergies:** Identifying potential cost savings and revenue enhancements that can result from the transaction. For example, merging two companies might reduce operating costs by consolidating facilities.
3. **Tax Implications:** Considering the tax consequences of various deal structures to optimize the financial outcome.
4. **Risk Profiles:** Analyzing and managing the risks associated with different financing options and deal terms.

Applications in Deal Structuring:

1. **Valuation Multiples:** These are used to set a fair transaction price based on market benchmarks.
2. **Financial Models:** Detailed models help simulate different deal structures and their impact on the company's financial health and strategic goals.
3. **Risk Assessment and Mitigation:** Through rigorous analysis, investment bankers can develop strategies to mitigate identified risks, ensuring a smooth transaction process.

Conclusion

Financial modeling and valuation are essential tools in investment banking, providing the quantitative backbone for strategic decision-making and deal structuring. They enable bankers to assess the viability of strategic alternatives, determine fair market value, and structure deals that optimize value for all stakeholders involved. Mastery of these techniques allows investment bankers to provide precise, strategic advice, facilitating successful transactions and long-term growth for their clients.

Chapter 64: How the Quantitative Side of Investment Banking Fits Together

Understanding the Quantitative Side of Investment Banking: A Comprehensive Guide

In the realm of investment banking, the quantitative side plays a crucial role in shaping financial strategies and making informed decisions. This blog post delves into the key components that integrate to form the quantitative framework within investment banking, exploring everything from financial modeling fundamentals to complex transaction-specific modeling.

Module 1: Fundamentals of Financial Modeling

Introduction to Corporate Finance Corporate finance forms the backbone of financial decision-making in investment banking. It encompasses a wide range of activities, including capital budgeting, capital structure management, and working capital management. The primary objective is to maximize shareholder value by making sound investment and financing decisions. Understanding these core concepts helps investment bankers assess the viability of potential investments and manage a company's financial resources effectively.

Accounting Fundamentals A solid grasp of accounting principles is vital for interpreting financial statements and building accurate financial models. Key concepts include the accounting equation (Assets = Liabilities + Equity), double-entry bookkeeping, and the preparation of financial statements. Investment bankers rely on these fundamentals to analyze a company's financial health, assess risk, and project future performance.

Excel Skills for Financial Modeling Excel is an indispensable tool in the investment banking industry due to its versatility and computational power. Mastery of essential functions and formulas, such as VLOOKUP, INDEX-MATCH, and SUMIF, is critical for efficient data manipulation and analysis. Investment bankers use Excel to create complex financial models, analyze data trends, and generate reports, all while ensuring accuracy and clarity.

Understanding and Utilizing Financial Statements Financial statements—comprising the income statement, balance sheet, and cash flow statement—are crucial for assessing a company's financial position. The income statement provides insights into profitability, the balance sheet offers a snapshot of financial stability, and the cash flow statement reveals liquidity and cash management. These documents are foundational for financial modeling and decision-making.

Module 2: Building Financial Statements

Constructing Financial Statements Building financial statements from scratch involves understanding the intricate details of each component. The income statement tracks revenues and expenses, the balance sheet lists assets and liabilities, and the cash flow statement connects these elements by showing cash inflows and outflows.

Accurate construction and linkage of these statements are essential for creating a cohesive financial model.

Forecasting Financial Performance Forecasting involves projecting a company's future financial performance based on historical data, market trends, and strategic plans. Investment bankers use various techniques, such as trend analysis and regression, to estimate future revenues, expenses, and cash flows. These forecasts help in planning and strategic decision-making.

Linking Financial Statements Linking the income statement, balance sheet, and cash flow statement ensures consistency and accuracy in financial models. For example, net income from the income statement affects retained earnings on the balance sheet, while changes in working capital impact the cash flow statement. This interconnectedness allows for a comprehensive view of a company's financial health.

Module 3: Valuation Techniques

Introduction to Valuation Valuation is the process of determining the present value of a company or asset. It is essential for making investment decisions, assessing mergers and acquisitions, and evaluating company performance. Common valuation methods include intrinsic valuation, which is based on the fundamental value of an asset, and relative valuation, which compares similar assets.

Discounted Cash Flow (DCF) Analysis DCF analysis estimates the value of an investment based on its expected future cash flows, discounted back to their present value. Key components include projecting cash flows, determining an appropriate discount rate, and calculating terminal value. This method provides a detailed view of an investment's potential profitability.

Comparable Company Analysis This technique involves valuing a company by comparing it with similar public companies. Key metrics, such as price-to-earnings and enterprise value-to-EBITDA ratios, are used to gauge relative value. This method is particularly useful for benchmarking and determining market value.

Precedent Transactions Analysis This approach involves analyzing past transactions involving similar companies to determine appropriate valuation multiples. It considers factors like deal size, industry, and market conditions, providing a historical benchmark for current valuations.

Module 4: Transaction-Specific Modeling

Leveraged Buyout (LBO) Modeling An LBO involves acquiring a company using a significant amount of debt. The model focuses on capital structure, cash flow projections, and debt repayment schedules. It helps investors assess the feasibility of the transaction and potential returns, considering the leverage and financial risk involved.

Merger and Acquisition (M&A) Modeling M&A modeling evaluates the financial impact of mergers and acquisitions. It includes valuation of the target company, purchase price allocation, and accretion/dilution analysis. This model helps in understanding the financial benefits and implications of a transaction, including how it will affect the acquiring company's earnings per share and overall financial position.

Conclusion

The quantitative side of investment banking integrates financial modeling, valuation, and transaction-specific analysis to provide a comprehensive view of financial health and potential. By mastering these skills, investment bankers can make informed decisions, offer valuable insights to clients, and drive successful transactions. The synergy between these quantitative tools enables investment bankers to navigate the complexities of corporate finance, from everyday financial analysis to major transactions like mergers and acquisitions.

NOTES:

Finance with Excel (Using Excel to run the data science process while solving for ROI)

Financial Accounting (The attribution rules and line items that aggregate to the different financial statements to display the descriptive data of the organization)

Corporate Finance (The Science behind the predictive relationships and prescriptive analytics in a strategic capital management context)

Financial Statement Reporting & Analysis (Where the descriptive data is housed and the basis for pulling into Excel)

Financial Statement Modeling (Pulling the attribution line items and reports into excel and interrelationships mathematically modeled to have a linked 3 statement model)

Financial Modeling (to find adjusted EBITDA proxy for Cash Flow)

Valuation: (To determine intrinsic and market value of the organization now and in the future)
- DCF Modeling (Intrinsic valuation)
- Comp Transactions Modeling (market valuation)
- Comp Companies Modeling (market valuation)

Transaction Specific Modeling: (To model the return from specific transactions given the sources and uses of capital)
- LBO Modeling (Financial sponsor)
- M&A Modeling (Strategic capital management)

NOTES:

Strategic Capital Management uses data science to solve for return as the prescriptive analytic.

Accounting provides the line itemed attribution structure necessary for capturing descriptive data. This descriptive data is aggregated in financial reports. In order to run our data science process (descriptive>predictive>prescriptive) we utilize excel to model the financial reports structure, drive predictive analytics and then ultimately utilize corporate finance valuation & Return concepts as the prescriptive analytic that we solve for.

Investment Banking University
All Rights Reserved

Chapter 65: Model Building Concepts

The Art and Science of Building Financial Models in Investment Banking

In investment banking, building a robust financial model is a critical skill. These models serve as essential tools for analyzing a company's financial performance, projecting future outcomes, and optimizing financial strategies. A well-constructed financial model comprises three core components: descriptive, predictive, and prescriptive analytics. Each plays a unique role in providing a comprehensive framework for decision-making. Let's delve into these concepts in greater detail.

1. Descriptive Analytics: Analyzing Historical Data

Laying the Foundation with Historical Data: The descriptive portion of a financial model involves gathering and analyzing historical financial data, typically spanning the last three to five years. This foundational step helps establish a clear picture of the company's past performance and provides insights into trends and patterns.

Key Elements:

- **Historical Financial Statements:** These include income statements, balance sheets, and cash flow statements, offering a detailed view of revenue, expenses, assets, liabilities, and equity.
- **Trend Analysis:** By examining historical data, analysts can identify trends in revenue growth, profit margins, and operating expenses. For instance, a consistent 10% annual revenue growth might indicate strong market positioning.
- **Benchmarking:** Comparing the company's metrics with industry averages and competitors helps highlight relative strengths and weaknesses.

Example & Visual: For example, if a company, ABC Corp., has shown consistent revenue growth of 10% annually, this positive trend can be visually represented in a line graph alongside profit margins and operating expenses over the past five years. Additionally, a table can compare ABC Corp.'s key financial metrics with industry benchmarks, providing a contextual understanding of its performance.

2. Predictive Analytics: Forecasting Future Performance

Projecting Financial Outcomes: The predictive portion focuses on forecasting the company's future financial performance. This involves creating pro forma financial statements for a defined projection period, typically five to ten years, including a terminal year.

Key Elements:

- **Pro Forma Financial Statements:** These projected statements include income, balance sheet, and cash flow forecasts based on historical trends and future assumptions.
- **Growth Assumptions:** These are based on historical data, industry analysis, and macroeconomic conditions. For

example, if ABC Corp. has grown revenues at 10% annually, a slightly lower future growth rate of 8% might be projected, considering market saturation.

- **Scenario Analysis:** This involves creating multiple scenarios (base, optimistic, pessimistic) to understand potential outcomes under different assumptions.

Example & Visual: ABC Corp.'s projections might show an 8% annual revenue growth over the next five years. A line graph can illustrate these projections under different scenarios, providing a visual representation of the expected financial trajectory.

3. Prescriptive Analytics: Optimizing Strategic Decisions

Optimizing for Success: The prescriptive portion focuses on analyzing various strategic options and determining the best course of action to achieve desired financial outcomes. This includes performing sensitivity analysis and using various valuation techniques.

Key Elements:

- **Optimization Strategies:** Analysts evaluate different financial strategies, such as cost reduction, pricing strategies, or investments in high-growth areas. For example, ABC Corp. might explore optimizing its supply chain to reduce costs.
- **Sensitivity Analysis:** Adjusting key assumptions (e.g., growth rates, discount rates) helps understand their impact on financial outcomes. This is crucial for identifying which factors most influence the company's valuation.
- **Valuation Techniques:** Methods like Discounted Cash Flow (DCF), Leveraged Buyout (LBO) analysis, and Comparable Company Analysis (CCA) provide a range of valuation estimates.

Example & Visual: For instance, conducting a sensitivity analysis for ABC Corp. with discount rates ranging from 8% to 10% can reveal how sensitive the company's valuation is to changes in the cost of capital. A chart can display this sensitivity, highlighting the most critical assumptions.

Conclusion

A comprehensive financial model integrates descriptive, predictive, and prescriptive analytics, providing a holistic view of a company's financial health and potential. The descriptive analysis offers a solid baseline, the predictive portion forecasts future performance, and the prescriptive analysis helps optimize strategic decisions. Together, these components enable investment bankers and analysts to make informed decisions, identify opportunities, and create value for clients. Understanding and effectively utilizing each component of the financial model is essential for success in investment banking.

Chapter 66: Introduction to Modeling Business Mathematics in Excel

Introduction to Modeling Business Mathematics in Excel

Mastering business mathematics in Excel is a fundamental skill for professionals in finance, analytics, and business decision-making. Excel's robust features allow users to automate calculations, manage data, and visualize complex relationships, making it an essential tool for modeling financial scenarios and business strategies. This post delves into the comprehensive use of Excel for business mathematics, covering everything from setting up equations to performing basic arithmetic operations.

Understanding Equations, Functions, & Numerical Processing

The Basics of Excel Equations

Equations in Excel are the foundation for performing calculations and data analysis. Every equation starts with an equals sign (=), which signals Excel to execute a calculation. The syntax typically consists of a **subject variable**, an **equality sign**, and an **expression** made up of **parameters** (cell references, numbers) and **operators** (such as +, -, *, /).

Components Explained:

- **Subject Variable:** This is the cell where the result of the equation will appear. For instance, in $A1 = B1 + C1$, A1 displays the sum of B1 and C1.
- **Equality Sign (=):** It indicates the start of a formula in Excel.
- **Expression:** The formula that performs the calculation, which can involve basic arithmetic or complex functions.

Understanding how these components work together allows users to automate data analysis tasks, simplifying complex calculations and improving efficiency.

Extending Business Mathematics to Algebra (Dynamic Variables)

Excel's power extends beyond basic arithmetic to handling algebraic relationships. Users can set up dynamic variables through cell references and formulas, enabling the creation of models that update automatically as input values change.

Steps to Set Up Algebraic Relationships:

1. **Cell References:** Use cell addresses to link data points dynamically. For example, $=A1 + B1$ will adjust automatically if the values in A1 or B1 change.
2. **Formulas:** These can range from simple operations to more complex functions, like $=B1*C1/D1$.
3. **Order of Operations:** Excel follows the standard mathematical order of operations (PEMDAS). It's crucial to structure formulas correctly to ensure accurate results. For example, in $=(A1 + B1) * C1$, the parentheses ensure that addition is performed before multiplication.

These capabilities are essential for financial modeling, where changes in assumptions must reflect immediately in output metrics.

Understanding Data Tables, Graphs & the Coordinate Plane

Visualizing Data Relationships

Excel allows users to visualize data through graphs and charts, making it easier to identify trends, patterns, and relationships between variables. This visual representation is critical for data-driven decision-making.

Creating Graphs:

1. **Select Data:** Highlight the data range you wish to visualize.
2. **Insert Chart:** Navigate to the Insert tab and select a chart type, such as a line, bar, or scatter chart.
3. **Customize:** Adjust elements like titles, labels, and legends to enhance clarity and readability.

For instance, a line chart depicting monthly sales data can reveal seasonal trends, helping businesses plan inventory and marketing strategies.

The Flow of Return Values & Input Parameters in a Fully Linked Model

In Excel, return values from one function can act as input parameters for another, creating a fully linked model. This interconnectedness ensures that any change in one part of the model propagates throughout, maintaining consistency and accuracy.

Building Linked Models:

1. **Define Inputs:** Identify key variables that influence the model.

2. **Create Formulas:** Link these inputs to derive output values using Excel functions.
3. **Ensure Consistency:** Use absolute references (e.g., A1) to maintain fixed references, or named ranges for clarity and error reduction.

For example, calculating a company's net income involves linking revenues, expenses, and tax rates across different worksheets, ensuring that updates in revenue projections automatically reflect in the net income calculation.

What Are You Solving For?

Determining the **subject variable** involves identifying the key output or metric you need to calculate, such as profit margins, break-even points, or return on investment.

Steps to Identify the Subject Variable:

1. **Define Objectives:** Understand the purpose of the analysis (e.g., maximizing profit).
2. **Set Up Equations:** Use relevant data and formulas to derive the subject variable.
3. **Validate Results:** Cross-check the results for accuracy and alignment with business objectives.

Modeling Basic Arithmetic Operations in Excel

Performing Basic Arithmetic Operations

Excel simplifies basic arithmetic through intuitive formulas.

Addition and Subtraction:

- =A1 + B1 for addition.
- =A1 - B1 for subtraction.

Multiplication and Division:

- =A1 * B1 for multiplication.
- =A1 / B1 for division.

Order of Operations: Excel adheres to PEMDAS, so ensure correct use of parentheses to control the order of calculations.

Excel Functions for Arithmetic Operations

Excel provides built-in functions to streamline arithmetic operations:

- **SUM:** Adds a range of numbers (e.g., =SUM(A1:A10)).
- **AVERAGE:** Calculates the average of a range (e.g., =AVERAGE(B1:B10)).
- **ROUND:** Rounds a number to a specified number of decimal places (e.g., =ROUND(C1, 2)).

Building Formulas: Combine cell references, constants, and operators to create complex, dynamic formulas that update automatically with changes in data.

Applying Absolute and Relative Cell References

Absolute References: Use dollar signs (A1) to fix a cell reference, ensuring it doesn't change when the formula is copied elsewhere.

Relative References: These adjust automatically when a formula is copied to another cell (e.g., A1 becomes B1 when moved one column to the right).

Named Ranges: Assign descriptive names to ranges (e.g., `SalesData`), making formulas easier to read and maintain (e.g., `=SUM(SalesData)`).

Conclusion

Mastering business mathematics in Excel is a critical skill for building robust financial models and performing accurate data analysis. Excel's functionalities enable dynamic, precise, and efficient calculations, supporting informed decision-making and driving business success. Understanding these concepts not only enhances your technical proficiency but also empowers you to tackle complex business challenges with confidence.

Chapter 67: How to Model Mathematical Variables & Formulas in Excel

How to Model Mathematical Variables & Formulas in Excel

Introduction to Excel Financial Modeling

In Excel financial modeling, accurately representing and manipulating variables is key to building dynamic and robust financial models. Variables in Excel are often represented as cell references within a spreadsheet, allowing for easy calculations and updates. This post explores the fundamentals of using variables and formulas in Excel, focusing on creating a dynamic and interconnected financial model.

Representing Variables with Cell References

What Are Cell References?

In Excel, each cell within a spreadsheet is uniquely identified by its column letter and row number, known as a cell reference. For instance, the cell located at the intersection of the first row and first column is referred to as A1. This referencing system allows users to easily pinpoint and manipulate specific data points within a large dataset.

Example of Basic Cell Reference Usage

Suppose you want to calculate revenue based on the price and volume of a product. You would use a formula referencing the cells containing these variables. For example, if the price per unit is located in cell B2 and the number of units sold is in cell C2, the formula for calculating revenue would be:

Copy code

```
=B2 * C2
```

In this example, B2 represents the price per unit, and C2 represents the volume sold. The formula multiplies these two values to compute the total revenue.

Linking Variables Across Multiple Cells and Formulas

Building a Comprehensive Financial Model

Financial models often consist of interconnected variables that flow through various calculations, reflecting the relationships between different financial metrics. For example, the revenue calculated in one part of the model might be used to determine gross profit, which, in turn, influences net income calculations.

Creating Dynamic Links

To build these connections, you reference the output of one formula as the input to another. For instance, if revenue (in cell B4) and the cost of goods sold (in cell B5) are already calculated, you can compute the gross profit using:

Copy code
```
=B4 - B5
```

Here, B4 (revenue) and B5 (cost of goods sold) are the input variables, and their difference gives the gross profit. If either revenue or costs change, the gross profit calculation will automatically update, showcasing the dynamic nature of the model.

Advanced Techniques for Financial Modeling

Using Named Ranges

For more complex models, it's often helpful to use named ranges instead of simple cell references. A named range is a descriptive name that you assign to a cell or range of cells. For example, you could name cell B2 as "PricePerUnit" and cell C2 as "UnitsSold." The formula for revenue would then become:

Copy code
```
=PricePerUnit * UnitsSold
```

Using named ranges makes formulas easier to read and manage, especially in large models.

Applying Financial Functions

Excel offers a wide range of built-in financial functions, such as **NPV (Net Present Value)**, **IRR (Internal Rate of Return)**, and **PMT (Payment for an annuity)**. These functions are useful for performing complex financial calculations and can be integrated into your models to provide deeper insights.

Scenario and Sensitivity Analysis

Excel allows for scenario and sensitivity analysis, which involves changing key variables to see how they affect outcomes. Tools like **Data Tables**, **Scenario Manager**, and **Goal Seek** are invaluable for this purpose, enabling you to simulate different financial situations and their potential impacts.

Conclusion

Excel is a powerful tool for financial modeling, allowing users to create dynamic and adaptable models by linking variables through cell references and formulas. By accurately representing financial relationships and using advanced techniques like named ranges and financial functions, you can build comprehensive models that provide valuable insights into various business scenarios. This flexibility is crucial for making informed financial decisions and adapting to changing market conditions.

Chapter 68: Most Important Finance with Excel Concepts for a Beginner to Know

Mastering Finance with Excel: Key Concepts for Beginners

Excel is an indispensable tool in the world of finance, providing the means to analyze data, create financial models, and present findings effectively. For beginners, mastering the basics can set a strong foundation for more advanced financial analysis. Here are the most important Excel concepts every finance newcomer should know:

1. Basic Excel Functions

SUM, AVERAGE, MIN, MAX, COUNT: These fundamental functions allow you to perform basic calculations such as adding, averaging, finding minimum and maximum values, and counting items in a data set. For instance, the SUM function helps in calculating the total revenue from different product lines, while AVERAGE can provide insights into the mean revenue per product.

Example:

- `=SUM(B2:B10)` calculates the total from cells B2 to B10.
- `=AVERAGE(C2:C10)` finds the average value in cells C2 to C10.

2. Formatting and Charting

Cell Formatting: Understanding how to format cells, rows, and columns is crucial for clarity and professionalism. This includes setting currency formats, adjusting decimal places, and using conditional formatting to highlight key data points.

Charts and Graphs: Visual representations such as bar charts, line graphs, and pie charts make it easier to interpret data and identify trends. They are invaluable for presenting financial data clearly and compellingly.

Example:

- Creating a bar chart to compare quarterly sales figures across different regions.

3. Pivot Tables

Pivot tables are powerful tools for summarizing and analyzing large datasets. They allow you to reorganize data dynamically, making it easy to identify trends and patterns.

Applications:

- Analyzing sales data by region, product line, or time period.
- Summarizing financial data to quickly assess performance metrics.

Example:

- A pivot table can help you summarize total sales by product category and region, providing a clear view of where the strongest sales are occurring.

4. Using Formulas

Formulas are the backbone of financial analysis in Excel. They allow for the calculation of various financial metrics, such as:

Compound Interest:

- $=PV*(1+r)^n$ where PV is the present value, r is the interest rate, and n is the number of periods.

Present Value (PV):

- $=FV\ /\ (1+r)^n$ where FV is future value.

Future Value (FV):

- $=PV*(1+r)^n$

These formulas help in evaluating investment opportunities, loan schedules, and more.

5. Sensitivity Analysis

Sensitivity analysis involves changing key variables in your model to see how these changes impact the outcome. This is essential for understanding the risk and potential variability in financial forecasts.

Applications:

- Assessing how changes in interest rates affect loan payments.
- Analyzing the impact of price changes on profit margins.

6. Financial Modeling

Financial modeling involves creating detailed models that represent a company's financial performance. Basic models include:

Income Statements:

- Detailing revenues, expenses, and profits.

Balance Sheets:

- Showing assets, liabilities, and equity.

Cash Flow Statements:

- Tracking cash inflows and outflows.

These models are used for forecasting future financial performance, conducting valuation analyses, and making investment decisions.

7. Macros

Macros are automated sequences that execute repetitive tasks, saving time and reducing errors. They are particularly useful for tasks like data cleaning, report generation, and complex calculations.

Example:

- Automating the update of a financial model with the latest data inputs.

8. Keyboard Shortcuts

Efficiency in Excel is greatly enhanced by using keyboard shortcuts. Some essential shortcuts include:

- **Ctrl + C:** Copy
- **Ctrl + V:** Paste
- **Ctrl + Z:** Undo

- **Ctrl + T:** Create a table
- **Alt + E, S, V:** Paste special values

Mastering these shortcuts can significantly speed up your workflow and improve productivity.

Conclusion

For beginners in finance, gaining proficiency in these essential Excel concepts provides a solid foundation for more complex financial analysis and modeling. By mastering basic functions, formatting, pivot tables, formulas, sensitivity analysis, financial modeling, macros, and keyboard shortcuts, you can unlock the full potential of Excel as a powerful tool in your finance toolkit. As you become more comfortable with these basics, you can explore more advanced features and techniques to further enhance your financial analysis capabilities.

Chapter 69: What is Excel and How is It Used in Investment Banking

The Crucial Role of Excel in Investment Banking

Excel, a versatile and powerful software program, plays an indispensable role in the finance industry, particularly in investment banking. It serves as a foundational tool for financial modeling, data analysis, and the creation of reports and presentations. This blog post explores the various ways Excel is utilized in investment banking and why it remains a go-to application for professionals in the field.

Financial Modeling and Analysis

One of the primary uses of Excel in investment banking is for financial modeling. Investment bankers build intricate financial models using Excel to forecast future earnings, assess the value of assets and companies, and evaluate the financial viability of potential investments. These models are crucial for making informed decisions, as they allow bankers to simulate different scenarios and understand the potential outcomes of various strategic options.

For example, an investment banker might use Excel to create a discounted cash flow (DCF) model, which helps in estimating the value of a company by projecting its future cash flows and discounting them to present value. This process involves complex calculations that Excel can handle efficiently, thanks to its built-in financial functions and the ability to create custom formulas.

Data Organization and Manipulation

Investment banking often involves analyzing vast amounts of financial data. Excel's capabilities in organizing, manipulating, and managing this data are invaluable. With features like pivot tables, data sorting, and filtering, investment bankers can quickly sift through large datasets to identify key trends and insights. This is particularly useful when dealing with data from financial statements, market analysis, and other sources.

For instance, pivot tables in Excel allow bankers to summarize large datasets dynamically, making it easier to analyze metrics like revenue growth, expense trends, or profit margins across different time periods or business units. This level of analysis is critical for making strategic recommendations and decisions.

Report and Presentation Generation

In addition to analysis, Excel is also a vital tool for creating reports and presentations. Investment bankers often need to present complex financial data to clients, investors, or internal stakeholders in a clear and concise manner. Excel facilitates the creation of charts, graphs, and other visual aids that help to distill complex information into easily understandable formats.

For example, a banker might use Excel to generate a comparative analysis chart, showing how a company's financial metrics stack up against its peers. This visual representation can be crucial in making persuasive arguments during client meetings or pitch presentations.

Customization and Flexibility

One of the most significant advantages of Excel is its flexibility and customizability. Investment banks can create their own custom templates, macros, and add-ins to automate repetitive tasks or streamline financial modeling processes. This customization can save significant time and reduce the risk of errors in complex calculations.

For instance, a custom Excel template for mergers and acquisitions (M&A) analysis might include pre-built models for valuation, synergy estimation, and transaction structuring. This allows bankers to focus on the analysis and strategic aspects rather than building models from scratch each time.

Conclusion

Excel remains an essential tool in investment banking due to its robust capabilities in financial modeling, data manipulation, and report generation. Its versatility and flexibility allow investment bankers to tailor their workflows and analyses to meet specific needs, making it an invaluable asset in the financial industry. Whether it's forecasting future earnings, organizing large datasets, or creating impactful presentations, Excel continues to be a cornerstone of investment banking operations.

Chapter 70: Data Science & the Analyst/Associate Role

The Integration of Data Science in the Analyst/Associate Role in Investment Banking

In the modern financial landscape, data science and analytics have become integral to the operations of investment banking. These disciplines are not just peripheral support functions but are central to decision-making processes that drive significant financial outcomes. This blog post explores how data science is applied within the roles of analysts and associates in investment banking, highlighting the methodologies, tools, and techniques used to derive actionable insights.

The Role of Data Science & Analytics

Data Science in Finance: Data science in finance involves using descriptive, predictive, and prescriptive analytics to make decisions that optimize return on investment (ROI). Investment banking, as a specialized field of finance, heavily relies on these analytics to evaluate deals, assess market conditions, and strategize client engagements.

Key Activities in Data Science:

1. **Data Cleaning & Organization:** The process begins with collecting and preparing data, often from diverse sources such as Excel and Access databases. This step is crucial for ensuring the accuracy and reliability of the analysis.

2. **Data Modeling & Analysis:** Analysts and associates use various analytic methodologies to model data, identifying patterns that can lead to actionable insights. These insights are crucial for driving high-level business decisions.
3. **Data Visualization (Dataviz):** Creating visual representations of data helps communicate complex patterns and trends clearly and concisely, making it easier for decision-makers to understand and act upon them.

Data Science Techniques in Investment Banking

Pivot Tables & Data Analysis in Excel: Excel remains a fundamental tool in investment banking. Analysts frequently use pivot tables to summarize, analyze, and explore data sets from multiple perspectives. This capability is vital for identifying trends and relationships within the data.

Analytic Methodologies:

- **Descriptive Analytics:** Involves summarizing historical data to understand what has happened in the past. This includes calculating statistical measures such as mean, median, mode, variance, and standard deviation.
- **Predictive Analytics:** Utilizes statistical models and machine learning techniques to forecast future events based on historical data. This could involve predicting market trends, company performance, or the likelihood of a successful merger.
- **Prescriptive Analytics:** Focuses on recommending actions based on predictive models. This is particularly useful in scenario planning and decision-making.

Key Excel Functions & Formulas: Investment banking analysts and associates must be proficient in Excel's syntax and functions, such as =COVAR for calculating covariance, which measures the degree to which two variables change together. Understanding and applying these formulas is critical for analyzing financial data and deriving insights.

Application in Investment Banking

Analysts & Associates as Data Scientists: In the context of investment banking, analysts and associates function as data scientists. Their roles involve:

- **Data Collection & Cleaning:** Ensuring data accuracy and reliability before analysis.
- **Financial Modeling:** Building models to forecast financial outcomes and assess the potential of different strategic alternatives.
- **Visualization & Communication:** Creating dashboards and visualizations to present findings to senior bankers and clients, aiding in decision-making.

Dealmaking & Data Science: While senior bankers (VP and above) focus on dealmaking and client relationships, analysts and associates provide the analytical backbone that supports these activities. They supply the necessary data-driven insights that inform strategic decisions and negotiations.

Conclusion

The integration of data science into the roles of analysts and associates in investment banking underscores the importance of technical skills and analytical thinking in the finance industry. As the field continues to evolve, proficiency in data analytics tools and methodologies will remain a critical component of success. Through a combination of descriptive, predictive, and prescriptive analytics, investment banking professionals can better understand market conditions, forecast outcomes, and recommend optimal strategies, ultimately enhancing client value and driving business growth.

Chapter 71: Financial Modeling & Valuation Steps

Financial Modeling & Valuation: A Step-by-Step Guide

In investment banking, financial modeling and valuation are critical processes, particularly during mergers and acquisitions (M&A). These processes provide the foundation for assessing the value of a target company, enabling informed decision-making. This blog post outlines the comprehensive steps involved in building a financial model and determining a company's valuation.

1. Gathering Historical Financial Data

Objective: The first crucial step is to collect the target company's historical financial data, typically covering the past three to five years. This data serves as the foundation for creating financial projections and conducting a thorough analysis.

Steps:

- **Collect Financial Statements:** Gather income statements, balance sheets, and cash flow statements. These documents provide a detailed overview of the company's financial health and performance.

- **Ensure Data Accuracy:** It's vital to verify the accuracy and completeness of the collected data, ensuring that all relevant financial transactions are correctly recorded.
- **Analyze Historical Trends:** Look for trends in revenue, expenses, profit margins, and cash flow. Understanding these trends helps in forecasting future performance.

Why It Matters: Accurate historical data enables investment bankers to construct reliable financial models, identify growth patterns, and assess the company's operational efficiency.

2. Building the Financial Statement Model

Objective: Develop a comprehensive financial statement model, including the income statement, balance sheet, and cash flow statement. This model serves as the basis for projecting future financial performance.

Steps:

- **Income Statement:** Detail revenues, cost of goods sold (COGS), operating expenses, and net income. This statement helps in understanding profitability.
- **Balance Sheet:** Document assets, liabilities, and shareholders' equity, providing a snapshot of the company's financial position.
- **Cash Flow Statement:** Track cash inflows and outflows, categorizing them into operating, investing, and financing activities.

Importance: The financial statement model allows for a holistic view of the company's financial health, necessary for making informed strategic decisions.

3. Calculating Adjusted EBITDA

Objective: Determine the Adjusted Earnings Before Interest, Taxes, Depreciation, and Amortization (EBITDA), which offers a clearer picture of the company's operational cash flow by excluding non-recurring and non-operational items.

Steps:

- **Standard EBITDA Calculation:** Start with net income and add back interest, taxes, depreciation, and amortization.
- **Identify Adjustments:** Include non-recurring expenses, such as restructuring costs or legal fees, and other adjustments like owner's compensation if above market rates.
- **Compute Adjusted EBITDA:** Adjust the standard EBITDA to reflect the true operational performance.

Importance: Adjusted EBITDA provides a more accurate measure of a company's operational efficiency and cash flow potential, crucial for valuation.

4. Valuation Methodologies Using Adjusted EBITDA

Objective: Use the Adjusted EBITDA to derive the company's valuation through various methodologies, providing a comprehensive valuation range.

Methodologies:

- **Comparable Company Analysis (Comps):**

- - **Process:** Identify public companies similar to the target in size and industry.
  - **Application:** Use valuation multiples (e.g., EV/EBITDA) from these companies to estimate the target's value.
- **Precedent Transactions Analysis:**
  - **Process:** Analyze past transactions involving similar companies.
  - **Application:** Apply the multiples from these transactions to the target company's Adjusted EBITDA.
- **Discounted Cash Flow (DCF) Analysis:**
  - **Process:** Project future cash flows and discount them to their present value using the company's weighted average cost of capital (WACC).
  - **Application:** This method focuses on the company's intrinsic value based on projected cash flows.

Importance: Using multiple valuation methodologies provides a range of values, ensuring a comprehensive assessment and minimizing biases.

5. Creating the Valuation Football Field

Objective: Visually represent the valuation range derived from the different methodologies to communicate the potential value spectrum effectively.

Steps:

- **Compile Valuation Estimates:** Gather results from Comps, Precedent Transactions, and DCF analyses.
- **Create Football Field Chart:** Illustrate the range of valuations to show high, low, and midpoint estimates.

- **Highlight Key Insights:** Use the chart to discuss the valuation range with stakeholders, providing a clear and visual representation of potential outcomes.

Importance: The valuation football field helps stakeholders understand the valuation spectrum and make informed decisions.

6. Customizing the Financial Model for Specific Transactions

Objective: Tailor the financial model for specific transactions, reflecting unique aspects and considerations of particular buyers or transaction scenarios.

Steps:

- **Identify Specific Considerations:** Determine buyer-specific factors like strategic fit, synergies, and financial structure.
- **Adjust Assumptions:** Modify the financial model to incorporate these factors, ensuring relevance to the transaction context.
- **Conduct Prescriptive Analysis:** Use the customized model to recommend optimal transaction structures and identify key value drivers.

Importance: Customization ensures the model reflects the specific dynamics of the transaction, aiding in accurate valuation and successful deal structuring.

Conclusion

Financial modeling and valuation are integral to investment banking, providing a robust framework for assessing company value. By following these detailed steps, investment bankers can create comprehensive and accurate financial models, helping clients make well-informed strategic decisions during M&A transactions. This meticulous approach ensures that all financial aspects are considered, leading to fair and objective valuations.

Chapter 72: The Analysis Process in Investment Banking

The Analysis Process in Investment Banking: Turning Data into Actionable Insights

In investment banking, the ability to analyze and interpret data is crucial for making informed decisions and maximizing return on investment (ROI). The analysis process involves a structured approach to collecting, analyzing, and reporting data to provide actionable insights. Here's a comprehensive breakdown of the process:

1. Planning: Strategizing Key Performance Indicators (KPIs)

The first step in the analysis process is to **strategize** and **identify the key performance indicators (KPIs)** or value drivers that are most likely to impact ROI. This involves:

- **Setting Objectives:** Clearly defining what the analysis aims to achieve, whether it's assessing the financial health of a company, forecasting future performance, or identifying potential investment opportunities.

- **Identifying Value Drivers:** Pinpointing the specific factors that can influence the business's value, such as revenue growth, cost efficiency, market share, and customer satisfaction.
- **Selecting KPIs:** Choosing measurable metrics that can accurately reflect the performance of these value drivers. For example, metrics like EBITDA, net profit margin, and return on equity (ROE) are commonly used in financial analysis.

By carefully planning and selecting the right KPIs, analysts can focus their efforts on the most relevant data, ensuring that the analysis is both efficient and effective.

2. Data Collection: Gathering Information from Various Sources

Once the KPIs are identified, the next step is to **collect data**. This involves gathering information from various attribution sources, including:

- **Internal Data:** Financial statements, sales records, and operational data from within the company.
- **External Data:** Market reports, economic indicators, and competitor analysis obtained from third-party research firms or public databases.
- **Real-Time Data:** For more dynamic analyses, real-time data feeds such as stock prices, economic news, and market sentiment can be incorporated.

Data collection must be meticulous to ensure accuracy and reliability. The quality of the data directly impacts the validity of the analysis.

3. Analysis: Exploring and Interpreting the Data

The analysis phase involves several **subprocesses** to model the data and uncover insights. These include:

- **Descriptive Analytics:** This involves summarizing historical data to understand what has happened in the past. It includes calculating averages, identifying trends, and creating data visualizations to depict past performance.
  Example: Analyzing quarterly earnings reports to identify seasonal trends in revenue.
- **Predictive Analytics:** This focuses on forecasting future outcomes based on historical data. Techniques like regression analysis, time series forecasting, and machine learning models are used to predict future trends and behaviors.
  Example: Predicting future stock prices based on historical trends and economic indicators.
- **Prescriptive Analytics:** This involves suggesting actions to optimize outcomes. It uses the insights gained from descriptive and predictive analytics to recommend strategies and actions.
  Example: Advising a company to diversify its product portfolio based on market trends and consumer preferences.

By leveraging these analytical techniques, investment bankers can interpret the relationships and trends in the data, providing a comprehensive understanding of the business environment.

4. Reporting: Communicating Insights Through Data Visualization

The final step is to **report the findings** in a clear and actionable manner. This is where the concept of **Data Visualization (Dataviz)** comes into play. Investment bankers use visually appealing and intuitive charts, graphs, and infographics to present the data. Effective reporting involves:

- **Clear Communication:** Presenting complex data in a straightforward manner that is easy to understand for stakeholders, including non-technical audiences.

- **Actionable Insights:** Highlighting key takeaways and recommendations based on the analysis. This could include strategic recommendations, potential risks, and investment opportunities.
- **Interactive Elements:** In some cases, interactive dashboards are used to allow stakeholders to explore the data and insights on their own, providing a more engaging experience.

For example, a report might use a combination of bar charts, line graphs, and heat maps to illustrate a company's financial performance, market trends, and competitive positioning.

Conclusion

The analysis process in investment banking is a systematic approach that transforms raw data into actionable insights. By strategically planning, collecting relevant data, conducting thorough analysis, and effectively reporting the findings, investment bankers provide valuable guidance to their clients. This process not only helps in making informed decisions but also in optimizing financial performance and achieving strategic objectives.

Chapter 73: Introduction to Financial Accounting

Introduction to Financial Accounting: A Foundation for Investment Banking

Financial accounting is the cornerstone of corporate reporting and financial analysis in investment banking. It provides a standardized framework for recording, summarizing, and communicating a company's financial information. This blog post explores the essential principles and concepts of financial accounting that investment bankers need to master to analyze and evaluate financial statements effectively.

Purpose of Financial Accounting

Overview: Financial accounting serves as the backbone of corporate reporting. It enables stakeholders to assess a company's financial health and performance by providing critical information about assets, liabilities, equity, revenue, and expenses.

Importance:

1. **Informed Decision-Making:** Financial accounting delivers detailed financial information that helps investors, analysts, and lenders make informed decisions about investing in, lending to, or doing business with a company. For instance, it

includes insights into a company's profitability, liquidity, and solvency.

2. **Standardization:** Financial accounting ensures consistency, comparability, and transparency in financial reporting. This standardization is crucial for accurate financial analysis across different companies and industries, enabling stakeholders to compare financial statements easily and make accurate assessments.

Examples:

- **Annual Reports:** Companies publish annual reports based on financial accounting principles. Stakeholders use these reports, which include financial statements and management discussions, to evaluate a company's financial health.
- **Financial Projections:** Investment bankers use historical financial data to create future financial projections, aiding in M&A, IPOs, and other financial activities. Accurate projections help assess potential growth and risks.

Generally Accepted Accounting Principles (GAAP)

Overview: GAAP is a set of standardized principles that ensure consistency, comparability, and transparency in financial reporting.

Key Principles:

- **Consistency:** Financial statements should be prepared using the same accounting methods from period to period, facilitating comparability over time.
- **Relevance:** Financial information must be relevant to the decision-making needs of users, providing useful insights for stakeholders.

- **Reliability:** Financial information should be free from material error and bias, presenting an accurate depiction of the company's financial status.
- **Comparability:** Financial information should be comparable across different companies and time periods, aiding in benchmarking and performance analysis.

Importance for Investment Bankers: Familiarity with GAAP is essential for interpreting financial statements accurately, allowing investment bankers to assess the financial health and performance of companies based on reliable data.

Examples:

- **Revenue Recognition:** GAAP provides guidelines on when revenue should be recognized, ensuring consistency in reporting.
- **Expense Matching:** GAAP requires expenses to be matched with related revenues, providing a clear picture of profitability.

Financial Statements

Overview: Financial accounting produces several key financial statements that investment bankers analyze to assess a company's financial position, profitability, cash flow generation, and changes in shareholders' equity over time.

Key Financial Statements:

- **Balance Sheet:** Provides a snapshot of a company's financial position at a specific point in time, listing assets, liabilities, and equity.
- **Income Statement:** Presents a company's revenues, expenses, gains, and losses over a specific period, showing the company's profitability.

- **Cash Flow Statement:** Tracks the inflow and outflow of cash from a company's operating, investing, and financing activities, highlighting liquidity and cash management.
- **Statement of Changes in Equity:** Shows changes in shareholders' equity over a period, including retained earnings, dividends, and other equity adjustments.

Examples:

- **Balance Sheet Analysis:** Evaluating liquidity and leverage by analyzing current assets versus current liabilities and debt-to-equity ratios.
- **Income Statement Analysis:** Assessing profitability by examining revenue trends, cost structures, and net income margins.
- **Cash Flow Statement Analysis:** Understanding cash generation and usage by reviewing operating cash flow, free cash flow, and cash flows from investing and financing activities.

Balance Sheet Analysis

Overview: The balance sheet provides a snapshot of a company's financial position at a specific point in time, including assets, liabilities, and equity.

Key Components:

- **Assets:** Resources owned by the company with economic value.
- **Liabilities:** Obligations the company owes to others.
- **Equity:** The residual interest in the company's assets after deducting liabilities.

Importance for Investment Bankers: Analyzing the balance sheet helps investment bankers evaluate a company's liquidity, leverage, and asset composition, using key ratios such as the current ratio, debt-to-equity ratio, and inventory turnover.

Steps:

- **Evaluate Liquidity:** Assess the company's ability to meet short-term obligations.
- **Analyze Leverage:** Determine the level of financial risk by examining the debt-to-equity ratio.
- **Review Asset Composition:** Understand the structure of the company's assets and their potential impact on financial health.

Examples:

- **High Debt-to-Equity Ratio:** Indicates higher financial risk due to increased reliance on debt financing.
- **Strong Current Ratio:** Suggests good short-term financial health, indicating the company can easily cover its short-term liabilities.

Income Statement Analysis

Overview: The income statement presents a company's revenues, expenses, gains, and losses over a specific period, typically a quarter or a year.

Key Metrics:

- **Revenue:** Total income generated from sales or services.
- **Gross Profit:** Revenue minus the cost of goods sold (COGS).
- **Operating Income:** Gross profit minus operating expenses.
- **Net Income:** Total profit after all expenses, taxes, and interest.

Importance for Investment Bankers: Assessing the income statement helps investment bankers understand a company's profitability, revenue sources, cost structure, and operating performance.

Steps:

- **Analyze Revenue Trends:** Evaluate the growth or decline in revenue over time.
- **Examine Cost Structure:** Identify major expenses and assess their impact on profitability.
- **Evaluate Profitability:** Use profitability ratios to measure the company's ability to generate profit from its operations.

Examples:

- **Increasing Operating Margin:** Indicates improved operational efficiency and cost management.
- **Declining Net Income:** May suggest rising expenses, declining sales, or other financial challenges.

Cash Flow Statement Analysis

Overview: The cash flow statement tracks the inflow and outflow of cash from a company's operating, investing, and financing activities.

Key Components:

- **Operating Activities:** Cash flows from core business operations.
- **Investing Activities:** Cash flows from the acquisition and disposal of long-term assets.
- **Financing Activities:** Cash flows from transactions with owners and creditors.

Importance for Investment Bankers: Focusing on cash flow analysis helps investment bankers evaluate a company's liquidity, cash generation, and ability to meet financial obligations.

Steps:

- **Review Operating Cash Flow:** Assess the cash generated from core business operations.
- **Analyze Investing Cash Flow:** Evaluate cash used for or generated from investing activities.
- **Examine Financing Cash Flow:** Understand cash flows related to financing activities.

Examples:

- **Positive Free Cash Flow:** Indicates the company generates sufficient cash from operations to fund its capital expenditures and other investments.
- **Negative Operating Cash Flow:** Suggests potential liquidity issues, indicating the company may struggle to generate cash from its core operations.

Conclusion

Summary: Financial accounting is a vital aspect of investment banking, enabling professionals to evaluate a company's financial health, profitability, and overall performance. By understanding accounting principles, analyzing financial statements, and interpreting key ratios, investment bankers can make informed decisions and provide valuable insights to stakeholders.

Key Takeaways:

- **Understanding GAAP:** Essential for accurate financial analysis and consistent reporting.

- **Analyzing Financial Statements:** Crucial for assessing a company's financial position, profitability, and cash flow.
- **Employing Financial Ratios:** Helps identify strengths, weaknesses, and potential risks in a company's financial performance.
- **Evaluating Revenue Recognition and Investments:** Ensures the reliability and accuracy of financial reporting.
- **Reviewing Disclosures and Footnotes:** Provides additional context and insights, leading to a comprehensive understanding of the financial statements.

By mastering these concepts, investment bankers can create robust financial models, perform thorough valuations, and offer well-informed recommendations, ultimately enhancing their ability to serve clients and make strategic investment decisions.

Chapter 74: Introduction to Financial Statements

Understanding Financial Statements: A Guide for Investment Bankers

Financial statements are the cornerstone of corporate financial reporting and are vital for stakeholders, including investment bankers, to assess a company's financial health and performance. This blog post delves into the critical aspects of financial statements, highlighting their purpose, key components, and the analytical techniques used by investment bankers to evaluate a company's financial position.

The Purpose of Financial Statements

Financial statements provide a comprehensive overview of a company's financial activities and condition. They serve multiple purposes:

1. **Profitability Assessment**: Analyzing how effectively a company generates profit from its operations.
2. **Liquidity Evaluation**: Determining the company's ability to meet short-term obligations.
3. **Solvency Analysis**: Assessing the company's capacity to handle long-term liabilities.
4. **Cash Flow Insight**: Understanding the flow of cash in and out of the business, crucial for operational efficiency.

For investment bankers, these documents are indispensable for making informed decisions about mergers and acquisitions (M&A), investment opportunities, and corporate strategies.

Key Financial Statements

1. **The Balance Sheet**
   Overview: The balance sheet offers a snapshot of a company's financial position at a specific point in time, detailing assets, liabilities, and shareholders' equity.
   - **Assets**: Divided into current (short-term) and non-current (long-term), including cash, inventory, and property.
   - **Liabilities**: Obligations, categorized into current (due within a year) and non-current (due after a year).
   - **Shareholders' Equity**: The residual interest in the assets after deducting liabilities.
2. **Analysis**:
   - **Liquidity**: Measured by ratios like the current ratio (current assets/current liabilities).
   - **Leverage**: Evaluated using the debt-to-equity ratio (total liabilities/shareholders' equity).
3. **The Income Statement**
   Overview: The income statement provides details on a company's revenues, expenses, and profits over a specified period.
   - **Revenue**: Total income from sales or services.
   - **Expenses**: Costs incurred in generating revenue, including cost of goods sold (COGS) and operating expenses.
   - **Net Income**: The profit after all expenses are deducted from revenues.
4. **Analysis**:

- o **Profitability**: Gross margin, operating margin, and net profit margin are key metrics.
- o **Cost Structure**: Insight into major expenses and their impact on profitability.

5. **The Statement of Cash Flows**
   Overview: This statement outlines the cash inflows and outflows categorized into operating, investing, and financing activities.
   - o **Operating Activities**: Cash from core business operations.
   - o **Investing Activities**: Cash flows from buying and selling long-term assets.
   - o **Financing Activities**: Cash flows related to debt and equity financing.

6. **Analysis**:
   - o **Liquidity**: Assessed through operating cash flow.
   - o **Cash Generation**: Measured by free cash flow, indicating the cash available after capital expenditures.

Analytical Techniques in Financial Statement Analysis

1. **Financial Ratio Analysis**
   Ratios provide insights into various aspects of a company's financial health:
   - o **Current Ratio**: Indicates liquidity.
   - o **Debt-to-Equity Ratio**: Assesses solvency and financial leverage.
   - o **Return on Equity (ROE)**: Measures profitability relative to shareholders' equity.

2. **Trend Analysis**
   Involves comparing financial statement items over multiple periods to identify growth patterns and performance trends. It

helps in understanding the company's growth trajectory and risk factors.

3. **Common-Size Analysis**
Expresses each financial statement item as a percentage of a base figure, such as total assets or total revenue, facilitating comparison across companies or industries.

4. **Vertical and Horizontal Analysis**
   - **Vertical Analysis**: Assesses the proportional size of items within a single financial statement.
   - **Horizontal Analysis**: Compares financial data across periods to identify growth trends and performance changes.

Limitations of Financial Statement Analysis

While financial statements are invaluable, they have limitations:

- **Historical Nature**: They reflect past performance and may not predict future conditions.
- **Accounting Policies**: Variations in accounting methods can affect comparability.
- **Qualitative Factors**: Financial statements often omit qualitative factors like market conditions, management quality, and industry changes.

Conclusion

Financial statements are essential tools for investment bankers, providing a wealth of information that guides investment decisions and strategic planning. By mastering financial statement analysis, investment bankers can offer comprehensive evaluations and insightful recommendations, aiding clients in navigating the complex financial landscape. Understanding these documents' nuances ensures that investment bankers can effectively assess companies' financial health and make informed decisions in a dynamic and competitive market.

Chapter 75: Introduction to Corporate Finance

Understanding Corporate Finance: A Guide for Investment Bankers

Corporate finance is a cornerstone of investment banking, focusing on the financial strategies and decisions of corporations. This field encompasses various aspects, from capital structure and cost of capital to valuation and risk management. In this blog post, we will delve into the core principles of corporate finance, offering a comprehensive overview for investment bankers to better analyze, evaluate, and advise on financial strategies and transactions.

Capital Structure: Balancing Debt and Equity

Capital structure is the blend of debt and equity that a company uses to finance its operations. A well-structured capital framework is crucial as it influences the company's risk profile and cost of capital. Investment bankers assess several key metrics when analyzing a company's capital structure:

1. **Leverage Ratios:** These ratios, such as the debt-to-equity ratio, help gauge the proportion of debt in a company's capital

structure. High leverage can increase financial risk but may also amplify returns on equity.

2. **Credit Ratings:** Credit ratings provided by agencies like Moody's or S&P assess a company's creditworthiness. Higher ratings usually result in lower borrowing costs, as they indicate a lower risk of default.

3. **Interest Coverage Ratios:** This ratio measures a company's ability to pay interest on its debt, indicating financial health. A higher ratio suggests a stronger ability to meet debt obligations.

Investment bankers use these factors to craft an optimal capital structure that minimizes costs while maintaining financial flexibility, thereby enabling companies to pursue growth opportunities.

Cost of Capital: The Benchmark for Investment Decisions

The **cost of capital** represents the expected return that investors demand for providing capital to the company. It serves as a critical benchmark for evaluating investment projects and strategic decisions. The **Weighted Average Cost of Capital (WACC)** is a common metric used, which combines the cost of equity and debt:

- **Cost of Equity:** This is the return required by equity investors, often estimated using the Capital Asset Pricing Model (CAPM), which accounts for the risk-free rate, market risk premium, and the company's beta (a measure of market volatility).

- **Cost of Debt:** This is the effective interest rate the company pays on its debt, adjusted for tax benefits from interest payments.

Understanding the WACC helps investment bankers determine the discount rate for valuing projects, ensuring that investment decisions align with shareholder expectations.

Capital Budgeting: Evaluating Investment Opportunities

Capital budgeting involves analyzing and selecting long-term investment projects. Key methods include:

1. **Net Present Value (NPV):** This calculates the difference between the present value of cash inflows and outflows. A positive NPV indicates a project that is expected to add value.
2. **Internal Rate of Return (IRR):** The IRR is the discount rate that makes the NPV of a project zero. It represents the expected rate of return and is compared against the WACC to determine the project's viability.
3. **Payback Period:** This metric measures the time required to recover the initial investment. Although it does not account for the time value of money, it provides a simple assessment of investment recovery.

These methods help in assessing the profitability and risk associated with different investment opportunities, guiding companies in their capital allocation decisions.

Valuation: Determining Company Worth

Valuation is a critical component of corporate finance, especially for transactions like mergers and acquisitions (M&A) or initial public offerings (IPOs). Common valuation methods include:

- **Discounted Cash Flow (DCF):** This method projects future cash flows and discounts them to present value using the WACC, providing an intrinsic value of the company.
- **Comparable Company Analysis (Comps):** This involves valuing a company based on the trading multiples of similar, publicly traded companies.
- **Precedent Transactions:** This approach looks at past M&A deals involving similar companies to gauge market valuations.

Accurate valuation is crucial for ensuring fair and reasonable transaction pricing.

Dividend Policy: Balancing Payouts and Growth

Investment bankers evaluate a company's **dividend policy** to determine how much profit should be distributed to shareholders versus reinvested in the business. Factors influencing dividend policy include:

- **Profitability:** Sustained earnings support regular dividends.
- **Cash Flow:** Positive cash flow ensures that dividends can be paid without compromising operations.
- **Growth Prospects:** High-growth companies may prefer reinvesting profits over paying dividends.
- **Capital Requirements:** Future investments may necessitate retaining earnings.

Risk Management: Mitigating Financial Risks

Effective **risk management** strategies are essential to safeguard a company's financial stability. Investment bankers help manage risks related to:

- **Interest Rate Fluctuations:** Hedging strategies can mitigate the impact of changing interest rates on borrowing costs.

- **Foreign Exchange Risks:** Tools like forward contracts and options protect against adverse currency movements.
- **Commodity Price Volatility:** Futures and options help stabilize costs associated with commodity purchases.

Corporate Restructuring: Enhancing Efficiency

Corporate restructuring involves significant changes to a company's structure or operations to improve efficiency and profitability. Common restructuring activities include:

- **Mergers and Acquisitions (M&A):** Combining with or acquiring other companies to achieve strategic goals.
- **Divestitures:** Selling off non-core assets to focus on core competencies.
- **Spin-offs:** Creating independent companies from existing units to unlock value.
- **Debt Restructurings:** Renegotiating debt terms to improve financial stability.

Working Capital Management: Ensuring Liquidity

Managing short-term assets and liabilities, or **working capital**, is crucial for maintaining liquidity. Key aspects include:

- **Accounts Receivable:** Efficient collection processes improve cash flow.
- **Inventory Management:** Balancing stock levels to optimize costs and service levels.
- **Accounts Payable:** Timely payments to suppliers while optimizing cash flow.

Corporate Governance: Ensuring Accountability

Strong **corporate governance** practices are vital for maintaining investor confidence and ensuring ethical conduct. Key areas include:

- **Board Structures:** Effective boards have a mix of independent and executive directors.
- **Executive Compensation:** Aligning management incentives with shareholder interests.
- **Governance Practices:** Clear reporting lines and compliance with regulations.

Financial Planning and Analysis: Supporting Strategic Decisions

Investment bankers assist in **financial planning and analysis**, creating financial models and forecasts that guide strategic decisions. This includes:

- **Developing Financial Strategies:** Planning for growth, market expansion, and operational improvements.
- **Assessing Performance:** Monitoring financial targets and identifying areas for improvement.
- **Providing Insights:** Offering data-driven recommendations based on market trends and competitive positioning.

Conclusion: Corporate finance is a comprehensive field that encompasses various aspects of financial management and strategy. Investment bankers play a crucial role in guiding companies through complex financial decisions, ensuring that they are well-positioned for growth and success. By mastering these core principles, investment bankers can effectively advise their clients and contribute to their long-term financial health.

Chapter 76: Introduction to Excel

Mastering Excel for Investment Banking: A Comprehensive Guide

Excel is a cornerstone tool for investment bankers, essential for a wide range of tasks from financial analysis to data management. Its versatility and powerful features make it an indispensable software in the finance industry. In this post, we'll delve into the various functionalities and techniques of Excel that investment bankers must master to perform their roles effectively.

Spreadsheet Fundamentals

Understanding the basics of Excel is crucial for any investment banker. This includes navigating through rows, columns, cells, and worksheets. Mastering the basics, such as entering data, formatting cells, and creating formulas, forms the bedrock upon which more advanced skills are built. Being adept at these tasks ensures that financial documents are organized, accurate, and easily understandable.

Mastering Formulas and Functions

At the heart of Excel's utility are its formulas and functions, which enable complex calculations and data manipulation. For investment bankers, familiarity with basic functions like SUM, AVERAGE, and more advanced ones like VLOOKUP and INDEX-MATCH is essential. These functions streamline data analysis, allowing bankers to efficiently manage large datasets and perform calculations with precision.

Advanced Data Analysis and Visualization

Investment bankers often work with large volumes of data. Excel's data analysis tools, such as PivotTables, are invaluable for summarizing data and extracting insights. Visualization tools, including various types of charts and conditional formatting, are crucial for presenting data in a clear and compelling manner. These skills are vital for interpreting market trends, financial performance, and making data-driven decisions.

Building Financial Models

Financial modeling is a core function in investment banking, used to project a company's financial future, evaluate investment opportunities, and conduct scenario analysis. Excel provides the tools needed to create detailed financial models, incorporating elements like cash flow analysis, balance sheet projections, and income statements. Mastering functions like IF statements, NPV, and IRR helps in constructing robust models that can adapt to changing inputs.

Data Manipulation and Cleansing

Handling and preparing data is a frequent task. Investment bankers need to be proficient in data manipulation techniques, including sorting, filtering, and using functions like TRIM and CONCATENATE for data cleansing. Ensuring data accuracy and consistency is critical for reliable analysis and decision-making.

Automation with Macros and VBA

Excel's automation capabilities, through macros and Visual Basic for Applications (VBA), can significantly enhance efficiency. Investment bankers can automate repetitive tasks, such as report generation and data processing, by recording macros or writing custom VBA scripts. This not only saves time but also reduces the risk of manual errors.

Sensitivity Analysis and Scenario Planning

In financial modeling, sensitivity analysis and scenario planning are used to understand the impact of varying key assumptions. Excel's data tables, goal seek, and scenario manager tools are invaluable for this purpose. They allow bankers to assess how changes in variables, like interest rates or sales volumes, affect financial outcomes, aiding in risk assessment and strategic planning.

Advanced Charting Techniques

Effective data presentation is key in investment banking. Excel offers advanced charting options, such as combination charts and trendlines, which help in conveying complex financial data visually. Customizing these charts, adding secondary axes, and integrating them into dashboards can significantly enhance the clarity and impact of presentations.

Collaboration and Sharing

Excel's features for collaboration, such as sharing workbooks, tracking changes, and using cloud-based solutions, are essential for team-based projects. Investment bankers often work in teams, requiring seamless collaboration and data sharing. Understanding how to manage permissions, protect sensitive data, and ensure that all team members are working with the most up-to-date information is crucial.

Leveraging Excel Add-ins and External Data Sources

Investment bankers often extend Excel's capabilities by using add-ins and connecting to external data sources. Add-ins can provide specialized tools for financial analysis and modeling, while data connections allow for the integration of real-time data from platforms like Bloomberg or databases. This capability is critical for maintaining up-to-date financial models and analysis.

Conclusion

Excel is not just a tool but a vital component of the investment banking profession. Proficiency in Excel allows investment bankers to efficiently analyze complex financial data, build sophisticated models, and make informed decisions. Mastering these skills is essential for success in the fast-paced and data-intensive world of finance. As investment banking continues to evolve, staying updated with the latest Excel features and techniques will ensure that bankers remain competitive and effective in their roles.

Chapter 77: Introduction to Financial Modeling

Introduction to Financial Modeling in Investment Banking

Financial modeling is an indispensable tool for investment bankers, enabling them to analyze financial data, forecast future performance, and make strategic decisions. This process involves creating a mathematical representation of a company's financial situation to evaluate investment opportunities, assess risks, and support decision-making. Here's a comprehensive guide to understanding the basics of financial modeling, its components, and its applications in investment banking.

Purpose and Importance of Financial Modeling

Financial modeling serves several critical functions in investment banking. It helps bankers and analysts:

1. **Evaluate Investment Opportunities**: By projecting future financial performance, models help determine the attractiveness of potential investments, mergers, or acquisitions.
2. **Support Strategic Decisions**: Models provide a quantitative basis for decisions regarding capital allocation, expansion, or restructuring.

3. **Assess Risks and Returns**: They allow for the analysis of different scenarios and sensitivities, helping to understand potential risks and rewards.
4. **Valuation**: Models are essential for determining the value of companies, assets, or projects, guiding pricing and negotiation strategies.

Model Design and Structure

A well-structured financial model is clear, consistent, and easy to update. It typically consists of:

- **Input Section**: This is where all assumptions and variables are entered. Inputs can include growth rates, cost assumptions, tax rates, and market conditions. Ensuring that inputs are clearly labeled and sourced is crucial for transparency.
- **Calculation Modules**: These sections perform the necessary computations, such as revenue projections, cost calculations, and cash flow generation. This part of the model is often divided into different sections for clarity, such as revenue drivers, cost schedules, and financing assumptions.
- **Output Section**: This displays the key results, including financial statements (income statement, balance sheet, and cash flow statement), valuation outputs, and key financial ratios. The output section is designed to provide a comprehensive view of the company's projected financial performance.

Assumptions and Inputs

Accurate and well-founded assumptions are the backbone of a reliable financial model. Inputs should be based on historical data, market research, and realistic expectations. Key assumptions might include:

- **Revenue Growth Rates**: Projections based on historical performance, market trends, and the company's business plan.
- **Cost Structures**: Including fixed and variable costs, cost of goods sold (COGS), and operating expenses.
- **Capital Expenditures**: Planned investments in property, plant, equipment, and other long-term assets.
- **Financing Assumptions**: Information on existing debt, interest rates, and potential equity issuances.

Building Financial Statements

A core component of financial modeling is the construction of financial statements. These include:

- **Income Statement**: Projects revenues, expenses, and profitability. Key metrics include gross profit, operating income, and net income.
- **Balance Sheet**: Provides a snapshot of the company's financial position, including assets, liabilities, and equity at a specific point in time.
- **Cash Flow Statement**: Tracks the cash inflows and outflows, highlighting the company's liquidity and cash management. It includes cash flows from operations, investing, and financing activities.

Sensitivity and Scenario Analysis

Sensitivity analysis tests the impact of changes in key assumptions on the model's outputs. For example, a sensitivity analysis might show how changes in sales growth rates affect profitability. Scenario analysis, on the other hand, involves creating different scenarios (e.g., best-case, worst-case, and base-case) to understand a range of possible outcomes and their implications.

Valuation Techniques

Financial models are crucial for various valuation methods, including:

- **Discounted Cash Flow (DCF) Analysis**: Calculates the present value of future cash flows to estimate the intrinsic value of an investment.
- **Comparable Company Analysis (Comps)**: Involves comparing the target company with similar companies in the industry based on metrics like P/E ratios, EV/EBITDA, etc.
- **Precedent Transaction Analysis**: Evaluates past transactions involving similar companies to estimate the value.

Model Auditing and Documentation

Ensuring the accuracy and reliability of a financial model involves thorough auditing. This includes:

- **Reviewing Assumptions**: Verifying the realism and consistency of the inputs.
- **Checking Calculations**: Ensuring all formulas and links between sheets are correct and functional.
- **Documenting the Model**: Clear documentation of assumptions, methodologies, and data sources enhances the model's credibility and usefulness. This documentation also facilitates communication with stakeholders and supports decision-making processes.

Conclusion

Financial modeling is an essential skill in investment banking, providing a quantitative foundation for strategic decision-making. By mastering the principles and techniques of financial modeling, investment bankers can deliver valuable insights, support transaction processes, and create value for their clients. Whether assessing a merger opportunity, projecting the impact of a new investment, or valuing a business, a robust financial model is a critical tool in the banker's toolkit.

Chapter 78: Introduction to Valuation

Introduction to Valuation in Investment Banking

Valuation is a fundamental aspect of investment banking, critical for assessing the worth of companies, assets, and investment opportunities. This comprehensive evaluation enables investment bankers to make informed decisions regarding mergers and acquisitions (M&A), initial public offerings (IPOs), and other financial strategies. In this blog post, we'll explore the importance of valuation, key methodologies, and the factors investment bankers consider during the valuation process.

The Importance of Valuation

Valuation is essential in investment banking as it provides a basis for determining the fair market value of a business or asset. Accurate valuations are crucial for various financial activities, including:

1. **Mergers and Acquisitions (M&A):** Determining the appropriate purchase price for target companies.
2. **Initial Public Offerings (IPOs):** Setting the price for public offerings of shares.
3. **Investment Analysis:** Assessing the potential return on investment opportunities.

4. **Strategic Decision-Making:** Helping companies decide on restructuring, divestitures, or expansions.

Accurate valuations help ensure that transactions are fair and beneficial to all parties involved, providing a foundation for negotiations and investment decisions.

Key Valuation Methodologies

1. Discounted Cash Flow (DCF) Analysis

DCF Analysis is a popular valuation method that calculates the present value of an entity's expected future cash flows. The steps include:

- **Projecting Future Cash Flows:** Estimating the company's future cash flows over a specific period, typically five to ten years.
- **Determining the Discount Rate:** Using the weighted average cost of capital (WACC) to discount future cash flows, reflecting the risk and time value of money.
- **Calculating Terminal Value:** Estimating the value of the business beyond the forecast period.
- **Summing Present Values:** Adding the present value of projected cash flows and terminal value to obtain the total valuation.

2. Comparable Company Analysis (Comps)

Comparable Company Analysis involves comparing the target company to similar publicly traded companies. This method uses valuation multiples such as:

- **Price-to-Earnings (P/E) Ratio:** Compares a company's current share price to its per-share earnings.

- **Enterprise Value-to-EBITDA (EV/EBITDA):** Compares a company's total value to its earnings before interest, taxes, depreciation, and amortization.

By analyzing these multiples, investment bankers estimate the target company's market value based on the valuations of comparable companies.

3. Precedent Transactions Analysis

Precedent Transactions Analysis looks at past M&A transactions involving similar companies. This method involves:

- **Identifying Comparable Transactions:** Finding historical deals within the same industry and of similar size.
- **Analyzing Transaction Multiples:** Reviewing metrics like EV/EBITDA or P/E ratios used in these deals.
- **Applying Multiples:** Using these multiples to estimate the value of the target company.

This approach provides a market-based valuation, reflecting what buyers have previously paid for similar businesses.

4. Asset-Based Valuation

Asset-Based Valuation calculates a company's value based on its net asset value (NAV). The process involves:

- **Assessing Tangible and Intangible Assets:** Valuing assets such as real estate, equipment, intellectual property, and goodwill.
- **Subtracting Liabilities:** Determining the net value by subtracting total liabilities from total assets.

This method is particularly useful for asset-heavy companies or in liquidation scenarios.

5. Real Options Valuation

Real Options Valuation considers the value of potential future opportunities, akin to financial options. This method is used when a company has the flexibility to make strategic decisions, such as expanding operations or entering new markets. Investment bankers use models like the Black-Scholes model to value these real options, factoring in variables such as volatility and time to maturity.

Qualitative Factors in Valuation

Beyond quantitative metrics, qualitative factors also play a significant role in valuation:

- **Industry Trends:** Understanding market trends, regulatory changes, and economic conditions.
- **Competitive Positioning:** Analyzing a company's market share, competitive advantages, and unique value propositions.
- **Management Quality:** Assessing the experience and track record of the management team.
- **Market Sentiment:** Gauging investor perceptions and market conditions that may affect valuation.

Conclusion

Valuation is a complex and nuanced process, essential for making informed investment decisions in the field of investment banking. By combining quantitative analysis with qualitative insights, investment bankers can provide accurate and comprehensive valuations. These valuations not only guide strategic decisions but also facilitate successful transactions, ensuring value creation for clients and stakeholders. Whether through DCF analysis, comps, precedent transactions, asset-based valuation, or real options, the goal remains the same: to determine a fair and accurate assessment of value.

Chapter 79: Introduction to Leveraged Buyouts

A Comprehensive Guide to Leveraged Buyouts

Leveraged buyouts (LBOs) are a cornerstone of investment banking, involving the acquisition of a company using a significant amount of borrowed funds. This financing method allows acquirers to maximize returns while utilizing the company's assets and future cash flows to secure the necessary debt. Let's delve into the intricate process and strategies behind LBOs, exploring the roles of key players, financing mechanisms, due diligence, valuation, deal structuring, risk management, and exit strategies.

Understanding Leveraged Buyouts

Leveraged buyouts are financial transactions where an investor, typically a private equity firm, acquires a company using a mix of equity and a substantial portion of debt. The acquired company's assets often serve as collateral for the borrowed funds, making this a high-risk, high-reward strategy. LBOs aim to restructure companies, enhance value, and achieve significant returns on equity through financial engineering and operational improvements.

Structure and Key Players in LBOs

An LBO involves multiple stakeholders, each playing a vital role:

1. **Private Equity Firms/Acquirers**: These entities initiate the LBO, providing the equity capital and strategic oversight necessary for the transaction. They focus on identifying undervalued or underperforming companies with potential for growth and improvement.
2. **Lenders**: Banks, institutional investors, and alternative financing providers supply the debt portion of the acquisition. They assess the company's creditworthiness and the potential risks involved.
3. **Management Team**: The existing or newly appointed management team is critical for executing post-acquisition strategies, driving operational efficiencies, and achieving growth objectives.
4. **Target Company**: The company being acquired, whose assets and future earnings are leveraged to finance the transaction.

LBO Financing Mechanisms

Investment bankers play a pivotal role in structuring the financing for LBOs. Key components include:

- **Senior Secured Loans**: These are the primary source of debt, secured by the company's assets and having the first claim on cash flows.
- **Subordinated Debt**: Higher-yield debt that is junior to senior loans, offering more risk but potentially higher returns.
- **Mezzanine Financing**: A hybrid of debt and equity, often with convertible features or warrants, providing additional capital with equity upside.
- **High-Yield Bonds**: Unsecured, high-interest debt used to raise substantial capital.

The equity contribution from the acquirers, often including management and co-investors, is crucial for aligning interests and ensuring commitment to the company's success.

Due Diligence and Valuation

Thorough due diligence is essential to assess the target company's viability and identify potential risks and opportunities. Key areas include:

- **Financial Performance**: Reviewing historical financial statements, cash flow projections, and financial health.
- **Operational Analysis**: Examining the efficiency of operations, management capabilities, and competitive positioning.
- **Market Assessment**: Understanding market dynamics, customer base, and industry trends.
- **Legal and Regulatory Review**: Ensuring compliance and identifying any legal challenges.

Valuation techniques specific to LBOs include:

- **Discounted Cash Flow (DCF) Analysis**: Estimating the present value of future cash flows.
- **Comparable Company Analysis**: Using valuation multiples from similar companies.
- **Precedent Transaction Analysis**: Looking at past similar transactions to gauge market norms.

Deal Structuring and Negotiation

Successful LBOs require careful deal structuring and negotiation:

- **Purchase Price Determination**: Arriving at a fair price for the acquisition, balancing risk and potential return.
- **Debt Covenants**: Setting financial covenants to protect lenders and ensure fiscal discipline.
- **Management Incentives**: Aligning the interests of management with the acquirers through equity participation and performance bonuses.
- **Exit Strategies**: Planning for eventual exits, whether through IPOs, secondary sales, or recapitalizations.

Post-Acquisition Integration and Value Creation

Post-acquisition, the focus shifts to integrating the target company and realizing value:

- **Operational Improvements**: Implementing cost reductions, optimizing operations, and improving efficiency.
- **Strategic Initiatives**: Launching new products, expanding into new markets, or enhancing customer relationships.
- **Synergies**: Realizing synergies, such as combining resources or eliminating redundancies, to increase profitability.

Risk Management in LBOs

Investment bankers and private equity firms meticulously assess and manage risks:

- **Market and Industry Risks**: Evaluating external factors, including economic conditions and market competition.
- **Financing Risks**: Monitoring leverage levels and interest rate exposure.
- **Operational Risks**: Addressing internal challenges, such as management capabilities and operational efficiency.

- **Regulatory Risks**: Ensuring ongoing compliance with legal and regulatory requirements.

Exit Strategies

Planning for exits is crucial in LBOs, with options including:

- **Initial Public Offerings (IPOs)**: Taking the company public to unlock value.
- **Secondary Offerings**: Selling stakes to other investors.
- **Sales to Strategic Buyers or Other Private Equity Firms**: Exiting through a sale to another interested party.
- **Recapitalization**: Refinancing to return capital to investors.

Conclusion

Leveraged buyouts are complex transactions that require a deep understanding of finance, strategy, and industry dynamics. Investment bankers play a critical role in every phase of the process, from deal origination and due diligence to structuring and post-acquisition management. By mastering these elements, investment bankers can facilitate successful LBOs that create significant value for investors and stakeholders.

Chapter 80: Introduction to Corporate M&A

Understanding Corporate M&A: A Comprehensive Overview

Introduction to Corporate M&A

Corporate mergers and acquisitions (M&A) are key strategies used by companies to achieve growth, expand market presence, diversify product offerings, and optimize operational efficiencies. Investment bankers play a crucial role in facilitating these transactions, offering expertise in various stages of the M&A process. This post delves into the fundamentals of corporate M&A, covering the types of transactions, stages of the M&A process, and the essential roles investment bankers play.

Types of M&A Transactions

1. **Horizontal Mergers**
   - These occur between companies in the same industry. The primary goal is to consolidate market share and reduce competition.
   - Example: Two competing tech firms merging to enhance their market position.
2. **Vertical Mergers**

- ○ Involve companies at different stages of the production process. This can streamline operations and reduce costs.
- ○ Example: A car manufacturer acquiring a tire company to ensure a steady supply of parts.

3. **Conglomerate Mergers**
   - ○ Occur between companies in unrelated businesses, often for diversification purposes.
   - ○ Example: A food processing company acquiring a tech startup to diversify its portfolio.

4. **Asset Acquisitions**
   - ○ One company purchases the assets of another. This type of transaction is often used when a company wants to acquire specific assets rather than the entire entity.

5. **Stock Acquisitions**
   - ○ Involve the purchase of another company's shares. The acquiring company gains control by buying a majority of the target's stock.

6. **Tender Offers**
   - ○ A company offers to buy shares directly from the shareholders of another company, often as a hostile takeover attempt.

The M&A Process and Key Stages

1. Target Identification and Screening

- **Target Identification:** Investment bankers use industry analysis and market research to identify potential acquisition targets. They focus on strategic fit and potential synergies.
- **Screening:** A thorough evaluation of targets to ensure they align with the acquirer's strategic goals. This involves preliminary financial analysis and compatibility assessments.

2. Due Diligence

- This critical phase involves a comprehensive review of the target's financial statements, operations, legal standings, and market position. Due diligence uncovers risks and opportunities, helping to refine valuation and negotiation strategies.

3. Valuation

- **Methods:**
  - **Discounted Cash Flow (DCF) Analysis:** Calculates the present value of future cash flows.
  - **Comparable Company Analysis (CCA):** Compares the target with similar companies.
  - **Precedent Transactions:** Examines past transactions of similar companies.
- Accurate valuation is essential for determining the fair price and structuring the deal effectively.

4. Deal Structuring and Negotiation

- Investment bankers design the deal structure, covering aspects like payment methods, legal terms, and conditions. Effective negotiation skills are crucial to align the interests of both parties and finalize the agreement.

5. Financing the Transaction

- Options include:
  - **Cash Reserves:** Using the acquiring company's internal funds.
  - **Debt Financing:** Loans or bonds.
  - **Equity Issuance:** Issuing new shares.

Investment Banking University
All Rights Reserved

- Hybrid Instruments: Combining elements of debt and equity.

6. Regulatory and Legal Considerations

- Ensuring compliance with antitrust laws, securities regulations, and other legal requirements is critical. Investment bankers work closely with legal experts to navigate these complexities.

7. Post-Merger Integration

- This involves integrating the operations, cultures, and systems of the merged entities. The goal is to realize synergies, streamline operations, and ensure the smooth functioning of the combined entity.

Role of Investment Bankers in M&A

Expert Guidance:

- Investment bankers provide expertise in market trends, valuation techniques, and deal structuring. They offer strategic advice tailored to the client's goals.

Facilitating Negotiations:

- They act as intermediaries, facilitating discussions and negotiations between buyers and sellers to reach mutually beneficial agreements.

Risk Management:

- Investment bankers identify potential risks and devise strategies to mitigate them, ensuring a smooth transaction process.

Post-Deal Support:

- They assist with post-merger integration, helping the combined entity achieve operational efficiencies and strategic goals.

Conclusion

Corporate M&A is a multifaceted process requiring deep industry knowledge, strategic insight, and meticulous execution. Investment bankers play a pivotal role in guiding clients through this complex landscape, from identifying opportunities to finalizing deals and ensuring successful integration. Mastery of the M&A process enables investment bankers to deliver significant value to their clients, driving growth and enhancing competitive positioning.

Chapter 81: Introduction to Investment Banking Deliverables

The Essential Deliverables in Investment Banking

In the world of investment banking, delivering high-quality outputs is a fundamental aspect of the job. These outputs, known as deliverables, are vital tools that facilitate transactions, attract clients, and support strategic decision-making. As an investment banking analyst, your role involves crafting various deliverables, each serving a distinct purpose in the banking process. This blog post delves into the key types of deliverables in investment banking, highlighting their importance and the expertise required to create them effectively.

1. Pitch Books

Definition and Purpose:
Pitch books are detailed presentations used to market the bank's services to potential clients. They are a blend of sales tool and informative guide, providing a comprehensive overview of the bank's capabilities and proposed financial solutions.

Components:

- **Market Analysis:** Includes data and insights on current market conditions, industry trends, and the competitive landscape. This helps the client understand the broader economic environment.
- **Financial Modeling:** Involves projections and valuations tailored to the client's business, illustrating potential financial outcomes.
- **Industry Trends:** Highlights emerging trends within the client's sector, demonstrating the bank's expertise.
- **Strategic Recommendations:** Proposes specific actions or strategies to address the client's challenges or goals.

Significance:
Pitch books are crucial for acquiring new business by demonstrating the bank's value proposition and expertise. They are often the first

detailed interaction a client has with the bank, making a strong, positive impression essential.

2. Financial Models

Definition and Purpose:
Financial models are intricate spreadsheets that forecast a company's financial performance. They are foundational tools used in evaluating the viability of transactions like mergers and acquisitions (M&A) or initial public offerings (IPOs).

Key Elements:

- **Revenue Projections:** Forecast future income based on historical data and market trends.
- **Expense Forecasting:** Predict operating costs and other financial outflows.
- **Capital Structure Analysis:** Examine the mix of debt and equity financing, assessing the company's leverage and financial health.
- **Cash Flow Projections:** Estimate future cash inflows and outflows, crucial for understanding liquidity.

Importance:
These models enable precise valuation and risk assessment, guiding decision-making processes for both clients and the bank. They provide a quantitative basis for strategic decisions, ensuring they are grounded in realistic financial expectations.

3. Confidential Information Memorandums (CIMs)

Definition and Purpose:
CIMs are detailed documents prepared for potential buyers when a company is being sold. They contain comprehensive information about the business, its financials, operations, and market position.

Sections Include:

- **Company Overview:** Background, mission, and historical context.
- **Financial Performance:** Detailed financial history, including revenue, profitability, and cash flow.
- **Operations and Management:** Structure and key personnel details.
- **Market Position:** Analysis of competitive standing and future growth prospects.

Utility:
CIMs serve as a critical marketing tool, providing potential buyers with the necessary information to evaluate the investment opportunity. They help facilitate due diligence and are integral to the M&A process.

4. IPO Prospectuses

Definition and Purpose:
An IPO prospectus is a legal document issued when a company intends to go public. It offers an exhaustive overview of the business, financials, and risks associated with the investment.

Core Components:

- **Business Overview:** Describes the company's operations and offerings.
- **Financial Statements:** Includes historical and current financial data.
- **Risk Factors:** Enumerates potential risks and uncertainties.
- **Use of Proceeds:** Details how the funds raised will be utilized.

Role:
IPO prospectuses provide transparency and essential information to

investors, helping them make informed decisions. They also ensure compliance with regulatory requirements.

5. Management Presentations

Definition and Purpose:
These are presentations used during meetings with clients or investors, focusing on the company's strategy, market position, and financial performance.

Key Aspects:

- **Market and Industry Analysis:** Insights into market trends and competitive dynamics.
- **Strategic Initiatives:** Overview of planned or ongoing strategic projects.
- **Financial Performance:** Highlight key metrics and achievements.
- **Q&A Preparation:** Anticipated questions and prepared answers.

Importance:
They support senior management in communicating the company's vision and strategy, reinforcing credibility and facilitating strategic discussions.

6. Industry Reports and Market Research Documents

Definition and Purpose:
These documents provide in-depth analysis of specific industries, covering market dynamics, competitive landscape, and emerging trends.

Content:

- **Market Overview:** Market size, growth rates, and key trends.
- **Competitive Analysis:** Insights into key players and market share.
- **Regulatory Environment:** Overview of industry regulations and their implications.
- **Future Outlook:** Projections and forecasts for market development.

Utility:
They serve as a resource for clients to understand their industry better and inform strategic decisions. These reports also establish the firm's thought leadership in the industry.

7. Transaction-Related Documents

Definition and Purpose:
These include documents like term sheets and offering memorandums, which outline the specifics of a deal.

Elements:

- **Deal Structure:** Details of the transaction, including payment and financing.
- **Pricing and Valuation:** Information on how the deal is priced.
- **Legal Provisions:** Key terms, representations, warranties, and covenants.
- **Risk Assessment:** Identifies potential risks and mitigation strategies.

Significance:
They are crucial for clearly defining the terms of a transaction, ensuring all parties have a clear understanding and agreement.

Conclusion

The creation of deliverables in investment banking is a multifaceted task that requires a blend of analytical skills, financial knowledge, and effective communication. These documents not only support strategic decision-making but also play a critical role in client engagement and transaction execution. Mastering the creation and presentation of these deliverables is essential for any investment banking professional, as they are key to the success of both the firm and its clients.

Chapter 82: What is EBITDA?

Understanding EBITDA: A Key Financial Metric in Investment Banking

EBITDA, short for "Earnings Before Interest, Taxes, Depreciation, and Amortization," is a crucial financial metric in the world of investment banking. It provides a clear view of a company's core operating performance, stripping away non-operational factors and accounting decisions that can cloud profitability assessments. This blog post delves into what EBITDA is, why it's important, its limitations, and how it's practically applied in various financial contexts.

What is EBITDA?

EBITDA is calculated using the following formula:

EBITDA=Net Income+Interest+Taxes+Depreciation+Amortization\text{EBITDA} = \text{Net Income} + \text{Interest} + \text{Taxes} + \text{Depreciation} + \text{Amortization}EBITDA=Net Income+Interest+Taxes+Depreciation+Amortization

This metric essentially focuses on the company's earnings from its core business operations before any financial deductions like interest and taxes, and non-cash items like depreciation and amortization are considered.

Importance of EBITDA in Investment Banking

1. **Assessing Operating Performance**: EBITDA provides a clear picture of a company's operational efficiency by excluding non-operational expenses. This makes it a valuable tool for comparing companies within the same industry, as it neutralizes the effects of differing capital structures and tax environments.
2. **Debt Servicing and Cash Flow Generation**: Investment bankers use EBITDA to gauge a company's ability to generate cash flow and service debt. A higher EBITDA indicates stronger operational earnings, suggesting that the company can comfortably meet its debt obligations and reinvest in its business.
3. **Valuation Tool**: The EV/EBITDA multiple is a popular valuation metric that compares a company's enterprise value (EV) to its EBITDA. This ratio helps determine if a company is overvalued or undervalued relative to its peers.
4. **Standardized Measure**: Because EBITDA removes the effects of financing and accounting choices, it serves as a more standardized measure for cross-company and cross-industry comparisons, allowing for a more apples-to-apples assessment.

Limitations of EBITDA

While EBITDA is a valuable metric, it is not without its drawbacks:

1. **Ignores Working Capital Changes**: EBITDA does not account for changes in working capital, which can significantly affect a company's cash flow situation. For instance, an increase in accounts receivable may inflate earnings without a corresponding increase in cash.

2. **Excludes Capital Expenditures (CapEx)**: Ignoring CapEx can lead to an overestimation of a company's cash-generating abilities, as it does not reflect the cash spent on maintaining or expanding the business.
3. **Non-Operating Items**: EBITDA excludes non-operating items such as restructuring costs, litigation expenses, and other one-time charges. These items, however, can significantly impact a company's financial health and should not be overlooked.
4. **Not a Cash Flow Measure**: Since EBITDA ignores actual cash outflows like taxes and interest payments, it does not provide a true picture of the cash available to the company.

Practical Application of EBITDA

1. **Debt Analysis**: Investment bankers use EBITDA to assess a company's debt capacity. Metrics like the interest coverage ratio (EBITDA/Interest Expense) and the debt/EBITDA ratio provide insights into a company's ability to manage its debt.
2. **Mergers and Acquisitions (M&A)**: In M&A transactions, EBITDA is crucial for valuing the target company. It helps in negotiating the purchase price by providing a clear view of the target's profitability.
3. **Performance Benchmarking**: Companies often benchmark their EBITDA against industry peers to evaluate their performance. This helps identify strengths and weaknesses and informs strategic decisions.
4. **Financial Forecasting**: EBITDA projections are vital for financial forecasting and planning. They help set financial targets and assess future profitability, guiding investment and operational decisions.

Conclusion

EBITDA is an essential tool in investment banking, offering a straightforward way to evaluate a company's operational profitability. However, it is crucial to understand its limitations and use it in conjunction with other financial metrics for a comprehensive analysis. By doing so, investment bankers can make more informed decisions and provide better strategic advice to their clients.

Chapter 83: What is an Internal Rate of Return (IRR)?

Understanding Internal Rate of Return (IRR)

Internal Rate of Return (IRR) is a fundamental metric in investment banking, pivotal for assessing the profitability of potential investments. Essentially, IRR represents the discount rate that makes the net present value (NPV) of all future cash flows from an investment equal to zero. In simpler terms, it is the expected annualized rate of return that an investment is projected to generate. Let's delve into its significance, calculation, practical applications, and limitations.

Importance of IRR in Investment Banking

1. **Investment Evaluation**: IRR is a critical tool for evaluating the attractiveness of investment opportunities, such as mergers, acquisitions, and new project developments. It helps investment bankers determine whether an investment is likely to meet or exceed the required rate of return, making it a key metric in the decision-making process.
2. **Comparative Analysis**: IRR provides a standardized measure to compare different investment opportunities. Regardless of

their scale, duration, or cash flow patterns, investments can be evaluated on a common basis, facilitating clear comparisons.

3. **Decision Making**: IRR assists in making crucial investment decisions. If the IRR exceeds the company's cost of capital or the minimum required rate of return, the investment is typically considered viable. Conversely, a lower IRR might indicate an unattractive investment.

Calculating IRR

Calculating IRR involves finding the discount rate that sets the NPV of all cash flows equal to zero. The formula is:

$$0=\sum(CF_t(1+IRR)t)-\text{Initial Investment}$$

Where:

- CF_t = Cash flow at time t
- IRR = Internal rate of return
- t = Time period

Given the complexity of the formula, especially with multiple cash flows, IRR is usually computed using financial software or iterative methods.

Practical Application of IRR

1. **Time Value of Money**: IRR accounts for the time value of money, ensuring that the timing of cash inflows and outflows is considered in the investment's profitability assessment.
2. **Project Viability**: An investment with a high IRR indicates strong potential returns. This is particularly important in

capital-intensive industries where the allocation of resources needs to be meticulously planned.
3. **Integrated Analysis**: While IRR is crucial, it is often used in conjunction with other metrics like NPV (which measures the dollar value added by the project) and the Payback Period (which measures how quickly the investment is recouped).

Limitations of IRR

1. **Reinvestment Assumption**: IRR assumes that intermediate cash flows can be reinvested at the same rate as the IRR, which is often unrealistic. This can lead to overly optimistic projections.
2. **Multiple IRRs**: For investments with fluctuating cash flows, IRR can produce multiple values, complicating the evaluation process. This occurs when cash flows change direction (from positive to negative) multiple times.
3. **Ignoring Project Size**: IRR does not account for the scale of a project. A small project with a high IRR might be less valuable in absolute terms than a larger project with a lower IRR.
4. **Risk Consideration**: IRR does not directly factor in the risk associated with an investment. Two projects may have similar IRRs but vastly different risk profiles, which should influence the final decision.

Conclusion

IRR is an essential metric in investment banking, offering insights into the expected profitability of investments while considering the time value of money. However, it is most effective when used alongside other financial metrics and qualitative assessments to provide a comprehensive view of an investment's potential. By effectively applying IRR, investment bankers can help clients optimize their investment strategies, balancing risk and return to achieve financial objectives.

Chapter 84: What is Weighted Average Cost of Capital (WACC)?

Understanding Weighted Average Cost of Capital (WACC) in Investment Banking

Weighted Average Cost of Capital (WACC) is a fundamental concept in corporate finance and investment banking. It represents the average rate of return a company is expected to pay to its capital providers, both debt holders and equity investors. WACC is crucial for evaluating investment opportunities, optimizing capital structures, and assessing the overall cost of financing. This blog post explores the significance of WACC, the methodology for calculating it, and its limitations.

Importance of WACC

1. Investment Decision-Making: WACC is a critical tool for evaluating the profitability of potential investments. It serves as a benchmark for comparing the expected return on an investment against its cost of capital. If the projected return exceeds WACC, the investment is likely to add value; otherwise, it may not be worth pursuing.

2. Capital Structure Optimization: Determining the optimal mix of debt and equity financing is vital for minimizing a company's cost of capital. WACC helps in assessing the impact of different financing strategies and finding a balance that maximizes the company's value.

3. Valuation: In discounted cash flow (DCF) analysis, WACC is used as the discount rate to calculate the present value of future cash flows. This calculation helps in valuing a company or project, providing insights into whether the investment is priced appropriately.

4. Risk Assessment: WACC also reflects the risk profile of a company. A higher WACC indicates higher risk, requiring higher returns to compensate investors, while a lower WACC suggests lower risk.

Calculating WACC

To calculate WACC, follow these steps:

1. **Determine the Cost of Equity (Re):** The cost of equity can be estimated using the Capital Asset Pricing Model (CAPM), which considers the risk-free rate, the equity market risk premium, and the company's beta (a measure of its stock volatility relative to the market). The formula is: Re=Risk-free rate+(Beta×Market risk premium)\text{Re} = \text{Risk-free rate} + (\text{Beta} \times \text{Market risk premium})Re=Risk-free rate+(Beta×Market risk premium)
2. **Determine the Cost of Debt (Rd):** This is the effective interest rate the company pays on its debt. Since interest expenses are tax-deductible, the after-tax cost of debt is considered: After-tax Rd=Rd×(1−Tax rate)\text{After-tax Rd} = \text{Rd} \times (1 - \text{Tax rate})After-tax Rd=Rd×(1−Tax rate)

3. **Calculate the Proportions of Debt and Equity:** Determine the market values of debt (D) and equity (E) in the company's capital structure.
4. **Compute WACC:** The WACC formula combines the costs of equity and debt, weighted by their respective proportions in the total capital structure:

$$\text{WACC} = \left(\frac{E}{E + D} \times \text{Re}\right) + \left(\frac{D}{E + D} \times \text{Rd} \times (1 - \text{Tax rate})\right)$$

Limitations of WACC

While WACC is a widely used metric, it has several limitations:

- **Assumption of Constant Capital Structure:** WACC assumes that a company's capital structure remains constant, which may not always be the case. Companies often adjust their mix of debt and equity over time.
- **Estimation Challenges:** Accurately estimating the components of WACC, such as the cost of equity, cost of debt, and market values, can be difficult and subject to market fluctuations.
- **Complex Capital Structures:** WACC may not accurately capture the cost of capital for companies with complex capital structures, such as those with significant preferred stock or convertible debt.

The Impact of Federal Reserve Policies

The Federal Reserve's decisions on interest rates can significantly influence WACC. An increase in interest rates raises the cost of debt, thereby increasing WACC. This rise in WACC can lead to a decrease in the valuation of future cash flows, potentially lowering stock prices.

Conclusion

WACC is a pivotal financial metric in investment banking, providing a comprehensive measure of a company's cost of capital. Despite its limitations, WACC remains essential for evaluating investments, optimizing capital structures, and conducting thorough financial analyses. Understanding and accurately calculating WACC enables investment bankers and corporate finance professionals to make informed strategic decisions, ultimately contributing to the growth and stability of the business.

Chapter 85: What is Free Cash Flow?

Understanding Free Cash Flow (FCF)

Free Cash Flow (FCF) is a fundamental financial metric in investment banking, representing the cash a company generates from its operations after accounting for capital expenditures necessary to maintain and expand its asset base. FCF is critical for assessing a company's financial health, determining its valuation, and making investment decisions. This blog post delves into the concept of Free Cash Flow, its calculation, significance, and practical applications.

Definition and Calculation of Free Cash Flow

Free Cash Flow is calculated by subtracting capital expenditures (CAPEX) from operating cash flow (OCF). Operating cash flow is the net cash generated from a company's core business operations, reflecting the firm's ability to produce cash through its regular activities. Capital expenditures refer to the funds used to acquire or upgrade physical assets such as property, plant, and equipment.

The formula for calculating Free Cash Flow is:

FCF=Operating Cash Flow (OCF)−Capital Expenditures (CAPEX)\text{FCF} = \text{Operating Cash Flow (OCF)} -

\text{Capital Expenditures (CAPEX)}FCF=Operating Cash Flow (OCF)−Capital Expenditures (CAPEX)

Example Calculation: Suppose a company reports an operating cash flow of $200 million and capital expenditures of $50 million. The calculation for FCF would be:

FCF=$200 million−$50 million=$150 million\text{FCF} = \$200\ \text{million} - \$50\ \text{million} = \$150\ \text{million}FCF=$200 million−$50 million=$150 million

This result indicates the company has $150 million available after covering its capital expenditures, which can be used for various strategic purposes.

Importance of Free Cash Flow in Investment Banking

Assessing Financial Health

Free Cash Flow is a vital indicator of a company's financial stability. A positive FCF signifies that a company generates more cash than needed to maintain and grow its business, suggesting good financial health. It reflects the company's capacity to generate cash, which can be used to pay dividends, buy back shares, reduce debt, or reinvest in the business.

Valuation

In investment banking, Free Cash Flow is crucial for valuing companies. The Discounted Cash Flow (DCF) model, a common valuation method, uses projected FCF to estimate the present value of a company. Since FCF represents the cash available to investors, it provides a reliable measure for determining a company's worth.

Investment Decisions

Investors prefer companies with high and consistent FCF because it suggests efficient capital management and a strong business model. A company with robust FCF is often seen as a safer investment, as it has the means to weather economic downturns and invest in growth opportunities.

Comparative Analysis

Free Cash Flow is also used for comparative analysis within an industry. Comparing the FCF of companies can reveal which firms are more efficient in generating cash and managing capital. A company with higher FCF relative to its peers may indicate better operational efficiency or more prudent capital expenditure management.

Uses of Free Cash Flow

1. **Dividends and Share Buybacks:** Companies with substantial FCF may return capital to shareholders through dividends or share buybacks. This not only provides income to shareholders but can also signal confidence in the company's financial strength.
2. **Debt Reduction:** Using FCF to pay down debt improves a company's balance sheet and reduces interest expenses, enhancing financial stability and flexibility.
3. **Reinvestment in Business:** FCF can fund research and development (R&D), acquisitions, or capital projects. Reinvesting in the business can drive future growth and enhance competitive positioning.
4. **Strategic Flexibility:** With a healthy FCF, companies have the financial flexibility to pursue new opportunities, manage economic fluctuations, and respond to unforeseen challenges without needing additional capital.

Conclusion

Investment Banking University
All Rights Reserved

Free Cash Flow is a critical metric in investment banking, offering insights into a company's ability to generate cash beyond its operational needs. It plays a pivotal role in company valuation, investment decision-making, and comparative analysis. By focusing on FCF, investors and analysts can gauge a company's financial health, strategic flexibility, and potential for sustainable growth. Understanding and effectively utilizing FCF can significantly enhance decision-making processes and investment outcomes.

Chapter 86: What is the Difference Between EBITDA, FCFF & FCFE?

Understanding the Differences: EBITDA, FCFF, and FCFE in Investment Banking

In the world of investment banking, understanding key financial metrics is essential for evaluating a company's performance and financial health. Three widely used metrics—EBITDA (Earnings Before Interest, Taxes, Depreciation, and Amortization), FCFF (Free Cash Flow to the Firm), and FCFE (Free Cash Flow to Equity)—each offer unique insights. Let's dive into what these metrics represent and how they differ from each other.

EBITDA: Measuring Core Operating Performance

What is EBITDA? EBITDA stands for Earnings Before Interest, Taxes, Depreciation, and Amortization. It is a measure that focuses on a company's operational profitability, excluding non-operational elements like financing costs, tax expenses, and non-cash charges.

Purpose and Usefulness: EBITDA provides a clear picture of a company's core operational efficiency. By excluding interest, taxes, depreciation, and amortization, it isolates the company's earnings from its operating activities. This makes it particularly useful for comparing companies across industries, as it eliminates the effects of different capital structures and tax situations. It's a popular metric in valuation, especially when calculating EV/EBITDA multiples, which help in assessing company value based on operational earnings.

Calculation: EBITDA = Net Income + Interest + Taxes + Depreciation + Amortization

FCFF: Evaluating Cash Flow for All Stakeholders

What is FCFF? Free Cash Flow to the Firm (FCFF) is a comprehensive measure of the cash generated by a company that is available to all capital providers—both debt and equity holders—after accounting for capital expenditures, changes in working capital, and taxes.

Purpose and Usefulness: FCFF provides a holistic view of a company's ability to generate cash flow from its operations, which can be used for debt repayment, reinvestment, or distribution to shareholders. It is a critical metric for valuing a company and assessing its ability to meet its financial obligations. Unlike EBITDA, FCFF considers capital expenditures and working capital changes, giving a more accurate reflection of the actual cash available.

Calculation: FCFF = EBIT * (1 - Tax Rate) + Depreciation & Amortization - Change in Working Capital - Capital Expenditures

FCFE: Focusing on Equity Investors' Returns

What is FCFE? Free Cash Flow to Equity (FCFE) measures the cash flow available to equity shareholders after accounting for all expenses, reinvestment needs, and debt servicing. It represents the potential cash that can be returned to equity holders either through dividends or share buybacks.

Purpose and Usefulness: FCFE is crucial for equity investors as it directly reflects the cash that can be distributed to them. This metric helps investors understand the company's ability to generate cash that can be paid out after fulfilling all other financial obligations. It's an essential component in equity valuation, especially in determining the value of a company's shares based on projected cash flows.

Calculation: FCFE = FCFF - Interest Expense * (1 - Tax Rate) - Net Debt Repayment

Key Differences Between FCFF and FCFE

1. **Recipients of Cash Flow:**
   - **FCFF:** Considers cash flow available to all capital providers, including both debt and equity holders.
   - **FCFE:** Focuses solely on the cash flow available to equity shareholders.
2. **Scope and Perspective:**
   - **FCFF:** Provides a comprehensive view of the company's ability to generate cash flow for all stakeholders.
   - **FCFE:** Specifically highlights the cash flow available to equity investors, making it a narrower but more focused measure for this group.
3. **Calculation Adjustments:**
   - **FCFF:** Does not consider the company's debt servicing in its calculation.
   - **FCFE:** Adjusts FCFF by deducting net debt repayments and after-tax interest expenses to reflect cash available solely to equity holders.

Conclusion

Each of these financial metrics—EBITDA, FCFF, and FCFE—serves a distinct purpose in financial analysis and valuation. EBITDA is a quick measure of operational performance, FCFF gives a broader picture of cash available to all stakeholders, and FCFE focuses on cash available to equity shareholders. Understanding these differences is crucial for investors, analysts, and investment bankers to make informed decisions and accurately value a company's financial health and potential returns.

Chapter 87: What is Enterprise Value?

Understanding Enterprise Value in Investment Banking

Enterprise Value (EV) is a fundamental concept in investment banking and corporate finance, offering a comprehensive measure of a company's total value. Unlike market capitalization, which only reflects equity value, EV provides a more holistic view by incorporating debt and cash into the valuation. This post delves into the significance, calculation, and application of Enterprise Value, explaining why it is crucial for accurately assessing a company's worth.

1. Comprehensive Measure of Company Value

Enterprise Value represents the total value of a company by including its equity and debt while subtracting cash and cash equivalents. The formula for EV is:

EV=Market Capitalization+Total Debt−Cash and Cash Equivalents\text{EV} = \text{Market Capitalization} + \text{Total Debt} - \text{Cash and Cash Equivalents}EV=Market Capitalization+Total Debt−Cash and Cash Equivalents

- **Market Capitalization**: This is calculated by multiplying the company's current share price by its total number of outstanding shares.

- **Total Debt**: Includes all interest-bearing liabilities such as bonds and loans.
- **Cash and Cash Equivalents**: Highly liquid assets that can be quickly converted to cash, such as treasury bills.

This formula ensures that all financial obligations and available liquid assets are considered, providing a more accurate representation of the company's value compared to just its market cap.

2. True Cost of Acquisition

Enterprise Value is crucial for potential acquirers as it represents the total cost of purchasing a company. It accounts for the company's debt obligations, which an acquirer would need to assume or pay off, and offsets this with the company's cash reserves. This makes EV a more realistic indicator of the financial commitment required to acquire a business, beyond just buying its equity.

For example, if a company has significant cash reserves, these can be used to pay down debt, reducing the net cost of acquisition. Conversely, high debt levels increase the acquisition cost, making EV a more precise measure for M&A activities.

3. Adjustment for Cash and Cash Equivalents

The inclusion of cash and cash equivalents in the EV calculation is a crucial adjustment. Cash is subtracted because it can be used to pay off debt, thereby reducing the overall financial burden on an acquirer. This adjustment provides a clearer picture of a company's net financial position, excluding liquid assets that can be readily used.

For instance, if a company has a market cap of $500 million, $200 million in debt, and $50 million in cash, its EV would be $650 million ($500M + $200M - $50M). This adjustment is essential for understanding the net value that would change hands in a transaction.

4. Standardized Comparison Across Companies

Enterprise Value allows for consistent comparison across companies, even those with differing capital structures. By including debt, EV normalizes companies that may have varying levels of leverage, making it easier to compare their true market value and performance. This is particularly useful when assessing companies in capital-intensive industries, where debt levels can vary significantly.

For example, two companies in the same industry might have similar market caps, but one could have much higher debt. EV takes this into account, providing a more accurate basis for comparison.

5. Impact on Valuation Multiples

Enterprise Value is integral to calculating key valuation multiples like EV/EBITDA and EV/Sales, which are used to assess a company's value relative to its earnings or sales. These multiples are critical for comparing companies' valuations and determining if they are overvalued or undervalued relative to peers.

A higher EV often corresponds with higher multiples, reflecting the company's market position, growth prospects, and profitability. For instance, a company with a higher EV/EBITDA ratio compared to its peers might be considered overvalued, suggesting investors expect significant growth.

Conclusion

Enterprise Value is a vital metric in investment banking, providing a more comprehensive measure of a company's worth than market capitalization alone. It accounts for the company's entire capital structure, including debt and cash, offering a true picture of its value. Understanding EV is essential for anyone involved in mergers and acquisitions, financial analysis, or investment decision-making, as it provides a standardized and accurate measure for comparing companies and assessing their financial health.

Investment Banking University
All Rights Reserved

Chapter 88: What Are Sources & Uses in a Financial Model?

What Are Sources & Uses in a Financial Model?

In the realm of investment banking, understanding the sources and uses of capital in a financial model is essential for evaluating how a company or project is financed and how these funds are deployed. This chapter will explore the key components of sources and uses, providing a detailed breakdown of the inflows and outflows of capital.

Sources of Capital

Sources of capital represent the various means through which a company raises funds to support its operations, investments, and growth initiatives. These include:

1. Equity Financing

- **Common Stock:** Issuing common shares to investors provides ownership stakes in the company and voting rights. This method dilutes existing ownership but raises significant capital.

- **Preferred Stock:** Issuing preferred shares, which often come with fixed dividends and have priority over common stock in the event of liquidation. Preferred shares provide a less risky investment option than common stock.
- **Additional Paid-In Capital:** Funds raised above the par value of shares issued, often through new share issuances, enhancing the equity base of the company.

2. Debt Financing

- **Bank Loans:** Borrowing from financial institutions can be short-term or long-term, secured or unsecured. These loans are often used for immediate capital needs.
- **Bonds:** Issuing debt securities to investors obligates the company to pay periodic interest and repay the principal at maturity. Bonds are a common way to secure large amounts of funding over extended periods.
- **Lines of Credit:** Access to flexible, revolving credit from banks allows the company to draw funds as needed, providing financial flexibility.

3. Retained Earnings

Profits generated by the company that are reinvested into the business instead of being distributed as dividends. This internal source of funding supports ongoing operations and growth, reducing the need for external financing.

4. Capital Contributions

Additional capital injected by existing shareholders or new investors to bolster the company's financial position. These contributions are often used for expansion or strategic initiatives.

5. Other Sources

- **Grants and Subsidies:** Non-repayable funds provided by governments or organizations to support specific projects or initiatives. These can significantly reduce project costs.
- **Asset Sales:** Selling non-core assets to raise funds, which can include real estate, equipment, or divisions of the business. This helps in focusing on core business areas and improving liquidity.

Uses of Capital

Uses of capital detail how the funds raised are allocated within the company or project. These allocations ensure the capital is effectively utilized to generate returns and support strategic goals. Key uses include:

1. Capital Expenditures (CapEx)

Investments in long-term assets such as property, plant, and equipment (PP&E). This includes purchasing new machinery, upgrading facilities, or acquiring new technology to enhance production capabilities.

2. Working Capital

Funds used to manage day-to-day operations, including maintaining inventory levels, financing accounts receivable, and managing accounts payable. Efficient working capital management ensures liquidity and operational efficiency.

3. Debt Repayment

Repaying principal and interest on existing debt obligations. This includes scheduled payments for bank loans, bonds, and other debt instruments, helping maintain the company's creditworthiness.

4. Dividends and Distributions

Cash payments made to shareholders as a return on their investment. Regular dividend payments can attract and retain investors by providing a steady income stream.

5. Acquisitions and Investments

Allocating funds for acquiring other companies or making strategic investments. These initiatives can expand the company's market presence, diversify its product offerings, or enhance its competitive position.

6. Interest Payments

Periodic payments made to service the interest on debt. Timely interest payments are crucial to maintaining good relationships with lenders and avoiding default.

7. Taxes

Payments made to fulfill tax obligations, including corporate income tax, property tax, and sales tax. Proper tax planning and compliance are essential to avoid legal issues and optimize financial performance.

8. Other Uses

Specific expenses relevant to the company or project, such as research and development (R&D) costs, marketing expenses, or restructuring charges. These allocations support innovation, market expansion, and organizational improvements.

Importance of Sources and Uses in Financial Modeling

The sources and uses of capital in a financial model provide a comprehensive view of a company's financing activities and how funds are deployed. They help investment bankers, analysts, and management evaluate:

- **Capital Structure:** Understanding the mix of debt and equity financing and its impact on the company's risk profile and cost of capital.
- **Funding Requirements:** Identifying the amount of capital needed to support strategic initiatives and operational needs.
- **Cash Flow Management:** Ensuring sufficient liquidity to meet obligations and fund growth.
- **Financial Performance:** Assessing how different financing scenarios impact profitability, return on investment, and overall financial health.

Conclusion

Understanding the sources and uses of capital is fundamental in financial modeling within investment banking. By providing a detailed breakdown of how funds are raised and allocated, these components help evaluate a company's financial strategy, ensure efficient capital deployment, and support informed decision-making. Accurate and thorough analysis of sources and uses is essential for optimizing a company's financial performance and achieving its strategic objectives.

Chapter 89: What is a Discounted Cash Flow (DCF) Model?

Understanding the Discounted Cash Flow (DCF) Model in Investment Banking

Introduction to the DCF Model

In investment banking, the Discounted Cash Flow (DCF) model is a vital tool for estimating the intrinsic value of an asset, company, or investment. The core principle of the DCF model is the *time value of money*, which posits that a dollar today is worth more than a dollar in the future. This principle underpins the process of discounting future cash flows back to their present value, providing a clear picture of an investment's potential worth.

Key Components of a DCF Model

1. Projecting Future Cash Flows

The first step in constructing a DCF model is to forecast the future cash flows that the investment is expected to generate. This involves:

- **Revenue Growth**: Estimating future sales growth based on historical data, market conditions, and the company's strategic initiatives.
- **Operating Expenses**: Forecasting costs related to day-to-day operations, such as production, administration, and marketing.
- **Capital Expenditures**: Predicting investments in long-term assets like machinery and infrastructure, which are crucial for sustaining business operations.
- **Working Capital Changes**: Assessing changes in assets and liabilities, such as accounts receivable, inventory, and accounts payable, which affect cash flow availability.
- **Taxes**: Calculating tax expenses based on projected earnings, tax laws, and the company's tax strategy.

2. Calculating the Discount Rate

The discount rate reflects the required rate of return for the investment, capturing the risk and time preferences of investors. Typically, this rate is derived from the company's Weighted Average Cost of Capital (WACC), which includes:

- **Cost of Equity**: The return required by equity investors, often estimated using the Capital Asset Pricing Model (CAPM). This model considers factors like the risk-free rate, the equity market risk premium, and the company's beta (a measure of volatility relative to the market).
- **Cost of Debt**: The effective interest rate the company pays on its debt, adjusted for the tax deductibility of interest expenses.
- **Capital Structure**: The mix of debt and equity used to finance the company, which affects the overall cost of capital.

3. Estimating the Terminal Value

To capture the value beyond the explicit forecast period, the DCF model includes a terminal value calculation. This value represents the future cash flows' value at the end of the forecast period. There are two primary methods to calculate the terminal value:

- **Perpetuity Growth Model**: Assumes that free cash flows will grow at a constant rate indefinitely. The formula is: Terminal Value=Final Year Free Cash Flow×(1+Growth Rate)Discount Rate−Growth Rate\text{Terminal Value} = \frac{\text{Final Year Free Cash Flow} \times (1 + \text{Growth Rate})}{\text{Discount Rate} - \text{Growth Rate}}Terminal Value=Discount Rate−Growth RateFinal Year Free Cash Flow×(1+Growth Rate)
- **Exit Multiple Method**: Applies a multiple (e.g., EBITDA multiple) based on industry norms to the final year's financial metric.

4. Discounting Cash Flows to Present Value

Future cash flows and the terminal value are discounted to their present value using the discount rate. The formula for discounting a cash flow is:

Present Value=Future Cash Flow(1+Discount Rate)t\text{Present Value} = \frac{\text{Future Cash Flow}}{(1 + \text{Discount Rate})^t}Present Value=(1+Discount Rate)tFuture Cash Flow

where ttt is the time period.

5. Summing the Present Values

The total value of the investment is found by summing the present value of the forecasted cash flows and the present value of the terminal value. This sum provides the total enterprise value (EV) of the business. From this value, subtracting the net debt gives the equity value.

Application of the DCF Model in Investment Banking

Investment bankers use the DCF model in various contexts, including:

- **Mergers and Acquisitions (M&A)**: Estimating the value of a target company and advising on appropriate purchase prices.
- **Initial Public Offerings (IPOs)**: Setting offering prices for new shares by assessing the intrinsic value of the company.
- **Investment Analysis**: Comparing the intrinsic value of potential investments with their current market prices to identify undervalued opportunities.

Advantages and Limitations of the DCF Model

Advantages:

- **Detailed Analysis**: Provides a comprehensive assessment of an investment's value by considering all cash flows.
- **Flexibility**: Can be adjusted to reflect various scenarios and assumptions, allowing for sensitivity analysis.

Limitations:

- **Assumption-Driven**: The accuracy of the DCF model heavily relies on the quality and accuracy of the input assumptions, which can introduce uncertainty.
- **Complexity**: Requires extensive data and a deep understanding of financial concepts, making it complex and time-consuming to construct.

Conclusion

The DCF model is a cornerstone of valuation in investment banking, offering a structured approach to estimating the value of an investment based on its future cash flows. Despite its reliance on assumptions and complexity, it remains a powerful tool for making informed financial decisions and guiding strategic planning in various financial contexts.

Chapter 90: What is a Leveraged Buyout (LBO) Model?

Understanding Leveraged Buyout (LBO) Models: A Comprehensive Guide

A Leveraged Buyout (LBO) model is a crucial financial tool in investment banking, used to evaluate the feasibility and potential returns of acquiring a company using a significant amount of debt. This post explores the key components and applications of LBO models, shedding light on their importance in assessing investment opportunities and structuring transactions.

What is an LBO Model?

An LBO model simulates the financial structure and performance of a company after a leveraged buyout. In an LBO, a firm is acquired primarily using borrowed funds, with the acquired company's assets often serving as collateral. The objective is to generate sufficient returns through operational improvements, asset sales, or other value-creating activities, enabling the repayment of debt and generating returns for equity investors.

Key Components of an LBO Model

1. Valuation of the Target Company

Purpose: Determine the company's worth to set a baseline for the acquisition.

Steps:

- **Project Future Cash Flows:** Estimate revenues, costs, capital expenditures, and working capital changes over a projection period, typically 5-10 years.
- **Discount Future Cash Flows:** Use the weighted average cost of capital (WACC) to discount these cash flows to present value.
- **Calculate Terminal Value:** Estimate the company's value at the end of the projection period using methods like perpetuity growth or exit multiples.
- **Total Enterprise Value (EV):** Sum the present value of projected cash flows and the terminal value to determine the EV.

2. Determining the Purchase Price

Purpose: Establish the acquisition cost, typically a multiple of the company's EBITDA.

Steps:

- **Apply EBITDA Multiple:** Use an appropriate industry multiple to the target's EBITDA.
- **Adjust for Negotiation Factors:** Consider strategic premiums, synergies, or negotiation dynamics that might adjust the final price.

3. Structuring the Financing

Purpose: Determine the mix of debt and equity to finance the acquisition.

Components:

- **Debt Financing:** Identify the types (senior debt, subordinated debt, etc.), amounts, interest rates, and repayment schedules.
- **Equity Contribution:** Calculate the equity required from investors, typically a smaller portion compared to the debt.

4. Projecting Financial Performance and Debt Repayment

Purpose: Assess the target's ability to generate cash flows for debt servicing and returns.

Projections:

- **Operating Performance:** Forecast post-acquisition revenue growth, expenses, and EBITDA.
- **Debt Amortization:** Detail the repayment schedule, including interest and principal.
- **Free Cash Flow:** Determine the cash available after operational and capital expenses, crucial for debt repayment.

5. Returns Analysis

Purpose: Estimate the potential returns to investors.

Metrics:

- **Internal Rate of Return (IRR):** The annualized return rate expected by investors.
- **Cash-on-Cash Return:** Total cash received relative to the initial equity investment.

- **Equity Multiple:** The ratio of total cash returns to initial equity investment.

Applications of LBO Models in Investment Banking

Investment bankers use LBO models to:

- **Determine the Appropriate Purchase Price:** Ensure the acquisition cost aligns with projected cash flows and valuation metrics.
- **Assess Debt Capacity:** Evaluate how much debt the target can handle without risking financial instability.
- **Estimate Potential Returns:** Provide investors with a clear view of expected returns, aiding in decision-making.
- **Strategic Planning:** Identify synergies and value-creation opportunities that can enhance returns.

Conclusion

An LBO model is an essential tool in the arsenal of investment bankers. By carefully projecting cash flows, determining the purchase price, structuring financing, and analyzing potential returns, bankers ensure that leveraged buyouts are financially sound and meet investors' return expectations. This meticulous process helps align investment opportunities with strategic goals, facilitating successful transactions and value creation.

Chapter 91: How to Build a Financial Statement Model?

How to Build a Financial Statement Model

Creating a comprehensive financial statement model is an essential skill in investment banking, as it provides a detailed projection of a company's financial future. This model integrates the income statement, balance sheet, and cash flow statement, giving a full view of the company's financial health. Here's an in-depth guide on how to build a financial statement model, covering each step in detail.

Step 1: Gather Historical Financial Data

Collect Financial Statements

1. **Income Statement**: Collect the past 3-5 years of income statements to understand trends in revenue, expenses, and profitability.
2. **Balance Sheet**: Gather balance sheets for the same period to examine assets, liabilities, and shareholders' equity.
3. **Cash Flow Statement**: Collect cash flow statements to analyze cash inflows and outflows, including operating, investing, and financing activities.

Analyze Historical Trends

- **Revenue Growth**: Assess historical growth rates and seasonal patterns.
- **Cost Structure**: Evaluate the consistency of cost of goods sold (COGS) and operating expenses relative to revenue.
- **Profit Margins**: Analyze changes in gross, operating, and net margins over time.

Step 2: Develop Assumptions

Industry and Market Trends

- **Economic Conditions**: Research economic indicators that may impact the industry, such as interest rates, inflation, and GDP growth.
- **Regulatory Environment**: Consider current and potential future regulations that could affect operations.

Company-Specific Factors

- **Revenue Growth**: Base projections on historical growth rates, market trends, and management's guidance.
- **Gross Margin**: Consider factors affecting COGS, such as raw material costs and production efficiency.
- **Operating Expenses**: Project expenses like SG&A, R&D, and others, taking into account fixed and variable components.
- **Capital Expenditures**: Estimate future investments in property, plant, and equipment.
- **Working Capital Changes**: Forecast changes in accounts receivable, inventory, and accounts payable.

Step 3: Build the Income Statement

Revenue Projections

- Use historical growth rates and market analysis to project future revenues.
- Segment revenue by product line, geographic region, or customer type if applicable.

Cost of Goods Sold (COGS) and Gross Margin

- Project COGS to calculate gross profit, ensuring consistency with historical margins.

Operating Expenses

- Forecast major expense categories, considering historical percentages of revenue and expected changes.

EBITDA and Net Income

- Calculate Earnings Before Interest, Taxes, Depreciation, and Amortization (EBITDA).
- Subtract depreciation, interest expenses, and taxes to derive net income.

Step 4: Build the Balance Sheet

Assets

- **Current Assets**: Include projections for cash, accounts receivable, and inventory.
- **Non-Current Assets**: Account for property, plant, and equipment (PP&E), considering depreciation and capital expenditures.

Liabilities

- **Current Liabilities**: Include accounts payable and short-term debt.
- **Non-Current Liabilities**: Project long-term debt and other long-term obligations.

Equity

- **Retained Earnings**: Update based on net income and dividend payments.
- **Common Equity**: Reflect any new equity issuance or repurchase.

Step 5: Build the Cash Flow Statement

Cash Flow from Operating Activities

- Start with net income and adjust for non-cash items and changes in working capital.

Cash Flow from Investing Activities

- Include capital expenditures and proceeds from asset sales.

Cash Flow from Financing Activities

- Account for debt issuance/repayment and equity transactions.

Net Change in Cash

- Ensure the net change reconciles with the beginning and ending cash balances on the balance sheet.

Step 6: Check the Model for Consistency

Reconciliation

- Verify that the model's outputs align with the inputs and that all statements are correctly linked.

Cross-Verification

- Double-check all figures and formulas for accuracy and consistency.

Step 7: Conduct Sensitivity Analysis

Identify Key Variables

- Determine which assumptions have the most significant impact on the financial model.

Scenario Planning

- Develop scenarios (best-case, worst-case, and base-case) to assess how changes in key assumptions affect the financial outlook.

Step 8: Create a Presentation

Summarize Financial Performance

- Provide a summary of historical and projected financial performance, highlighting key metrics.

Visualize Data

- Use graphs and charts to illustrate financial trends, assumptions, and scenarios.

Provide Strategic Recommendations

- Offer actionable insights based on the financial model, including potential risks and opportunities.

Conclusion

Building a comprehensive three-statement financial model is an intricate process that requires a thorough understanding of a company's financials, industry dynamics, and market conditions. By following these detailed steps, investment bankers can create robust financial models that inform strategic decisions and support financial planning and analysis. This skill is indispensable for evaluating a company's financial health and strategic opportunities, providing a foundation for informed decision-making in investment banking.

Chapter 92: How Are Line Items Linked in the Three Financial Statements

How Line Items are Linked in the Three Financial Statements: A Comprehensive Overview

In financial statement modeling, the accurate linkage of line items across the income statement, balance sheet, and cash flow statement is fundamental to understanding a company's financial health. These linkages ensure consistency and clarity, allowing analysts to see how transactions affect various aspects of the business. This blog post explores the detailed interconnections between these three financial statements, explaining how specific line items interact and influence each other.

1. Net Income

Income Statement:

- **Function:** Net income represents the company's total earnings after all expenses, taxes, and costs are deducted from revenues.
- **Importance:** It is a key indicator of profitability.

Balance Sheet:

- **Linkage:** Net income flows into the retained earnings section under shareholders' equity. Retained earnings reflect the cumulative amount of net income retained in the company after dividends are paid.

Cash Flow Statement:

- **Connection:** Net income is the starting point in the cash flow from operations section. Adjustments are made for non-cash items and changes in working capital to reconcile it with net cash provided by operating activities.

Example:
A net income of $100,000 increases retained earnings and forms the baseline for calculating operating cash flow, which is adjusted for items like depreciation and changes in working capital.

2. Revenue

Income Statement:

- **Function:** Revenue is the top line, showing total sales before any deductions.
- **Importance:** It reflects the company's ability to generate sales.

Balance Sheet:

- **Linkage:** Revenue affects accounts receivable if sales are made on credit, indicating cash not yet collected.

Cash Flow Statement:

- **Connection:** The cash flow statement adjusts for changes in accounts receivable to reflect cash actually received from sales.

Example:
A company with $500,000 in revenue and a $50,000 increase in accounts receivable has collected $450,000 in cash, impacting the operating cash flow.

3. Cost of Goods Sold (COGS)

Income Statement:

- **Function:** COGS represents the direct costs of producing goods sold.
- **Importance:** It affects gross profit and indicates efficiency in production.

Balance Sheet:

- **Linkage:** COGS impacts inventory levels, showing the cost of inventory sold during the period.

Cash Flow Statement:

- **Connection:** Changes in inventory and accounts payable related to COGS affect cash flow from operations.

Example:
With COGS of $200,000 and a $20,000 increase in inventory, cash flow from operations shows additional cash tied up in inventory.

4. Depreciation and Amortization

Income Statement:

- **Function:** These are non-cash expenses that reduce taxable income.
- **Importance:** Reflects the allocation of asset costs over time.

Balance Sheet:

- **Linkage:** Accumulated in the accumulated depreciation account, reducing the net book value of fixed assets.

Cash Flow Statement:

- **Connection:** Added back to net income in operating activities, as they do not involve actual cash outflows.

Example:
A depreciation expense of $30,000 reduces net income but is added back in the cash flow statement, as it doesn't impact cash.

5. Working Capital

Income Statement:

- **Function:** Impacts operating efficiency and profitability indirectly.
- **Importance:** Reflects short-term financial health.

Balance Sheet:

- **Linkage:** Includes accounts receivable, accounts payable, and inventory.

Cash Flow Statement:

- **Connection:** Adjustments for changes in working capital reconcile net income to operating cash flow.

Example:

An increase in accounts receivable by $10,000 reduces cash flow from operations, indicating more sales made on credit.

6. Long-term Debt and Interest Expense

Income Statement:

- **Function:** Interest expense is recorded as a cost, reducing net income.
- **Importance:** Reflects the cost of borrowed funds.

Balance Sheet:

- **Linkage:** Long-term debt is listed under liabilities, and interest payable may appear as a current liability.

Cash Flow Statement:

- **Connection:** Interest payments are included in cash flows from operating activities, while principal repayments and new borrowings affect cash flows from financing activities.

Example:

A $1,000,000 loan with a $50,000 interest expense reduces net income and reflects on both the balance sheet (debt) and cash flow statement (interest paid).

7. Capital Expenditures (CapEx)

Income Statement:

- **Function:** CapEx is not directly recorded but affects future depreciation expenses.
- **Importance:** Indicates investment in long-term assets.

Balance Sheet:

- **Linkage:** Increases property, plant, and equipment (PP&E).

Cash Flow Statement:

- **Connection:** Recorded as outflows in investing activities, reducing the total cash balance.

Example:
Purchasing machinery for $200,000 increases PP&E and shows as an investing outflow.

8. Dividends

Income Statement:

- **Function:** Dividends are not recorded here.
- **Importance:** Impact shareholder returns.

Balance Sheet:

- **Linkage:** Reduce retained earnings under shareholders' equity.

Cash Flow Statement:

- **Connection:** Recorded as outflows in financing activities.

Example:
Paying $50,000 in dividends reduces retained earnings and appears as a cash outflow.

Conclusion

Understanding the intricate links between the income statement, balance sheet, and cash flow statement is crucial for accurate financial modeling and analysis. These interconnections provide a holistic view of a company's financial health, ensuring that all aspects of its operations and financial activities are accurately reflected. Mastering these relationships allows for more reliable financial forecasts, better strategic planning, and more informed decision-making.

Chapter 93: What Are the Most Common Drivers Used in Financial Modeling

Understanding the Most Common Drivers Used in Financial Modeling

In the realm of investment banking, financial modeling is an indispensable tool used to forecast a company's financial future. By leveraging a variety of drivers, analysts can predict financial outcomes and provide strategic insights. These drivers are critical components that influence the accuracy and reliability of financial models. Let's delve into some of the most common drivers used in financial modeling, highlighting their importance and the factors that influence them.

1. Revenue Growth Rate

Definition and Importance: The revenue growth rate indicates the percentage increase in a company's sales over time. It's a foundational metric because it directly impacts the company's overall financial health and profitability. Accurately forecasting revenue growth is crucial for understanding future performance.

Influencing Factors:

- **Market Demand:** Changes in consumer preferences and economic conditions.
- **Industry Trends:** Growth rates within the broader industry.
- **Product Pricing:** Adjustments in product or service pricing strategies.
- **New Product Launches:** Introduction of new offerings can drive significant revenue increases.
- **Marketing and Sales Efforts:** Effectiveness in attracting and retaining customers.

Sources for Projections:

- Historical data on past sales growth.
- Industry benchmarks and market research reports.
- Company management forecasts and strategic plans.

2. Cost of Goods Sold (COGS) Ratio

Definition and Importance: COGS refers to the direct costs associated with producing goods or services sold by a company. The COGS ratio, calculated as COGS divided by revenue, is essential for assessing gross profit margins.

Influencing Factors:

- **Raw Material Costs:** Fluctuations in the prices of inputs.
- **Labor Costs:** Wages and salaries of production staff.
- **Operational Efficiency:** Improvements in production processes that reduce costs.
- **Economies of Scale:** Cost reductions achieved through increased production levels.

Sources for Projections:

- Historical COGS data.
- Industry averages and benchmarks.
- Future cost estimates provided by the company's management.

3. Operating Expense Ratios

Definition and Importance: Operating expenses include costs related to selling, general, and administrative activities. These expenses are typically expressed as a percentage of revenue and are crucial for calculating operating profit.

Influencing Factors:

- **Marketing Expenses:** Costs associated with promoting products.
- **Research and Development (R&D):** Investments in innovation.
- **Administrative Costs:** Overheads like salaries for administrative staff and office expenses.

Sources for Projections:

- Past operating expense ratios.
- Industry standards.
- Budget forecasts from the company.

4. Gross Margin

Definition and Importance: Gross margin is calculated as (Revenue - COGS) / Revenue. It indicates the proportion of revenue remaining after accounting for COGS, which is used to cover operating expenses and generate profit.

Influencing Factors:

- **COGS Management:** Ability to control production costs.
- **Pricing Strategy:** Pricing adjustments to maintain or improve margins.
- **Product Mix:** The impact of different products with varying profitability.

Sources for Projections:

- Historical gross margin data.
- Industry comparisons.
- Strategic initiatives like cost-cutting measures.

5. Operating Margin

Definition and Importance: Operating margin is calculated as Operating Income / Revenue. It shows the efficiency of a company's core business operations in generating profit.

Influencing Factors:

- **Revenue Growth:** Higher sales can lead to better utilization of fixed costs.
- **Cost Control:** Effective management of operating expenses.
- **Scale of Operations:** Larger operations can achieve efficiencies.

Sources for Projections:

- Historical operating margins.
- Management forecasts.
- Comparisons with industry peers.

6. Working Capital Ratios

Definition and Importance: Working capital ratios include metrics like the accounts receivable turnover, accounts payable turnover, and inventory turnover. These ratios are vital for assessing a company's liquidity and operational efficiency.

Influencing Factors:

- **Credit Terms:** The terms extended to customers and received from suppliers.
- **Inventory Management:** Efficiency in managing stock levels.
- **Cash Flow Management:** The timing of cash inflows and outflows.

Sources for Projections:

- Historical working capital ratios.
- Industry norms and best practices.
- Company-specific policies.

7. Capital Expenditure (CapEx) as a Percentage of Revenue

Definition and Importance: CapEx refers to funds used by a company to acquire, upgrade, and maintain physical assets. It's often expressed as a percentage of revenue and indicates the level of investment in long-term assets.

Influencing Factors:

- **Growth Strategies:** Expansion plans that require new assets.
- **Technology Upgrades:** Investments in new technology.
- **Maintenance Requirements:** Ongoing maintenance and replacement of existing assets.

Sources for Projections:

- Historical CapEx spending.
- Industry standards.
- Company management's investment plans.

8. Debt Ratios

Definition and Importance: Debt ratios, such as the debt-to-equity ratio and interest coverage ratio, measure a company's financial leverage and its ability to meet debt obligations.

Influencing Factors:

- **Interest Rates:** The cost of borrowing.
- **Debt Levels:** The amount of outstanding debt.
- **Cash Flow:** The company's ability to generate cash to service debt.

Sources for Projections:

- Current debt levels.
- Future borrowing plans.
- Economic conditions affecting interest rates.

Conclusion

These common drivers in financial modeling are critical for developing accurate financial forecasts. They provide a comprehensive view of a company's financial health and future prospects, guiding strategic decisions and investment evaluations. By understanding and correctly applying these drivers, investment bankers can offer valuable insights and recommendations, ultimately supporting informed decision-making and strategic planning.

Chapter 94: How to Build a DCF Model?

How to Build a DCF Model

Building a Discounted Cash Flow (DCF) model is a fundamental task in investment banking, providing an estimate of a company's intrinsic value based on its projected future cash flows. Here's a detailed, step-by-step guide to constructing a DCF model, covering everything from projecting future cash flows to performing sensitivity analysis.

Step 1: Project Free Cash Flows

Estimating Future Free Cash Flows (FCF)

1. **Revenue Projections:**
   - **Historical Data Analysis:** Review the company's historical revenue growth rates.
   - **Industry Trends:** Analyze industry growth trends and market conditions.
   - **Company-Specific Factors:** Consider the company's market position, product pipeline, and competitive advantages.
2. **Gross Margin and Operating Expenses:**
   - **Gross Margin:** Project based on historical trends and industry benchmarks.

- **Operating Expenses:** Forecast SG&A, R&D, and other operating costs, considering the company's past expense patterns and future plans.
3. **Capital Expenditures (CapEx):**
   - **Historical CapEx:** Review past capital expenditures.
   - **Future Growth Plans:** Consider the company's future investment plans.
4. **Working Capital Changes:**
   - **Components:** Estimate changes in accounts receivable, accounts payable, and inventory.
   - **Historical Trends:** Use past working capital cycles as a reference.
5. **Tax Rates:**
   - **Applicable Tax Rates:** Apply the current tax rate or expected changes in tax legislation.

Calculating Unlevered Free Cash Flow (UFCF)

1. **EBITDA Calculation:**
   - **Revenue - Operating Expenses:** Determine Earnings Before Interest, Taxes, Depreciation, and Amortization (EBITDA).
2. **Interest Expense and Taxes:**
   - **EBIT:** Subtract interest expenses and taxes from EBITDA.
3. **Non-Cash Charges:**
   - **Depreciation and Amortization:** Add back non-cash charges to EBIT.
4. **UFCF Calculation:**
   - **Formula:** UFCF = EBIT - Taxes + Non-Cash Charges - CapEx - Changes in Working Capital.

Step 2: Calculate the Terminal Value

Estimating Terminal Value

1. **Perpetuity Growth Method:**
   - **Formula:** Terminal Value = FCF in Final Year × (1 + Growth Rate) / (WACC - Growth Rate).
2. **Exit Multiple Method:**
   - **Comparable Analysis:** Apply an exit multiple to the terminal year's EBITDA or cash flow based on industry standards.

Discounting Terminal Value

1. **Present Value Calculation:**
   - **Formula:** Present Value of Terminal Value = Terminal Value / (1 + WACC) ^ Number of Years.

Step 3: Determine the Cost of Capital

Calculating WACC

1. **Cost of Equity (CAPM):**
   - **Formula:** Cost of Equity = Risk-Free Rate + Beta × (Market Risk Premium).
2. **Cost of Debt:**
   - **Formula:** After-Tax Cost of Debt = Cost of Debt × (1 - Tax Rate).
3. **WACC Calculation:**
   - **Formula:** WACC = (E / (E + D)) × Cost of Equity + (D / (E + D)) × After-Tax Cost of Debt.
   - **Where:** E = Market value of equity, D = Market value of debt.

Step 4: Calculate the Enterprise Value

Present Value of Cash Flows

1. **Discounting Cash Flows:**
   - **Formula:** Present Value of FCF = $\sum$ (FCF in Year t / $(1 + WACC)^t$).

Enterprise Value Calculation

1. **Summing Present Values:**
   - **Formula:** Enterprise Value = Present Value of Projected FCF + Present Value of Terminal Value.

Step 5: Calculate the Equity Value

1. **Net Debt Adjustment:**
   - **Formula:** Equity Value = Enterprise Value - Net Debt.

Step 6: Calculate the Share Price

1. **Share Price Determination:**
   - **Formula:** Share Price = Equity Value / Shares Outstanding.
2. **Market Comparison:**
   - **Compare Valuations:** Evaluate the calculated share price against the current market price to identify overvaluation or undervaluation.

Step 7: Perform Sensitivity Analysis

Assessing Impact of Assumptions

1. **Key Drivers:**

- Identify Variables: Focus on revenue growth, discount rate, and terminal growth rate.
2. **Scenario Analysis:**
    - **Different Scenarios:** Assess how changes in assumptions affect valuation.

Sensitivity Analysis Tools

1. **Data Tables and Tornado Charts:**
    - **Visualization:** Use Excel to create data tables and tornado charts, illustrating the sensitivity of the valuation to different assumptions.

Conclusion

Building a DCF model involves projecting future free cash flows, calculating terminal value, determining the cost of capital, calculating enterprise and equity values, and performing sensitivity analysis. Each step is critical for developing an accurate valuation of a company. By following this structured approach, investment bankers can provide valuable insights into a company's intrinsic value, aiding in informed investment decisions and strategic planning.

Chapter 95: What is M&A Modeling?

What is M&A Modeling?

Mergers and Acquisitions (M&A) modeling is a specialized area of financial modeling used in investment banking to analyze and project the financial impact of potential M&A transactions. This involves constructing detailed financial models to assess how the merger or acquisition will affect the combined company's financial statements, such as the income statement, balance sheet, and cash flow statement. The ultimate goal is to determine whether the transaction will be financially beneficial and strategically sound.

The Purpose of M&A Modeling

M&A modeling serves several crucial purposes:

1. **Financial Feasibility Assessment**: It helps determine whether a proposed merger or acquisition is financially viable.
2. **Valuation**: It estimates the value of the target company and the potential combined entity.
3. **Synergy Analysis**: It identifies and quantifies potential synergies that could result from the transaction.
4. **Risk Assessment**: It evaluates the risks associated with the deal and how they could impact the combined entity.

5. **Decision Support**: It provides critical information that helps decision-makers understand the financial implications of the transaction.

Key Steps in M&A Modeling

1. Analyzing Industry and Market Trends

Understanding the Market Landscape: Investment bankers start by examining the industry in which the target company operates. This involves understanding market dynamics, competitive positioning, and identifying key growth drivers and challenges. For example, they may analyze the impact of regulatory changes or technological advancements on the industry.

Market Trends Analysis: Bankers assess current trends and forecast future developments. This analysis helps in identifying companies that could be attractive targets for M&A, based on market positioning and potential for growth or consolidation.

2. Conducting Due Diligence

Financial Review: This involves a thorough examination of the target company's financial statements to assess historical performance and current financial health. Key financial metrics, such as revenue, profit margins, and cash flow stability, are analyzed.

Operational and Strategic Evaluation: The target's business model, revenue streams, cost structure, and competitive strengths are scrutinized. Investment bankers also evaluate the target's management team and their ability to execute post-transaction strategies.

3. Building a Financial Model

Data Collection: Historical financial data for both the acquirer and target is gathered. This data includes financial statements and other relevant metrics that provide a baseline for projections.

Projections: The model projects the financial performance of the combined entity, considering factors like expected revenue growth, cost savings, capital expenditures, and changes in working capital. These projections are typically laid out over a multi-year horizon.

4. Valuation Analysis

Valuation Techniques: Investment bankers use various methods to value the target company and the combined entity:

- **Discounted Cash Flow (DCF) Analysis**: This method involves estimating the present value of expected future cash flows, using a discount rate that reflects the risk profile of the business.
- **Comparable Company Analysis (CCA)**: This involves comparing the target company to similar publicly traded companies, using multiples such as EV/EBITDA, P/E, and P/S ratios.
- **Precedent Transactions Analysis (PTA)**: This method looks at past transactions involving similar companies to derive valuation multiples.

5. Synergy Analysis

Cost Synergies: These include potential savings from eliminating redundancies, achieving economies of scale, and optimizing operations.

Revenue Synergies: These could arise from cross-selling opportunities, expanded market reach, or enhanced product offerings.

Tax Benefits: Potential tax efficiencies, such as the utilization of tax loss carryforwards, are also considered.

6. Performing Sensitivity Analysis

Scenario Analysis: Investment bankers create various scenarios to test how changes in key assumptions, such as growth rates or discount rates, impact the valuation. This analysis helps identify the range of possible outcomes and assess the risks involved.

7. Creating a Presentation

Comprehensive Presentation: The final step involves preparing a detailed presentation that summarizes the financial analysis, valuation findings, and strategic recommendations. This presentation is crucial for communicating the value and rationale behind the proposed transaction to stakeholders, including company management and investors.

Conclusion

M&A modeling is an intricate and essential process in investment banking that provides a comprehensive analysis of potential mergers and acquisitions. It involves multiple stages, from industry analysis and due diligence to financial modeling and valuation. By meticulously assessing the financial and strategic implications, investment bankers can provide valuable insights that aid in making informed decisions, ultimately aiming to create long-term value for stakeholders.

Chapter 96: How to Build an M&A Model?

How to Build an M&A Model: A Comprehensive Guide for Investment Bankers

Building a mergers and acquisitions (M&A) model is a crucial skill in investment banking, as it allows professionals to evaluate potential deals and provide informed advice to clients. This process involves a series of meticulous steps, each requiring careful analysis and financial acumen. Here's a detailed breakdown of how to construct an M&A model, from understanding market dynamics to calculating the financial impact on the acquirer and target companies.

1. Industry and Market Analysis

Understanding Industry Dynamics: Start by analyzing the industry in which the target company operates. This involves understanding the overall economic environment, key growth drivers, regulatory landscape, competitive forces, and current trends. Determine how these factors influence the target's market position and potential for future growth.

Identifying Value-Creating Opportunities: Identify strategic opportunities within the industry, such as market expansion, diversification, or technological advancements. Assess how these opportunities can create value for the acquirer, whether through enhancing market share, cost synergies, or access to new technologies.

2. Due Diligence

In-Depth Review of Target Company: Conduct a thorough review of the target company's historical financial statements, including the income statement, balance sheet, and cash flow statement. Analyze revenue streams, profitability margins, cost structures, and capital expenditures. Assess operational efficiency and management capabilities.

Risk Assessment: Identify potential risks, including financial vulnerabilities, operational inefficiencies, and regulatory issues. Evaluate how these risks could impact the target's value and the success of the transaction.

3. Building the Financial Model

Integration of Financial Statements: Input historical financial data for both the acquirer and the target. Project future performance based on assumptions about growth rates, cost savings, and capital expenditure. The model should include:

- **Income Statement:** Project revenues, costs, taxes, and net income.
- **Balance Sheet:** Forecast assets, liabilities, and shareholders' equity.
- **Cash Flow Statement:** Calculate cash flows from operating, investing, and financing activities.

4. Valuation Analysis

Valuation Techniques:

- **Discounted Cash Flow (DCF) Analysis:** Estimate the present value of future cash flows, considering a discount rate reflective of the risk.
- **Comparable Company Analysis (CCA):** Use valuation multiples from similar companies to value the target.
- **Precedent Transactions Analysis (PTA):** Derive valuation multiples from comparable past M&A deals.

Determining Enterprise Value (EV): Calculate the target's enterprise value, adjusting for debt and cash, to derive equity value. Consider how different valuation methods compare and reconcile them to arrive at a fair value estimate.

5. Synergy Identification

Cost and Revenue Synergies: Identify potential cost savings and revenue enhancements from combining the two companies. This can include streamlined operations, expanded market reach, and increased product offerings. Quantify these synergies and incorporate them into the financial projections.

6. Sensitivity Analysis

Testing Assumptions: Conduct sensitivity analysis to understand how changes in key assumptions (e.g., growth rates, discount rates) affect the valuation. This helps in assessing the robustness of the financial model under different scenarios.

Scenario Planning: Develop best-case, worst-case, and base-case scenarios to evaluate potential risks and returns. This analysis helps in understanding the range of possible outcomes and preparing for different market conditions.

7. Transaction Structuring

Deal Considerations: Determine the form of consideration (cash, stock, or a mix) and structure the deal accordingly. This involves negotiating the purchase price, payment terms, and financing arrangements.

Financing Strategy: Decide on the mix of debt and equity financing. Consider the impact on the acquirer's leverage and overall financial health.

8. Accretion/Dilution Analysis

Earnings Impact: Create pro forma financial statements to assess the impact of the transaction on the acquirer's earnings per share (EPS). Determine whether the deal is accretive (increases EPS) or dilutive (decreases EPS).

Key Metrics: Calculate pro forma EPS and the accretion/dilution percentage to quantify the financial benefits or costs of the transaction.

Conclusion

Building an M&A model involves a detailed and structured approach, integrating industry analysis, financial modeling, valuation, and strategic planning. By following these steps, investment bankers can provide comprehensive and accurate assessments, guiding clients through complex transactions and helping them make informed decisions. The ultimate goal is to create a model that not only reflects the current financial standing of the companies involved but also provides a roadmap for future growth and value creation.

Chapter 97: What is the Difference Between LBO Modeling & M&A Modeling?

Understanding the Key Differences Between LBO Modeling and M&A Modeling

Investment banking utilizes various financial modeling techniques to assess and evaluate complex transactions. Two critical methodologies are Leveraged Buyout (LBO) modeling and Mergers & Acquisitions (M&A) modeling. While both are essential tools, they serve distinct purposes, focus on different aspects of transactions, and involve unique methodologies. Let's explore the intricacies of each to understand their differences better.

LBO Modeling: A Deep Dive into Leveraged Buyouts

Definition and Purpose:

LBO modeling is primarily used to assess the viability and profitability of acquiring a company using a significant amount of borrowed funds. The core objective is to determine whether the cash flows generated by the target company can sufficiently cover debt obligations and yield an attractive return on equity.

Key Elements:

1. **Capital Structure:**
   - **Debt and Equity Mix:** The model focuses on structuring the acquisition's financing, typically involving a high level of debt relative to equity.
   - **Leverage Ratio:** It assesses the optimal balance between debt and equity to minimize the cost of capital while maximizing returns.
   - **Interest Rates:** The cost of debt financing is a critical factor, influencing the overall feasibility of the buyout.
2. **Purchase Price:**
   - **Valuation:** The target company's value is determined using valuation techniques, which sets the baseline for negotiation.
   - **Equity Contribution:** The equity stake provided by the private equity firm is calculated to understand the risk-return profile.
3. **Debt Financing:**
   - **Types of Debt:** The model incorporates various debt instruments, such as senior debt, subordinated debt, and mezzanine financing, each with different priority levels and risk profiles.
   - **Interest and Principal Payments:** Detailed projections of interest expenses and debt repayment schedules are included.
4. **Cash Flow Projections:**
   - **Forecasting Cash Flows:** The model projects the company's cash flows, considering historical

performance, market trends, and future growth initiatives.

5. **Returns Analysis:**
   - **Metrics like IRR, ROI, and Cash-on-Cash Returns** are used to evaluate the financial performance of the investment and its attractiveness.

M&A Modeling: Analyzing Mergers and Acquisitions

Definition and Purpose:

M&A modeling focuses on the financial and strategic assessment of merging two companies or acquiring one company by another. The primary goal is to evaluate the potential synergies, financial impact, and overall value creation from the transaction.

Key Elements:

1. **Valuation Analysis:**
   - **Valuation Methods:** Various techniques, such as Discounted Cash Flow (DCF), Comparable Company Analysis, and Precedent Transactions Analysis, are used to value the target company.
2. **Purchase Price Allocation:**
   - **Goodwill and Intangible Assets:** The purchase price is allocated among tangible and intangible assets, identifying the premium paid over the fair value of net identifiable assets.
3. **Pro Forma Financial Statements:**
   - **Combined Financials:** The model integrates the financials of both companies, adjusting for synergies, cost savings, and revenue enhancements.
   - **Synergies Assessment:** The analysis includes identifying and quantifying potential synergies that

can arise from the transaction, such as cost reductions and cross-selling opportunities.

4. **Accretion/Dilution Analysis:**
   - **Impact on EPS:** The model assesses whether the transaction will be accretive (increasing EPS) or dilutive (decreasing EPS) to the acquiring company's shareholders.

5. **Financing Considerations:**
   - **Financing Mix:** The model evaluates the mix of debt and equity used to finance the transaction and its impact on the acquirer's capital structure.
   - **Debt Issuance:** If new debt is raised, the model projects the impact on the company's balance sheet and interest expenses.

6. **Integration Costs:**
   - **One-Time Costs:** The model accounts for the costs associated with integrating the companies, such as restructuring expenses and technology integration.

Comparative Summary

LBO Modeling is centered around leveraging a high amount of debt to acquire a company, with a focus on cash flow projections, debt servicing, and generating high returns for equity investors. The model is heavily reliant on the target company's ability to generate sufficient cash flows.

M&A Modeling, on the other hand, focuses on the strategic and financial benefits of combining two companies. It involves a comprehensive analysis of valuation, synergies, financing structures, and the impact on financial metrics such as earnings per share. The emphasis is on value creation through synergies and strategic fit rather than purely financial engineering.

Both models require a deep understanding of financial analysis, market conditions, and strategic planning, and are essential tools for investment bankers in guiding clients through complex transactions. Understanding the differences between LBO and M&A modeling is crucial for professionals in the field to accurately assess and execute these financial strategies.

Chapter 98: Comparable Companies Analysis

Comparable Companies Analysis: A Deep Dive into Valuation Methodology

Comparable Companies Analysis, often referred to as "comps analysis," is a fundamental valuation technique used in investment banking. This method involves comparing the financial metrics and valuation multiples of a target company with those of similar publicly traded companies. The goal is to derive an estimated value for the target company based on market data. This blog post will walk through the detailed steps and considerations involved in conducting a comps analysis.

Selecting Comparable Companies

Initial Selection Criteria:

The process begins with identifying a set of comparable companies. These companies should operate in the same industry as the target company and share similar characteristics. Key factors to consider include:

1. **Industry and Sector:** Companies should be in the same industry to ensure that they face similar market dynamics and regulatory environments.

2. **Size and Scale:** Comparable companies should have similar revenue, market capitalization, and operational scale.
3. **Geographic Focus:** Companies operating in similar regions often face similar market conditions and regulatory challenges.
4. **Growth Prospects:** Firms with similar growth trajectories and market potential should be selected.

Ensuring Accurate Comparability:

It's crucial to ensure that the selected companies are truly comparable. Analysts should consider:

- **Business Model Similarities:** Comparable companies should have similar business models, product lines, and service offerings.
- **Financial Metrics:** Key metrics like revenue, EBITDA, and net income should be within a comparable range.

Gathering Financial Data and Valuation Metrics

Data Collection:

Once comparable companies are selected, the next step is to gather financial data. This includes:

- **Historical Financial Statements:** Income statements, balance sheets, and cash flow statements.
- **Market Data:** Stock prices, trading volumes, and market capitalization.
- **Valuation Multiples:** Key multiples such as P/E, EV/EBITDA, and P/S ratios.

Sources of Data:

Analysts typically use several sources for data collection, including:

- **Public Filings:** SEC filings like 10-Ks and 10-Qs provide comprehensive financial data.
- **Financial Databases:** Tools like Bloomberg, Capital IQ, and FactSet are invaluable for accessing up-to-date financial information and market data.
- **Industry Reports:** These provide context on industry trends and benchmarks.

Calculating and Analyzing Valuation Multiples

Determining Multiples:

Valuation multiples are calculated for each comparable company. Key multiples include:

1. **P/E Ratio:** Market price per share divided by earnings per share. It indicates how much investors are willing to pay per dollar of earnings.
2. **EV/EBITDA Ratio:** Enterprise value divided by EBITDA. It is a measure of a company's overall value relative to its earnings.
3. **P/S Ratio:** Market price per share divided by sales per share. This ratio is useful for companies with low or volatile earnings.

Benchmarking and Averaging:

The analyst calculates the median or average multiples for the group of comparable companies. This provides a benchmark that can be applied to the target company's financial metrics.

Applying Valuation Multiples to the Target Company

Application Process:

The calculated benchmark multiples are applied to the target company's financial metrics. For instance:

- **P/E Multiple Application:** If the median P/E ratio is 15x and the target company's earnings per share is $2, the estimated market price per share would be $30.
- **EV/EBITDA Application:** Similarly, if the target company's EBITDA is $10 million and the median EV/EBITDA multiple is 8x, the implied enterprise value would be $80 million.

Deriving the Valuation Range:

The application of multiples results in a valuation range for the target company. This range reflects the estimated value based on market data and comparable companies.

Refining the Valuation

Adjustments and Sensitivity Analysis:

To refine the valuation, analysts may:

- **Weight Multiples Differently:** Depending on the industry or the specific circumstances of the target company, some multiples may be given more weight than others.
- **Perform Sensitivity Analysis:** This involves adjusting key assumptions and observing how these changes impact the valuation.

Considering Qualitative Factors:

Beyond the quantitative analysis, qualitative factors such as management quality, market position, and potential growth opportunities are considered. These factors can significantly influence the final valuation.

Presenting and Interpreting the Analysis

Final Presentation:

The results of the comps analysis are presented to clients or senior management. This presentation includes:

- **Summary of Comparable Companies:** A detailed overview of the selected companies and their key metrics.
- **Valuation Range:** The estimated valuation range for the target company based on the analysis.
- **Supporting Data and Assumptions:** A comprehensive explanation of the data used, assumptions made, and any adjustments applied.

Conclusion:

Comparable Companies Analysis is a vital tool in investment banking for estimating the value of a company. By comparing a target company to its peers, analysts can derive a market-based valuation that reflects current market conditions and industry trends. However, it's important to supplement this analysis with other valuation methods and qualitative assessments to ensure a comprehensive valuation.

By following these detailed steps, investment banking analysts can provide clients with a well-supported, data-driven valuation estimate, helping them make informed strategic decisions.

Chapter 99: Precedent Transactions Analysis

Precedent Transactions Analysis: A Guide for Investment Bankers

Precedent Transactions Analysis is a key valuation method used in investment banking to estimate the value of a company based on the valuation of similar companies in recent transactions. This approach provides a market-based perspective, offering insights into how the market currently values comparable businesses. Here's a step-by-step guide on how investment bankers perform this analysis:

1. Identifying Relevant Transactions

The first step involves selecting a set of comparable transactions within the same industry as the target company. The criteria for selection include:

- **Industry Similarity**: The transactions should involve companies operating in the same industry as the target. This ensures the comparability of market dynamics, regulatory environment, and competitive pressures.
- **Company Characteristics**: Similarities in size, business model, market position, and growth prospects are crucial. For

example, a technology startup's valuation would not be compared to a mature industrial firm.

- **Transaction Attributes**: The size, nature (merger, acquisition, buyout), and strategic rationale of the transactions should align with the potential transaction for the target company.
- **Timing and Market Conditions**: Recent transactions are preferred, as they reflect current market conditions and investor sentiment.

2. Data Collection and Transaction Metrics

Once relevant transactions are selected, detailed data collection follows:

- **Transaction Values**: This includes the total consideration paid, including cash, stock, debt assumed, and any contingent payments.
- **Deal Structures**: Information on how the deal was structured, such as payment methods and any earn-out agreements.
- **Financial Metrics**: Key financial figures such as revenue, EBITDA (Earnings Before Interest, Taxes, Depreciation, and Amortization), and net income at the time of the transaction.

Data sources often include public filings (like SEC documents), financial databases (Capital IQ, Bloomberg), industry reports, and press releases.

3. Calculation of Valuation Multiples

With the data collected, the next step is calculating the relevant valuation multiples:

- **Transaction Value/Revenue**: Measures how much was paid per unit of revenue.

- **Transaction Value/EBITDA**: Shows the value paid relative to EBITDA, a measure of operating performance.
- **Transaction Value/Earnings**: Reflects the price paid per dollar of net income.

These multiples are calculated for each transaction and then averaged or medians are taken to mitigate the impact of outliers.

4. Application of Valuation Multiples

The derived multiples are then applied to the financial metrics of the target company to estimate its valuation:

- **Selecting the Right Metric**: Depending on the nature of the target company and industry, bankers choose the most appropriate multiple (e.g., EBITDA for cash flow-generating companies).
- **Calculating Valuation Range**: By applying the selected multiple to the target's corresponding financial metric, a range of valuations is derived, providing a benchmark based on market comparables.

5. Interpretation and Conclusion

The final step involves interpreting the results and contextualizing them within the broader market and company-specific context:

- **Valuation Range**: The analysis provides a range of potential valuations, highlighting the lower and upper bounds based on comparable transactions.
- **Consideration of Unique Attributes**: Investment bankers take into account unique factors of the target company that might not be fully reflected in the multiples, such as brand value, intellectual property, or strategic partnerships.

- **Cross-Validation**: It's often beneficial to cross-check the results with other valuation methods like Discounted Cash Flow (DCF) analysis or Comparable Company Analysis (CCA) for a comprehensive valuation perspective.

Conclusion

Precedent transactions analysis offers a practical, market-based valuation approach, crucial for making informed investment decisions and strategic recommendations. While it provides valuable insights, it's important to recognize its limitations, such as the availability of comparable transactions and the potential for market conditions to change. By combining this method with other valuation techniques, investment bankers can provide a more nuanced and accurate valuation for their clients.

Chapter 100: Discounted Cash Flow (DCF) Analysis

Discounted Cash Flow (DCF) Analysis: A Comprehensive Guide

Introduction to DCF Analysis

Discounted Cash Flow (DCF) analysis is a cornerstone technique in investment banking, used to estimate the intrinsic value of a company. By forecasting future cash flows and discounting them to their present value, DCF provides a clear picture of what a company is worth today based on its expected future earnings. Here's a detailed breakdown of the DCF process, highlighting the key steps and considerations involved.

1. Projecting Future Cash Flows

Understanding the Projections

The first step in a DCF analysis is to project the company's future free cash flows. These projections typically cover a period of five to ten years, depending on the predictability of the company's earnings and the stability of its industry.

Key Considerations

- **Revenue Forecasting**: Analysts start by estimating the company's future revenues based on historical growth rates, market trends, and economic conditions.
- **Expense Estimation**: Operating expenses, cost of goods sold, and other costs are forecasted to determine future profitability.
- **Capital Expenditures**: Projected capital expenditures (CapEx) are considered, reflecting the company's plans for investments in property, plant, and equipment.
- **Working Capital Changes**: Changes in working capital are forecasted, as they affect the cash flow available to the company.

Sources of Assumptions

These projections are grounded in historical financial data, industry reports, market analyses, and insights from company management. For instance, if a company operates in a growing industry like renewable energy, projections might assume an increasing growth rate due to favorable market conditions.

2. Determining the Discount Rate

The Role of WACC

The discount rate in a DCF analysis is critical as it accounts for the time value of money and investment risk. The Weighted Average Cost of Capital (WACC) is commonly used as the discount rate, blending the costs of equity and debt financing.

Components of WACC

- **Cost of Equity**: Often calculated using the Capital Asset Pricing Model (CAPM), which considers the risk-free rate, the stock's beta (a measure of volatility relative to the market), and the equity risk premium.

- **Cost of Debt**: Determined by the interest rates on the company's existing debt, adjusted for tax benefits since interest payments are tax-deductible.
- **Capital Structure**: The mix of debt and equity financing, reflecting the company's financial strategy and risk profile.

3. Calculating Present Value of Future Cash Flows

Present Value Calculation

Each projected cash flow is discounted back to its present value using the discount rate. The formula for discounting future cash flows is:

$$PV = CFt(1+r)tPV = \frac{CF\_t}{(1 + r)^t} PV = (1+r)tCFt$$

where $PVPVPV$ is the present value, $CFtCF\_tCFt$ is the cash flow in year ttt, and rrr is the discount rate.

Summing Present Values

The sum of the present values of all projected cash flows provides the total present value of the company's expected cash flows over the projection period.

4. Estimating the Terminal Value

Significance of Terminal Value

The terminal value accounts for the company's value beyond the projection period, often representing the largest portion of the DCF valuation.

Calculation Methods

- **Perpetuity Growth Model**: Assumes the company will continue to grow at a stable rate indefinitely. The formula is:
$$TV=FCFn+1r-gTV = \frac{FCF\_{n+1}}{r - g}TV=r-gFCFn+1$$
where $TVTVTV$ is the terminal value, $FCFn+1FCF\_{n+1}FCFn+1$ is the free cash flow in the first year after the projection period, rrr is the discount rate, and ggg is the perpetual growth rate.
- **Exit Multiple Method**: Applies a multiple to the company's financial metric (e.g., EBITDA) at the end of the projection period, using comparable company data to determine the multiple.

Discounting the Terminal Value

The terminal value is then discounted back to the present value using the discount rate, just like the projected cash flows.

5. Summing and Concluding the Valuation

Total Enterprise Value

The final step in DCF analysis is to sum the present value of the projected cash flows and the discounted terminal value. This sum represents the estimated total enterprise value of the company.

Equity Value Calculation

To derive the equity value, subtract the net debt (total debt minus cash) from the total enterprise value. This provides the value attributable to the shareholders.

Comparative Analysis

The resulting equity value is compared to the company's current market capitalization. If the calculated value is higher than the market value, the stock may be undervalued, presenting a potential investment opportunity. Conversely, if the calculated value is lower, the stock may be overvalued.

6. Sensitivity Analysis and Validation

Testing Assumptions

To validate the DCF results, analysts often conduct sensitivity analyses. This involves altering key assumptions, such as growth rates and discount rates, to see how changes impact the valuation.

Cross-Verification

Additionally, analysts may use other valuation methods, such as Comparable Company Analysis (CCA) or Precedent Transactions Analysis (PTA), to cross-check the DCF results and ensure a comprehensive valuation perspective.

Conclusion

DCF analysis is a comprehensive valuation method that provides an estimate of a company's intrinsic value based on projected cash flows and the time value of money. By meticulously calculating and analyzing each component, investment bankers can offer valuable insights into the true worth of a business, guiding investment decisions and strategic planning. This detailed approach, combined with sensitivity analyses and comparative methods, ensures a well-rounded understanding of a company's valuation and market potential.

Chapter 101: What is a Valuation Football Field?

Understanding the Valuation Football Field in Investment Banking

A **valuation football field**, also known as a valuation matrix, is a crucial visual tool in investment banking. It provides a comprehensive representation of a company's potential valuation by considering various scenarios and methodologies. This visualization helps stakeholders understand the range of possible valuation outcomes, making it easier to make informed decisions. In this blog post, we'll delve into what a valuation football field is, its purpose, and the step-by-step process of creating one.

What is a Valuation Football Field?

A valuation football field is essentially a chart that displays the range of possible valuations for a company. It aggregates different valuation methods and scenarios to present a comprehensive overview of a company's worth under varying assumptions. This tool is especially valuable during mergers and acquisitions, IPOs, and other strategic financial decisions, as it helps visualize the potential value of a transaction.

Steps to Building a Valuation Football Field

Step 1: Determine the Key Drivers of Value

The first step in creating a valuation football field is identifying the key factors that significantly influence the company's value. These key drivers typically include:

- **Revenue Growth**: The rate at which the company's sales are expected to grow over a specific period.
- **Profit Margins**: This measures the company's profitability, often using metrics like EBITDA (Earnings Before Interest, Taxes, Depreciation, and Amortization) margin.
- **Capital Expenditures (CapEx)**: Investments necessary for maintaining or expanding the company's operational capabilities.
- **Working Capital**: The company's operational liquidity, which reflects its ability to cover short-term liabilities with short-term assets.

Investment bankers work closely with the company's management team to accurately identify and understand these drivers, ensuring that all relevant factors influencing future performance are considered.

Step 2: Define the Range of Possible Outcomes

After identifying the key drivers, the next step is to establish a range of possible outcomes for each:

- **Best-Case Scenario**: Assumes optimal performance, where all key drivers reach their highest potential.
- **Base Case Scenario**: Reflects the most likely outcomes based on realistic assumptions, historical data, and current market conditions.
- **Worst-Case Scenario**: Considers a conservative outlook, where key drivers underperform.

This step involves using market expertise and historical data to develop credible and realistic scenarios for each driver.

Step 3: Assign Probabilities to Each Outcome

Investment bankers then assign probabilities to each scenario to reflect the likelihood of each outcome. This process involves:

- **Analyzing Market Trends**: Understanding the broader economic and market conditions.
- **Evaluating Competitive Dynamics**: Assessing the competitive landscape and potential changes in market share.
- **Reviewing Historical Performance**: Considering the company's past performance as an indicator of future potential.

For instance, a best-case scenario might be given a 20% probability, a base case 60%, and a worst-case 20%.

Step 4: Calculate the Implied Valuation

The next step is to calculate the implied valuation for each scenario. This is typically done using a Discounted Cash Flow (DCF) analysis, which involves:

- **Projecting Future Cash Flows**: Estimating the company's future cash flows based on each scenario's assumptions.
- **Determining the Discount Rate**: Applying a discount rate that reflects the company's cost of capital and inherent risks.
- **Calculating Present Value**: Finding the present value of the projected cash flows to determine the company's valuation under each scenario.

These valuations are then plotted on a chart, illustrating the range from the worst-case to best-case scenarios.

Step 5: Analyze the Results

Finally, investment bankers analyze the valuation football field to draw conclusions about the company's worth:

- **Identify Valuation Range**: Determine the most probable valuation range based on the plotted scenarios.
- **Highlight Key Drivers**: Identify the primary drivers of value and how variations in these drivers impact the valuation.
- **Assess Risks and Opportunities**: Evaluate the risks associated with each scenario and their potential impact on the company's value.

This analysis helps stakeholders understand the full spectrum of potential valuation outcomes and the factors influencing them.

Example of a Valuation Football Field

Imagine a technology company with the following scenarios:

- **Best-Case Scenario**: The company expands into new markets with a 15% annual revenue growth rate, leading to a $1 billion valuation.
- **Base Case Scenario**: Steady growth at 8% with a valuation around $750 million.
- **Worst-Case Scenario**: Limited growth due to market saturation, resulting in a valuation of $500 million.

The valuation football field visually represents these scenarios, providing a clear picture of the potential value range. The chart would show a range from $500 million to $1 billion, with a base case of $750 million being the most likely outcome.

Conclusion

A valuation football field is a powerful tool in investment banking, offering a nuanced view of a company's potential value under various scenarios. By incorporating multiple valuation methods and assumptions, it helps stakeholders understand the range of possible outcomes and make informed strategic decisions. This tool not only aids in negotiations but also provides a clear framework for assessing risk and opportunity in potential transactions.

Chapter 102: Analyzing EBITDA/EV Multiples by Industry

Understanding EBITDA/EV Multiples by Industry

In the realm of investment banking, the EBITDA/EV (Earnings Before Interest, Taxes, Depreciation, and Amortization to Enterprise Value) multiple is a key metric used for valuing companies across various industries. It helps investors compare the value of similar companies, assess the attractiveness of investment opportunities, and understand the market's valuation of a company's earnings potential. This blog post delves into the analysis of EBITDA/EV multiples across several major industries, highlighting the typical range of multiples, key drivers, and notable outliers.

Technology Industry

Range of Multiples:
In the technology sector, EBITDA/EV multiples typically range from **10x to 30x**, with certain high-growth companies exceeding this range.

Key Drivers:

1. **Revenue Growth:** Rapid growth rates in revenue are highly valued, as they indicate future earnings potential.
2. **Profitability and Scalability:** Companies with high profit margins and scalable business models, like SaaS firms, often command higher multiples.
3. **Intellectual Property and Competitive Advantage:** Firms with unique technologies or strong intellectual property portfolios are more attractive, as they offer competitive advantages.

Notable Outliers:
SaaS companies, due to their recurring revenue models and high customer retention rates, often achieve EBITDA/EV multiples above **40x**. This is driven by their strong growth prospects and stable cash flows.

Healthcare Industry

Range of Multiples:
Healthcare companies generally exhibit EBITDA/EV multiples ranging from **10x to 25x**, with biotechnology firms occasionally reaching higher levels.

Key Drivers:

1. **Regulatory Approvals:** Successful clinical trials and regulatory approvals significantly enhance valuations by reducing risk.

2. **Patents and Exclusivity:** Companies with exclusive rights to market products, such as drugs or medical devices, benefit from limited competition.
3. **Market Demand:** An aging population and increasing prevalence of chronic diseases drive demand for healthcare services and products.

Notable Outliers:
Biotech companies with promising drug pipelines or those nearing product launches can see multiples exceeding **30x**, reflecting their potential for substantial future revenues.

Consumer Goods Industry

Range of Multiples:
Consumer goods companies typically have EBITDA/EV multiples ranging from **5x to 15x**, depending on factors like brand strength and market position.

Key Drivers:

1. **Brand Value and Loyalty:** Strong, established brands often command premium valuations due to consistent consumer demand.
2. **Market Share:** Companies with dominant market positions and economies of scale are generally valued higher.
3. **Growth Prospects:** Innovations and successful market expansions can enhance a company's valuation.

Notable Outliers:
Luxury goods companies, such as those in the high-end fashion or premium beverage sectors, can have multiples exceeding **20x** due to strong brand equity and high profit margins.

Energy Industry

Range of Multiples:
Energy companies' EBITDA/EV multiples typically range from **5x to 15x**, heavily influenced by commodity prices.

Key Drivers:

1. **Commodity Prices:** The value of energy firms fluctuates with prices of oil, gas, and other resources.
2. **Reserves and Production Levels:** Companies with large reserves and efficient production processes are more highly valued.
3. **Operational Efficiency:** Lower operational costs can significantly impact profitability and valuation.

Notable Outliers:
Renewable energy companies, particularly those in solar and wind, are increasingly valued higher (sometimes above **20x**) due to growing demand for clean energy and favorable regulatory environments.

Applying EBITDA/EV Multiples in Investment Banking

Valuation Analysis:
EBITDA/EV multiples are crucial for financial models, helping estimate a company's market value. They are used in relative valuation, where companies within the same industry are compared.

Due Diligence and Risk Assessment:
Investment bankers use these multiples to assess fair value, identify risks, and develop mitigation strategies. For example, understanding industry-specific risks, such as regulatory challenges in healthcare, is essential for accurate valuation.

Strategic Advisory and Recommendations:
Knowledge of EBITDA/EV multiples and their drivers allows investment bankers to advise clients on optimizing their operations and strategic positioning. For example, a consumer goods company might be advised to strengthen its brand to achieve higher valuation multiples.

Conclusion

Analyzing EBITDA/EV multiples across industries provides valuable insights into market valuations and helps in making informed investment decisions. While these multiples vary widely across sectors due to different risk factors and growth potentials, they remain a fundamental tool in the valuation process. A comprehensive understanding of the factors influencing these multiples allows investment bankers and investors to navigate the complexities of financial markets and identify valuable investment opportunities.

Chapter 103: Understanding Value Drivers

Understanding Value Drivers in Investment Banking

Introduction to Value Drivers

In investment banking, value drivers are the critical elements that influence a company's financial and operational performance, ultimately impacting its valuation and strategic positioning. Identifying and understanding these drivers are essential for making informed investment decisions, advising clients, and structuring deals. This blog post delves into what value drivers are, their importance, and specific examples across various industries.

What Are Value Drivers?

Value drivers are specific factors that significantly affect a company's success. They can be internal, such as management quality and operational efficiency, or external, like market conditions and regulatory changes. These drivers are pivotal in determining a company's worth and potential for growth, making them crucial for investment bankers to assess and leverage.

Importance of Value Drivers

1. **Assessing Company Strengths and Weaknesses:**
   - ○ Identifying key value drivers helps in evaluating a company's strengths and areas for improvement. For instance, a strong intellectual property portfolio in a tech company can be a major strength, while weak customer satisfaction can be a potential area for enhancement.
2. **Strategic Decision-Making:**
   - ○ Understanding these drivers allows investment bankers to make strategic recommendations, such as mergers, acquisitions, or divestitures, based on what will most likely enhance the company's value.
3. **Valuation Accuracy:**
   - ○ Accurate valuation models depend heavily on understanding a company's value drivers. This understanding helps in forecasting future performance and setting realistic price targets.

Key Value Drivers by Industry

1. Technology Industry

- **Innovation and R&D:** Continuous innovation and a robust R&D pipeline are crucial for staying competitive.
- **Market Share:** The extent to which a company dominates its market.
- **Scalable Business Models:** The ability to grow revenue without a corresponding increase in costs.
- **Data Analytics:** Leveraging big data and AI for decision-making and operational efficiency.

2. Healthcare Industry

- **Regulatory Approvals:** Crucial for bringing new drugs and medical devices to market.
- **R&D Pipeline:** Indicates future growth potential through new product development.
- **Patient Outcomes:** Quality of care and patient satisfaction can drive demand and reputation.

3. Consumer Goods Industry

- **Brand Strength:** A strong, recognizable brand can command premium pricing and customer loyalty.
- **Supply Chain Efficiency:** Reduces costs and ensures timely product availability.
- **Product Quality:** High-quality products lead to customer satisfaction and repeat business.

4. Energy Industry

- **Proven Reserves:** The quantity and quality of a company's energy reserves.
- **Commodity Prices:** Fluctuations in oil, gas, or other energy prices can significantly impact revenues.
- **Technological Advancements:** In extraction and production efficiency.

5. Financial Services Industry

- **Capital Adequacy:** Strong capital base and liquidity position.
- **Risk Management:** Effective practices to mitigate financial risks.
- **Regulatory Compliance:** Ensuring adherence to financial regulations.

Application of Value Drivers in Investment Banking

1. **Valuation Analysis:**
   - Value drivers are integral to financial models like Discounted Cash Flow (DCF) and Comparable Company Analysis, helping to estimate a company's worth.
2. **Due Diligence and Risk Assessment:**
   - Thorough understanding of value drivers enables comprehensive due diligence, identifying potential risks and opportunities.
3. **Strategic Advisory:**
   - Investment bankers use value drivers to advise clients on potential growth strategies, including acquisitions, partnerships, or market expansions.

Conclusion

Understanding value drivers is fundamental in the realm of investment banking. They form the backbone of accurate valuations, strategic decision-making, and risk management. By focusing on the key value drivers relevant to each industry, investment bankers can provide clients with tailored advice and insights, helping them achieve their business objectives and maximize shareholder value.

This comprehensive understanding of value drivers not only aids in identifying and seizing opportunities but also in navigating the complexities of the business landscape.

Chapter 104: Valuation Analysis of Apple (AAPL)

The Comprehensive Valuation Analysis of Apple Inc. (AAPL)

Valuation analysis is a cornerstone of investment banking, offering crucial insights into a company's worth. For a global giant like Apple Inc. (AAPL), accurate valuation is vital for investors, analysts, and corporate strategies. This post delves into three primary valuation methodologies used to estimate the value of Apple: Discounted Cash Flow (DCF) Analysis, Comparable Companies Analysis, and Precedent Transactions Analysis. Each method provides a unique lens through which to view Apple's financial health and market position.

Discounted Cash Flow (DCF) Analysis

1. Forecasting Future Cash Flows

- **Revenue Growth:** The starting point involves projecting Apple's future revenue based on past performance, market conditions, and industry trends. Analysts consider factors like product innovation (e.g., new iPhone models), market expansion (such as growth in Asia), and competitive pressures.

- **Operating Expenses:** Estimations include cost of goods sold (COGS), research and development (R&D) expenses, and selling, general, and administrative expenses (SG&A). This helps in calculating the net cash flow.
- **Capital Expenditures (CapEx) and Working Capital:** These are forecasted to understand the necessary investments in infrastructure and the liquidity needs to support operations.

2. Calculating Free Cash Flows (FCF)

- FCF is derived by subtracting CapEx and changes in working capital from operating cash flows. It represents the cash available for distribution to all investors.

3. Determining Terminal Value

- **Gordon Growth Model:** Terminal value can be estimated by assuming a perpetual growth rate for free cash flows.
- **Exit Multiple Approach:** Alternatively, the final year's EBITDA is multiplied by an appropriate market multiple.

4. Discounting Cash Flows

- The present value of future cash flows, including the terminal value, is calculated using the Weighted Average Cost of Capital (WACC), which considers the risk and cost of Apple's debt and equity.

5. Summing the Present Values

- The total value obtained represents Apple's enterprise value, indicating the intrinsic worth based on future cash flows.

Comparable Companies Analysis

1. Selecting Comparable Companies

- The choice of comparable firms involves identifying companies with similar business models, market presence, and financial metrics. For Apple, this includes tech giants like Microsoft, Google (Alphabet), and Amazon.

2. Gathering Financial Data

- Key metrics such as revenue, EBITDA, net income, and market capitalization are collected for these comparables.

3. Calculating Valuation Multiples

- Multiples like Price-to-Earnings (P/E), Price-to-Sales (P/S), and Enterprise Value-to-EBITDA (EV/EBITDA) are calculated based on the financial data of these companies.

4. Applying Multiples to Apple

- The derived multiples are applied to Apple's financial metrics to estimate its market value. For example, if the average P/E ratio of comparable companies is 30x, and Apple's EPS is $5, then Apple's implied market price per share would be $150.

Precedent Transactions Analysis

1. Identifying Relevant Transactions

- This method involves analyzing past M&A transactions of companies similar to Apple in size, industry, and market position.

2. Collecting Transaction Data

- Data on transaction values, revenue, EBITDA, and other financial metrics of acquired companies are compiled.

3. Calculating Transaction Multiples

- Multiples from these transactions, such as EV/Revenue and EV/EBITDA, are calculated.

4. Applying Multiples to Apple

- These multiples are then applied to Apple's financials to estimate its value based on how the market has valued similar companies in past transactions.

Conclusion

A comprehensive valuation analysis of Apple Inc. provides a multi-faceted view of the company's worth. The DCF analysis offers an intrinsic value based on expected cash flows and growth, while Comparable Companies Analysis and Precedent Transactions Analysis provide a relative valuation perspective grounded in market conditions and historical data.

Key Takeaways:

- **DCF Analysis:** Focuses on Apple's future cash flows, providing a foundational intrinsic value.

- **Comparable Companies Analysis:** Offers a market-based view by comparing Apple with peers.
- **Precedent Transactions Analysis:** Reflects investor sentiment through historical deal values.

Using these methodologies collectively ensures a robust and well-rounded valuation, enabling stakeholders to make informed investment and strategic decisions. This comprehensive approach is crucial for understanding Apple's market position, growth prospects, and potential risks.

STEP X: PACKAGING & SECURITIZING THE STRATEGIC ALTERNATIVE

Chapter 105: The Securitization Process

The Securitization Process: Transforming Illiquid Assets into Tradable Securities

Securitization is a cornerstone process in investment banking, enabling the transformation of illiquid assets into liquid, marketable securities. This complex process not only enhances liquidity in the financial system but also provides a mechanism for risk management and capital allocation. Investment bankers play a pivotal role throughout this journey, from asset selection to the final distribution of securities. Let's delve into each stage of the securitization process, exploring the crucial contributions of investment bankers.

1. Origination: Identifying and Selecting Assets

The securitization process begins with the origination phase, where investment bankers identify and select the pool of assets to be securitized. This step is foundational, as it determines the quality and nature of the securities that will eventually be issued.

- **Types of Assets**: Commonly securitized assets include residential and commercial mortgages (RMBS and CMBS),

credit card receivables, auto loans, and student loans. These assets are chosen for their predictable cash flows.
- **Criteria for Selection**:
    - **Credit Quality**: Preference is given to assets with high credit quality to minimize default risk.
    - **Cash Flow Predictability**: Steady and predictable cash flows are essential for investor confidence.
    - **Homogeneity and Diversification**: Grouping similar assets together enhances predictability, while diversification reduces risk by spreading it across different sectors or geographies.

2. Structuring: Packaging and Tranching the Assets

Once the assets are selected, the structuring phase involves creating the framework for securitization. This phase determines how the assets will be bundled and converted into securities.

- **Segmentation**: The assets are divided into tranches, each with different risk and return profiles. This segmentation caters to various investor appetites, from those seeking low-risk, steady returns to those willing to accept higher risks for potentially higher rewards.
    - **Senior Tranches**: These have the highest claim on cash flows and are typically rated highly due to lower risk.
    - **Mezzanine and Junior Tranches**: These bear higher risk and offer higher potential returns. Junior tranches are often the first to absorb losses.
- **Creating Securities**: The tranches are then structured into various types of securities, such as Mortgage-Backed Securities (MBS), Asset-Backed Securities (ABS), and Collateralized Debt Obligations (CDOs).

3. Obtaining Ratings: Assessing Creditworthiness

An essential part of the securitization process is obtaining credit ratings for the securities from rating agencies like Moody's, S&P, and Fitch. These ratings provide an independent assessment of the credit risk associated with each tranche.

- **Criteria for Ratings**:
    - **Credit Quality of Underlying Assets**: Evaluation of the asset pool's overall risk.
    - **Securitization Structure**: Examination of how the tranches are structured and the protections in place for investors.
    - **Credit Enhancements**: Consideration of features like overcollateralization, reserve funds, or guarantees that enhance the credit quality.

4. Underwriting: Marketing and Risk Management

In the underwriting phase, investment bankers market the securities to potential investors. This phase involves crafting a compelling value proposition for the securities.

- **Marketing Strategies**: Bankers develop marketing materials, conduct roadshows, and engage in direct outreach to potential investors, such as institutional investors and hedge funds.
- **Risk Management**: Investment bankers manage the risks associated with the issuance, ensuring that the terms are favorable and compliant with regulatory requirements.

5. Issuance: Legal and Financial Documentation

The issuance phase involves preparing all necessary legal and financial documents. This documentation provides transparency and details about the securitization.

- **Legal Documentation**: Includes prospectuses, offering circulars, and legal opinions. These documents outline the specifics of the securitization and are essential for regulatory compliance.
- **Financial Statements**: Accurate financial documentation is crucial for investor confidence and regulatory compliance.

6. Distribution: Selling and Ensuring Liquidity

The final stage in the securitization process is the distribution of securities to investors.

- **Distribution Channels**: Securities are sold through a network of brokers, dealers, and financial advisors. In some cases, securities may be directly placed with large institutional investors.
- **Ensuring Liquidity**: Investment bankers ensure that the securities remain liquid, allowing for easy trading in the secondary market. This liquidity is vital for maintaining the attractiveness of the securities to investors.

Conclusion

The securitization process is a sophisticated and intricate mechanism that transforms illiquid assets into tradable securities, thereby enhancing liquidity and risk management in financial markets. Investment bankers are integral to this process, guiding the selection of assets, structuring securities, obtaining ratings, and managing the sale and distribution of the final products. As the financial landscape continues to evolve, the role of securitization and the expertise of investment bankers remain critical in facilitating capital flows and promoting financial stability.

Chapter 106: Packaging the Strategic Alternative

Understanding the Role of Packaging in Investment Banking: Crafting Effective Marketing Materials

In investment banking, the creation and presentation of marketing materials is a crucial aspect of the deal-making process. These materials serve to inform, persuade, and engage potential clients and investors. They are meticulously crafted to convey the value proposition, financial health, and strategic opportunities associated with various financial products or transactions. This post explores the primary types of marketing materials used in investment banking, detailing their purposes, contents, and strategic applications.

1. Pitch Books

Purpose and Functionality: Pitch books are comprehensive presentations that investment bankers use to showcase their services and transaction ideas to potential clients. The goal is to demonstrate the bank's expertise, provide insights into market conditions, and outline potential strategies or deals.

Key Components:

- **Cover Page:** Displays the bank's branding, the title of the presentation, and the date, setting a professional tone.
- **Executive Summary:** Offers a concise overview of the pitch, summarizing key points and the presentation's purpose.
- **Market Analysis:** Provides an in-depth look at market trends, industry conditions, and economic factors relevant to the client.
- **Service Offerings:** Details the specific services offered by the bank, such as M&A advisory, capital raising, and more.
- **Case Studies:** Highlights past successful transactions, demonstrating the bank's capability and experience.
- **Team Profiles:** Introduces the key team members who will work with the client, emphasizing their expertise and experience.
- **Financial Projections:** Presents tailored financial data and analysis, showcasing potential growth and return scenarios.

Example Application: A technology company's pitch book might include a detailed analysis of tech industry trends, successful tech IPOs managed by the bank, and profiles of team members specializing in tech transactions.

2. Information Memorandums

Purpose and Functionality: An information memorandum is an exhaustive document provided to potential investors, offering in-depth details about a specific investment opportunity. It helps investors make informed decisions by presenting a complete picture of the business and its potential.

Key Components:

- **Company Overview:** Provides a thorough description of the company's history, mission, products, and market position.
- **Market Analysis:** Delivers detailed insights into industry conditions and competitive dynamics.
- **Financial Performance:** Includes comprehensive financial statements, historical data, and future projections.
- **Management Team:** Introduces the key personnel, highlighting their qualifications and experience.
- **Risk Factors:** Identifies and discusses potential risks associated with the investment.
- **Transaction Details:** Outlines the specifics of the proposed deal, including valuation, terms, and timeline.

Example Application: For a retail company seeking investment, an information memorandum might detail the company's market share, financial health, growth strategy, and profiles of the executive team.

3. Teaser Documents

Purpose and Functionality: Teaser documents are concise summaries designed to spark initial interest in an investment opportunity. They provide a high-level overview and encourage potential investors to seek more detailed information.

Key Components:

- **Overview:** A brief introduction to the investment opportunity.
- **Key Highlights:** The most attractive aspects of the opportunity, such as market position or financial metrics.
- **Call to Action:** Instructions for obtaining more detailed information, usually by signing a confidentiality agreement.

Example Application: A teaser for a healthcare startup might emphasize its innovative product, significant market potential, and recent financial performance.

4. Roadshow Presentations

Purpose and Functionality: Roadshow presentations are used to promote investment opportunities to a broader audience, typically in a series of live presentations to potential investors.

Key Components:

- **Introduction:** Sets the stage by introducing the investment opportunity and the presenting team.
- **Detailed Analysis:** Covers the business model, market conditions, and strategic plans in depth.
- **Financial Performance:** Provides detailed financial data, supported by visuals like charts and graphs.
- **Growth Prospects:** Discusses future opportunities and strategic initiatives.
- **Q&A Session:** Engages the audience, allowing them to ask questions and clarify details.

Example Application: For an upcoming IPO, a roadshow presentation would include the company's growth plans, competitive advantages, and detailed financial projections.

5. Offering Memorandums

Purpose and Functionality: Offering memorandums, or prospectuses, are detailed documents outlining the terms and conditions of securities being offered. They provide all necessary information for potential investors to evaluate the offering.

Key Components:

- **Executive Summary:** A concise overview of the offering.
- **Financial Information:** Detailed financial statements and projections.
- **Use of Proceeds:** Explains how the funds raised will be utilized.
- **Legal and Regulatory Information:** Includes disclosures necessary for regulatory compliance.
- **Terms of the Offering:** Specifies the conditions, including pricing, timing, and investor qualifications.

Example Application: For a bond issuance, the offering memorandum would detail the issuer's financial health, bond terms, and how the proceeds will be used.

Conclusion

In investment banking, effective packaging of marketing materials is essential for communicating value, building trust, and facilitating successful transactions. Each type of material serves a unique purpose in the engagement process, from sparking initial interest to providing comprehensive transaction details. By carefully crafting these documents, investment bankers can effectively engage potential clients and investors, paving the way for successful deals and long-term partnerships.

NOTES:
Why Packaging?
After underwriting the financial product (ex. M&A), we can move forward with packaging in the form of various marketing material including a teaser and Confidential Information Memorandum (CIM).

After finding adjusted EBITDA and determining valuation, the investment banker can build the marketing material for the target company which includes a teaser and a CIM. The teaser is a summary of the client's key selling points.

Packaging Process
1. Teaser Creation
2. Confidential Information Memorandum (CIM)

Chapter 107: What Are the Transaction-Specific Documents Used in Investment Banking?

Understanding the Transaction-Specific Documents Used in Investment Banking

In the world of investment banking, various transaction-specific documents play a pivotal role in the deal-making process. These documents provide crucial information, facilitate communication, and help in the execution of financial transactions. Let's delve into the most commonly used documents in investment banking, their purposes, contents, and how they contribute to the overall process.

1. Pitch Books

Purpose:
Pitch books are comprehensive presentations used by investment

bankers to showcase their services, market analysis, and strategic ideas to potential clients. The primary objective is to win new business by demonstrating the bank's expertise and suggesting strategic alternatives.

Contents:

- **Cover Page:** Displays the bank's logo, presentation title, and date.
- **Table of Contents:** Lists sections for easy navigation.
- **Executive Summary:** Brief overview of the pitch's main points.
- **Investment Thesis:** Justification for the proposed transaction, highlighting potential benefits and strategic fit.
- **Market Analysis:** In-depth look at the industry, including trends, opportunities, and competitive landscape.
- **Financial Projections:** Future financial performance estimates based on different scenarios.
- **Valuation Analysis:** Valuation methods like DCF (Discounted Cash Flow), Comps (Comparable Company Analysis), and precedent transactions.
- **Potential Value Creation:** Discussion of how the transaction could enhance value through synergies or other means.
- **Transaction Structure:** Proposed deal structure, including financing options and potential risks.
- **Appendices:** Supplementary information, such as detailed financials or additional market research.

Example:
A pitch book for a potential merger in the pharmaceutical industry might include a comprehensive market analysis, projected financial synergies, and a strategic fit with the client's portfolio.

2. Offering Memorandums (Information Memorandums or Prospectuses)

Purpose:
Offering memorandums are detailed documents provided to potential investors, offering a thorough overview of the company or asset being sold. They are critical in public offerings, private placements, and M&A transactions.

Contents:

- **Cover Page:** Document title, date, and confidentiality disclaimer.
- **Executive Summary:** High-level overview of the business and the investment opportunity.
- **Company Overview:** History, business model, and key products/services.
- **Industry Analysis:** Market size, trends, and competitive dynamics.
- **Operational Overview:** Details on production, supply chain, and distribution.
- **Financial Performance:** Historical financials and key metrics.
- **Management Team:** Profiles of key executives and board members.
- **Risk Factors:** Potential risks, including market, operational, and regulatory risks.
- **Transaction Details:** Specific terms, including pricing and payment structure.
- **Appendices:** Additional detailed financials and legal documents.

Example:
An offering memorandum for a tech startup might detail the company's innovative products, financial performance, and market positioning, alongside risks like technology adoption barriers.

3. Financial Models

Purpose:
Financial models are quantitative tools used to forecast a company's future financial performance and value. They are essential for valuation analysis and decision-making.

Contents:

- **Introduction and Assumptions:** Overview of the model's purpose and key assumptions.
- **Historical Financial Data:** Past financial performance as a baseline.
- **Projected Financial Statements:** Income statement, balance sheet, and cash flow projections.
- **Valuation Techniques:** Application of methods like DCF and Comps.
- **Sensitivity Analysis:** Impact of changing key assumptions on outcomes.
- **Output and Summary:** Key findings, including valuation ranges and financial metrics.

Example:
A financial model for an energy company may include projections based on oil price scenarios, capital expenditures, and regulatory changes, with a valuation based on projected cash flows.

4. Term Sheets

Purpose:
Term sheets outline the preliminary terms and conditions of a proposed transaction. They serve as a basis for negotiations before a formal agreement is drafted.

Contents:

- **Transaction Overview:** Summary of the deal and involved parties.
- **Key Deal Terms:** Purchase price, payment structure, and earn-out provisions.
- **Representations and Warranties:** Statements of facts and assurances.
- **Covenants:** Commitments and restrictions on actions pre-closing.
- **Conditions Precedent:** Requirements to be met before closing.
- **Indemnification:** Provisions for dealing with potential losses.
- **Governance Provisions:** Post-transaction management and control.
- **Exclusivity and Confidentiality:** Clauses to protect the negotiation process.

Example:
A term sheet for a private equity investment might specify a $50 million investment for a 30% equity stake, contingent on due diligence and regulatory approval.

5. Transaction Summaries (Deal Summaries or Executive Summaries)

Purpose:
Transaction summaries provide a concise overview of a transaction, highlighting essential details for senior management or external stakeholders.

Contents:

- **Transaction Rationale:** Strategic reasons for the deal.

- **Parties Involved:** Key players in the transaction.
- **Financial Impact:** Overview of financial effects, including costs and returns.
- **Key Deal Terms:** Summary of major terms and conditions.
- **Significant Risks:** Key risks and considerations.
- **Next Steps:** Timeline and responsibilities for moving forward.

Example:
A transaction summary for an asset sale might outline the asset's valuation, the buyer's background, the sale price, and expected closing date.

Conclusion

These transaction-specific documents are fundamental in investment banking, providing the necessary information, structure, and clarity required for successful deal execution. Mastery of these documents enables investment bankers to guide their clients through complex transactions, ensuring informed decision-making and optimal outcomes.

Chapter 108: The Pitch Book

The Pitch Book: An Essential Tool in Investment Banking

In the world of investment banking, a pitch book is a crucial marketing presentation that showcases a bank's services, expertise, and capabilities to potential clients. It serves as a comprehensive introduction to the bank, aimed at persuading prospective clients to engage in business relationships. The creation of a pitch book is a collaborative effort, typically involving a team of analysts and associates who work meticulously to ensure it effectively communicates the bank's value proposition.

Structure of a Pitch Book

A well-structured pitch book typically includes several key sections, each serving a specific purpose:

1. **Introduction to the Investment Bank**
   - ○ **Objective**: To establish the bank's credibility and showcase its expertise.
   - ○ **Contents**:
     - ■ **History and Background**: Overview of the bank's founding, growth, and key

milestones, highlighting its legacy and achievements.

- **Size and Scale**: Information on the bank's global presence, including the number of offices, employees, and financial metrics such as assets under management (AUM) and revenue.
- **Core Capabilities**: Description of the bank's primary services, such as mergers and acquisitions (M&A), equity and debt underwriting, and financial restructuring.

2. *Example*: A bank might highlight its origins in the early 1900s, its expansion to a global financial institution with over 20,000 employees, and its leadership in M&A advisory.

3. **Description of the Target Market**
   - **Objective**: To demonstrate the bank's deep understanding of the client's industry and the broader market environment.
   - **Contents**:
     - **Client Types**: Overview of the types of clients the bank serves, such as corporations, private equity firms, and government entities.
     - **Industry Expertise**: Detailed analysis of specific industries where the bank has significant experience, including market trends, regulatory factors, and competitive landscapes.
     - **Market Dynamics**: Insights into market trends, key drivers, and potential challenges within the industry.

4. *Example*: For a client in the renewable energy sector, the pitch book might include analysis of market trends like increasing

investment in green technology, regulatory support for clean energy, and the competitive landscape.

5. **Description of the Investment Bank's Services**
    - ○ **Objective**: To highlight the specific services offered by the bank and how they can address the client's needs.
    - ○ **Contents**:
        - ■ **M&A Advisory**: Description of the bank's capabilities in advising on mergers and acquisitions, including strategic planning and deal execution.
        - ■ **Equity and Debt Underwriting**: Overview of the bank's experience in raising capital through public and private markets, detailing past IPOs, secondary offerings, and bond issuances.
        - ■ **Financial Restructuring**: Services related to restructuring, including distressed asset management and bankruptcy advisory.

6. *Example*: For a healthcare client, the pitch book might detail the bank's experience in healthcare M&A, IPOs for biotech companies, and restructuring services for financially distressed healthcare providers.

7. **Summary of Recent Transactions**
    - ○ **Objective**: To provide evidence of the bank's successful track record and reliability.
    - ○ **Contents**:
        - ■ **Deal Summaries**: Brief descriptions of recent deals, including transaction size, involved parties, and outcomes.
        - ■ **Case Studies**: In-depth analysis of notable transactions, showcasing the bank's role, challenges faced, and solutions provided.

- **Testimonials and References**: Positive feedback from past clients, reinforcing the bank's credibility and effectiveness.

8. *Example*: The pitch book might showcase a successful acquisition deal in the technology sector, highlighting the bank's role in negotiating favorable terms and achieving strategic goals for the client.

Customization for Specific Clients

Each pitch book is tailored to address the specific needs and interests of the prospective client. This customization involves:

- **Client-Specific Analysis**: Detailed market analysis and financial modeling tailored to the client's industry and situation.
- **Targeted Solutions**: Highlighting how the bank's services can meet the client's unique challenges and goals.
- **Relevant Experience**: Showcasing past experiences and successes that are relevant to the client's sector and objectives.

Example: A pitch book for a retail company might include an analysis of consumer spending trends, potential expansion markets, and the bank's experience with similar retail transactions.

Creating a Compelling Pitch Book

To create an effective pitch book, investment bankers focus on:

- **Understanding Client Needs**: Conducting extensive research on the client's business, industry, and strategic goals.
- **Clear and Concise Content**: Presenting information in a clear, logical manner with easy-to-understand language and avoiding unnecessary jargon.

- **Professional Design**: Utilizing high-quality visuals, consistent formatting, and a professional layout to enhance readability and impact.
- **Effective Storytelling**: Crafting a narrative that connects the bank's capabilities to the client's needs, emphasizing how the bank can add value and help achieve strategic goals.

Conclusion

The pitch book is an indispensable tool in the investment banking toolkit. It not only introduces the bank's capabilities and expertise but also serves as a key component in securing new business. By carefully crafting a pitch book that addresses the specific needs and goals of prospective clients, investment bankers can effectively communicate their value proposition, build strong client relationships, and ultimately drive business success.

Chapter 109: The Teaser

The Teaser: A Key Tool in Investment Banking

In the world of investment banking, a **teaser** is an essential document used to pique the interest of potential investors or buyers in an investment opportunity. It serves as a brief and enticing overview of a deal, providing just enough information to attract interest while maintaining confidentiality. This blog post delves into the critical elements of creating an effective teaser and its role in the investment process.

Purpose of a Teaser

Capturing Initial Interest

The primary function of a teaser is to capture the attention of potential investors or buyers. It acts as the first introduction to the investment opportunity, offering a snapshot that highlights why the deal is worth considering. The teaser is designed to be distributed widely among potential investors, including institutional investors, private equity firms, venture capitalists, and high-net-worth individuals. Its concise nature allows for a broad outreach, maximizing the chance of attracting interested parties.

Creating Excitement and Momentum

An effective teaser not only informs but also excites. It creates a buzz around the investment opportunity, making it appear as an attractive and potentially lucrative proposition. The excitement generated by a well-crafted teaser can propel potential investors to the next step, typically signing a confidentiality agreement (NDA) to access more detailed information through a Confidential Information Memorandum (CIM).

Key Components of a Teaser

High-Level Overview

The teaser begins with a brief introduction to the company or asset being offered. It includes:

- **Company Overview**: A summary of the company's history, mission, and core business.
- **Investment Highlights**: Key selling points such as unique features, competitive advantages, and market position.

Growth Prospects

This section outlines the potential for future growth, detailing:

- **Expansion Opportunities**: Information about new markets, product lines, or technological advancements that the company may pursue.
- **Market Trends**: An overview of the market dynamics and industry trends that support the company's growth potential.

Financial Metrics

A teaser includes essential financial information to give potential investors a snapshot of the company's financial health:

- **Revenue and Earnings**: Key financial figures such as revenue, EBITDA, and profit margins.
- **Historical Performance**: A brief overview of financial performance over recent years, demonstrating stability and growth.

Potential Returns

To entice investors, the teaser provides an initial indication of potential returns:

- **ROI Projections**: Preliminary estimates of return on investment.
- **Valuation Context**: Suggested valuation ranges or multiples based on industry standards.

Call to Action

A crucial part of the teaser is the call to action, guiding interested parties on how to proceed:

- **Next Steps**: Information on how to express interest, typically involving contacting the investment banker or signing an NDA.
- **Contact Information**: Details of the investment banker or deal manager responsible for the transaction.

Crafting an Effective Teaser

Compelling Content

The content of the teaser must be compelling and concise. It should tell a captivating story about the investment opportunity, emphasizing what makes it unique and attractive. The language used should be persuasive but grounded in factual data.

Professional Presentation

The design and format of the teaser are also crucial. It should be visually appealing, with a clean layout and high-quality graphics. The use of charts and infographics can help convey complex information quickly and effectively.

Compliance and Confidentiality

It's essential to ensure that the teaser does not disclose sensitive or proprietary information. Legal review is often necessary to protect both the seller's and potential buyers' interests and comply with regulatory requirements.

Example of a Teaser Structure

1. **Executive Summary**:
    - Introduction and investment highlights.
2. **Investment Highlights**:
    - Unique selling points and market position.
3. **Market Opportunity**:
    - Market overview and growth prospects.
4. **Financial Overview**:
    - Key financial metrics and historical performance.
5. **Strategic Initiatives**:
    - Current and future strategic initiatives.
6. **Potential Returns**:
    - ROI projections and valuation multiples.
7. **Next Steps**:
    - Call to action and contact information.

Conclusion

The teaser is a vital initial step in the investment process, serving as the first point of contact with potential investors. By presenting a clear, concise, and compelling overview of the investment opportunity, it sets the stage for deeper engagement and further exploration. A well-crafted teaser can significantly enhance the likelihood of attracting serious interest and facilitating a successful transaction.

Teaser

After creating the teaser, the investment banker goes into greater detail in a marketing document called a CIM. This document is distributed to buyers after the teaser and is for the serious buyers to do an in depth analysis of the target.

Building the Teaser

The teaser is a summary of the client's key selling points. The teaser can be broken down in the following manner along selling points including:

1. Overall financial profile: three years of historical revenue and EBIT/EBITDA and at least two years of projected revenue and EBIT/EBITDA
2. Indicate type of transaction
3. Indicate sustainable growth potential based upon competitive advantage:
   a. Customer entrenchment and high switching costs
   b. Long term contracts
   c. Brand recognition
   d. Intellectual property
   e. Stable management teams
   f. Culture

Chapter 110: The Confidential Information Memorandum (CIM)

The Confidential Information Memorandum (CIM): A Comprehensive Guide for Investment Bankers

In the realm of mergers and acquisitions (M&A), the Confidential Information Memorandum (CIM) is a pivotal document. It serves as the cornerstone for presenting a company to potential buyers, offering an in-depth view of the company's operations, financial health, market position, and future prospects. This blog post delves into the importance of the CIM, its construction, and the critical information it must convey to attract and inform potential buyers.

Importance of the CIM

The CIM is crucial for several reasons:

1. **Informing Potential Buyers**: It provides detailed information that helps buyers understand the investment opportunity, facilitating informed decision-making.

2. **Facilitating Due Diligence**: It lays the groundwork for the buyer's due diligence process, offering comprehensive data and insights about the company.
3. **Enhancing Credibility**: A well-prepared CIM demonstrates the seriousness and professionalism of the sale process, potentially attracting more qualified and serious buyers.

Building the CIM

Creating a CIM involves meticulous planning and attention to detail. Below are the key sections typically included in a CIM:

1. Overview and Key Investment Highlights

Objective: To provide a succinct introduction to the company and highlight its most compelling attributes.

Contents:

- **Company Overview**: A brief history and mission statement.
- **Key Investment Highlights**: Includes growth prospects, operational improvements, and timing, showcasing why now is an ideal time to invest.

Example: For a tech startup, the CIM might emphasize its innovative products, market traction, and strategic partnerships, outlining why these factors make it a lucrative investment.

2. Products and Services

Objective: To offer a detailed account of what the company sells and how it stands out in the market.

Contents:

- **Product/Service Descriptions**: Detailed explanations of offerings.
- **Unique Selling Propositions (USPs)**: Key differentiators.
- **Development Roadmap**: Future product or service enhancements.

Example: A software company's CIM would detail its core applications, unique features, and upcoming updates or new launches.

3. Market Analysis

Objective: To provide a thorough understanding of the market landscape.

Contents:

- **Market Analysis**: Overview of the industry, trends, and future outlook.
- **Market Size and Growth**: Data on market dimensions and projected growth.
- **Competitive Landscape**: Analysis of key competitors and market positioning.

Example: A healthcare company's CIM might include market size projections, key demographic trends, and a competitive analysis highlighting its strong market position.

4. Sales & Marketing Strategy

Objective: To explain how the company generates revenue and attracts customers.

Contents:

- **Sales Strategy**: Description of sales channels and approach.

- **Marketing Strategy**: Overview of marketing tactics and branding.
- **Customer Segments**: Breakdown of the customer base.

Example: For a consumer goods company, this section would outline retail and online sales strategies, marketing campaigns, and target demographics.

5. Management Team

Objective: To showcase the expertise and leadership driving the company.

Contents:

- **Leadership Profiles**: Backgrounds and contributions of key executives.
- **Organizational Structure**: Key departments and team roles.

Example: A manufacturing firm's CIM might profile the CEO's industry experience and the COO's efficiency in scaling production.

6. Financial Results and Projections

Objective: To present the company's financial health and future outlook.

Contents:

- **Historical Financials**: Past financial statements and key metrics.
- **Financial Projections**: Forecasts of future performance.
- **Key Metrics**: Revenue, EBITDA, cash flow, etc.
- **CAPEX and WC Requirements**: Future capital expenditure and working capital needs.

Example: Financial projections might illustrate a company's expected revenue growth, margin improvements, and cash flow sustainability.

7. Appendices

Objective: To provide supplementary information that supports the main content.

Contents:

- **Supporting Documents**: Detailed reports and documents.
- **Market Research**: In-depth market studies.
- **Product Brochures**: Detailed descriptions of products.
- **Legal and Regulatory Information**: Compliance documents.

Example: A biotech company's CIM appendices might include clinical trial results, market research reports, and regulatory filings.

Demonstrating Key Aspects

Future Growth Prospects: Emphasize the company's potential for growth and operational enhancements.

Timing: Highlight why the current moment is optimal for investment.

Financial Health: Demonstrate strong financial metrics, including growth rates, margins, and cash flow.

Market Leadership: Showcase the company's leading position in its market.

Defensible Business Model: Present a robust business model with competitive advantages.

Conclusion

A well-crafted CIM is essential for effectively marketing a company in the M&A process. It provides potential buyers with a detailed, accurate, and compelling portrayal of the company, helping to facilitate a smooth transaction. By meticulously detailing each section and conveying key aspects clearly, investment bankers can attract serious buyers and ensure a successful sale process.

PART XI: BUYER LIST

Chapter 111: Buyer List

Creating a Comprehensive Buyer List in M&A: A Detailed Guide

In the realm of mergers and acquisitions (M&A), crafting a comprehensive and targeted buyer list is crucial for maximizing the chances of a successful transaction. This process involves meticulous research, evaluation, and strategic outreach to ensure the best possible match between the seller and potential buyers. Let's delve into the step-by-step process of creating an effective buyer list, focusing on the methodology and critical considerations.

Step 1: Identify Potential Buyers

Objective:
The initial step involves identifying potential buyers who might be interested in acquiring the target company. This foundational phase sets the trajectory for the entire M&A process.

Methods:

1. **Industry Research:**
    Conduct a thorough investigation of companies within the same industry or related sectors. Look for organizations that

could benefit from expanding their market share, diversifying their product lines, or enhancing their geographic footprint.

2. **Review of Recent M&A Activity:**
   Analyze recent transactions to identify active buyers who have demonstrated interest in similar deals. This helps pinpoint companies currently pursuing acquisitions.

3. **Identify Private Equity and Strategic Investors:**
   Seek out private equity firms and strategic investors with investment mandates that align with the opportunity. These entities often have specific acquisition criteria based on their portfolio strategies.

Example:
For a company in the healthcare services sector, potential buyers might include larger healthcare providers, private equity firms focusing on healthcare investments, and companies in adjacent fields such as medical equipment suppliers.

Step 2: Evaluate Potential Buyers

Objective:
Once potential buyers are identified, it's essential to evaluate their suitability for the deal. This evaluation ensures alignment with the seller's objectives and maximizes the likelihood of a successful transaction.

Criteria for Evaluation:

1. **Financial Position:**
   Assess the financial health of the potential buyer, including liquidity, debt capacity, and overall financial stability.

2. **Previous M&A Activity:**
   Examine the buyer's history with mergers and acquisitions,

focusing on their experience and success in similar transactions.

3. **Strategic Objectives:**
Understand the strategic goals of the buyer, such as entering new markets, acquiring technology, or consolidating their position in the industry.

Example:
A tech company could be evaluated based on its robust financial position, history of acquiring complementary tech firms, and a strategic objective to expand its software offerings.

Step 3: Prioritize Potential Buyers

Objective:
After evaluation, prioritize the buyers based on their alignment with the seller's objectives and the likelihood of a successful transaction.

Scoring System:

1. **Financial Strength:**
Rate buyers based on their ability to finance the acquisition.
2. **Strategic Fit:**
Evaluate how well the target aligns with the buyer's strategic goals.
3. **Likelihood of Success:**
Consider factors such as the buyer's management team, current market position, and previous acquisition success.

Example:
A private equity firm might rank higher due to its substantial available capital and focus on expanding in the target's industry.

Step 4: Reach Out to Potential Buyers

Objective:
Initiate contact with the prioritized buyers to gauge their interest in the acquisition opportunity.

Activities:

1. **Send Teasers:**
    Distribute high-level, anonymized summaries that highlight the key attributes of the target company.
2. **Information Memorandums:**
    Provide detailed documents containing comprehensive information about the target, including financials, market positioning, and growth potential.
3. **Initial Contact:**
    Reach out via emails, phone calls, or through networking events to engage key decision-makers within the potential buyer organizations.

Example:
An investment bank might send a teaser to a selected group of strategic buyers, followed by a more detailed information memorandum after signing confidentiality agreements.

Step 5: Manage the Bidding Process

Objective:
As potential buyers show interest, manage the bidding process to secure the best possible deal for the seller.

Activities:

1. **Solicit Formal Bids:**
    Request detailed offers from interested buyers, outlining their proposed terms and conditions.

2. **Negotiation:**
   Engage in negotiations with multiple buyers to refine their offers and achieve favorable terms.
3. **Final Selection:**
   Choose the preferred buyer based on the financial terms, strategic fit, and other relevant factors.

Example:
In receiving multiple bids for a manufacturing firm, an investment bank might negotiate with top bidders to enhance the purchase price and secure better deal terms.

Conclusion

The creation of a comprehensive buyer list is a strategic and systematic process that involves identifying, evaluating, prioritizing, and reaching out to potential buyers. This meticulous approach not only enhances the likelihood of closing a deal but also helps in achieving the best possible outcome for the seller. By managing the bidding process effectively and maintaining clear communication, investment bankers ensure that all parties involved are well-informed and that the transaction progresses smoothly. This process is crucial for building long-term relationships and fostering a successful M&A environment.

NOTES:
Why Buyer List Creation?
After landing the M&A engagement, the investment banker will need to build a buyer list and then begin outreach to the buyer list to generate interest. In order to build a buyer list, the investment banker uses a database service to pull a list of likely strategic and financial buyers along with contact information in order to run the M&A process and build a market for control of the business.

After finalizing the buyer list from the database, the investment banker can then begin contacting each prospective buyer in the list. Contacts should be to the corporate M&A representative for large corporations or CEOs and owners for lower middle market companies.

Buyer List Process
1. Database Utilization
2. Strategic Buyers
3. Financial Buyers
4. Initial Outreach

Chapter 112: Buyer Profiles

Understanding Buyer Profiles in M&A Transactions

In the realm of mergers and acquisitions (M&A), understanding the profiles of potential buyers is crucial for crafting successful deals. Investment bankers play a pivotal role in identifying and matching these buyers with suitable opportunities. This blog post delves into the different types of buyers, their typical deal characteristics, and how investment bankers navigate the M&A landscape to optimize outcomes for all parties involved.

1. Individuals & Search Funds

Overview

- **Typical Deal Size:** Individuals and search funds usually target businesses with less than $1 million in EBITDA, looking for deals in the 3x to 4x EBITDA range.
- **Qualification:** It's essential to pre-qualify these buyers to ensure they fit the size and nature of the deal.

Characteristics

- **Deal Size:** These buyers focus on smaller businesses, often preferring passive investment roles rather than active management.
- **Operational Preference:** They are generally not interested in being involved in day-to-day operations, preferring businesses that can operate independently.

- **Expectation Management:** Their investment criteria often align with smaller, simpler business structures, as they typically do not have the resources or desire to manage complex operations.

Example: An individual buyer might be interested in a small manufacturing business generating $600k in EBITDA, aiming to own and grow the business without direct involvement in daily operations.

2. Lower Middle Market Private Equity (LMM PE)

Overview

- **Typical Deal Size:** Focus on businesses with $1M to $3M in EBITDA, often around 5x EBITDA.
- **Investment Horizon:** Generally aim for a 3 to 8-year investment period, with the goal of growing the business and eventually selling it at a profit.

Characteristics

- **Strategic Fit:** Seek businesses with solid fundamentals that can be scaled up through operational improvements and strategic growth initiatives.
- **Financial Strength:** These firms typically have access to substantial capital and expertise to drive growth.
- **Exit Strategy:** Often plan to exit through strategic sales or secondary buyouts.

Example: An LMM PE firm may acquire a healthcare services company with $2M in EBITDA, intending to enhance its operations and market reach before selling it at a higher valuation.

3. Middle Market Private Equity (MM PE)

Overview

- **Typical Deal Size:** Targets companies with a minimum of $2M in EBITDA, usually looking at multiples starting at 7x EBITDA.
- **Platform Strategy:** Often pursue platform acquisitions to facilitate roll-ups in specific industries.

Characteristics

- **Growth Potential:** MM PE buyers seek companies with strong growth prospects that can serve as a foundation for further acquisitions.
- **Sector Focus:** They often specialize in certain industries, leveraging their expertise to identify and capitalize on sector-specific opportunities.
- **Investment Strategy:** Focus on building significant value through consolidation and synergy realization.

Example: An MM PE firm may acquire a logistics company as a platform, with plans to acquire smaller competitors to expand its service offerings and geographic reach.

4. Strategic Buyers

Overview

- **Typical Deal Size:** Engage in deals starting at ~$500k in EBITDA, often with a valuation floor of 5x EBITDA.
- **Motivation:** Aim to enhance their competitive position, achieve synergies, or enter new markets.

Characteristics

- **Synergies:** Look for acquisitions that can create value through integration, such as cost savings, increased revenue, or enhanced operational efficiencies.
- **Strategic Alignment:** Focus on targets that complement their existing operations and strategic goals.
- **Market Expansion:** Often seek acquisitions to diversify their product lines or expand into new markets.

Example: A technology firm might acquire a smaller company with $1M in EBITDA to gain access to new technologies and enhance its product offerings.

Understanding M&A Multiples in the Market

Investment bankers use multiples as a quick valuation tool to assess potential M&A deals:

- **General Multiples:** Companies with more than $25M in Total Enterprise Value (TEV) generally see multiples of 7x - 7.5x EBITDA, while smaller companies typically have multiples around 5x - 5.5x EBITDA.
- **Lower Middle Market Multiples:** For companies with <$1M EBITDA, multiples are around 4x; for those with $1M EBITDA, around 5x; and for those with $1M - $2M EBITDA, around 6x. Companies with >$2M EBITDA often command 7x or higher.

Application: Investment bankers use these multiples to set realistic expectations during initial discussions and to provide growth advisory services, helping businesses achieve their valuation targets.

Conclusion

Understanding the profiles and preferences of different types of buyers is essential for investment bankers when crafting M&A deals. Whether dealing with individuals, private equity firms, or strategic buyers, each profile has distinct characteristics and expectations. By leveraging this knowledge, investment bankers can effectively match opportunities with the right buyers, facilitating successful transactions and achieving optimal outcomes for all parties involved.

Chapter 113: Tapping into the Buyer Database

Leveraging the Buyer Database for Successful M&A Transactions

In the world of investment banking, tapping into a well-maintained buyer database is essential for executing successful mergers and acquisitions (M&A). This blog post explores how investment bankers effectively use their buyer databases to align investment opportunities with the mandates of strategic and financial buyers, maximizing transaction success.

Importance of a Comprehensive Buyer Database

A robust buyer database is an invaluable resource for investment bankers. It contains detailed information about potential buyers, including their investment mandates and acquisition criteria. The key objective is to identify which buyers' mandates align with the current M&A opportunity, ensuring a targeted and efficient outreach.

Steps to Utilize the Buyer Database

1. **Identify Buyer Mandates:** Understand the specific investment criteria and strategic goals of potential buyers.
2. **Match Mandates to Opportunity:** Align the characteristics of the M&A opportunity with the identified buyer mandates.
3. **Prioritize Potential Buyers:** Rank buyers based on the strength of the match, their financial capacity, and their likelihood of executing the transaction.
4. **Initiate Outreach:** Engage with prioritized buyers through tailored marketing materials and discussions.

Understanding Strategic Buyers

Definition and Importance

Strategic buyers are companies that pursue acquisitions to enhance their competitive position, achieve synergies, or enter new markets. They typically include larger competitors, suppliers, customers, and companies in related industries. By maintaining relationships and understanding the strategic goals of key players in a specific vertical, investment bankers can identify the most likely strategic buyers for a given opportunity.

Types of Strategic Buyers

1. **Larger Competitors:** Companies looking to increase market share, eliminate competition, or achieve economies of scale.
    o   **Example:** A leading software company acquiring a smaller competitor to consolidate its market position.
2. **Suppliers:** Companies that can benefit from acquiring their downstream partners to secure supply chains and reduce costs.
    o   **Example:** A manufacturing firm acquiring a key supplier to ensure a steady supply of raw materials.
3. **Customers:** Companies that might acquire suppliers to control product quality and supply reliability.
    o   **Example:** An electronics company acquiring a chip manufacturer.
4. **Related Industries:** Companies looking to diversify into adjacent markets or enhance their product offerings.
    o   **Example:** A consumer goods company acquiring a packaging firm.

Evaluation Criteria for Strategic Buyers

*   **Strategic Fit:** How well the target company complements the buyer's existing operations and goals.
*   **Synergy Potential:** The ability to achieve cost savings, revenue enhancements, or operational efficiencies.

Understanding Financial Buyers

Definition and Importance

Financial buyers, typically private equity firms, acquire companies to improve their financial performance and exit at a profit within a specific timeframe, usually 3 to 8 years. Investment bankers assess whether the M&A opportunity aligns with the financial criteria and investment strategies of private equity firms.

Evaluation Criteria for Financial Buyers

- **Cash Flow Characteristics:** Companies with strong, predictable cash flows.
- **Growth Potential:** The ability of the target company to grow through organic expansion or add-on acquisitions.
- **Exit Strategy:** Potential to sell the company to a strategic buyer or another financial buyer at a higher valuation.
  - **Example:** A private equity firm acquiring a profitable healthcare services company with steady cash flow for growth and eventual sale.

Matching Mandates to Opportunity

Process

1. **Review Buyer Database:** Analyze the database to identify buyers whose mandates align with the M&A opportunity.
2. **Criteria Matching:** Match the strategic goals and financial criteria of potential buyers with the target company's attributes.
3. **Prioritization:** Prioritize buyers based on the strength of the match, their financial capacity, and their likelihood of executing the transaction.

Example

For a mid-sized technology firm looking to sell, the investment banker might prioritize larger tech companies seeking to expand their product lines and private equity firms focused on tech investments.

Initiating Outreach

Steps

1. **Prepare Marketing Materials:** Develop teasers, information memorandums, and other materials tailored to highlight the target company's strategic fit and financial attractiveness.
2. **Confidentiality Agreements:** Ensure that confidentiality agreements are signed before sharing detailed information.
3. **Engage in Discussions:** Initiate contact with prioritized buyers, provide them with initial information, and facilitate discussions to gauge interest and proceed with the M&A process.

Example

An investment banker might send a teaser to a prioritized list of strategic and financial buyers, followed by detailed information after signing confidentiality agreements, leading to initial meetings and further negotiations.

Conclusion

Key Takeaways

- **Strategic and Financial Buyers:** Understanding the distinct goals and evaluation criteria of strategic and financial buyers is crucial for successful M&A outreach.
- **Database Utilization:** A well-maintained buyer database allows for efficient matching of M&A opportunities with the right buyers, increasing the likelihood of a successful transaction.
- **Targeted Outreach:** Effective outreach involves identifying, prioritizing, and engaging buyers whose mandates align with the target company's characteristics.

By leveraging a comprehensive buyer database and understanding the motivations of potential buyers, investment bankers can optimize the M&A process, ensuring that the right buyers are targeted and engaged, leading to successful and value-creating transactions.

Chapter 114: Outreach to Buyers

Outreach to Buyers: A Comprehensive Guide for Investment Bankers

Reaching out to potential buyers is a critical phase in the mergers and acquisitions (M&A) process, playing a vital role in ensuring successful transactions. Investment bankers must meticulously plan and execute this phase to identify the most suitable buyers, effectively communicate the investment opportunity, and ultimately secure a favorable deal for their clients. This post delves into the detailed steps involved in outreach to buyers, emphasizing best practices and strategic considerations.

Step 1: Identifying Potential Buyers

Importance of Buyer Identification

Identifying potential buyers is foundational to the M&A process. It ensures that the investment opportunity is presented to entities that are most likely to have the strategic interest and financial capability to proceed with a transaction.

Methods for Identification

1. **Industry Research:** Begin with a comprehensive analysis of the industry. Look for companies within the same sector or those in related industries that could benefit from the acquisition. Consider competitors, suppliers, and customers as potential buyers.
2. **Review Recent M&A Activity:** Examine recent transactions to identify active buyers. These entities are often in acquisition mode and may be interested in similar opportunities.
3. **Private Equity and Strategic Investors:** Identify private equity firms with a history of investing in the target's sector and strategic investors seeking specific assets or capabilities.

Example: For a tech company, potential buyers might include large technology firms expanding their product lines, private equity firms with tech-focused portfolios, and corporations seeking technological innovations.

Step 2: Prioritizing Potential Buyers

Criteria for Prioritization

Not all identified buyers are equal in their suitability and readiness. Prioritize based on:

1. **Financial Strength:** Ensure buyers have the necessary financial resources to complete the transaction, assessing liquidity, debt levels, and capital availability.

2. **Strategic Fit:** Evaluate how well the target aligns with the buyer's strategic goals, such as expanding into new markets or acquiring new technologies.
3. **Likelihood of Success:** Consider the buyer's acquisition history, management stability, and reputation. Assess the probability of a successful negotiation and transaction.

Scoring System

Develop a scoring system to rank potential buyers, assigning weights to various factors like financial capacity, strategic alignment, and market position.

Example: Assign scores based on criteria like acquisition budget, previous acquisition successes, and strategic interests. Focus outreach efforts on high-scoring entities.

Step 3: Contacting Potential Buyers

Materials for Initial Contact

1. **Teasers:** A brief, anonymous overview of the target company to pique interest without revealing sensitive information.
2. **Information Memorandums (IMs):** A more detailed document provided under confidentiality agreements, outlining the company's financials, operations, and market positioning.

Contact Methods

- **Emails and Calls:** Direct outreach to key decision-makers, such as corporate development executives or M&A heads.
- **Networking Events:** Utilize industry conferences and events to establish initial contact and gauge interest.

Example: Send a teaser to a senior executive followed by a phone call to discuss the opportunity and gauge preliminary interest.

Step 4: Securing Confidentiality Agreements

Importance

Confidentiality agreements are crucial to protect sensitive information about the target company during the M&A process.

Process

1. **Draft Agreement:** Ensure the confidentiality agreement covers non-disclosure, use of information, and return of materials.
2. **Execution:** Have all potential buyers sign the agreement before sharing detailed information.

Key Clauses

- **Non-Disclosure:** Prohibits sharing confidential information with unauthorized parties.
- **No-Shop Clause:** May restrict the seller from engaging with other potential buyers for a specified period.

Example: Before disclosing financial projections, ensure the buyer signs a confidentiality agreement to protect sensitive data.

Step 5: Conducting Meetings and Due Diligence

Importance

Face-to-face meetings and thorough due diligence are essential for validating the potential deal and building trust.

Activities

- **Meetings:** Arrange detailed discussions between the seller and potential buyers to clarify any questions and outline the strategic rationale.
- **Due Diligence:** Facilitate access to financial records, legal documents, and other relevant information.

Tools and Resources

- **Data Rooms:** Secure online platforms where sensitive documents can be shared.
- **Due Diligence Checklists:** Lists outlining all necessary documents and information for comprehensive evaluation.

Example: A secure data room is set up to provide access to audited financial statements, contracts, and market research reports.

Step 6: Managing the Bidding Process

Importance

A well-managed bidding process ensures competitive tension, maximizing value for the seller.

Activities

- **Soliciting Bids:** Request formal offers from interested buyers, specifying terms and conditions.
- **Negotiation:** Engage with bidders to refine offers, aiming to optimize deal terms.
- **Final Selection:** Evaluate offers based on financial terms, strategic fit, and other factors.

Example: The investment bank negotiates with multiple buyers, leveraging the competitive process to enhance the terms of the sale.

Conclusion

Outreach to buyers is a strategic and multi-faceted process that requires meticulous planning and execution. Investment bankers must identify the right buyers, prioritize them, engage effectively, and manage the process to ensure a successful transaction. By following a structured approach and leveraging their expertise, investment bankers can maximize value for their clients and achieve successful outcomes in the M&A process.

NOTES:

Initial Outreach

Initial outreach follows a pattern where the high level teaser will be distributed to generate interest in learning more. From there the investment banker will get an NDA signed with the buyer to then review the CIM.

    I.   Distributing the teaser
    II.   Signing the NDA
    III.   Confidential Information Memorandum (CIM)

PART XII: DEAL STRUCTURING

Chapter 115: Deal Structuring

The Art and Science of Deal Structuring in Investment Banking

Deal structuring is a critical aspect of investment banking, determining how a transaction is organized to meet the needs and objectives of both the buyer and the seller. This process involves multiple steps, each requiring careful analysis and negotiation to ensure a successful outcome. This blog post delves into the comprehensive steps involved in deal structuring, offering insights into the strategic considerations that investment bankers must navigate.

1. Evaluating Strategic Goals of Both Parties

Understanding Objectives:
The initial step in deal structuring is to clearly understand the strategic goals of both the buyer and the seller. For the buyer, objectives may include expanding market share, acquiring new technologies, or diversifying product lines. Sellers, on the other hand, might aim to maximize sale proceeds, exit a non-core business, or secure a future role within the company.

Financial and Operational Considerations:
This step also involves examining the financial targets, such as expected sale price and acceptable payment structures, alongside any legal or regulatory constraints. For example, a company may need to adhere to antitrust laws or industry-specific regulations.

Example: A tech firm looking to acquire a startup might seek not just technology but also the startup's talent, while the startup may prioritize securing funding for product development.

2. Determining the Deal Structure

Forms of Payment:
Investment bankers must decide on the payment method—cash, stock, or a combination. Cash offers immediate liquidity but can strain the buyer's finances. Stock can provide sellers with potential future upside but may dilute existing shareholders.

Timing and Structure of Payments:
Payments can be structured as upfront payments, earn-outs based on future performance, or deferred payments. These options help balance risk and reward for both parties.

Example: A deal might involve an initial cash payment followed by stock options, aligning the interests of both buyer and seller over the long term.

3. Conducting Due Diligence

Financial, Legal, and Operational Due Diligence:
This comprehensive review includes examining financial statements, legal contracts, and operational capabilities to ensure there are no hidden liabilities or issues. It's crucial for validating the business's value and understanding any potential risks.

Example: Due diligence on a manufacturing company may involve checking compliance with environmental regulations and the efficiency of production processes.

4. Negotiating the Terms of the Deal

Key Negotiation Points:
Negotiations cover the purchase price, payment terms, conditions and covenants, and warranties and representations. Investment bankers must balance these aspects to protect their clients' interests and ensure fair terms.

Example: In a merger, the negotiation might focus on determining an appropriate valuation multiple and structuring earn-outs based on achieving specific financial targets.

5. Drafting the Legal Documents

Key Documents:

- **Purchase Agreement:** Outlines the terms of sale, including price, payment method, and representations and warranties.
- **Shareholders' Agreement:** If applicable, details the rights and obligations of shareholders post-transaction.
- **Ancillary Documents:** Non-compete agreements, employment contracts, and intellectual property transfers.

Example: A purchase agreement might include clauses addressing potential indemnities for breaches of representations.

6. Closing the Transaction

Finalizing the Deal:
The final steps involve ensuring all legal and regulatory requirements

are met, completing financial transactions, and officially transferring ownership. This phase often includes complex logistical arrangements, such as the transfer of funds and updating corporate registries.

Example: Completing an acquisition may require regulatory approvals, transferring cash payments, and issuing new stock.

Conclusion

Deal structuring in investment banking is a multifaceted process that requires strategic thinking, detailed analysis, and adept negotiation skills. By meticulously following these steps, investment bankers can craft deals that align with the strategic goals of both buyers and sellers, ensuring successful and mutually beneficial outcomes. This process not only involves technical expertise but also the art of understanding and aligning the different motivations and constraints of the involved parties.

NOTES:
Why Deal Structuring?
After building & executing on a buyer list, it is up to the investment banker to work with the buyer and seller to structure a deal. This means negotiating the valuation range and deal terms.

Deal Structuring Process
1. Valuation Range
2. Deal Terms

Chapter 116: Valuation Range & Deal Terms

Understanding the Role of Valuation Range & Deal Terms in Investment Banking

Introduction In investment banking, valuation range and deal terms are critical components that form the foundation of any financial transaction, whether it's a merger, acquisition, or other strategic investment. These elements help determine the value of a company and establish the conditions under which a transaction will occur. This blog post explores the intricacies of these concepts, their methodologies, and their interplay in structuring successful deals.

Valuation Range

Definition and Significance

The valuation range refers to the spectrum of potential values assigned to a company or asset. This range is derived from various financial analyses and serves as a benchmark for negotiations. It's essential because it sets the expectations for both buyers and sellers and forms the basis for initial offer prices and subsequent negotiations.

Methodologies for Determining Valuation Range

1. **Discounted Cash Flow (DCF) Analysis**
   - *What it is:* DCF analysis involves projecting the target company's future cash flows and discounting them to their present value using the weighted average cost of capital (WACC).
   - *Key Considerations:* Accurate cash flow projections and appropriate discount rates are crucial. This method provides an intrinsic valuation based on the company's fundamental financial health.
   - *Example Use:* Used frequently in industries with stable cash flows, such as utilities.

2. **Comparable Company Analysis (CCA)**
   - *What it is:* This method compares the target company with similar publicly traded companies, using multiples like P/E (Price-to-Earnings) or EV/EBITDA (Enterprise Value to Earnings Before Interest, Taxes, Depreciation, and Amortization).
   - *Key Considerations:* Identifying truly comparable companies can be challenging. It reflects market sentiment and current industry benchmarks.
   - *Example Use:* Often used in technology sectors where peer group comparisons are relevant.

3. **Precedent Transactions Analysis**
   - *What it is:* Analyzes previous transactions involving similar companies to understand the multiples paid.
   - *Key Considerations:* Market conditions at the time of past transactions may differ from the current market, affecting the relevance of this analysis.
   - *Example Use:* Useful in assessing industries with frequent M&A activities, like pharmaceuticals.

Factors Affecting Valuation Range

- Assumptions about future growth and profitability.
- Current market conditions, including economic indicators and investor sentiment.
- Risk factors such as operational risks, market competition, and financial stability.

Deal Terms

Definition and Importance

Deal terms define the specific conditions under which a transaction will take place. They include the purchase price, payment methods, warranties, representations, covenants, and indemnities. Properly structured deal terms ensure that both parties' interests are protected and that the transaction is fair and balanced.

Key Components of Deal Terms

1. **Purchase Price and Payment Structure**
   - *Components:* May include upfront payments, deferred payments, and earnouts.
   - *Example:* In a tech acquisition, a buyer might pay 60% upfront and 40% in earnouts based on future revenue targets.
2. **Warranties and Representations**
   - *Definition:* Statements of fact and assurances provided by the seller regarding the state of the business.
   - *Purpose:* Protects the buyer from undisclosed liabilities or risks.
3. **Indemnities**

- o *Purpose:* Provides compensation for losses due to breaches of warranties or other specified issues.
- o *Example:* Indemnification clauses might cover legal liabilities arising from previous business activities.

4. **Covenants**
  - o *Types:* Can be affirmative (actions to take) or negative (actions to avoid).
  - o *Example:* A negative covenant might prevent the seller from engaging in competitive activities post-transaction.

Interrelationship Between Valuation Range and Deal Terms

Negotiation Framework

The valuation range provides a starting point for determining the purchase price. As negotiations progress, the initial valuation may be adjusted based on findings from due diligence, market shifts, or new financial data.

Influence on Deal Structuring

Valuation and deal terms are interdependent:

- A higher valuation might lead to more complex payment structures, including earnouts or stock options, to align interests.
- Deal terms are crafted to manage risks identified during valuation and due diligence, balancing the benefits and protections for both parties.

Alignment of Interests

The goal is to align the interests of buyers and sellers, ensuring that the final agreement reflects the true value of the target and is structured to minimize risks and maximize benefits for both parties.

Role of Investment Bankers

Advisory and Analytical Expertise

Investment bankers play a critical role in:

- Advising clients on appropriate valuation methodologies and deal terms.
- Conducting due diligence and financial analysis to support valuation assessments.
- Negotiating and structuring transactions to align with market conditions and client objectives.

Negotiation and Execution

Investment bankers leverage their market knowledge and transaction experience to negotiate favorable terms and ensure a smooth execution of the deal. They act as intermediaries, facilitating communication and resolving disputes to achieve a successful transaction.

Conclusion

Understanding and effectively managing the interplay between valuation range and deal terms is crucial for structuring successful transactions in investment banking. These elements not only set the framework for negotiations but also ensure that both parties' interests are adequately protected, leading to value creation and strategic alignment.

By providing detailed analysis and expert advice, investment bankers help clients navigate complex financial landscapes, making informed decisions that align with their long-term goals. The careful crafting of valuation and deal terms ultimately leads to successful and mutually beneficial transactions.

NOTES:

Valuation Range

Deal structures initially involve a rough range of valuation to make sure that both parties are in the sphere of reasonability. Reasonable deals typically look like the following:

- 4x <$1M EBITDA
- 5x ~$1M EBITDA
- 6x $1M - $2M EBITDA
- 7x >$2M EBITDA

Deal Terms

From there we should get an understanding of whether this is:

- Asset Sale vs. Stock Sale
- Cash vs. Stock vs. Cash & Stock
- Going to be a majority or minority ownership deal
- Whether the owner plans on staying as a CEO after the transaction or whether there is existing management in place
- Owner financing is available
- Earn outs

Asset Sale vs. Stock Sale

An asset sale in M&A does not mean distressed but rather is where a buyer acquires the assets of a company rather than the stock.

In a stock sale, the depreciation schedule is transferred to the new buyer.

Purchase Price Allocation

The purchase price allocation forms points of negotiation where hard assets are stepped up to the purchase price.

Investment Banking University
All Rights Reserved

Chapter 117: Dealing with Sellers in the Lower Middle Market/Middle Market

Navigating the Lower Middle Market and Middle Market as an Investment Banker

Dealing with sellers in the lower middle market (LMM) and middle market (MM) presents unique challenges and opportunities for investment bankers. These segments consist of companies with annual revenues ranging from $5 million to $500 million. Due to their size, these companies often face different operational, financial, and strategic dynamics than larger corporations. Investment bankers play a crucial role in guiding these companies through the complexities of mergers and acquisitions (M&A), capital raising, and strategic planning. This blog post explores the key steps and considerations involved in working with sellers in the LMM/MM, from understanding market dynamics to managing the transaction process.

Understanding Market Dynamics

Defining the Lower Middle Market and Middle Market

- **Lower Middle Market (LMM):** Companies with annual revenues between $5 million and $50 million.

- **Middle Market (MM):** Companies with annual revenues between $50 million and $500 million.

Importance of Market Knowledge Investment bankers must have a deep understanding of the industries they operate in, including growth drivers, competitive landscapes, and regulatory environments. This knowledge helps them provide accurate advice and tailor their services to the specific needs of each client.

Valuation Multiples

- **Industry-Specific Multiples:** Different industries have varying valuation benchmarks. For instance, technology firms may command higher multiples due to their growth potential, while manufacturing firms might have lower multiples.
- **Common Multiples in LMM/MM:**
  - Companies with EBITDA between $500k and $1 million: approximately 4x EBITDA.
  - Companies with EBITDA around $1 million: typically 5x EBITDA.
  - Companies with EBITDA between $1 million and $2 million: generally 6x EBITDA.
  - Companies with EBITDA over $2 million: around 7x EBITDA.

Advising Clients

Initial Discussions and Strategic Planning

- **Timing Considerations:** Many sellers in these markets are 1 to 5 years away from selling. They might be waiting for optimal market conditions or aiming to achieve specific business milestones before entering the market.

- **Developing a Roadmap:** Investment bankers assist clients in preparing for a future sale. This preparation may involve enhancing operational efficiency, ensuring accurate financial records, and implementing growth strategies.

Patience and Relationship Building

- **Long-Term Engagement:** Building a relationship with potential sellers can take years. Investment bankers need patience and persistence to maintain these connections.
- **Fee Agreements:** It's crucial to establish clear fee agreements early to ensure compensation for the banker's time and expertise.

Identifying Acquisition Targets or Buyers

Types of Buyers

- **Strategic Buyers:** Companies seeking acquisitions for synergies, such as entering new markets, acquiring technologies, or realizing cost efficiencies.
- **Financial Buyers:** Private equity firms and other financial investors looking for investment opportunities that offer potential for operational improvements and financial returns.

Market Research and Proactive Outreach

- **Industry Analysis:** Using industry reports and databases, investment bankers identify potential buyers or acquisition targets.
- **Engaging Buyers:** Proactive outreach to potential buyers helps generate interest and can lead to competitive bidding, which benefits the seller.

Negotiating Deal Terms

Structuring the Deal

- **Payment Structures:** Deciding between cash, stock, or a combination of payments, each with different risk and reward profiles.
- **Earnouts and Contingencies:** Including earnouts can help bridge valuation gaps and align the interests of buyers and sellers.
- **Warranties and Indemnities:** Establishing terms to protect buyers against potential future liabilities.

Balancing Interests

- **Risk Allocation:** Striking a fair balance in risk-sharing between buyer and seller.
- **Value Maximization:** Ensuring that the deal structure maximizes value for the seller while remaining attractive to buyers.

Managing the Transaction Process

Due Diligence and Transparency

- **Comprehensive Review:** Thorough due diligence involves a deep dive into the financial, operational, legal, and market aspects of the target company.
- **Transparency:** Maintaining open communication and transparency helps build trust and facilitates smoother negotiations.

Legal Documentation and Closing

- **Drafting Agreements:** Preparing and reviewing all necessary legal documents, such as purchase agreements and shareholder agreements.
- **Closing the Deal:** Ensuring all conditions are met and the transaction is executed efficiently.

Post-Transaction Integration and Support

Transition Planning

- **Integration Support:** Assisting with the integration of the acquired business into the buyer's operations, addressing cultural, operational, and strategic alignment.

Conclusion

Key Takeaways Working with sellers in the LMM/MM requires specialized knowledge of market dynamics, valuation multiples, and the nuances of different industries. Investment bankers must be adept at relationship building, patient in their approach, and skilled in navigating the complexities of dealmaking. By providing expert guidance, they help sellers achieve their strategic and financial goals, ensuring successful transactions in a highly competitive market.

This comprehensive understanding and strategic approach enable investment bankers to add significant value to their clients, whether they are exploring a sale, seeking acquisitions, or looking to raise capital. The role of the investment banker is crucial in managing the intricacies of these transactions and ensuring favorable outcomes for all parties involved.

Chapter 118: Dealing with Buyers in the Lower Middle Market/Middle Market

Navigating Transactions with Buyers in the Lower Middle Market and Middle Market

The lower middle market (LMM) and middle market (MM) are unique spaces in the investment banking landscape, often characterized by nuanced buyer and seller dynamics. Engaging effectively with buyers in these markets involves a blend of strategic communication, rigorous qualification, and managing expectations. This blog post delves into the intricate process investment bankers follow to successfully navigate these transactions, focusing on setting up buyer/seller calls, qualifying buyers, and managing expectations.

Setting Up Buyer/Seller Calls

Initial Communication: Establishing Trust and Engagement

Building Initial Rapport: The first step in engaging with potential buyers is to establish a line of communication that builds trust. Investment bankers initiate preliminary calls, where the focus is not on exchanging detailed financial information but on understanding the buyer's interest and aligning it with the seller's offerings. This initial engagement is crucial as it sets the tone for the entire transaction.

Providing Market Insights: During these initial calls, bankers provide insights into current market trends, industry dynamics, and recent M&A activities. This not only showcases the banker's expertise but also helps potential buyers understand the broader context of the transaction. It's an opportunity to discuss the strategic value of the business, setting a foundation for deeper discussions.

Requesting Buyer Questions: Before delving into financial specifics, bankers request potential buyers to submit their questions. This allows the seller to prepare and provides a focused agenda for the upcoming discussions. Typically, these questions center around key financial metrics like revenue and EBITDA over the past few years.

Scheduling and Conducting Calls: With the questions in hand, investment bankers schedule buyer/seller calls. These meetings are critical as they allow both parties to assess compatibility and build a preliminary understanding of the potential transaction. It's during these calls that sellers often become more comfortable sharing sensitive financial data, having established a basic level of trust with the buyer.

Qualifying Buyers

The Screening Process

Initial Inquiry and Classification: A significant part of the process involves determining whether the buyer is an individual investor or represents a corporate entity. This distinction is crucial as individual buyers typically have different financial capabilities and strategic interests compared to corporate buyers or private equity firms.

Key Screening Questions:

- Are you buying individually or on behalf of a corporation?
- What is your acquisition history and investment criteria?
- How do you typically finance acquisitions?

Understanding Buyer Capacity: Individual buyers, for example, may offer lower multiples, typically in the range of 3x to 4x EBITDA, compared to corporate buyers who might offer higher multiples. Understanding these dynamics helps in setting realistic expectations for the seller and ensures that the discussions are with serious and capable buyers.

Example: For a technology firm seeking acquisition, an investment banker might discern early on that an interested buyer is a strategic acquirer looking for specific technological synergies. This early qualification helps streamline the process, ensuring only relevant buyers are engaged further.

Managing Expectations

Setting Realistic Seller Expectations

Seller's Perspective: Sellers often have high expectations regarding the valuation of their business. It is crucial for investment bankers to manage these expectations by providing a clear understanding of market realities, potential deal structures, and valuation methodologies.

Buyer's Perspective: Buyers, particularly those looking for strategic acquisitions, may be willing to pay a premium for synergies or strategic fit. However, they need to be assured that the valuation aligns with the potential value addition.

Communicating Value: Investment bankers articulate the value proposition of the business clearly, emphasizing aspects such as market position, growth potential, and unique selling points. They use industry benchmarks, comparable transactions, and financial analysis to justify the proposed valuation multiples.

Example: For a healthcare services provider, an investment banker might emphasize the company's strong patient retention rates, specialized services, and favorable market conditions as justifications for a higher multiple.

Conclusion

Key Takeaways: Navigating transactions in the LMM and MM requires a strategic approach that blends communication skills, market knowledge, and a deep understanding of the client's business. By carefully setting up buyer/seller calls, qualifying buyers, and managing expectations, investment bankers can facilitate successful transactions that align with the strategic and financial goals of both buyers and sellers. This structured approach not only ensures a smooth transaction process but also fosters long-term relationships and trust between all parties involved.

Chapter 119: The Different Types of Financial Instruments Used in Investment Banking

Understanding the Different Types of Financial Instruments in Investment Banking

Investment banking plays a crucial role in the financial ecosystem by helping corporations, governments, and institutions raise capital and manage financial risk. One of the core functions of investment banking is the creation, issuance, and trading of various financial instruments. These instruments serve as vehicles for investment, financing, and risk management. In this blog post, we'll delve into the various types of financial instruments commonly used in investment banking, exploring their features, purposes, and the roles investment bankers play in their issuance and management.

1. Equity Instruments

Definition and Purpose

Equity instruments represent ownership stakes in a company. Investors who purchase these instruments become shareholders, gaining voting rights and a claim on the company's profits in the form of dividends. Equity instruments are vital for companies looking to raise capital without incurring debt.

Types of Equity Instruments

- **Common Shares**: These are the most prevalent form of equity. Common shareholders have voting rights and may receive dividends, though they are the last to be paid in the event of liquidation.
- **Preferred Shares**: Preferred shareholders typically do not have voting rights but have a higher claim on assets and earnings than common shareholders. They often receive fixed dividends.

Role of Investment Bankers

Investment bankers assist companies in issuing equity instruments through initial public offerings (IPOs) or secondary offerings. They help price the shares, underwrite the issuance, and market them to potential investors.

2. Debt Instruments

Definition and Purpose

Debt instruments are financial assets that entail a borrower repaying a lender with interest over a specified period. These instruments are essential for entities seeking capital without diluting ownership.

Types of Debt Instruments

- **Bonds**: Long-term debt securities that pay periodic interest and return the principal at maturity.
- **Debentures**: Unsecured bonds that rely on the creditworthiness of the issuer.
- **Commercial Paper**: Short-term unsecured promissory notes typically used for immediate financing needs.
- **Loans**: Direct borrowings from financial institutions, which can be structured as term loans or revolving credit facilities.

Role of Investment Bankers

Investment bankers help structure debt offerings, set the terms, and find investors. They also provide advisory services to optimize the capital structure.

3. Convertible Securities

Definition and Purpose

Convertible securities are hybrid instruments that can be converted into another form, typically common stock. They offer the benefits of both debt and equity, providing fixed income with the potential for capital appreciation.

Types of Convertible Securities

- **Convertible Bonds**: Bonds that can be converted into a set number of common shares.
- **Convertible Preferred Stock**: Preferred shares with an option to convert into common shares.

Role of Investment Bankers

Investment bankers design and market these instruments, helping companies attract investors who are interested in both income and growth potential.

4. Derivatives

Definition and Purpose

Derivatives are financial contracts whose value is derived from an underlying asset, such as stocks, bonds, commodities, or currencies. They are primarily used for hedging risks or speculative purposes.

Types of Derivatives

- **Options**: Contracts that give the holder the right, but not the obligation, to buy or sell an asset at a predetermined price.
- **Futures**: Agreements to buy or sell an asset at a future date at a predetermined price.
- **Swaps**: Contracts to exchange cash flows or financial instruments, often used for interest rate or currency risk management.

Role of Investment Bankers

Investment bankers facilitate the creation and trading of derivatives, providing risk management solutions and speculative opportunities for clients.

5. Structured Products

Definition and Purpose

Structured products are customized financial instruments created to meet specific investor needs, often combining different financial instruments such as derivatives and debt.

Features of Structured Products

- **Customization**: Tailored to specific investment goals and risk profiles.
- **Diverse Payoffs**: Can offer capital protection, income, or leverage.

Role of Investment Bankers

Investment bankers design structured products to meet the unique needs of institutional and retail investors, often incorporating derivatives to offer complex payoff structures.

6. Syndicated Loans

Definition and Purpose

Syndicated loans involve multiple lenders pooling resources to provide a large loan to a single borrower. This allows for risk distribution and access to more substantial funding.

Features of Syndicated Loans

- **Shared Risk**: Multiple lenders share the credit risk.
- **Large Capital Access**: Suitable for significant projects requiring substantial capital.

Role of Investment Bankers

Investment bankers organize the syndicate, structure the loan terms, and facilitate the transaction.

7. Asset-Backed Securities (ABS)

Definition and Purpose

Asset-backed securities (ABS) are financial instruments backed by a pool of assets, such as loans or receivables. They allow issuers to raise capital while offloading the risk associated with the underlying assets.

Features of ABS

- **Credit Risk Transfer**: Passes the risk of the underlying assets to investors.
- **Cash Flow**: Investors receive payments derived from the cash flows of the underlying assets.

Role of Investment Bankers

Investment bankers assist in the securitization process, structuring the ABS, and finding investors.

8. Mezzanine Financing

Definition and Purpose

Mezzanine financing is a hybrid of debt and equity financing, often used in situations where senior debt is insufficient. It typically includes subordinated debt with warrants or options to convert into equity.

Features of Mezzanine Financing

- **High Risk and Return**: Subordinated status means higher risk, but potential equity conversion offers high returns.
- **Flexible Terms**: Can be customized to meet the needs of the issuer and investors.

Role of Investment Bankers

Investment bankers arrange mezzanine financing, helping companies bridge the gap between debt and equity funding.

Conclusion

Investment bankers play a vital role in the financial ecosystem, providing a range of financial instruments that cater to diverse funding needs and risk profiles. By leveraging these instruments, they help companies raise capital, manage risk, and achieve strategic objectives. Understanding the different types of financial instruments is crucial for investors and companies alike, as it enables informed decision-making and effective financial management.

Investment Banking University
All Rights Reserved

PART XIII: M&A PROCESS

Chapter 120: The Rationale for Mergers & Acquisitions (M&A)

The Rationale for Mergers & Acquisitions (M&A)

Introduction Mergers and acquisitions (M&A) are key strategies companies employ to grow, diversify, and enhance their competitive positioning. This post explores the various rationales behind M&A activities, shedding light on the motivations and benefits companies seek through these transactions.

Synergies: The Power of Combined Forces Understanding Synergies Synergies occur when two companies merge, creating value greater than the sum of their parts. These can manifest in several forms:

- **Cost Synergies:** By eliminating redundant operations, such as overlapping departments or facilities, companies can reduce expenses and achieve economies of scale. For instance, two manufacturing firms merging can consolidate their production facilities, reducing overhead costs.

- **Revenue Synergies:** These arise when companies combine their products, services, or market reach to enhance sales. For example, a merger between a tech firm with strong hardware capabilities and another with software expertise can lead to integrated products that appeal to a broader customer base.
- **Operational Synergies:** These include improvements in supply chain management, production processes, and overall operational efficiency. An example is a retail chain acquiring a logistics company to streamline its distribution network.

Market Expansion: Reaching New Frontiers Geographical Expansion M&A can provide instant access to new geographic markets, bypassing the time and regulatory hurdles associated with organic expansion. For example, an American company acquiring a European firm can leverage the latter's established presence to quickly enter the European market.

Target Market Expansion Companies also use M&A to diversify into new customer segments or industries. This strategy helps mitigate risks associated with dependency on a single market. For instance, a beverage company might acquire a snack manufacturer to broaden its product portfolio and appeal to a wider audience.

Product and Service Diversification: Broadening Horizons Expanding Product Lines Mergers can allow companies to diversify their product offerings, reducing reliance on a single revenue stream. This is particularly beneficial in industries where innovation is rapid, and customer preferences change frequently.

Gaining Technological Edge Acquiring firms with advanced technologies can accelerate innovation and enhance a company's competitive advantage. For example, a traditional automaker acquiring an electric vehicle startup gains access to cutting-edge battery technology and expertise.

Vertical Integration: Strengthening Supply Chains Upstream and Downstream Integration Vertical integration involves acquiring companies at different stages of the supply chain. This can provide greater control over production inputs or distribution channels, leading to cost savings and improved margins. For example, a fashion brand acquiring a fabric manufacturer ensures a steady supply of high-quality materials.

Enhancing Competitive Advantage Owning more of the supply chain can also provide a competitive edge by securing key resources or distribution networks, making it harder for competitors to replicate the business model.

Talent Acquisition and Intellectual Property: Gaining Expertise and Assets Acquiring Skilled Talent M&A can be a strategic move to acquire top talent, especially in industries where skilled professionals are scarce. This is common in tech and pharmaceuticals, where companies acquire startups to gain access to specialized skills.

Securing Intellectual Property Acquiring intellectual property, such as patents and trademarks, can provide a competitive edge and open new revenue streams through licensing or product development.

Financial Considerations: Enhancing Shareholder Value Boosting Profitability M&A can lead to significant cost savings, increased market share, and improved profitability. By consolidating operations, companies can reduce costs and increase their pricing power.

Optimizing Capital Structure M&A can also improve a company's capital structure, providing better access to capital markets and reducing the cost of capital. This is achieved by balancing debt and equity in the company's financial framework.

Strategic Alliances and Joint Ventures: Collaborative Growth Forming Alliances In addition to full-scale mergers, companies may pursue strategic alliances or joint ventures to achieve specific goals while maintaining independence. This can involve joint product development, marketing collaborations, or shared infrastructure.

Benefits and Challenges While these partnerships can provide significant benefits, such as shared risk and resources, they also require careful management to align goals and prevent conflicts.

Conclusion Mergers and acquisitions are driven by a myriad of strategic, operational, and financial rationales. Whether aiming to achieve synergies, expand market presence, diversify products, integrate vertically, acquire talent and intellectual property, or improve financial standing, M&A remains a critical tool for companies striving for growth and competitive advantage. Investment bankers play an essential role in these processes, guiding companies through complex transactions to achieve their strategic objectives. Understanding these rationales provides a deeper insight into the world of corporate strategy and finance.

Chapter 121: Navigating the M&A Deal Lifecycle

Navigating the M&A Deal Lifecycle: A Comprehensive Guide

Navigating the M&A (Mergers and Acquisitions) deal lifecycle is a complex process that involves multiple stages, each requiring careful consideration and strategic planning. Investment bankers play a crucial role in guiding companies through this process, ensuring that transactions align with their long-term goals and create value. In this blog post, we'll explore the detailed steps involved in the M&A deal lifecycle, highlighting the key activities and considerations at each stage.

1. Strategic Planning

Defining Objectives and Goals: The first step in the M&A process is to define clear objectives that align with the company's long-term strategy. This involves understanding the company's growth ambitions, whether through expanding market share, acquiring new technologies, or entering new markets.

Market and Industry Analysis: Investment bankers assist in conducting a thorough analysis of market trends, competitive landscapes, and regulatory environments. This helps identify potential opportunities and threats, setting the groundwork for identifying suitable acquisition targets.

Setting Clear Criteria: Based on the analysis, specific criteria are established for the ideal acquisition targets, including factors such as size, industry, geographic presence, and financial performance.

2. Target Identification

Comprehensive Research: Identifying potential targets involves extensive research using various databases, industry reports, and market intelligence. Investment bankers leverage their networks and expertise to uncover companies that fit the established criteria.

Competitor and Market Dynamics: Understanding the target's position within its market and relative to competitors is crucial. This includes evaluating the target's market share, growth potential, and strategic fit with the acquiring company.

Preliminary Screening: A shortlist of potential targets is created, which includes a preliminary assessment of their financial health, business model, and alignment with the acquiring company's strategic goals.

3. Due Diligence

In-Depth Investigation: Due diligence is a comprehensive examination of the target's operations, financials, legal standing, and potential risks. It aims to uncover any hidden liabilities or issues that could affect the deal's value.

Key Areas of Focus:

- **Financial Review:** Detailed analysis of financial statements, including historical performance and future projections.
- **Operational Assessment:** Evaluation of the target's business processes, supply chain, and management capabilities.
- **Legal and Compliance:** Examination of any legal issues, intellectual property rights, and regulatory compliance.

Risk Identification and Mitigation: Identifying potential risks and developing strategies to mitigate them is a critical part of due diligence. This includes assessing market risks, operational risks, and financial risks.

4. Valuation Analysis

Determining the Target's Value: Valuation involves estimating the fair value of the target using various methods, including:

- **Discounted Cash Flow (DCF) Analysis:** Projecting future cash flows and discounting them to present value.
- **Comparable Company Analysis (CCA):** Comparing the target to similar companies based on key financial metrics.
- **Precedent Transactions Analysis:** Reviewing past M&A transactions in the same industry to determine valuation multiples.

Establishing a Fair Purchase Price: The valuation helps establish a fair purchase price, ensuring that the acquirer pays an appropriate amount based on the target's value and potential synergies.

5. Negotiation and Deal Structuring

Negotiating Terms: Investment bankers facilitate negotiations between the buyer and the target, focusing on key terms such as purchase price, payment structure (cash, stock, or a combination), and any contingent considerations like earn-outs.

Structuring the Deal: The deal structure is carefully crafted to align with the strategic objectives and financial constraints of both parties. This includes determining the appropriate financing mix and addressing any regulatory or legal requirements.

Finalizing Agreements: Once the terms are agreed upon, the final legal documents are drafted, including the purchase agreement, representations and warranties, and any covenants.

6. Regulatory Approvals and Closing

Obtaining Necessary Approvals: Depending on the deal's nature, various regulatory approvals may be required, such as antitrust clearance. Investment bankers work with legal advisors to navigate these requirements.

Finalizing the Transaction: The closing involves completing all legal and financial documentation, transferring ownership, and issuing payments. Investment bankers ensure that all conditions are met and that the transaction is finalized smoothly.

7. Post-Closing Integration

Integrating Operations: Post-closing integration is crucial for realizing the anticipated synergies. This involves aligning the target's operations, systems, and cultures with the acquiring company.

Change Management: Effective communication and change management strategies are essential to ensure a smooth transition, maintain employee morale, and minimize disruption.

Monitoring and Evaluation: Investment bankers continue to provide support by monitoring the integration process and evaluating the deal's success based on predefined metrics.

Conclusion

The M&A deal lifecycle is a multifaceted process that requires careful planning, strategic insight, and meticulous execution. Investment bankers play a pivotal role in guiding companies through each stage, from initial planning to post-closing integration. By understanding the complexities and key considerations of each stage, companies can navigate the M&A process more effectively, achieving their strategic objectives and creating long-term value.

Chapter 122: M&A Process

The Comprehensive M&A Process: A Step-by-Step Guide

Mergers and acquisitions (M&A) are vital operations in investment banking, enabling companies to grow, consolidate, or enter new markets. The M&A process involves a series of well-defined steps that investment bankers meticulously follow to ensure successful transactions. This blog post explores the M&A process in detail, from initial interest to the final closing and transfer of funds, highlighting key stages and essential documents.

Understanding the M&A Process

The M&A process can vary in complexity and duration, depending on the size and nature of the deal. However, the following are the typical stages involved in a standard M&A transaction:

1. **Indication of Interest (IOI) from Buyer**
   - **Definition**: The IOI is an initial document where a potential buyer expresses interest in purchasing the target company after reviewing preliminary information, such as a teaser or summary financials.
   - **Purpose**: It sets the stage for more detailed discussions, providing a framework for the proposed transaction without binding commitment.
2. **Buyer-Seller Meeting**

- ○ **Setup**: An in-person meeting is ideal, but phone or video calls are used if necessary due to logistics.
- ○ **Purpose**: This meeting allows both parties to establish rapport, discuss strategic fits, and outline preliminary terms. It is crucial for gauging mutual interest and seriousness.

3. **Purchase Agreement Proposal**
   - ○ **Action**: Following the initial discussions, the buyer submits a draft purchase agreement.
   - ○ **Purpose**: This document outlines the proposed terms, including price, payment structure, and conditions, serving as a foundation for further negotiations.

4. **Negotiation and Signing of Terms**
   - ○ **Negotiation**: The seller reviews the proposed terms and may suggest revisions. This negotiation process refines the agreement's details.
   - ○ **Outcome**: The final agreement reflects both parties' commitments and conditions, including any specific contingencies.

5. **Due Diligence**
   - ○ **Start**: The signing of the revised purchase agreement, which is legally binding contingent on the completion of due diligence.
   - ○ **Process**: This phase involves a thorough examination of the target's financial, legal, operational, and strategic aspects. The buyer's team confirms each aspect to ensure no surprises post-acquisition.

6. **Completion of Due Diligence**
   - ○ **Completion**: Once all due diligence checks are verified, the parties finalize preparations for closing.
   - ○ **Outcome**: Necessary documents are prepared and reviewed, ensuring all conditions are met for the transaction's completion.

7. **Closing and Flow of Funds**

- Execution: The final stage involves the signing of the closing documents.
- Funds Transfer: The agreed funds are transferred, and any M&A fees are paid. The transaction is then officially completed.

Key Documents in the M&A Process

1. **Letter of Intent (LOI)**
   - **Nature**: Generally non-binding except for clauses on confidentiality and exclusivity.
   - **Content**: Includes the proposed purchase price, transaction structure, and other key terms, serving as a roadmap for final negotiations.
2. **Purchase Agreement**
   - **Drafting**: This detailed document outlines the final terms and conditions, incorporating findings from due diligence and any negotiated changes.
   - **Content**: Covers representations, warranties, indemnities, covenants, and closing conditions.
3. **Due Diligence Documentation**
   - **Purpose**: Ensures all representations made by the seller are accurate and identifies any potential risks.
   - **SMB vs. LMM and MM**: The scope and detail of due diligence vary depending on the deal's size and complexity. Smaller deals might involve simpler checks, while larger transactions require comprehensive reviews.

Financial Information Required

Investment bankers typically request the following financial documents:

- Profit and Loss (P&L) statements for the last three years.
- Year-to-Date (YTD) P&L statement.
- Last Twelve Months (LTM) adjusted EBITDA.

These documents are essential for assessing the company's financial health and determining a fair purchase price.

M&A Process for Middle Market and Above

In more extensive transactions, the process includes additional steps such as:

- **Teaser**: An initial summary to attract potential buyers.
- **Non-Disclosure Agreement (NDA)**: Protects the confidentiality of shared information.
- **Confidential Information Memorandum (CIM)**: A detailed document providing comprehensive information about the target.
- **Term Sheet and Letter of Intent (LOI)**: Outlines the agreed terms before moving to due diligence and final agreements.

Conclusion

Understanding the M&A process is crucial for both buyers and sellers. Investment bankers play a pivotal role in guiding clients through each stage, ensuring that all aspects are thoroughly considered and that the transaction aligns with the strategic goals of the involved parties. From initial interest to closing, the structured approach of the M&A process helps mitigate risks and enhance the potential for a successful outcome.

APPLICATIONS

Chapter 123: How to Break into Investment Banking

How to Break into Investment Banking: An Alternative Approach

Breaking into investment banking traditionally involves rigorous academic preparation, often from top universities, coupled with networking and internships to secure an entry-level analyst position. However, Investment Banking University (IBU) proposes a different path that can be more accessible and practical, especially for those who may not have the conventional academic background or networking opportunities. Here's a comprehensive guide to an alternative route into the investment banking industry, focusing on gaining practical experience in Small and Medium-sized Business (SMB) and Lower Middle Market (LMM) Mergers and Acquisitions (M&A).

The Traditional Route: A Quick Overview

1. **Academic Excellence**: Typically, candidates come from top-tier universities with strong backgrounds in finance, economics, or business.
2. **Internships**: Securing internships at prestigious firms is a critical step for gaining relevant experience.

3. **Networking**: Building a network of industry contacts is essential for landing interviews and offers.
4. **Technical Skills**: Mastery of financial modeling, valuation, and other technical skills is crucial.

While this path can be effective, it's also highly competitive and can be limiting for those who don't fit the traditional mold.

The Alternative Path: Gaining Practical M&A Experience

Instead of focusing solely on technical skills and hoping for an entry-level position, consider the following approach:

1. **Start in SMB & Lower Middle Market M&A**:
   - **Why SMB & LMM?** These markets are less competitive and offer more opportunities for hands-on experience. Deals are smaller, and firms often have fewer resources, allowing you to take on more responsibilities.
   - **Roles and Responsibilities**: You'll likely be involved in all aspects of the deal process, from initial client meetings to deal structuring and execution. This broad exposure is invaluable and typically not available at larger firms for entry-level positions.
2. **Form Your Own M&A Firm**:
   - **Entrepreneurial Approach**: If you have the drive and resources, consider starting your own M&A advisory firm. This route allows you to work directly with clients, manage deals, and build a track record.
   - **Skill Development**: Running your own firm forces you to develop a wide range of skills, from business development and client management to financial analysis and deal execution.

3. **Building Experience and Credibility**:
    - ○ **Hands-On Experience**: Working in SMB or starting your own firm provides practical, hands-on experience in deal-making. This experience is often more valuable than theoretical knowledge or technical skills alone.
    - ○ **Scaling Up**: Once you've proven your ability to manage deals successfully, you can leverage this experience to move into larger markets and more complex transactions.

Why This Alternative Path Works

1. **Diverse Skill Set**: Working in smaller markets or running your own firm forces you to wear many hats. You'll develop a broader skill set, including client management, negotiation, and strategic thinking.
2. **Proven Track Record**: Unlike traditional entry-level candidates, you'll have a proven track record of managing deals and creating value, making you a more attractive candidate for higher positions.
3. **Stronger Positioning**: Entering the investment banking world from a position of strength—with real-world experience and a track record—gives you an edge over candidates who only have theoretical knowledge.

Moving Forward: Scaling Up

As you gain experience, you can aim to:

1. **Join Larger Firms**: With practical M&A experience, you can transition into larger investment banks or boutique advisory firms, often in more senior roles than those offered to traditional entry-level candidates.

2. **Specialize**: Use your experience to specialize in a particular industry or type of transaction, further differentiating yourself in the market.
3. **Expand Your Network**: Continuously build and expand your network within the industry, leveraging your experience and success stories to connect with influential professionals.

Conclusion

Breaking into investment banking doesn't have to follow the traditional path of academic excellence, internships, and networking at prestigious firms. By gaining practical experience in SMB and LMM M&A, or by starting your own advisory firm, you can build a strong foundation of skills and experience. This alternative route not only prepares you for a career in investment banking but positions you as a versatile and experienced professional capable of handling complex transactions and strategic decisions.

Chapter 124: How to Land Your First Buy Side Relationship

How to Land Your First Buy-Side Relationship in M&A

Breaking into the world of mergers and acquisitions (M&A) as an investment banker involves mastering several critical steps, with one of the most vital being the establishment of buy-side relationships. These relationships are foundational for securing M&A deals, as they involve working with potential acquirers or investors looking to purchase companies or assets. Here's a detailed guide on how to effectively land your first buy-side relationship, focusing on establishing a solid foundation, targeted outreach, and building credibility.

1. Internalize the Investment Banking Process

Master the Fundamentals

Before reaching out to potential buy-side clients, it's crucial to have a strong grasp of the front office investment banking process. This involves understanding how to:

- **Conduct Financial Analysis**: Learn to analyze financial statements, create financial models, and assess company valuations.
- **Identify Strategic Alternatives**: Be able to propose various strategies, such as mergers, acquisitions, joint ventures, and divestitures, that align with client goals.
- **Prepare Pitchbooks and Presentations**: Develop skills in creating compelling pitchbooks that clearly communicate value propositions and strategic recommendations.

2. Establish Your Coverage Area

Define Your Niche

To effectively target buy-side clients, you need to establish your coverage area based on specific criteria. This includes:

- **Geographic Region**: Decide whether to focus on local, regional, national, or international markets. Your choice may depend on your knowledge, network, and language skills.
- **Company Size**: Determine whether you will target small businesses, middle-market companies, or large corporations. This decision will shape the nature of the deals you pursue.
- **Industry Vertical**: Choose a specific industry or set of industries where you have expertise or interest. This could range from technology to healthcare, manufacturing, consumer goods, and more.

By defining these parameters, you can focus your efforts on a more manageable and strategic segment of the market.

3. Targeted Outreach to Corporate M&A Departments and Financial Sponsors

Research and Identify Prospects

Once you have established your coverage area, the next step is to identify potential buy-side clients. This involves:

- **Corporate M&A Departments**: Reach out to companies with dedicated M&A teams. These are often large corporations looking to expand through acquisitions.
- **Financial Sponsors**: Target private equity firms, venture capitalists, and other investment entities that regularly invest in or acquire companies.

Initial Contact

When making initial contact, it's essential to demonstrate your understanding of the industry and the specific needs of the potential client. Your outreach should:

- **Be Personalized**: Address the specific challenges and opportunities the client may be facing. Show that you've done your homework by referencing recent news, transactions, or strategic initiatives related to the prospect.
- **Highlight Your Value Proposition**: Clearly articulate how your services can help the client achieve their strategic objectives. This could include identifying undervalued assets, optimizing capital structure, or finding synergies through acquisitions.

4. Build Credibility and Trust

Demonstrate Expertise

Building trust is crucial, and one of the most effective ways to do this is by demonstrating your expertise. This can be done through:

- **Thought Leadership**: Publish articles, whitepapers, or research reports on industry trends and strategic insights. Share these with potential clients to showcase your knowledge and analytical capabilities.
- **Case Studies and Success Stories**: Share examples of past successes, highlighting how you've helped other clients achieve their M&A goals. If you're new to the field, leverage experiences from internships, previous roles, or academic projects.

Develop Relationships

Developing relationships with potential buy-side clients requires consistent and meaningful engagement:

- **Regular Updates**: Provide clients with regular updates on market trends, relevant transactions, and industry news. This keeps you top-of-mind and positions you as a valuable resource.
- **Follow-Up**: After initial meetings or communications, follow up with tailored insights or additional information that may be of interest to the client.

5. Leveraging Networks and Referrals

Network Within the Industry

Networking is a powerful tool in investment banking. Attend industry conferences, seminars, and networking events to meet potential clients and industry peers. Building a strong network can lead to referrals and introductions, which are invaluable when establishing buy-side relationships.

Utilize Professional Platforms

Utilize platforms like LinkedIn to connect with decision-makers in your target companies. Engage with their posts, join relevant groups, and share your own content to increase visibility and establish yourself as a thought leader.

6. Continuous Learning and Adaptation

The M&A landscape is constantly evolving, and staying current is essential. Continuously educate yourself on new trends, market conditions, and regulatory changes. This ongoing learning will enhance your ability to provide valuable insights and advice to your clients.

Conclusion

Landing your first buy-side relationship in M&A requires a strategic approach, thorough preparation, and the ability to build and maintain strong relationships. By mastering the fundamentals, targeting the right clients, demonstrating your expertise, and leveraging your network, you can successfully establish yourself in the competitive world of investment banking. As you gain experience and build your reputation, you'll find that these initial relationships will serve as the foundation for a successful career in M&A.

Chapter 125: How to Land Your First M&A Engagement

How to Land Your First M&A Engagement

Landing your first mergers and acquisitions (M&A) engagement can be a challenging but rewarding endeavor. It requires a combination of understanding buy-side mandates, identifying suitable targets, establishing relationships, and effectively communicating with business owners. Here's a detailed guide to help you navigate this process:

Understanding Buy-Side Mandates

1. **Define Buy-Side Mandates**:
   - **Clarify Objectives**: Begin by understanding the specific goals and investment criteria of potential buyers, whether they are strategic buyers or financial investors like private equity firms.
   - **Investment Criteria**: Key factors include the target company's industry, size (revenue and EBITDA), geographic location, and specific operational or strategic attributes desired by the buyer.
2. **Build Relationships with Buyers**:
   - **Networking**: Establish and nurture relationships with potential buyers. Attend industry conferences, join

professional organizations, and leverage LinkedIn to connect with key decision-makers.

- ○ **Regular Communication**: Keep buyers updated with market trends, potential opportunities, and insights that may interest them. This demonstrates your expertise and keeps you top-of-mind when they are ready to make acquisitions.

Identifying Suitable Targets

1. **Research and Analysis**:
   - ○ **Industry Analysis**: Perform a comprehensive analysis of the target industries to identify trends, growth opportunities, and key players.
   - ○ **Target Identification**: Use databases, industry reports, and your network to compile a list of potential acquisition targets that match the criteria defined in the buy-side mandates.
2. **Evaluating Targets**:
   - ○ **Financial Health**: Assess the financial health of potential targets, including profitability, revenue growth, and debt levels.
   - ○ **Strategic Fit**: Evaluate how well the target aligns with the buyer's strategic goals, such as expanding into new markets, acquiring technology, or achieving economies of scale.

Reaching Out to Business Owners

1. **Initial Contact**:
   - ○ **Personalized Outreach**: Craft personalized outreach messages that clearly articulate the potential benefits of exploring strategic alternatives. Highlight your

understanding of their business and the value you can bring as an advisor.
- ○ **Leveraging Networks**: Use mutual connections and industry contacts to facilitate introductions and establish credibility.

2. **Gauging Interest**:
   - ○ **Open Dialogue**: Initiate conversations with business owners to understand their openness to exploring a sale or other strategic alternatives. Discuss their long-term goals and concerns.
   - ○ **Value Proposition**: Clearly communicate the value proposition of working with you, including your expertise, market knowledge, and network of potential buyers.

Negotiating Engagement Terms

1. **Fee Structure**:
   - ○ **Success Fee Basis**: The standard fee structure in M&A advisory is a success fee, which is contingent upon the successful completion of the transaction. This aligns your incentives with the client's goals and reduces upfront costs for the business owner.
   - ○ **Additional Fees**: In some cases, you may negotiate a retainer or a minimum fee to cover initial costs and effort.

2. **Formalizing the Engagement**:
   - ○ **Engagement Letter**: Draft and agree upon an engagement letter that outlines the scope of work, fee structure, confidentiality terms, and any other relevant conditions. This document formalizes the advisory relationship and sets clear expectations.

Building Credibility and Trust

1. **Demonstrate Expertise**:
   - **Case Studies**: Share case studies or examples of past successful transactions (if applicable) to demonstrate your expertise and track record.
   - **Market Knowledge**: Regularly provide insights and updates on market conditions, industry trends, and potential opportunities.
2. **Transparency and Communication**:
   - **Regular Updates**: Keep the business owner informed throughout the process, providing updates on buyer interest, market feedback, and any challenges encountered.
   - **Ethical Standards**: Uphold high ethical standards and transparency in all dealings, reinforcing trust and confidence in your advisory services.

Conclusion

Landing your first M&A engagement requires a strategic approach, deep industry knowledge, and strong relationship-building skills. By understanding buy-side mandates, identifying suitable targets, effectively engaging with business owners, and negotiating clear engagement terms, you can position yourself as a trusted advisor and successfully secure your first M&A mandate. This journey not only helps you build credibility but also lays the foundation for future success in the competitive world of investment banking.

Chapter 126: How to Build a Lower Middle Market/Middle Market M&A Practice Methodology

Building a Lower Middle Market/Middle Market M&A Practice: A Comprehensive Guide

Building a successful M&A (Mergers and Acquisitions) practice in the Lower Middle Market (LMM) and Middle Market (MM) requires a meticulous and strategic approach. This guide outlines the essential steps and methodologies for establishing a thriving M&A practice, focusing on defining the investment product, selecting industry coverage, creating indices, generating marketing materials, and leveraging research and relationships to drive deal origination.

Defining the Investment Product

Core Services

To begin, it's crucial to define the core services your M&A practice will offer. These services can include:

1. **Mergers & Acquisitions (M&A)**: Facilitating the buying and selling of businesses.
2. **Financing**: Arranging debt or equity financing for corporate clients.
3. **Growth Advisory**: Providing strategic advice to companies looking to expand.

Industry Focus

Choosing the right industries and sub-industries to cover is vital. Your firm's expertise should align with market demand and your team's experience. Typical industry verticals include:

1. **Manufacturing**:
   - Durable Consumer Goods
   - Non-durable Consumer Goods
   - Aerospace & Defense
   - Building Products
   - Industrial Products
   - Medical Devices
2. **Software**:
   - Traditional Software
   - Software as a Service (SaaS)
   - Internet-based Solutions
3. **Business Services**:
   - Education & Training

- Business Process Outsourcing (BPO)
- Facility and Industrial Services
- Human Resources
- Information Services
- Marketing Services
- Real Estate Services
- IT Services
- Specialty Consulting

4. **Healthcare**:
- Dental Products and Providers
- Medical Devices & Products
- Medical Product Distribution
- Specialty Providers
- Pharma Services
- Practice Management
- Provider Services
- Long-Term & Behavioral Care

Building Indices for Vertical and Sub-Vertical Coverage

Public Comps Analysis

To effectively track market trends and benchmark potential deals, build indices using publicly traded comparables (public comps). This involves:

1. **Data Collection**:
- Gather financial data for public companies in the chosen verticals and sub-verticals.

- Use financial statement models to analyze revenue growth, EBITDA margins, debt levels, and valuation multiples.
2. **Index Construction**:
   - Create indices that reflect the median and average performance metrics within each vertical and sub-vertical.
   - Track metrics such as growth rates, profit margins, debt-to-equity ratios, and market multiples.

Research and Reporting

Leverage the indices to generate proprietary research, including:

- **Industry Reports**: Comprehensive analysis of market trends, competitive dynamics, and financial benchmarks.
- **Newsletters**: Regular updates on market activities, notable transactions, and industry developments.

These materials not only inform potential clients but also demonstrate your firm's expertise and thought leadership in the industry.

Generating Marketing Materials

Teasers and Presentations

Use data from your indices and research to create compelling marketing materials:

- **Teasers**: Brief documents that provide an overview of potential deals, used to gauge initial interest from buyers.

- **Presentations**: Detailed documents that delve into market analysis, strategic rationale, and financial projections, used in formal pitches.

Pitchbooks and CIMs

- **Pitchbooks**: Tailored presentations for specific clients, detailing strategic alternatives and showcasing the firm's capabilities.
- **Confidential Information Memorandums (CIMs)**: In-depth documents that provide comprehensive information about a business being marketed for sale, including its financials, operations, and market positioning.

Leveraging Relationships for Deal Origination

Building Networks

Establish relationships with both strategic and financial buyers, including private equity firms, venture capitalists, and corporate acquirers. This involves:

- **Networking**: Attending industry events, conferences, and networking sessions.
- **Direct Outreach**: Regular communication with potential buyers to understand their investment criteria and strategic goals.

Ongoing Monitoring and Analysis

Continuously monitor market conditions and adjust your strategies accordingly. This involves:

- **Tracking Market Trends**: Keeping abreast of changes in market valuations, regulatory developments, and industry disruptions.
- **Benchmarking**: Regularly updating your indices and benchmarking potential deals against market standards.

Advising on Strategic Alternatives

Analysis and Recommendations

Using the insights gained from your indices and market analysis, advise clients on the best strategic alternatives, such as:

- **Timing for Exits**: Based on market multiples and industry trends, recommend the optimal timing for selling a business.
- **Strategic Acquisitions**: Identify acquisition targets that align with the client's growth strategy and market positioning.

Execution and Support

Provide end-to-end support, from initial strategy discussions to deal execution, including negotiation and closing.

Conclusion

Building a successful Lower Middle Market/Middle Market M&A practice requires a comprehensive approach, combining industry expertise, robust research capabilities, and strong client relationships. By defining your services, building detailed indices, producing insightful research, and leveraging a network of buyers, your firm can effectively originate and execute high-quality M&A transactions. This methodology not only positions your firm as a trusted advisor but also ensures a steady flow of business opportunities and long-term success in the competitive M&A landscape.

Chapter 127: Case Study of an Example Capital Raise

Case Study: Capital Raise for Company A by Bank X

Introduction

Raising capital is a critical step for companies looking to scale operations, develop new products, or enter new markets. This blog post examines a real-world example of a capital raise, focusing on the role of Bank X in helping Company A, a mid-sized tech firm, secure the necessary funding to expand its business.

Background

Company A developed a cutting-edge software platform that was rapidly gaining market traction. However, to capitalize on this momentum and expand its customer base, the company needed additional capital. They engaged Bank X, an investment bank with expertise in tech sector financings, to assist in raising funds through a private placement.

Preparation and Strategy

1. **Developing the Confidential Information Memorandum (CIM):**

- **Objective:** The CIM is a comprehensive document that outlines Company A's business model, financial performance, market position, and growth prospects. It serves as a key marketing tool for potential investors.
- **Contents:** The CIM included detailed descriptions of the software platform, target market analysis, competitive landscape, historical financials, and projected financial performance. This document provided potential investors with a thorough understanding of the company's value proposition and future potential.
- **Customization:** Bank X tailored the CIM to highlight the aspects of Company A's business most likely to appeal to different types of investors, such as growth potential for venture capitalists or profitability metrics for private equity firms.

2. **Targeting Potential Investors:**
   - **Investor List:** Bank X identified a select group of potential investors, including private equity firms, venture capitalists, and strategic investors. The selection was based on the investors' industry focus, investment track record, and strategic interests.
   - **Distribution:** The CIM was distributed to these potential investors, initiating a competitive process that maximized Company A's chances of securing favorable terms.

Evaluation and Negotiation

1. **Evaluating Offers:**
   - **Multiple Offers:** Company A received several offers, reflecting various terms and conditions. Bank X's role was crucial in assessing these offers based on

valuation, investment structure, and the strategic value of the investor's involvement.
- ○ **Detailed Analysis:** Bank X conducted a thorough analysis of each offer, considering not only the financial terms but also the potential for strategic partnerships, market expansion, and operational synergies.

2. **Selecting the Right Partner:**
- ○ **Firm Y's Offer:** Among the offers, a private equity firm, Firm Y, stood out. Firm Y had a strong track record in the tech industry and could provide not only capital but also strategic guidance and industry connections.
- ○ **Investment Terms:** Firm Y proposed a $50 million investment for a significant minority stake in Company A. The investment was structured as convertible preferred stock, providing Firm Y with an option to convert to common stock upon meeting certain milestones, thus aligning their interests with the company's growth.

3. **Negotiation Process:**
- ○ **Valuation and Structure:** Bank X led negotiations on the valuation of Company A and the structure of the investment. Key considerations included the conversion ratio for the preferred stock, governance rights, and exit provisions for Firm Y.
- ○ **Governance and Control:** Negotiations also covered the extent of control and influence Firm Y would have post-investment, including board representation and voting rights.

Execution and Closure

1. **Finalizing the Transaction:**

- Legal and Regulatory Compliance: Bank X ensured that all legal and regulatory requirements were met, facilitating a smooth closing process. This included coordinating with legal counsel, regulatory bodies, and financial auditors.
- Documentation: All necessary legal documents, including the stock purchase agreement, shareholder agreements, and other relevant contracts, were prepared and executed.

2. Post-Investment Strategy:
   - Use of Funds: The $50 million investment provided Company A with the necessary capital to scale operations, including expanding its sales and marketing efforts, accelerating product development, and exploring new market opportunities.
   - Ongoing Support: Bank X continued to provide advisory support post-transaction, helping Company A leverage Firm Y's expertise and network to drive growth.

Conclusion

This case study illustrates the critical role that investment bankers play in capital raising. Bank X's comprehensive approach—from preparing the CIM and targeting investors to evaluating offers and closing the deal—was instrumental in helping Company A secure the capital needed to achieve its growth objectives. The partnership with Firm Y not only provided financial resources but also strategic value, positioning Company A for long-term success. This example underscores the importance of a well-executed capital raise process in achieving a company's strategic goals.

Chapter 128: Case Study of an Example M&A

A Strategic Acquisition: How Company A Expanded Through M&A

In the world of mergers and acquisitions (M&A), strategic transactions are often the key to unlocking growth and gaining competitive advantages. This post explores a real-world example where Company A, a prominent healthcare services provider, leveraged an acquisition to expand its market presence and achieve strategic goals, with the assistance of an investment bank, Bank X.

Identifying the Right Target

Company A, aiming to enhance its footprint in a specific geographic region, identified the acquisition of a local player as a viable strategy. Through a collaborative process, Bank X's investment bankers helped Company A shortlist potential targets, focusing on those with a strong market presence and complementary services. Company B, a smaller yet respected healthcare provider, emerged as the top candidate due to its established customer base and reputation in the region.

The Due Diligence Process

The due diligence phase was crucial. Bank X's team meticulously analyzed Company B's financial statements, operational metrics, and market positioning. This included evaluating potential risks, such as regulatory compliance issues and operational challenges, and identifying opportunities for synergies post-acquisition.

For instance, the team assessed how integrating Company B's facilities and workforce could streamline operations and reduce costs. They also explored how Company B's existing contracts and customer relationships could be leveraged to enhance Company A's service offerings and market reach.

Structuring the Deal

After thorough analysis and due diligence, Company A decided to proceed with the acquisition, valuing Company B at $150 million. The deal structure was carefully crafted to balance cash and stock components, considering Company A's capital structure and strategic priorities.

Bank X played a pivotal role in negotiating the deal terms. This included determining the purchase price, outlining the financing arrangements, and defining the governance structure for the newly combined entity. The negotiation process was intricate, requiring careful consideration of both companies' interests to ensure a fair and beneficial agreement.

Navigating Legal and Regulatory Hurdles

M&A transactions often involve complex regulatory scrutiny, and this deal was no exception. Bank X's legal and compliance teams guided Company A through the regulatory landscape, ensuring that all necessary approvals were secured. This involved preparing comprehensive filings and engaging with regulatory authorities to address any concerns.

Successful Integration and Value Creation

With the deal closed, Company A embarked on integrating Company B into its operations. This integration phase was critical for realizing the anticipated synergies. Company A achieved significant cost savings by consolidating administrative functions and optimizing operational processes. Additionally, the acquisition expanded Company A's customer base and strengthened its competitive position in the region, aligning perfectly with its strategic growth objectives.

The Role of Bank X in the Transaction

Bank X's expertise was instrumental throughout the transaction lifecycle. From identifying the target to structuring the deal and navigating the regulatory process, their guidance ensured that the acquisition was completed smoothly and efficiently. Their strategic insights and financial acumen enabled Company A to make informed decisions, ultimately leading to a successful acquisition that created value for all stakeholders.

Conclusion

This case study underscores the critical role of investment bankers in facilitating strategic M&A transactions. By providing comprehensive analysis, expert negotiation, and seamless execution, they help companies like Company A navigate the complexities of acquisitions and achieve strategic growth. The successful acquisition of Company B not only expanded Company A's market presence but also positioned it for long-term success in a competitive industry. This example illustrates how strategic M&A can be a powerful tool for companies looking to grow and strengthen their market position.

Chapter 129: Case Study of an Example IPO

Case Study of an Example IPO: The Journey of Company A

Introduction: Company A, an innovative and rapidly growing technology firm, had made significant strides in developing a groundbreaking software platform. Having successfully raised several rounds of funding from venture capitalists and other private investors, the company reached a pivotal moment where accessing the public markets became essential. This move was aimed at raising additional capital and providing liquidity to existing shareholders. To navigate this complex process, Company A enlisted the expertise of Bank X, a reputable investment bank, to guide them through the Initial Public Offering (IPO) process.

Preparation for the IPO: The journey toward the IPO began with a meticulous preparation phase, where Bank X's team of investment bankers collaborated closely with Company A's management. The primary tasks included:

1. **Registration Statement and Prospectus:**
    - **Objective:** The creation of these documents was crucial to provide potential investors with a comprehensive understanding of Company A's

business model, financial health, market position, and growth prospects.

- **Process:** Bank X's team meticulously drafted the registration statement, including detailed financial statements, management's discussion and analysis (MD&A), and disclosures about potential risks. The prospectus was crafted to highlight the company's value proposition, market opportunity, and competitive advantages.

2. **Roadshow Preparation:**
    - **Objective:** The roadshow was an essential phase where Company A's management presented the investment opportunity to potential investors, including institutional investors, mutual funds, and retail investors.
    - **Process:** Bank X guided Company A's executives in developing a compelling narrative and presentation materials. They conducted mock presentations to refine the management's delivery and ensure they were prepared to address any investor concerns or questions.

Targeting Investors and Pricing the IPO: Bank X leveraged its extensive network and market expertise to identify and target potential investors. The bank's team utilized a strategic approach to market the IPO:

1. **Investor Targeting:**
    - **Objective:** Ensuring a diverse and robust investor base was crucial for the success of the IPO.
    - **Process:** Bank X identified key institutional investors, mutual funds, and potential retail investors, reaching out to gauge their interest and secure

commitments. This targeted approach helped create a broad and stable investor base.

2. **Setting the IPO Price:**
   - **Objective:** Determining the IPO price was a critical step, balancing the need to raise capital with offering an attractive valuation to investors.
   - **Process:** Bank X conducted a thorough valuation analysis, considering market demand, comparable company valuations, and Company A's financials. The IPO price was ultimately set at $20 per share, resulting in a total raise of $250 million.

Executing the IPO and Post-IPO Support: The IPO process culminated in a highly successful offering:

1. **Execution:**
   - **Outcome:** The IPO was oversubscribed, indicating strong investor demand. The high interest in the shares underscored confidence in Company A's growth potential and the market's positive reception of the offering.
2. **Aftermarket Performance:**
   - **Post-IPO Support:** Bank X continued to support Company A in the aftermarket, helping manage investor relations and market perception. This ongoing support was crucial in maintaining a stable and positive stock performance.
   - **Impact:** Following the IPO, Company A's stock price performed well, and its market capitalization increased significantly. The capital raised provided the necessary resources to invest in research and development, expand the customer base, and accelerate growth initiatives.

Conclusion: This case study of Company A's IPO illustrates the critical role investment bankers play in guiding companies through the IPO process. Bank X's expertise in strategic planning, market positioning, investor targeting, and execution was instrumental in the successful public debut of Company A. The IPO not only provided the company with essential capital but also positioned it for sustained growth and long-term success, benefiting all stakeholders involved.

Investment Banking University
All Rights Reserved

Chapter 130: Case Study of an Example Restructuring

Restructuring Success: A Case Study of Company A and Bank X

Overview: Company A, a prominent manufacturing firm, faced severe financial distress due to a combination of declining revenues and rising costs. The company was burdened with significant debt and was on the brink of defaulting on its loans. To address these challenges, Company A sought the expertise of Bank X, an investment bank renowned for its restructuring capabilities. This case study details how Bank X guided Company A through a complex restructuring process, culminating in a debt-for-equity swap that revitalized the company's financial health.

Initial Assessment and Challenges

Financial Evaluation: Upon engagement, Bank X's investment bankers conducted a thorough analysis of Company A's financial statements, debt obligations, and overall market position. This evaluation revealed:

1. **High Debt Levels:** Company A had accumulated substantial debt, resulting in high interest payments that strained cash flow.

2. **Decreasing Revenue:** A downturn in market demand and competitive pressures had led to a consistent decline in revenues.
3. **Operational Inefficiencies:** Increased costs and inefficiencies within the manufacturing process exacerbated the financial strain.

Key Challenges:

- **Imminent Loan Default:** The company was at risk of defaulting on its loans, which could lead to severe legal and financial repercussions.
- **Creditor Negotiations:** With a diverse group of creditors, reaching a consensus on restructuring terms would require careful negotiation and coordination.

The Restructuring Plan

Debt-for-Equity Swap: Bank X proposed a debt-for-equity swap as the central component of the restructuring plan. This strategy involved creditors exchanging a portion of their debt holdings for equity in Company A. The key elements included:

1. **Debt Reduction:** The swap aimed to reduce the company's debt burden, thereby lowering interest expenses and freeing up cash flow.
2. **Equity Issuance:** Creditors received equity in Company A, giving them a stake in the company's future success and aligning their interests with the company's long-term growth.
3. **Capital Injection:** The reduced debt load allowed Company A to access additional capital for operational improvements and strategic investments.

Negotiation Process: Negotiating the terms of the debt-for-equity swap was a complex process. Bank X's team played a pivotal role in facilitating these discussions, leveraging their expertise in restructuring and debt negotiations. Key negotiation points included:

- **Valuation of Equity:** Determining the value of equity offered to creditors required careful consideration of the company's future prospects and market conditions.
- **Creditor Agreement:** Reaching an agreement among a diverse group of creditors, each with different priorities and risk tolerances, was challenging. Bank X's team had to balance these interests to secure a consensus.

Implementation and Results

Successful Execution: After meticulous planning and negotiation, the debt-for-equity swap was successfully executed. The outcomes were significant:

1. **Improved Financial Health:** The restructuring substantially reduced Company A's debt, lowering interest payments and improving cash flow.
2. **Operational Investment:** With a stronger balance sheet, Company A was able to invest in operational efficiencies and growth initiatives, setting the stage for long-term success.
3. **Stakeholder Alignment:** The involvement of creditors as equity holders aligned their interests with the company's success, fostering a more cooperative relationship.

Post-Restructuring Support: Bank X continued to support Company A post-restructuring, offering guidance on optimizing operations and capitalizing on new opportunities. This ongoing partnership ensured that the company maintained its positive trajectory.

Conclusion

This case study illustrates the crucial role that investment bankers play in navigating complex financial restructurings. Bank X's expertise enabled Company A to overcome a dire financial situation, restructure its debt, and set a foundation for future growth. The success of this restructuring underscores the value of strategic financial planning and skilled negotiation in achieving favorable outcomes for all stakeholders involved.

Chapter 131: Case Study of an Example LBO

A Case Study: Leveraged Buyout of Company A

In the world of private equity, leveraged buyouts (LBOs) are a common strategy to acquire companies by using a combination of debt and equity. This blog post details a case study of an LBO involving Company A, a mature manufacturing firm, and Firm X, a private equity firm, facilitated by the investment bank, Bank Y. The story highlights the critical role of investment bankers in structuring and executing successful LBO transactions.

Background on Company A and Firm X

Company A, known for its consistent cash flow generation, faced stagnation in growth. Recognizing an opportunity, Firm X approached Company A with a proposition to acquire the company through an LBO. The goal was to enhance Company A's growth prospects and eventually generate substantial returns on investment.

Role of Investment Bankers in the LBO Process

Initial Assessment and Strategy Development

Bank Y was brought in by Firm X to assist in the financial evaluation and structuring of the deal. The investment bankers at Bank Y conducted a comprehensive analysis of Company A's financials. This involved assessing historical cash flows, market position, and potential for operational improvements. The team's objective was to determine the optimal capital structure that could maximize the value of the acquisition while minimizing risk.

Structuring the Financing Package

The cornerstone of any LBO is its financing package, typically involving a significant portion of debt. Bank Y recommended a financing structure that balanced debt and equity to optimize the deal's leverage. The investment bankers proposed several financing options, including:

1. **Senior Debt**: This was the primary source of financing, secured by the assets of Company A, providing a lower-cost capital source due to its lower risk profile.
2. **Subordinated Debt**: To fill the gap between the senior debt and equity, subordinated debt was used, albeit at a higher interest rate due to its lower priority in the capital structure.
3. **Equity Contribution**: Firm X also had to contribute equity, ensuring they had skin in the game and aligning their interests with the company's success.

Bank Y's role was crucial in negotiating favorable terms with lenders, ensuring that the debt structure was manageable for Company A and provided enough flexibility for future growth investments.

Execution and Post-Acquisition Strategy

Securing Financing and Acquisition

Once the financing structure was agreed upon, Bank Y facilitated the closing of the financing by coordinating with various lenders and investors. This included drafting and finalizing loan agreements and other necessary legal documentation. After securing the necessary funds, Firm X completed the acquisition, taking Company A private.

Operational Improvements and Value Creation

Post-acquisition, Firm X implemented a series of operational and strategic initiatives to enhance Company A's performance. This included optimizing supply chain operations, expanding into new markets, and leveraging technology for efficiency improvements. These initiatives, guided by Firm X's expertise and the strategic insights provided by Bank Y, aimed to increase the company's market share and profitability.

Successful Exit and Returns

Over the following years, Company A's performance improved significantly. The combined efforts led to enhanced cash flows, a stronger market position, and an overall increase in company value. Eventually, Firm X exited the investment through a sale, yielding substantial returns for its investors. This successful exit underscored the effectiveness of the LBO strategy and the critical role of the investment bankers at Bank Y in structuring and executing the transaction.

Conclusion

This case study illustrates the vital role investment bankers play in LBO transactions. From financial evaluation to structuring complex financing packages and supporting post-acquisition strategies, their expertise is crucial in navigating the intricacies of such deals. For Firm X, the partnership with Bank Y was instrumental in transforming Company A into a more valuable enterprise, achieving a win-win outcome for all parties involved.

Chapter 132: Case Study of an Example Merger

Case Study: The Merger of Company A and Company B in the Technology Industry

When two leading technology companies, Company A and Company B, decided to merge to form a more robust and competitive entity, they turned to the expertise of Bank Z. This case study illustrates the critical role investment bankers play in facilitating successful mergers, from initial evaluation to post-merger integration.

Initial Evaluation and Strategic Planning

Engagement and Preliminary Analysis: The journey began with Company A and Company B approaching Bank Z, an investment bank known for its proficiency in mergers and acquisitions (M&A). Bank Z's team of investment bankers initiated the process by engaging in detailed discussions with the management teams of both companies. The primary objective was to understand the strategic motivations behind the merger and to gather comprehensive data for analysis.

Financial and Market Analysis: Bank Z's team conducted a thorough examination of the financial statements, market positions, and growth prospects of both companies. This involved:

- **Financial Health Assessment:** Reviewing income statements, balance sheets, and cash flow statements to determine the financial stability and performance of each company.
- **Market Position Analysis:** Analyzing market share, competitive advantages, and positioning within the technology industry to assess how the merger would enhance market strength.
- **Growth Potential:** Identifying synergies that could be leveraged post-merger to drive growth and profitability.

Structuring the Merger

Recommendation of Stock-for-Stock Merger: Based on their analysis, Bank Z recommended a stock-for-stock merger. This approach involved the exchange of shares between the two companies to complete the merger, rather than a cash transaction. The benefits of this structure included:

- **Alignment of Interests:** Both sets of shareholders would benefit from the combined entity's future success.
- **Capital Preservation:** The companies could preserve their cash reserves for future growth initiatives and operational needs.

Negotiation of Terms: The investment bankers facilitated negotiations between Company A and Company B to agree on the terms of the merger. Key aspects included:

- **Exchange Ratio:** Determining the appropriate exchange ratio for the stock swap, ensuring fair value for shareholders of both companies.
- **Governance Structure:** Deciding on the composition of the new board of directors and executive team to ensure a smooth leadership transition.

- **Integration Plan:** Developing a detailed plan for integrating the operations, cultures, and systems of the two companies to maximize synergies.

Execution and Post-Merger Integration

Closing the Deal: Once the terms were finalized, Bank Z's team worked diligently to structure the deal and prepare the necessary legal and regulatory documents. This included:

- **Regulatory Approvals:** Securing approvals from relevant regulatory bodies to ensure compliance with antitrust laws and other regulations.
- **Shareholder Approvals:** Organizing meetings and communications to obtain the necessary approvals from shareholders of both companies.

Post-Merger Integration: Following the successful completion of the merger, the newly formed entity focused on integrating operations. Bank Z continued to play a vital role by:

- **Integration Support:** Assisting with the integration of systems, processes, and corporate cultures to achieve seamless operations.
- **Performance Monitoring:** Providing ongoing advisory services to monitor the performance of the merged company and identify further opportunities for growth.

Conclusion

This case study exemplifies the comprehensive role of investment bankers in orchestrating mergers. Bank Z's team was instrumental in guiding Company A and Company B through the complex process of merging, from initial evaluations and strategic planning to execution and integration. By leveraging their expertise in financial analysis, negotiation, and strategic advisory, Bank Z helped create a larger, more competitive company positioned for long-term success.

This merger not only enhanced the market position of the newly formed company but also demonstrated how strategic M&A can drive growth and value creation in the technology industry. Investment bankers, with their deep industry knowledge and transaction experience, are crucial partners in navigating the complexities of such significant corporate transformations.

Chapter 133: What Are the Best Books on Financial Modeling & Valuation

The Best Books on Financial Modeling & Valuation

If you're looking to deepen your understanding of financial modeling and valuation, there are several authoritative books that offer valuable insights and practical knowledge. These resources are essential for anyone interested in investment banking, corporate finance, private equity, or valuation analysis. Below is a detailed look at some of the most highly recommended books in this field.

1. "Financial Modeling" by Simon Benninga

This comprehensive guide is a staple for those interested in financial modeling using Excel. The book covers a wide range of topics, including:

- **Accounting and Financial Statements:** Understanding the basics of financial statements and how to model them.
- **Corporate Finance Concepts:** Techniques like discounted cash flow (DCF) analysis and capital budgeting.

- **Excel Modeling:** Step-by-step tutorials on building models from scratch, with practical examples and exercises.

Benninga's work is praised for its clarity and hands-on approach, making it suitable for both beginners and experienced professionals looking to refine their skills.

2. "Valuation: Measuring and Managing the Value of Companies" by McKinsey & Company

This book is a go-to resource for understanding the complexities of valuation. Key topics include:

- **Discounted Cash Flow (DCF) Analysis:** Detailed guidance on how to perform DCF valuations, including cash flow forecasting and terminal value calculation.
- **Relative Valuation:** Techniques for valuing companies based on comparable firms, using multiples like P/E and EV/EBITDA.
- **Advanced Valuation Techniques:** Includes discussions on real options and other advanced methods.

The book includes numerous case studies and real-world examples, providing practical applications of the valuation theories discussed.

3. "Investment Banking: Valuation, Leveraged Buyouts, and Mergers & Acquisitions" by Joshua Pearl and Joshua Rosenbaum

A comprehensive guide that covers a wide array of investment banking topics:

- **Valuation Techniques:** Detailed walkthroughs of various valuation methods, including DCF, precedent transactions, and comparable company analysis.
- **Leveraged Buyouts (LBOs):** Step-by-step LBO modeling, including structuring and financing.
- **Mergers & Acquisitions (M&A):** Insight into M&A processes, deal structuring, and negotiation tactics.

The authors use practical examples and case studies, making complex topics more accessible. The book is often accompanied by an *Investment Banking Workbook* for hands-on practice.

4. "Financial Statement Analysis and Security Valuation" by Stephen H. Penman

Penman's book offers a rigorous approach to financial statement analysis and valuation:

- **Cash Flow Analysis:** Techniques for analyzing cash flows and assessing financial health.
- **Ratio Analysis:** Comprehensive coverage of various financial ratios and their implications.
- **Forecasting and Valuation:** Methods for projecting future financial performance and valuing companies based on these projections.

The book is well-suited for those looking to understand the intricacies of financial statements and how they relate to security valuation.

5. "The Art of Company Valuation and Financial Statement Analysis" by Nicolas Schmidlin

Focused on value investing, this book provides:

- **Valuation Techniques:** Covers both traditional and modern approaches to valuing companies.
- **Financial Statement Analysis:** Offers a deep dive into analyzing financial statements with a value investor's perspective.
- **Case Studies:** Real-life case studies that demonstrate practical applications of the concepts discussed.

Schmidlin's work is particularly useful for those interested in value investing and long-term financial strategies.

6. "Financial Modeling and Valuation: A Practical Guide to Investment Banking and Private Equity" by Paul Pignataro

A practical guide that combines theoretical knowledge with practical application:

- **Investment Banking Focus:** Includes sections on M&A, LBOs, and other investment banking activities.
- **Private Equity Insight:** Offers a perspective on private equity investments and valuation.
- **Hands-On Exercises:** Practical exercises and case studies help readers apply the concepts in real-world scenarios.

Pignataro's guide is ideal for those looking to understand both the investment banking and private equity landscapes.

7. "Business Analysis and Valuation: Using Financial Statements" by Krishna Palepu and Paul Healy

This book blends theoretical concepts with practical case studies:

- **Financial Statement Analysis:** Offers techniques for analyzing financial statements and understanding business economics.
- **Valuation:** Covers various valuation methods and how to apply them using financial statement data.
- **Real-World Applications:** Includes case studies that show how these techniques are used in practice.

Palepu and Healy's book is suitable for both students and professionals looking to deepen their understanding of business analysis and valuation.

8. "Financial Modeling for Business Owners and Entrepreneurs" by Tom Y. Sawyer

A practical guide designed for business owners and entrepreneurs:

- **Excel-Based Models:** Focuses on developing Excel models for various business scenarios.
- **Capital Raising:** Techniques for using financial models to raise capital and plan business strategies.
- **Operational Planning:** Models for improving cash flow, planning projects, and making informed business decisions.

Sawyer's book is particularly valuable for entrepreneurs looking to apply financial modeling to their business strategies.

Conclusion

These books offer a wealth of knowledge and practical insights into financial modeling and valuation. Whether you're a student, a professional in finance, or an entrepreneur, these resources provide valuable tools and techniques to master these critical aspects of investment banking and corporate finance. By leveraging the lessons and methodologies presented in these books, readers can enhance their financial analysis skills and make informed investment decisions.

Chapter 134: Practicing Investment Banking & Equity Research

Practicing Investment Banking & Equity Research: A Comprehensive Guide

Investment banking and equity research are two critical components in the financial industry. They involve analyzing financial data, building valuation models, and making informed recommendations. This blog post outlines the essential steps in practicing investment banking, from pulling and analyzing financials to writing a comprehensive equity research report.

1. Pulling the Financials

Objective: The first step is to gather the company's financial data.

Sources:

- **Annual Reports (10-K):** These are comprehensive reports filed annually by publicly traded companies to the SEC, providing a detailed overview of their financial performance.

- **Quarterly Reports (10-Q):** These filings offer more frequent updates on the company's financial condition and performance, filed quarterly.

Action Steps:

- Access the company's latest 10-K and 10-Q filings through financial databases like EDGAR (SEC's database), Bloomberg, or Yahoo Finance.
- Download the financial statements, including the income statement, balance sheet, and cash flow statement.

2. Reading the Financials

Objective: Understand the company's financial health and operational performance.

Key Areas to Focus:

- **Management's Discussion and Analysis (MD&A):** Provides the management's perspective on the financial results, including insights into revenue trends, expenses, and future outlook.
- **Income Statement:** Analyzes the company's profitability over a specific period.
- **Balance Sheet:** Provides a snapshot of the company's assets, liabilities, and shareholders' equity.
- **Cash Flow Statement:** Details the cash inflows and outflows, highlighting the company's liquidity and cash management.

Action Steps:

- Thoroughly review each section to understand the company's financial position, growth drivers, and potential risks.

3. Spreading the Financials into Excel

Objective: Organize financial data systematically.

Action Steps:

- **Data Entry:** Input the historical financial data into an Excel spreadsheet. Create separate sheets for the income statement, balance sheet, and cash flow statement.
- **Ensure Accuracy:** Double-check the data for accuracy, ensuring that the figures match the reported numbers in the financial statements.

4. Building an Integrated Financial Statement Model

Objective: Forecast future financial performance.

Action Steps:

- **Linking Financial Statements:** Develop an integrated model that links the income statement, balance sheet, and cash flow statement. This allows for dynamic forecasting based on various assumptions.
- **Key Assumptions:** Incorporate assumptions for revenue growth rates, profit margins, capital expenditures, working capital changes, and other relevant metrics.
- **Projections:** Use these assumptions to project future financial statements over a specified forecast period (e.g., 5-10 years).

5. Building a Valuation Model

Objective: Determine the intrinsic value of the company.

Valuation Methods:

- **Discounted Cash Flow (DCF):** Calculates the present value of expected future cash flows.
- **Comparable Company Analysis (CCA):** Valuation based on metrics from similar companies.
- **Precedent Transactions Analysis (PTA):** Valuation based on prices paid in similar past transactions.

Action Steps:

- **DCF Model:** Develop a DCF model by discounting future free cash flows back to their present value using a discount rate (usually the weighted average cost of capital, WACC).
- **Comparables and Precedents:** Select appropriate comparable companies and precedent transactions to establish valuation multiples.
- **Valuation Summary:** Combine the results from different valuation methods to determine a range of fair values for the company.

6. Writing an Equity Research Report

Objective: Provide a comprehensive analysis and investment recommendation.

Structure:

- **Executive Summary:** Brief overview of the company and your recommendation (buy, hold, or sell).
- **Company Analysis:** In-depth analysis of the company's business model, industry context, and financial health.
- **Valuation:** Detailed presentation of the valuation models used, including key assumptions and resulting valuation range.
- **Investment Thesis:** Clearly state the rationale behind your recommendation, supported by data and analysis.

- **Risks and Considerations:** Highlight potential risks that could impact the investment thesis and valuation.

Action Steps:

- **Data Presentation:** Use charts, graphs, and tables to present data clearly.
- **Recommendation:** Provide a clear and concise investment recommendation based on the analysis.

Conclusion

Practicing investment banking and equity research requires a systematic approach to analyzing financial statements, building models, and making informed investment recommendations. By following the steps outlined in this guide, you can develop a comprehensive understanding of these critical financial practices and enhance your skills in the field. Continuous practice and real-world application will further hone your expertise as an investment banker.

Appendix

Introduction to Data Science

Introduction to Data Science: Maximizing Business Potential through Intelligent Systems

In today's digital age, data science has emerged as a crucial discipline, transforming how businesses operate and make decisions. At its core, data science involves leveraging data and advanced analytics to uncover insights, automate processes, and optimize performance. This blog post explores the fundamental concepts of data science, its applications in creating intelligent work systems, and how businesses can harness its power to achieve superior outcomes.

Intelligent Work Systems: These are technological systems designed to solve specific problems, allowing businesses to optimize processes and capitalize on arbitrage opportunities. By integrating data science, these systems become capable of making intelligent decisions and automating actions, thus driving efficiency and effectiveness.

The Role of Intelligent Technology

Intelligent technology plays a pivotal role in unlocking or automating arbitrage opportunities. This involves using data to drive intelligent work systems that optimize performance. The flow of intelligence within these systems can be broken down into several key components:

1. **Data Collection and Analysis:** The foundation of any intelligent work system is data. This includes gathering data from various sources and applying analytics to extract valuable insights.
2. **Conditional Logic (Decision Making):** Once data is collected, the next step involves applying conditional logic to make decisions. This includes using descriptive, predictive, and prescriptive analytics to determine the best course of action. Descriptive analytics helps in understanding what has happened, predictive analytics forecasts what might happen, and prescriptive analytics suggests actions to achieve desired outcomes.
3. **Augmentation and Automation (Tasks):** Based on the insights derived from the data, tasks can be augmented or automated. This means that certain actions can be carried out automatically, reducing the need for human intervention and increasing efficiency.

Building Autonomous Intelligent Work Systems

An autonomous intelligent work system is built upon a foundation of data and analytics. It operates at various levels of analysis:

- **Descriptive Analytics:** This involves summarizing past data to understand what has happened. It is akin to traditional Business Intelligence (BI) and provides a historical view of data.
- **Predictive Analytics:** This uses statistical models and machine learning techniques to forecast future events based on historical data. It helps businesses anticipate trends and make proactive decisions.
- **Prescriptive Analytics:** This goes a step further by recommending actions based on the analysis. By suggesting specific actions, it helps businesses optimize their operations.

These levels of analytics work together to form a cohesive system that can make intelligent decisions and automate tasks. For instance, an AI-powered product might use prescriptive analytics to automatically adjust marketing strategies based on real-time data, thus optimizing campaign performance.

The Flow of Intelligence: From Data to Action

The process of intelligence in data science follows a clear flow:

1. **Data:** The raw information collected from various sources.
2. **Conditional Logic:** The decision-making framework that determines which actions to take based on data analysis.
3. **Augmentation & Automation:** The execution of tasks, either through augmentation (enhancing human abilities) or automation (carrying out tasks without human intervention).

Data science focuses on finding new variables and metrics that serve as better predictors of performance. By identifying these, businesses can optimize their strategies and achieve superior results. The application of computing power in data science is threefold: understanding and recording reality (data), making decisions (conditional logic), and executing tasks (doing).

The Process of Data Science: From Data Model to Intelligent Action

To implement data science effectively, businesses must follow a structured process:

1. **Build the Data Model:** Define the data requirements and collect relevant data.
2. **Build the Analytic Model:** Apply analytic algorithms to analyze the data and derive insights.

3. **Evaluate the Model:** Assess the model's accuracy and effectiveness in predicting outcomes.

Business Intelligence (BI) typically involves descriptive analytics, while data science encompasses predictive and prescriptive analytics. The key to success in data science lies in developing and applying analytic algorithms that can process and analyze data to solve business problems.

The Future of Intelligent Systems: AI and Automation

As artificial intelligence (AI) continues to evolve, it is increasingly integrated into products, making them "intelligent products." These products use prescriptive insights to automate decision-making processes, enabling businesses to turn optimization over to machines. This not only enhances efficiency but also allows for real-time adjustments and improvements.

In conclusion, data science offers a powerful framework for businesses to leverage data and technology to achieve their strategic objectives. By building intelligent work systems that integrate descriptive, predictive, and prescriptive analytics, companies can optimize their operations, automate processes, and drive superior performance. The future lies in harnessing the full potential of data science to create intelligent, autonomous systems that continuously learn and adapt, paving the way for innovation and growth.

Analytic algorithms (analysis)
The analysis process with models and analytic algorithms
Business problems of deciding (conditional logic) - apply analytic algorithms
Data requirements mapping
Analytic requirements mapping

Ai bakes prescriptive insights and automation relative to those insights into the product to turn optimization over to the machines and enable intelligent actions automatically for the client.

Made in the USA
Las Vegas, NV
12 January 2025

16284923R00435